3124300 496 8631
Lake Forest Library
360 E. Deerpath
Lake Forest, IL 60045
847-234-0636
www.lakeforestlibrary.org

W9-ABP-614

The City of Akhenaten and Nefertiti

NEW ASPECTS OF ANTIQUITY

General Editor: COLIN RENFREW

Consulting Editor for the Americas: JEREMY A. SABLOFF

BARRY KEMP

The City of Akhenaten and Nefertiti

AMARNA AND ITS PEOPLE

287 illustrations, 53 in color

To my daughters, Nickie, Vicky and Frances

Frontispiece: A symbol of Akhenaten's mind? Obsessive literalism and a scale of piety that must be seen to be believed: banks of offering-tables at the Great Aten Temple. Part of the Boston model of Amarna.

First published in 2012 in hardcover in the United States of America by Thames & Hudson Inc., 500 Fifth Avenue, New York, New York 10110

thamesandhudsonusa.com

Library of Congress Catalog Card Number 2011945993

ISBN 978-0-500-05173-3

Printed and bound in China by Toppan Leefung Printing Limited

CONTENTS

PROLOGUE

On 25 January 1977, I set out from the clinic building on the edge of the village of El-Amariya (which lies towards the southern end of Amarna), accompanied by one inspector of antiquities (the late Mohammed Abd el-Aziz Awad), several antiquities guards armed with elderly shotguns and rifles, a few donkeys and the basic sundries of an archaeologist taking a first look at a major ancient site. Some days later, I stood on the whitish dusty track linking El-Amariya with other villages further north, discovering that (in a pre-electronic age) the optical theodolite I had borrowed had a minor fault that would require pages of hand-written calculations to correct. My first purchase of a pocket calculator still lay in the future.

Thirty-five years on, I sit in the dig house typing into my laptop, printer and scanner at hand, digital camera ready to download the day's pictures, an internet connection in the next room. With patience it will download, free of charge, sharply detailed satellite images of Amarna that, not so many years ago, I might have been in trouble with the Egyptian security services for possessing. I have lived through a scientific revolution (as well as Egypt's latest political revolution, which began as I put the finishing touches to the manuscript of the book). I am a piece of oral history who can talk about the way things were at Amarna in 'the old days'.

Barry Kemp

ACKNOWLEDGMENTS

The Amarna expedition and its team of people represent a collective endeavour, with the highs and lows of long periods of enforced togetherness at the Amarna dig house. Field archaeology, especially when conducted outside one's country of birth, employs an odd little misfit fragment of society. People throw themselves with extraordinary passion, talent and self-sacrifice into the pursuit of abstract research goals for minimal recompense. The public likes archaeology and especially Egyptian archaeology, but, apart from dedicated groups of enthusiasts, views it as free entertainment. As a result, far too many good research projects have been left unfinished as their enthusiastic proponents have found it necessary to move on into the 'real' world of salaries and pensions. I wish I could have helped them more.

It is not possible to mention all those who have contributed their time and skills to the expedition, often as site supervisors on whom the progress of the excavation depends. The list of those who represent other specialist areas comprises (in no particular order): Salvatore Garfi, Helen Fenwick and Corinna Rossi (survey of Amarna); Howard Hecker, Rosie Luff, Martha Moreno Garcia, Pippa Payne and Tony Legge (animal bones); Tony Leahy and Marc Gabolde (hieratic texts); Jane Renfrew, Delwen Samuel, Wendy Smith, Alan Clapham and Chris Stevens (plant remains); Rainer Gerisch (charcoal and wood specimens); Paul Buckland and Eva Panagiotakopulu (insect remains); Michael Mallinson, Surésh Dhargalkar, Kate Spence, Simon Bradley and Bill Erickson (repairs to ancient buildings and discussions on architecture and the ancient urban experience); Andy Boyce (beautiful artwork and a deep appreciation of small finds); Pamela Rose and Boris Trivan (pottery); Carolyn Graves-Brown (flints); Malcolm Williamson, Christopher Goodmaster, Stephanie Sullivan and Jason Herrmann (University of Arkansas geophysics team); Ian Mathieson (geophysics); Mary Shepperson, Wendy Dolling and Melinda King-Wetzel (cemetery analysis); Ian Shaw (spatial analysis of artifacts); Sarah Parcak (coring and remote sensing); Paul Nicholson and Mark Eccleston (everything to do with heating things in kilns: pottery, glass, faience, metal); Jerry Rose, Melissa Zabecki and Gretchen Dabbs (University of Arkansas anthropology team); Gwil Owen (photography, in the studio and in the air); Willeke Wendrich (basketry and cordage); Gillian Vogelsang-Eastwood (textiles); Andre Veldmeijer (leather); Barbara Garfi (drawing of finds); Ann Cornwell (organization of the antiquities storehouse); Michael Jones and Miriam Bertram (work on the excavation archives); Fran Weatherhead (wall paintings); Julie Dawson and Lucy Skinner (conservation of finds); Margaret

Serpico (resin samples and relief fragments); Kristin Thompson and Marsha Hill (statue fragments); Jackie Williamson (relief fragments); Vicky Kemp (publication support). For the last few years, the expedition has been fortunate in having Anna Stevens first as research assistant and then as assistant director. I have benefited much from our discussions.

There is a whole side to the archaeology of Amarna not otherwise mentioned in this book, that of early Christian communities. The abundant traces of their determination to live ascetic lives have been the province of Gillian Pyke, Jane Faiers and Sarah Clackson.

I could not have worked at Amarna if the Egypt Exploration Society (EES), in whose name the expedition for long gained its annual permit from the Egyptian government, had not annually allocated a portion of its meagre British government grant (since withdrawn) to support it. Beginning in 2005, the Amarna Trust has taken over the responsibility for funding the expedition, benefiting from the guidance and good sense of Alf Baxendale, Alison Gascoigne and Shirley Priest. The Trust's supporters, and those of the Amarna Research Foundation of Denver (begun in 1995 by Bob Hanawalt and maintained by its own board of trustees), have become the principal means by which the work at Amarna continues. I am profoundly grateful to them. Along the way, the expedition's research has benefited from grants from various bodies, most notably the British Academy, The Leverhulme Foundation, The McDonald Institute for Archaeological Research, the Gerald Avery Wainwright Fund, the Seven Pillars of Wisdom Trust, the Robert Kiln Trust and, through the good offices of Jim Merrington, Scottish and Newcastle Brewery, who funded an investigation into the making of beer at Amarna.

I am one of the lucky few, salaried from the beginning by the University of Cambridge. For nearly all the time, as a member of the Faculty of Oriental Studies (and for a good part of the time a member also of the McDonald Institute for Archaeological Research), I was allowed, through what in retrospect seems an enlightened lightness of employer's touch, to manage my own time and so devote a good deal of it to the pursuit of the Amarna expedition. I am thankful for that.

Equally, nothing could have happened at all without the annually renewed agreement of the Egyptian government body responsible for archaeological sites and monuments, the Supreme Council of Antiquities (since 2011 the Ministry of Antiquities). Through its numerous officials, including the inspectors who temporarily become members of the team, I have received goodwill and respect to a degree that often I feel is undeserved. Egyptian antiquities law is comprehensive and its bureaucratic procedures are potentially stifling. It works out all right in the end because, with patience and respect given, one benefits from the submerged flexibility in the face of 'routine' (by now a colloquial Egyptian-Arabic word), which enables Egypt to function.

The constant employment of and general dealings with the inhabitants of the villages at Amarna, and of Egypt in general, have introduced me to an endless stream of good humour and hospitality, as well as fortitude in the face of living conditions much harsher than I myself experience. I must single one of them out for special mention: Mohammed Omar Osman. From the beginning, he has faithfully looked after the dig house and been a bridge of good understanding with the local communities and their authorities. His sceptical face and demeanour have helped me to understand the difference between acting the part of a director and being regarded with deference, and treating people as human beings and thus earning a little of their respect. There is a difference.

I was invited to write this book at the initiative of Colin Renfrew (who, along with Jane Renfrew, participated in the 1986 Amarna season) and with the continued patient encouragement of Colin Ridler at Thames & Hudson. It has taken far longer than expected. Along the way, my thoughts have been helped by being part of a research project, 'Investing in Religion in Akhenaten's Amarna', funded by a grant from the Templeton Foundation, by being asked by Bob Partridge to write a series of articles for *Ancient Egypt* magazine for 2008 and by many opportunities to lecture to enthusiastic audiences and to respond to their questions. At the end, Corinne Duhig most generously read through and commented upon the manuscript. Alice Reid's careful editing and perceptive questioning further smoothed and clarified the text. I am grateful also to Rowena Alsey, who did the layout of the book, and Celia Falconer for overseeing its production.

Illustrations

The Sources of Illustrations section at the end of this volume includes credits to those who have supplied them and allowed them to be used, most notably the Egypt Exploration Society, owner of the Lucy Gura Archive. EES archive photographs from the earlier seasons were numbered on a yearly basis, for example, 21/56 is negative 56 from the 1921 season. In later seasons, the photographs were separated into two groups by the prefixes A (for architecture) and O (for object); for example, 33/O 56 is negative 56 in the object series for the season 1933–34 (note that this labelling of photographic negatives is different from that of the objects themselves, which are referred to as 'obj. 33/56' etc.).

Some illustrations are of models showing parts of Amarna. The one that I have termed the 'Boston' model, which covers the Central City and half the housing area to the south, was made in the summer of 1999, in London, by the company Tetra, to designs by Mallinson Architects, Kate Spece and myself. The Boston Museum of Fine Arts, through the agreement of Rita Freed, the Norma-Jean Calderwood Curator, had commissioned it for the exhibition *Pharaohs of the Sun*, which opened in Boston in November 1999. It currently resides at Amarna awaiting the completion of the Amarna Visitor Centre, a project of the Supreme Council of Antiquities designed by Mallinson Architects. A separate set of models of individual buildings, also destined for the Visitor Centre, has been made by the company Eastwood Cook. I am grateful to all concerned for their agreement that I could use pictures of the models.

EXPLANATORY NOTES

The System of Numbering Amarna Buildings

The German expedition that worked at Amarna in 1907 and between 1911 and 1914, and was directed by Ludwig Borchardt, devised a system for numbering each building as it was excavated. Borchardt's surveyor, Paul Timme, laid a grid of squares over his map of Amarna, each square 200 m (656 ft) in extent and aligned to the north. He gave to each grid square a unique alphanumeric designation. Numbers ran in ascending order from north to south, and letters proceeded from west to east. The houses in each square, as they were excavated, were numbered starting from 1.

Later excavators maintained this system. Thus the house of the sculptor Thutmose is the second house in square P47, so P47.2; and house Q44.1 is a large house near the Central City for which we have no owner's name. A listing of all numbers used and maps showing where they are located are in B. J. Kemp and S. Garfi, *A Survey of the Ancient City of El-'Amarna* (London, EES 1993). The 200-m grid squares are, however, too large to be of practical use when conducting a small-scale excavation. The excavations that have been carried out since 1979 are within local 5-m grids, numbered from 1, although individual houses within the main part of Amarna are subsequently given the next number in the Timme–Borchardt system. The only grid referred to in this book is Grid 12, of which a detailed account is in B. Kemp and A. Stevens, *Busy Lives at Amarna: Excavations in the Main City (Grid 12 and the House of Ranefer, N49.18)* (2 vols. London, EES 2010).

Amarna Objects

In unhappy contrast with the buildings, no agreed system of numbering objects that transcends the work of individual expeditions has been devised, and the temptation to start new numbered catalogues beginning with 1 is hard to resist. Objects from the EES excavations of 1921–37 were given catalogue numbers on a yearly basis, for example, 21/56 is object 56 from the 1921 season, with separate catalogues for hieratic labels and sometimes for decorated stonework. A database of the EES numbered objects is available online at www.amarna project.com/pages/recent_projects/material_culture/small_finds/. The objects from the German excavations of the DOG (Deutsche Orient-Gesellschaft) were catalogued similarly, with a simple number sequence started each season. Objects from the excavations begun in 1979 have a continuous series of numbers that runs across the seasons for small finds, but have separate sequences for stones (beginning with S-), textiles, leather fragments and so on.

The huge quantities of finds from the Petrie–Carter excavation of 1891–92 were not numbered at all, and the very large share that went to Carter's then sponsor, Lord Amherst, were sold at public auction in 1923, having never been catalogued other than in the sales brochure where most form parts of 'lots'.

Objects from Amarna excavations can be found in museums throughout the world. Of those found prior to the last EES season in 1936–37, few remain in Egypt (mostly in the Egyptian Museum, Cairo, plus quantities buried by the excavators in unmarked caches beside the two Amarna dig houses, and of which only portions have so far been recovered). The rest are scattered worldwide like confetti, the result of distributions following the division of finds with the Egyptian Museum, Cairo, at the end of each season's work. Some people in the world of museums and private collections still hanker after those days, when it was possible to acquire newly found objects legally, maintaining that if the divisions system were restored it would also reduce looting.

The seeming reasonableness of their arguments is compromised when one looks at what actually happened. The 1920s and '30s were a golden age of archaeology, with generous divisions of finds that benefited foreign expeditions and their sponsors, but they were no less one of robbery. Submissions to an EES committee in 1935 on the conduct of their Amarna expedition observed: 'that the general agreement in Egypt is that anything from 10–20% of the total number of finds is stolen, whatever one may do', something reflected by 'the large number of Amarna objects being offered for sale, [and] the fact that dealers produce the greatest number of objects either during or just after the excavations'. The strict policy that the Egyptian government now maintains towards objects found in excavation and the feeling of unease that this generates among archaeologists is probably a reasonable safeguard in view of the still insatiable market for antiquities. When robberies take place now, the circumstances usually suggest that they would have happened whether or not a divisions system were in place.

Moreover, the wish to spread finds among as many museums as possible led to the splitting up not only of groups of objects that should have stayed together, but of wall and floor paintings into handy individual sections each of which could go to a different place. And in time, museum curators experienced déjà vu, as yet more Amarna objects headed their way. John Pendlebury commented near the end of his directorship of the Amarna expedition in the 1930s: 'I'm sorry Museums don't want scraps. It always seems funny that they are willing to buy things in the market for hundreds of pounds – yet if they subscribe to a dig a fiver they expect a Nefertiti head.'

The Nefertiti head, in the Ägyptisches Museum, Berlin, illustrates another of the dangers of the divisions system, the inevitable competition between the Egyptian government and foreign expeditions to get the best out of the situation. Exactly how Ludwig Borchardt finished up with the Nefertiti head in his share of the 1913 division will probably never be settled, but the obscured circumstances had already in the 1920s led the Egyptians to demand for it to be returned. The affair and subsequent fate of the head are discussed in R. Krauss, '1913–1988: 75 Jahre Büste der NofretEte/Nefret-iti in Berlin', *Jahrbuch Preußischer Kulturbesitz* 24 (1987), 87–124; the same, 'Zweiter Teil', *Jahrbuch Preußischer Kulturbesitz* 29 (1992), 123–57, and more generally in C. Wedel, *Nofretete und das Geheimnis von Amarna* (Mainz, von Zabern 2005). After the head had been recovered from a deep salt mine at the end of World War II, a scheme to send it to the USA for a temporary exhibition, after which it would have been returned to Egypt, was thwarted by the US army unit charged with safeguarding German art treasures. The story is told by the unit head, Walter I. Farmer, in *The Safekeepers: A Memoir of the Arts at the End of World War II* (Berlin and New York, de Gruyter 2000) (thanks are due to Luisa Wagner for sending me a copy).

The Nefertiti head was supposedly balanced in the 1913 division by a stela showing the royal family, which went to the Egyptian Museum, Cairo. Both have now been declared fakes, by separate investigators, creating a surreal picture of what might have happened at the time, see H. Stierlin, *Le buste de Néfertiti: Une imposture de l'égyptologie?* (En Crausaz and Paris, Infolio 2009); R. Krauss, 'Nefertiti's final secret.' *Kmt* 20, no. 2 (Summer 2009), 18–28. Archaeology and art masterpieces do not mix. Having participated in two divisions (one of them not Amarna objects), I am thankful that they are no longer allowed, even though great works of art were lacking in these instances (none having been found).

Note on Identifications

The principal metal used in ancient Egypt was copper, often mixed with other minerals, either from accidents of geology or through deliberate alloying. By the Amarna period, bronze (an alloy of copper and tin) was widespread, but it requires laboratory analysis for confirmation in individual cases. 'Bronze' has been used in this book for convenience, but should not be taken as a definitive identification.

The rock that used to be called alabaster is now, in the opinion of geologists, better called travertine. Likewise, in the plant realm, lily is now to be preferred to lotus.

THE CAST OF CHARACTERS

ROUGHLY IN THEIR ORDER OF APPEARANCE IN HISTORY

AMENHOTEP III Ruler of Egypt between about 1388 and 1348 BC, and representative of the line of kings whose family origin lay in Thebes and who had ruled Egypt for the previous century and a half. They had succeeded other lines of kings for whom Thebes was the family home as far back as the ending of the civil wars of the First Intermediate period, in *c.* 2050 BC.

QUEEN TIYE Daughter of a prominent family whose home was the Upper Egyptian city of Akhmim. She became Amenhotep III's chief wife and mother of Akhenaten. Her parents were the couple Yuya and Tjuiu, buried in the Valley of the Kings. The 'God's Father' Ay was another relative and so perhaps was Nefertiti.

AKHENATEN Son of Amenhotep III and Queen Tiye, and evidently not the first in the line of succession. He became king following the death of the intended heir, Thutmose. Crowned as another Amenhotep, he changed his name to Akhenaten to mark the change he effected in the name – from Amen/Amun to Aten – of the god who presided over Egypt's ruling house and over the universe in general. The dates of his reign are approximately 1348 to 1331 BC. He is possibly to be identified with the person buried in a reused coffin found in the Valley of the Kings at Thebes, tomb 55.

NEFERTITI Principal wife of Akhenaten. Her parentage is nowhere stated. The wife of the god's father Ay was her nurse, and this might suggest that she was related to Ay's family. She might, or might not, have died while the court was resident at Amarna and might, or might not, have been buried at Amarna, Thebes, Medinet el-Ghurab and other possible locations. The ambiguity of her position at Amarna vis-à-vis her eldest daughter Meryetaten (who was accorded honours we might expect to be Nefertiti's, see below) invites speculation. Was there a rift in the royal family or did Nefertiti represent the royal family's rule at Memphis, for example, which retained an important part of the country's administration?

MERYETATEN AND HER SISTERS The sources document the existence of six children by Akhenaten and Nefertiti, all of them girls. Meryetaten was the eldest and became the heiress. Her name, and the title 'King's Daughter', appear on the stonework of a few of the royal buildings at Amarna, particularly Maru-Aten and the North Palace. She evidently had a place of exceptional prominence at Amarna, acting virtually as Akhenaten's consort in the latter part of his reign (though this was not without precedent: such a position, accompanied by variations on the title 'Queen', was held in her father's court by a daughter of Amenhotep III, Satamun – and later also by at least three daughters of Ramesses II during his reign). Letters to Akhenaten written by Near Eastern rulers refer to Meryetaten as the 'mistress' of Akhenaten's household. Perhaps she was given responsibility for running the royal household. Her name, now in a cartouche, alongside that of a King Ankhkheperure Smenkhkare, identifies a royal couple in one of the rock tombs at Amarna (that of Meryre [II], no. 2). The second daughter, Meketaten, died during the occupation of Amarna and was buried in an annexe to the tomb intended for Akhenaten. The third daughter, Ankhsenpaaten eventually became, as Ankhsenamun, the wife of Tutankhamun. Other than by their names the other three daughters are undocumented in the historical record.

KIYA A secondary wife of Akhenaten, whose existence emerged only through scholarly identifications in the latter part of the last century. She has greatly intrigued people, who sense a participant in an episode of harem politics. She has been credited, on weak evidence, with being the mother of Tutankhamun. She bore the title 'Wife, greatly beloved of the king'.

ANKHKHEPERURE (with the second cartouche name, or nomen, **Nefernefruaten** or **SMENKHKARE**) The successor of Akhenaten and probably a son; he used two nomens. He was married to Meryetaten. In their brief reign, the last additions and alterations to the city were made, and theirs are the last recorded royal names in the rock tombs. A female form of the first part of his name has excited much modern interest, and perhaps points to a very short time when the legitimate ruler was a woman (who could only be Nefertiti or Meryetaten). He is the alternative, and stronger, possible candidate for the person buried in the reused coffin found in the Valley of the Kings, tomb 55.

TUTANKHAMUN The successor to Ankhkheperure Smenkhkare, originally crowned as Tutankhaten and married to Ankhsenpaaten. He was probably also a son of Akhenaten, though, like Smenkhkare, he does not appear among the royal family groups. Amarna was still occupied when he was crowned king, but it is unlikely that he ever presided over the court there. The change in the last element in his name from Aten to Amun is a sign of his rejection of his father's ideas (which were also partly embodied in the distinctive way by which Akhenaten had himself portrayed). In his reign, the court abandoned Amarna, and the bulk of the population left, too. His Restoration Decree (issued from Memphis) classes the immediately preceding period as a time of alienation from the gods. He reigned for nine years, was only about nineteen at his death and was buried in the Valley of the Kings at Thebes.

AY With the title 'God's Father', he lived at Amarna and oversaw the start of a conspicuous tomb there (no. 25), but must have left Amarna at the time of its abandonment, becoming king for a short time after Tutankhamun. He was buried in the Valley of the Kings. A probable member of the Akhmim family, he was, in effect, the last of the Upper Egyptian line of kings.

HOREMHEB A military officer evidently based at Memphis, he emerged as king after the death of Ay. In his reign, the demolition of Akhenaten's stone buildings began.

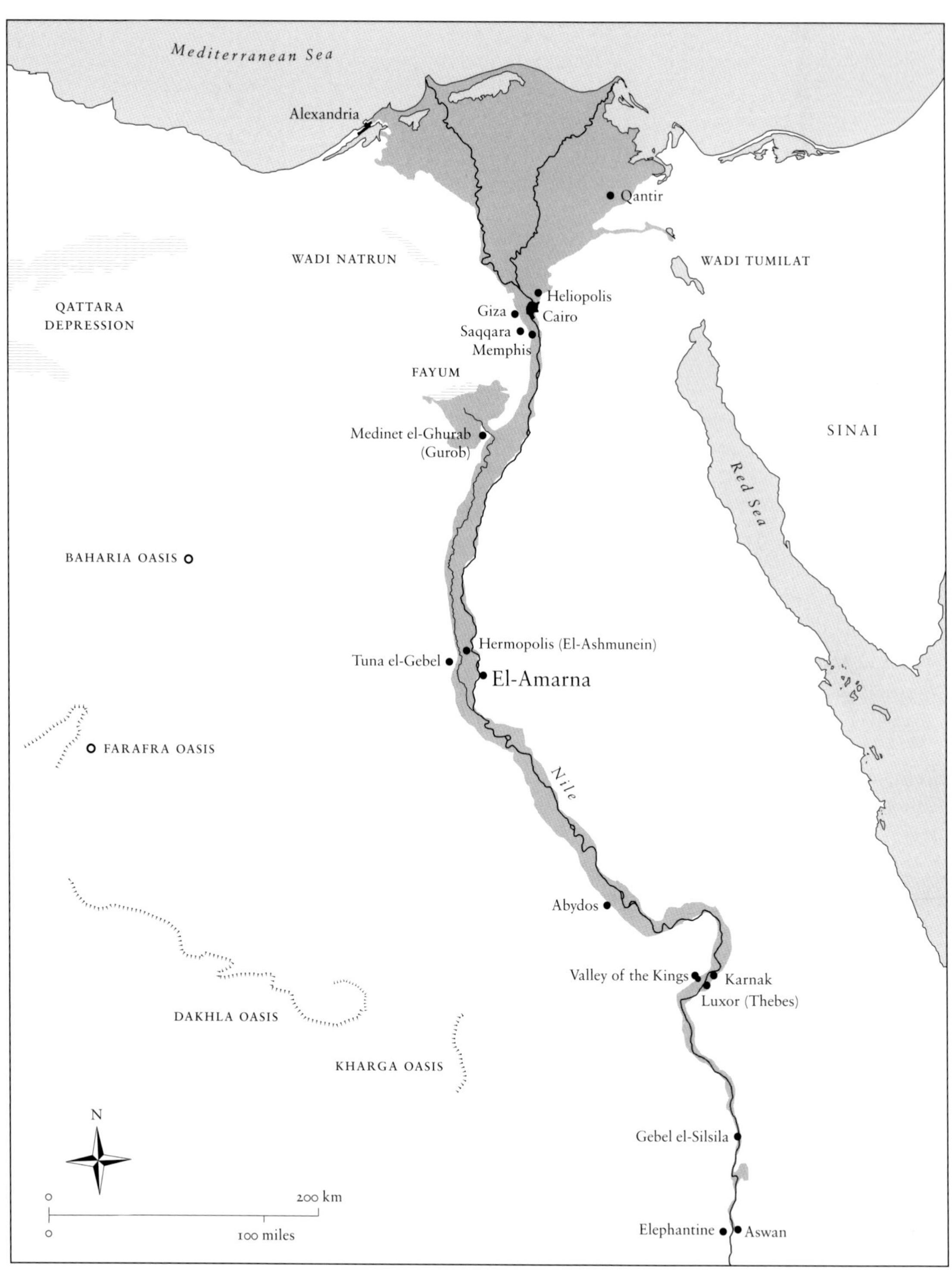

0.1 *Map of Egypt showing the location of Amarna and other sites mentioned in the text.*

INTRODUCTION

THE CITY OF THE HORIZON

Some thirty-three centuries ago, perhaps 20,000 Egyptians, or maybe twice that number, followed their king to what was then an empty stretch of desert beside the Nile and built a city. To their king, Akhenaten, the land was part of a sacred territory called 'The Horizon of the Sun's Disc' (or Akhetaten). We know it as Tell el-Amarna (or more simply El-Amarna or Amarna) [0.1; **Pl. IX**]. Within twenty years, following his death and that of at least one short-lived successor, they had left, never to return. Gangs of workmen systematically dismantled the stone temples and transported the blocks away for re-use elsewhere. The centuries then settled down to reducing the remainder to one and a half square miles of sandy hillocks, which never quite lost the semblance of a city [0.3]. It remains by far the largest area of readily accessible domestic occupation from ancient Egypt. It is the only city you can go and see.

In Akhenaten we have a king who initiated a major change in how the nation's divine patron should be approached and depicted. It was a change using language and images that together imply a wish to simplify and to cleanse. Akhenaten appears to represent an early example of a widespread trend in the history of piety, towards greater austerity in conceptions of the divine. The life-giving power of god was only what could be seen by all, the light shining in the disc of the sun (the Aten). But only two minds could comprehend it fully [0.2]. One was that of the king, the Aten's unique earthly agent. The other was that of his wife Nefertiti, who – however she really looked – was translated by the king's artists into a model of austere feminine beauty.

Akhenaten's character and motives, and the personal relationships within his family, have been debated at great length for more than a century. Was he a dreamer or a tyrant? The evidence we have does not take us far. The sketchy outlines of his reign have the makings of an appealing tale, of dreams, tragedy and unscrupulous women. I am reminded of the case of the English king Richard III (who reigned 1483–85). In William Shakespeare's play, written a century after the king's death, he is a villain. In a modern reaction, the Richard III Society has been brought into existence to exonerate him, in the belief (according to its mission statement) 'that many features of the traditional accounts of the character and career of Richard III are neither supported by sufficient evidence nor reasonably tenable'. The modern tendency to vilify Akhenaten could be countered in the same way, through the formation of an Akhenaten Society, and have the same inconclusive result. We will never know.

Two separate and different stories – or lines of research – come together at Amarna. One concerns Akhenaten, his family and his ideas. Much of it is the speciality of historians. At the same time, Akhenaten has a place among the not inconsiderable ranks of eccentric builder–kings of history, rulers for whom a major preoccupation was self-expression through architecture and landscape. Once we see Akhenaten in this guise, Amarna offers a unique opportunity for studying what such a figure could accomplish within the cultural tradition of ancient Egypt. We might not understand the full symbolism of the buildings or be able to reconstruct exactly how they were used (or how often), but together they offer an impressive lesson in just how varied were the combinations that could be built from the architectural and decorative repertoire of ancient Egypt. Akhenaten the creator of architectural conceits stands alongside the Akhenaten of the 'Hymn to the Aten', the poetic distillation of the universal power of the sun, and the one who can be studied through archaeology to greater effect.

The other story is the life of the city, as it can be reconstructed by archaeology. In writing this book, I began by telling myself that I had no new insights into Akhenaten's character or family life. My remit was to put the city first, and to present it as it has appeared to me, an archaeologist working there for a good part of my life (35 years). My intention was to take Akhenaten as the initiator of the city, and then, by and large, leave the man and his ideas in the background. As I worked on the text, however, I came to realize that certain aspects of the archaeology can best be explained as commentaries upon how

0.2 *The founder and his wife: Akhenaten (right) and Nefertiti (left). Both heads, found in the house of the sculptor Thutmose at Amarna in 1912, are now in Berlin.*

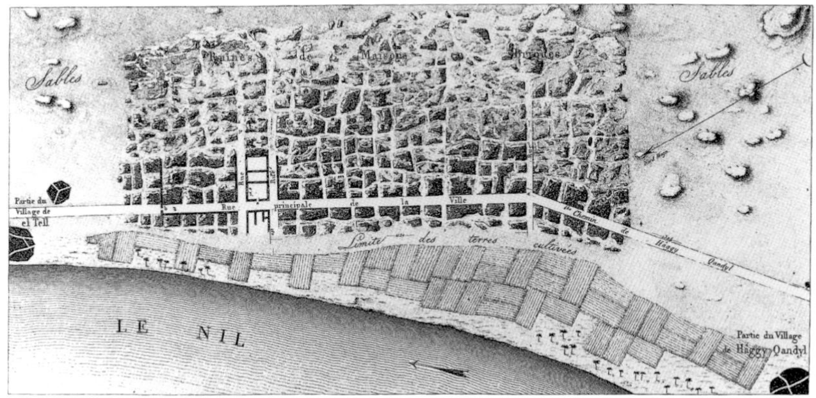

0.3 *The first known map of Amarna, made by the Napoleonic expedition in 1798–99.*

Akhenaten implemented his ideas. Conversely, the society that can be reconstructed (or conjured) from the archaeology is the society on which Akhenaten wrought his designs. Its particular character suggests limitations on what we should imagine appeared possible in his mind.

His vision has intrigued people since it was first rediscovered in the nineteenth century AD [0.3]. Amarna is where he put his vision into practice. The place itself ought also to tell us something about transformation, about converting dreams into reality.

Much in the book is inevitably descriptive, an attempt at the distillation of the results of exploration that began with surveys in the first half of the nineteenth century AD. The architecture of Amarna always communicates strongly. It is like a library of building types, covering the houses of the poor and the rich, palaces, temples and tombs. There is enough material here for a thick book on its own. Archaeological excavation has also covered more ground at Amarna than at any other habitation site from ancient Egypt. The number and the range of objects found are huge (and on the whole poorly published or not published at all), and with them has come extensive evidence for how they were made. But just letting the material speak for itself, by means of extensive description and illustration, underestimates what archaeology can do. I have woven into the text a number of themes where the archaeology sets up a dialogue with the written sources, and leads, I believe, to a better understanding of both Akhenaten and the society of his day. It seems scarcely necessary to add that the more one seeks to make sense of the past, the more one has to imagine. I have made big leaps of imagination in this book, but they should be fairly obvious.

The following is my summary of themes:

1. Akhenaten was obliged to make choices in implementing his vision. The archaeology makes clear that in doing so he was pushing against the limits of the resources available to him. Even rich countries and pharaohs are not boundlessly wealthy.

2. His vision took shape in a society where the village horizon still predominated. The scale of living was mostly modest, ostentation stood out sharply against muted and drab backgrounds, and society revolved around neighbourhoods of dependants and patrons where personal relationships with those in authority, and the accessibility of those in authority, mattered a great deal. Amarna was simultaneously a city and a continuous series of mud villages, intimately networked, above which the king raised a relatively small number of grand monuments.

3. The city as a whole depended on the king not only through the way it had come into existence, but because a significant portion of the population were recipients of benefactions, especially distributions of food. This was something of a fixation for the ancient Egyptians at both the mundane and spiritual levels. The 'House of the Aten' (the Great Aten Temple) and its dependencies that spread across the adjacent ground are particularly important for understanding this. Akhenaten presided over a system that created a channel of populism for his policies that the written sources barely hint at. At this level, the city itself was a dependant of its patron, the king, and the language and mindset of the day placed a high value on gratitude.

4. Through this pattern of nested dependency, the city was a hive of people busy making things for the court and incidentally for themselves. In its layout and in its industries, it shows a fine balance between direction from above and self-organization from below. The whole sprawling residential part of Amarna was 'a vast but loosely structured factory serving the state'.[1] As such, it exemplifies a stage in the history of the city, as broadly conceived. It is sufficiently different from the well-known model of the 'preindustrial city' as to suggest a separate term: the 'pre-preindustrial city' or, less unwieldy, 'the urban village'.

5. In its appearance, the city is a tribute to what self-organization can achieve in a society whose leaders are at ease with this way of doing things. It looks, in much of its plan, like a modern squatter settlement, yet its rich officials were incorporated within its framework. It is the antithesis of modern governmental over-regulation.

6. The people who populated Amarna arrived with minds shaped by the traditions of their upbringing. They balanced interest in the new spiritual environment against their own beliefs, which addressed different and more urgent needs than the intellectual concerns of the king. Here we run into an episode in the history of sponsored cult and popular belief, sometimes diverging, sometimes converging, something that could be claimed as one of the main themes in the history of human spirituality.

'Religion' is the theme that I find the most difficult for Amarna. It is difficult because we are acutely aware of religion whereas the Egyptians were not, having no word for it. The evolution of consciousness has given human beings the strangest of powers, that of invention within the mind, the power of imagination. Those things we invent, we arrange into patterns, the links taking the form of stories or logical flows of data. Gossip, religion, epic tales, philosophy, scientific constructs: they all flower in the imagination, cohabiting and intermingling. Modern knowledge – the list of '-ologies' – is an attempt to bring order by introducing partitions and definitions. Consciousness also delivers to the individual a personal measure of detachment and evaluation. An abundance brings the realization that the meaning of many things exists only in the imagination, and that many apparent truths are actually metaphors. At the other end of the scale stands belief, a condition in which something of what lies within the imagination is perceived as a reality that is also external, a truth that exists independent of humanity.

Among the peoples of the eastern Mediterranean, the last centuries BC saw the appearance of self-consciousness in belief, when people began to distinguish between beliefs that seemed true to them and beliefs that, while true to others, were false in their view. In this way 'religions' emerged, collecting followers and thus the means to divide society. Writing in the fifth century BC, Herodotus said of the Egyptians that they were 'religious to excess, beyond any other nation in the world'.[2] But a thousand years earlier, the Egyptians of the New Kingdom and of the Amarna period would not have said this of themselves or of anyone else. They were not conscious of religion as a separate aspect of existence, and thus had no urge to distinguish between truth and falsehood in beliefs, or between followers and the unfaithful. They lived with a less partitioned mind than we do. The gods were there, to be honoured, used, doubted and even mocked, a natural take-it-for-granted part of the universe and of a person's inner experience. How innocent it now seems!

'Religion' is thus one of the many creations of the Hellenistic period. Akhenaten's replacement of one form of an all-powerful creator god (Amun or Amun-Ra) by another (the Aten) is an early pointer to one way in which the world's conflicts would develop in the future. Had he been successful, in time an Atenist religion might have developed. In this sense it is not unreasonable to see him as a prophet. Yet, in living when he did, Akhenaten developed his ideas in a milieu that is very different from anything we are familiar with. His world tolerated inconsistency of thought to an extent that is uncomfortable in the modern world, and so provided less of a basis for intolerance and persecution. The normal terminology of religion (which includes the word 'monotheism') does not work very well. I have come to conclude that the very word 'religion', when applied to the ancient Egypt of this time, is mischievous. It brings into play unhelpful associations that belong to later times. I have therefore tried to avoid it, and to present instead a synopsis of an ancient approach to life that was rooted partly in the material world and partly in the imagination.

CHAPTER ONE

BUILDING A VISION

Akhenaten's Crime

A common interpretation of why we find Akhenaten so interesting and special is that he engaged in theological conflict. According to this view, a battle line lay between his form of monotheism and the traditional polytheism of his country. In the place of the crowded pantheon that the Egyptians had allowed to build up over the centuries, he aspired to the worship of one god, the disc of the sun, the source of light and life, the Aten [1.2]. How many gods did the Egyptians have who were thereby made redundant? Estimates run up to 2,000. It is a conflict that resonates with Old Testament Judaism and the Christian missionary outlook of the nineteenth century. Akhenaten has been linked or even identified with the Biblical Moses. This sits uneasily with his promotion of himself as sole intermediary with the Aten, something that shows a side of his character – megalomania? – that seems to be a fatal flaw in what might otherwise have been a spiritually heroic reputation, and a likely sign of intolerance and despotic rule. Many modern writers about Akhenaten seem not to like him.

Akhenaten belonged, however, within a culture for which judgments of this kind might not be appropriate. Moreover, the evidence for almost any interpretation of his reign is not consistent, though there is little enough that is specific. There clearly was a conflict. The most significant ancient statements that point to this are two remarks made in passing in legal texts that belong a century and more afterwards.[1] One of them refers to 'the time of the enemy of Akhetaten' (thus of Akhenaten who had made Akhetaten his home). The other records that a certain individual died 'in regnal year nine of the rebellion', which is generally taken to be an oblique reference to Akhenaten's reign. The words used belong more to the vocabulary of civil war. On their own, these statements could be read as indicating that Akhenaten was not the rightful heir and seized power by force of arms and that the matter was not quickly resolved. The omission of his name and those of his three successors (Smenkhkare, Tutankhamun and Ay) from later king lists parallels the omission of Queen Hatshepsut from a century earlier, her crime having apparently been that she was not part of the legitimate line of succession.

1.1 *Akhenaten as he wished his followers to regard him: the otherwise incomprehensible power of the sun now close and radiant as human flesh. The picture is of the royal family at the Window of Appearance. From the tomb of Ay (no. 25). Compare figure 1.13.*

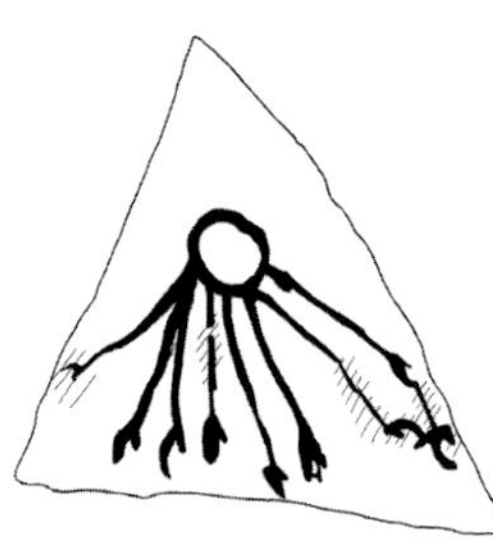

1.2 *The picture of the Aten's disc and its rays, which ended in human hands, very rarely appears on monuments other than royal ones, even at Amarna. This version, sketched on a potsherd from the Workmen's Village (obj. 836), is one of few exceptions. Width 8.5 cm (3.3 in.).*

Disapproval of a different kind is present in a pious memorial issued from Memphis by Tutankhamun after the abandonment of the Aten cult. It commemorated generous benefactions from the king to the cults of the gods, and especially to those of Amun of Thebes and Ptah of Memphis. The preamble reads:

> ... the temples and the cities of the gods and goddesses, starting from Elephantine [as far] as the Delta marshes ... were fallen into decay and their shrines were fallen into ruin, having become mere mounds overgrown with grass.... The gods were ignoring this land. If an army was sent to Syria to extend the boundaries of Egypt it met with no success at all. If one prayed to a god, to ask something from him, he did not respond at all. If one beseeched any goddess in the same way, she did not respond at all. Their hearts were faint in their bodies, and they destroyed what was made.[2]

Akhenaten, who is identified only by implication, had evidently offended those who maintained the traditional language of respect in which inscriptions of this kind were composed. He had become a failed king, and a powerful way of expressing this was to claim that the gods had withdrawn their favours. Akhenaten had, indeed, promoted the Aten to replace the old state god of Egypt, Amun-Ra, who combined in human form the ancient local god of Thebes (Amun) with the cult of the sun and its creative powers (Ra). Replacement took the form of obliteration of images and names of Amun and Amun-Ra. Akhenaten evidently hoped that the devotional landscape of the future would exclude Amun altogether. But this policy was not extended much further to other gods, as we shall see. Tutankhamun's decree was probably exaggerating; a piece of black propaganda.

Furthermore, we should not lose sight of a broader drama being played out, that of one family losing control of its personal empire – in this case the kingship of Egypt – to another. This was the end of an era. Not only was Akhenaten the last major king of the dynasty that had originated in Thebes and ruled the country and an empire for the previous century and a half, but also Thebes had been the family and spiritual seat of power in Egypt for far longer. The next dynasty, the 19th, which successfully took over the rule of Egypt, was originally a military family from the north. It is quite likely that as many established interests were adversely affected as was the case under Akhenaten. In some ways, the 19th Dynasty marks a return to 'traditionalism', but in others it represents a new order, including a reversal of geographic priority (from the south to the north), and the building of yet another new capital city (Per-Ramesses), this time in the Nile delta. The subsequent damning of Akhenaten could have had as much to do with the reinforcement of the claim to power by the house of Ramesses as dislike of his ideas. His presumed villainy was worth keeping in popular memory (as in the case of Richard III and the Tudors).

The fate of Amarna itself has a role in our assessment of Akhenaten's offence. The city was abandoned, but most likely because it had not been built in a place with a sustainable future. Houses, the brightly painted mud-brick palaces and the mud-brick pylons (monumental gates) of the Aten temples were left standing, so there was no attempt to pretend that Amarna had never existed. The boundary stelae in the surrounding cliffs, which were to fix for all time the limits of Akhetaten, were hardly touched at all and so kept alive a record of his reign for any curious passer-by. All the stone buildings were demolished, but the stones were re-used, mostly unaltered, in new religious buildings on other sites (especially those in the city of Hermopolis, modern El-Ashmunein, across the river). Many a temple must have contained (unseen) named images of Akhenaten and the Aten. While Akhenaten had the name and images of Amun eliminated, the same fate was not meted out subsequently to the Aten and to its image of sun rays spreading out from the central disc. They remained generally untouched. The kind of anger that is assuaged by the destruction of images was reserved for Akhenaten and Nefertiti themselves, and concentrated on their numerous fine statues in hard stones that were erected in some of the buildings at Amarna. These were methodically reduced to rubble. Their names and faces were attacked in most of the tombs of Akhenaten's officials, but not too thoroughly (1.1 is a fine exception, in one of the most important of the tombs).

What Lay in his Mind?

Even if we discount the possibility of civil war arising from disputed succession, there is room to question whether the conflict was theological in the polarized sense that is familiar from the much later history of Christian schism. In trying to understand Akhenaten we are, in fact, investigating the nature of the imagination – the Egyptian imagination and, as a point of comparison, our own – and the many outlets that people find for mental energy, prominent among them being religious devotion.

Take the blurry subject of gods. The property of 'being divine' in ancient Egypt – of attracting awe – was common to gods, to kings and also to those human individuals who were worthy of respect: prominent heads of households, thus urban patriarchs. Statues of all three were to be found in temples where they received the same kinds of offerings, presented in what was basically the same way. The cult of local civic leaders – men with the titles 'Nomarch' and 'Mayor' – reached its height during the Middle Kingdom (*c.* 2066–1750 BC), to the extent that theirs were some of the largest of the statues that people would see in their towns, with portable counterparts that were carried in festival processions, their cult supported by permanent endowments at temple-like tombs or other memorials. In the New Kingdom (*c.* 1549–1069 BC), the practice became muted, but even so Amenhotep III's chief builder, Amenhotep son of Hapu, was represented by statues in the temple at Karnak, where they acted as intermediaries for the petitions of common people to the god Amun. The divine aura surrounding human individuals becomes more understandable through the text of a prayer in the tomb of a scribe of the 18th Dynasty, Amenemhat. He asks that all the following parts of himself will live on in the afterlife: his spirit (*ka*), the memorial tablet at his tomb (through which his name would be kept alive), his soul (*ba*), his destiny, his life, his 'illumination', his body, his shadow, his place of origin, his upbringing, his personal creator-god (Khnum) and (in a final summary phrase) 'all his modes of being'. Each and every one of them is described as a 'god'.[3]

When we say that the Egyptians worshipped many gods, and were polytheists, we simplify and coarsen a subtle and sophisticated view of how, in the world around them, they saw the forces that brought life and purpose. Akhenaten was not necessarily assaulting all of this. In their houses, the citizens of Amarna might pay respect to Akhenaten through images, but they did the same to their own heads of household and also to helpful spirits from the world of the 'gods' (see Chapter 7).

An essential characteristic of being human is to tolerate inconsistency, an aspect of the fuzziness of the mind that allows new ideas to form that require to be tested, perhaps only to be rejected. Since the time of the ancient Greeks, however, thinking in the West has put firmer restrictions on inconsistency (though it still abounds in our personal lives). We expect significant ideas to apply universally. While the nature of mathematics excludes inconsistency, religious leaders can achieve consistency of belief only by imposition. The lure of consistency justifies, to them, intolerance and persecution. The Egyptians, by contrast, acquiesced more readily to inconsistency (insofar as they were aware of it as an identifiable phenomenon). They expected logic to have only local application, to come in small packets. Akhenaten's monotheism is a case in point. It had validity in that particular sphere in which the king was responsible for the welfare and stability of Egypt, the sphere that was 'state religion' and felt the full force of his vision. He wished to cleanse the solar cult of inappropriate imagery, the man-shaped sun-god Amun-Ra, leaving a simple direct channel of visual perception between himself and the remote and austere disc-image of the sun. But Akhenaten did not see that the same logic extended across the board to all manifestations of divinity. So, yes, he was a monotheist on his own ground, but not in the way that monotheism later developed.

According to the decree of Tutankhamun quoted above (or the way that modern readers are inclined to interpret it), Akhenaten's devotion to the Aten was to the detriment of the traditional temples throughout Egypt: in his time, they had been neglected, even closed and abandoned. The contemporary evidence does not match up to this, however. A source from Karnak early in Akhenaten's reign lists the (relatively modest) amounts of 'tax' that certain established temples in Egypt had to pay to support simultaneously the cult of the Aten and a large community of people (6,800 'subordinates of the House of the Aten' is the figure of the one preserved part).[4] Then, from shortly before the accession of Tutankhaten/Tutankhamun, we have a prayer to Amun written in a tomb at Thebes for the benefit of a priest who served in a temple of Amun.[5] So here we have, at either end of the Amarna period, statements that some of the old temples were functioning. For the intervening years, when we expect the king to have been at the height of his powers, we have to turn to less explicit sources to find out what happened.

Many temples belonging to the reigns of Akhenaten's predecessors have survived – an interesting sign in itself. Akhenaten's successors were quick to demolish his temples and to re-use the stones, leaving nothing standing. Akhenaten did not act like this. He left the existing temples in place, subjecting them to adjustments in their decoration. As yet, no full assessment of this practice has been made, the main reason being that the results would be largely negative (contradicting the theory that he opposed traditional temples) and therefore disappointing as source material for dramatic narratives.

One case concerns the temple of the god Horus, Lord of Buhen, built just over a century before Akhenaten, during the time of Hatshepsut and Thutmose III, in one of the colonial temple towns in Nubia. Its god, a local form of Horus (and thus a form of the sun-god), was left untouched, as were images and hieroglyphic references to the goddesses Satis and Anukis, and references to the plural word 'gods'. On one pillar, however, Amun-Ra had been depicted and named, and both his image and name had been scraped off (to be recarved again after the Amarna period). A significant find in the temple ruins at Buhen was of fragments of a text recording a violent attack upon raiding Nubians from the eastern desert made by the Viceroy of Kush on behalf of Akhenaten. It is dated probably to the king's twelfth regnal year. Its presence suggests (though it does not prove) that the temple of Horus at Buhen was functioning throughout Akhenaten's reign, having been purged of its Amun connection and thereby made acceptable. A temple built under Amenhotep II at Amada, 150 km (93 miles) downstream, reveals a similar pattern of studied alterations (rather than a savage attack). The figure of Amun was erased, along with his name and his epithet 'king of the gods'. Other figures and names of gods were, however, left untouched, as again was the plural word 'gods' in the king's title 'protector of the gods'. The same record of victory against Nubians was also set up there.[6]

It could be, therefore, that the general run of temples in Egypt and Nubia, once they had been cleansed of Amun references, were left to carry on as before, although here and there (including in Nubia) new shrines to the Aten were built as well. The statement on Tutankhamun's decree of restoration then looks to have been tendentious, even malicious. Even the other main beneficiary of Tutankhamun's restoration edict, the god Ptah of Memphis, did not attract hostility, despite being a creator-god and thus, from the point of view of consistency, a rival to the Aten. Akhenaten's restricted fervour becomes even more apparent at Amarna itself, where a tradition of honouring and appealing for assistance to spiritual beings in the domestic sphere (largely ignoring the Aten in the process) was generally maintained across the social spectrum (see Chapter 7, pp. 234–38).

Akhenaten's object of devotion, the Aten, was not new to Egypt, and neither was its identification with the king. Years before Akhenaten, King Thutmose III had been described as 'Ra, the lord of heaven, the king of the two lands when he rises, the Aten when he reveals himself'.[7] This is a neat example of the use of divine imagery in the service of pious flattery of kings, where the names of gods are metaphors. In Akhenaten's much-reduced vocabulary of god's names, Ra remained acceptable, as well as Horus (whose form was often that of a falcon, or a falcon-headed man) and Shu. This last spiritual being, also usually shown in human form, was the element in the universe that we experience as light and air, and who (or which) belonged to one particular theory that the Egyptians had developed about how matter in the universe had been created (centred on the creator-god Atum).

Akhenaten gave to the Aten its own pair of names written in cartouches as if they were the names of a king [1.3]. For the first years at Amarna, the cartouches identified the sun-disc as 'The living-one, Ra-Horus of the Horizon, who rejoices on the horizon, in his name of "Shu who is the Aten"'. Egyptians would have naturally drawn upon their existing traditional knowledge of what these terms meant. Later in his reign, Akhenaten changed the names of the Aten to read 'The living-one, Ra, ruler of the two horizons, who rejoices on the horizon, in his name of sunlight that comes from the Aten'. One can interpret this as a refinement, expressing a greater degree of abstraction, but the old form of the Aten's names was evidently not offensive, since they were generally not altered in places where they had been previously carved.

1.3 *A full set of Amarna cartouches. The larger pair on the left are those of the Aten in their earlier form and read, from right to left: '(The living-one, Ra-Horus of the Horizon, who rejoices on the horizon) (in his name of Shu who is the Aten).' The curved brackets show the start and end of each cartouche. The three smaller ones are, from left to right, the first and second cartouche names of Akhenaten, and the name of Nefertiti. From the tomb of Ay (no. 25), east thickness of the entrance doorway.*

Metaphors and symbols are natural forms of human expression, and religions allow them to blossom. Although Akhenaten retained some, he seems to have preferred a literalism that rejected the clutter that imagination supplies to fill the gaps in people's perception of how the universe works. The sun moved across the sky on its own; it did not voyage in a boat; it was not propelled by a divine scarab-beetle. There was no nighttime realm through which the sun journeyed, beset by dangers. There was no kingdom of Osiris. What existed was what you saw. Herein we can see the seeds of Akhenaten's self-destruction. The austerity of his vision was too dull and lacking in delightful poetic complexity and inconsistency for it to satisfy most people (though there are bound to have been exceptions: a seeming one of them, an 'unguent preparer' named Ramose, is introduced below, p. 30).

Akhenaten the Teacher

In their tomb inscriptions, some of Akhenaten's courtiers refer to him as the author of a teaching on righteous conduct in life. This was a powerful concept, to the extent that the word for truth and justice, *maat*, was regularly credited with being a goddess, her name Maat, the daughter of the sun-god Ra. The Aten was now called 'The Prince of Maat (Truth)', the 'mountain of Akhetaten, the place of Maat'.

> He has placed Maat in my innermost being. My abomination is falsehood, for I know that Waenra [Akhenaten's first cartouche name], my lord, rejoices in Maat.... My lord instructed me just so that I might practise his teaching ... my lord, who constructs people, brings lifetime into being and makes a good fate for his favourite, [whose] heart is satisfied with Maat, whose abomination is falsehood. How prosperous is he who hears your teaching of life....
>
> God's Father, Ay[8]

> I do not do what His Majesty hates. My abomination in my inmost being is wrongdoing, the great abomination of Waenra [the king]. Because I know he lives on them, I have elevated righteous things to His Majesty. You are Ra, who begat Maat.... I do not receive the reward of wrongdoing in order to suppress Maat falsely. I do what is righteous to the king.... Every day he rises early to instruct me, inasmuch as I carry out his teaching....
>
> Chamberlain Tutu[9]

Akhenaten as teacher appears in brief texts (neither of them in tombs) of both the sculptor Bak and the builder Maanakhtuef. These men recorded that they were, in their respective skills, disciples taught by the king.[10]

It is believable that Akhenaten wrote down his teachings on good conduct, and perhaps on other subjects, on papyrus. The intensity of vision that is conveyed by the art style that he adopted and the single-mindedness by which he must have pursued his agenda of change implies, at the very least, a person almost overwhelmed by his own thoughts. He would have been acting within the traditions of Egyptian kingship if he did, and the attempt to express difficult philosophical and moral dilemmas was a long-standing function of Egyptian literature. No set of teachings written by Akhenaten has survived, only carved stone texts, which are not the most fluent medium. The impression that they leave of superficiality in thinking might not be fair, however.

A teaching that emphasized the immediacy of concern for righteous living perhaps explains the quiet disappearance of Osiris from funerary beliefs. Traditionally, Osiris presided over the final judgment of a person's lifetime conduct, where the heart was weighed against the symbol of Maat. Perhaps Akhenaten was trying to make people answerable for their conduct in the face of the Aten, a daily vision of 'The Prince of Truth'. An example of the successful effect of the teaching appears in personal letters written by an unguent preparer in the household of Princess Meryetaten, named Ramose. He more than once refers to the Aten as a source of guidance in the making of personal decisions, as if the Aten were an extension to his conscience.[11]

People who took to heart the king's teaching were still not followers of an Aten religion, however. No such thing had been defined. People might have been encouraged to think a bit differently, but were not asked to abandon their way of life or wholly to suppress cherished notions of where, within the spirit world, they should look for protection.

Akhenaten's Appearance

To the modern world (and probably to his contemporaries) the most difficult aspect of Akhenaten's reign is the way he had himself portrayed. What should we make of the exaggerated physiognomy, so dramatically expressed in the sandstone colossal statues from Karnak made very early in his reign [1.5]? What did his contemporaries make of it? The shape he gave himself is a radical departure from the established forms of the period that, though they could surprise at the level of the technical skills employed, did not set out to challenge the viewer's assumptions about kingship. Were it to be true that, in the human remains discovered in the early-twentieth-century in tomb 55 in the Valley of the Kings, we have the actual body of Akhenaten, a body that shows no abnormalities, we would be obliged to look for an explanation within his own thoughts. The likelihood that the remains are not his scarcely lessens that obligation, in my view.[12]

The images are a wake-up call that here is someone not in the mainstream of humanity. He is one of a kind, on the edge. He wants you to feel uncomfortable and yet – as conveyed through the relaxed poses and overt affection for his family shown in other contexts – to love him at the same time. He is opposing himself to the preferred muscular images of kings and thus, presumably, to what they stood for (1.1, 1.4; but see 3.25 for an exception). This is not a king ruling through aggression. But does one read that face as malevolent (as many would have his character) or earnest? Is it the face of the would-be teacher trying to reach out beyond the awkward paraphernalia of rule and doing so in an experimental style? Has that style originated from intense introspection

1.4 *(above) The chariot was normally a king's military vehicle. Here Akhenaten subverts that image. As he bids farewell to his officials (the one at the top none other than his chief of police, Mahu) he creates a pose of intimacy with Nefertiti. From the tomb of Mahu (no. 9).*

1.5 *(right) Colossal statue of Akhenaten, sandstone, from Karnak, now in the Egyptian Museum, Cairo. Height 2.39 m (7 ft 9 in.).*

and from a personal preoccupation with the shape and functions of his own body? That is the Akhenaten that I see.

The Amarna period ended with a power struggle, whether involving armed combat we do not know, in which the final victors were military families from the north of the country. It is a reasonable presumption that the families associated with Akhenaten fell from official favour and many of their dependants would, as a consequence, have found themselves assigned to new masters. That was how ancient Egypt worked. A wider persecution of people sympathetic to his ideas is unlikely, however. They would not have mattered. To those who sought to replace his power, however, Akhenaten's eccentric style clearly caused great offence. He was the ultimately unacceptable role model, a style criminal where it mattered most, in the negotiated power transfers between the creator-god and his son on earth, the king of Egypt.

Akhenaten's Vision: The Written Version

Akhenaten acted like a man with a vision, a vision that gave him a practical agenda to follow. Nowadays he is mostly discussed in terms of his beliefs, considered in abstract. Close attention is paid to how his 'theology' related to the prevailing consensual system. His own statements, however, show that the full expression of his beliefs demanded the creation of physical sacred landscape. The creation of Akhetaten – which embraces the modern archaeological site of Amarna – was an essential defining act. Discussions about Akhenaten that are limited to theology separate themselves from a major part of the original medium through which he expressed himself. The buildings and the landscape were essential to the message; they defined it, as he himself makes clear in the foundation decrees carved into the cliffs that surround Amarna on the east, and into the low escarpment that faces Amarna from across the river on the west. They are the most extensive personal testimony we have as to what was in his mind.

1.6 *Map of the Nile valley at Amarna, showing the locations of the boundary stelae of the first and second sets, and the areas that they define. The stelae are given letters, as shown in the key. The first set defines the area shaded dark grey; in this initial vision, the eastern desert bay alone is the place Akhetaten. The second set define the area shaded paler grey; now the boundaries of Akhetaten have been redrawn to take in the land on the west side of the Nile.*

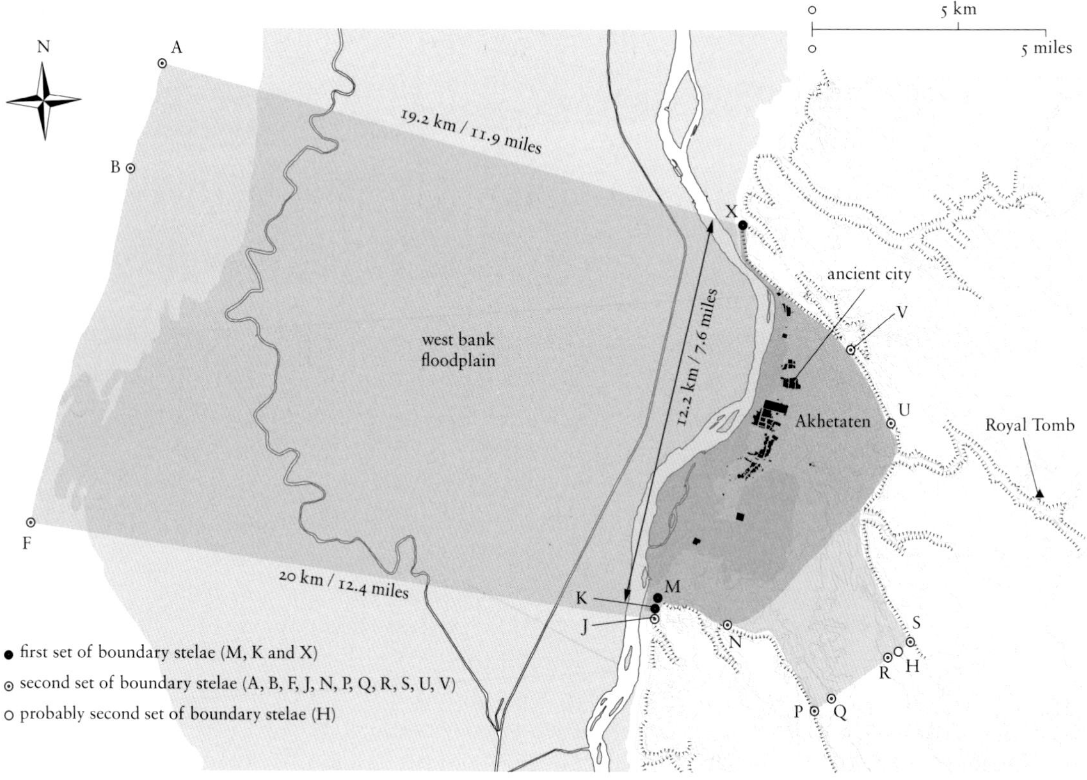

1.7 *Boundary stela U, of the second set, dated to year 6. Statues of Akhenaten, Nefertiti and two of the daughters stand on either side. The stela is 8.37 m (27.5 ft) high.*

A total of sixteen of these boundary tablets or stelae have been discovered [**1.6, 1.7; Pl. VIII**]. They were not all made at the same time, but belong to two sets, with different texts, made with an interval of a year between them. The first set is dated to the king's fifth year and the second to his sixth. At the end of the text on the second set, an additional passage (the 'colophon') commemorates the king's visit and oath in his eighth year. When freshly cut they would have been a dazzling white (though with the details picked out in bright colours) and visible from afar. It was also intended that they would be visited, for broad paths made by clearing stones to each side ran up to several of them.

The date of the first proclamation is regnal year 5, 4th month of Peret, day 13.

> On this day, when One was in Akhet[aten], His Majesty [appeared] on the great chariot of electrum.... Setting [off] on a good road [toward] Akhetaten, his [i.e. the Aten's] place of creation, which he made for himself that he might set within it every day.... There was presented a great offering to the Father, the Aten, consisting of bread, beer, long- and short-horned cattle, calves, fowl, wine, fruits, incense, all kinds of fresh green plants and everything good, in front of the mountain of Akhetaten....

The king addresses his gathered courtiers:

> As the Aten is beheld, the Aten desires that there be made for him [... (damaged passage)] as a monument with an eternal and everlasting name. Now, it is the Aten, my father, who advised me concerning it, [namely] Akhetaten. No official has ever advised me concerning it, not any of the people who are in the entire land has ever advised me concerning it, to suggest making Akhetaten in this distant place. It was the Aten, my fath[er, who advised me] concerning it, so that it might be made for him as Akhetaten.... Behold, it is Pharaoh who has discovered it: not being the property of a god, not being the property of a goddess, not being the property of a ruler, not being the property of a female ruler, not being the property of any people to lay claim to it....
>
> I shall make Akhetaten for the Aten, my father, in this place. I shall not make Akhetaten for him to the south of it, to the north of it, to the west of it, to the east of it. I shall not expand beyond the southern stela of Akhetaten toward the south, nor shall I expand beyond the northern stela of Akhetaten toward the north, in order to make Akhetaten for him there. Nor shall I make [it] for him on the western side of Akhetaten, but I shall make Akhetaten for the Aten, my father, on the east of Akhetaten, the place that he himself made to be enclosed for him by the mountain....
>
> I shall make the 'House of the Aten' for the Aten, my father, in Akhetaten in this place. I shall make the 'Mansion of the Aten' for the Aten, my father, in Akhetaten in this place. I shall make the Sun-Temple of the [Great King's] Wife [Nefernefruaten-Nefertiti] for the Aten, my father, in Akhetaten in this place. I shall make the 'House of Rejoicing' for the Aten, my father, in the 'Island of the Aten, Distinguished in Jubilees' in Akhetaten in this place.... I shall make for myself the apartments of Pharaoh, I shall make the apartments of the Great King's Wife in Akhetaten in this place.
>
> Let a tomb be made for me in the eastern mountain [of Akhetaten]. Let my burial be made in it, in the millions of jubilees that the Aten, my father, has decreed for me. Let the burial of the Great King's Wife, Nefertiti, be made in it, in the millions of yea[rs that the Aten, my father, decreed for her. Let the burial of] the King's Daughter, Meryetaten, [be made] in it, in these millions of years. If I die in any town downstream, to the south, to the west, to the east in these millions of years, let me be brought back, that I may be buried in Akhetaten. If the Great

> King's Wife, Nefertiti, dies in any town downstream, to the south, to the west, to the east in these millions [of years, let her be brought back, that] she [may be buried in Akhetaten. If the King's Daughter, Meryetaten, dies] in any town downstream, to the south, to the west, to the east in these millions of years, let her be brought back, that [she] may be buried in Akhetaten. Let a cemetery for the Mnevis Bull [be made] in the eastern mountain of Akhetaten, that he may [be buried] in it. Let the tombs of the Chief of Seers, of the God's Fathers of the [Aten ...] be made in the eastern mountain of Akhetaten, that they may be buried in it. Let [the tombs] of the priests of the [Aten] be [made in the eastern mountain of Akhetaten] that they may b[e bur]ied in it.[13]

The text of the second set of boundary stelae is largely concerned with stating, in the form of an oath by Akhenaten and with laborious repetition, that the boundary stelae fix absolute limits for Akhetaten. Akhetaten must never be extended beyond them and everything contained within them belongs absolutely to the Aten. The final addition, in year 8, repeats the oath.

People imagine cities. The Egyptians gave their city of Thebes a mythical status. It was 'the pattern for every city. Water and earth were in her from the beginning of time, when the sands came to limit the fields and to create her ground upon the high place at the earth's beginning.'[14] Here the image is of how the world of Egypt commenced as a series of mounds that emerged from a primeval flood and upon which the gods first made their abodes, and which in turn became the sites of the leading temples and places of creation. By contrast, Akhetaten is not given the characteristics of a city and has no prior history. It is a tract of newly discovered land, uncontaminated by prior ownership, which, in the first proclamation, is desert and mountain where the Aten can feel fully at home, without competition. It is the Aten's reservation and, as we shall see in Chapter 5, was protected from trespass.

Akhenaten's Vision: The Implementation

In the stelae, the implementation of the vision begins with the proclamation at the chosen site, the presentation of offerings and the fixing of the boundaries. There is the promise of major buildings to come. Akhenaten had already had, however, a trial run: at Thebes. Thousands of stone blocks from the first years of his reign, decorated in his distinctive style, have been recovered from later buildings in the temple enclosures at Karnak and Luxor where they were reused as convenient filling materials. The foundations of one of his buildings have been partially excavated, along with a number of striking colossal statues of the king that have become, in modern times, the most familiar image of his reign [**1.5, Pl. 1**]. It is clear that Akhenaten began his reign by building one or more large temples to the Aten beside the existing temple to Amun, which he allowed to stand. Amarna was thus a fresh start in a programme to which considerable resources had already been devoted. Whether he envisaged this at the outset, or developed the idea of Akhetaten, a new place, as he pursued his vision, is not clear.

On the ground at Amarna, we have the remains of a number of major buildings that, both from their size and often from the extensive use of stone, are obviously 'royal' and ought to be the ones Akhenaten promised in his list on the earlier proclamation. Two that are obviously temples to the Aten lie not far from one another in the centre of the city [1.8–1.10]. They are presumably the 'House of the Aten' and the 'Mansion of the Aten', and are the subject of Chapter 3, as are several buildings that are less temple-like, but also served the Aten. Some of them were called 'sun-temples' (the literal term is 'sunshades'). There were several buildings that attract the term 'palace'. One of them, in modern nomenclature the Great Palace, was of unusually large size and built mostly of stone. Whether the phrase 'House of Rejoicing', which features prominently in the building list of the boundary stelae, was applied to it as a single name is debatable. The palaces are the subject of Chapter 4.

1.8 *Aerial view, looking towards the north, of the Central City at Amarna, taken on 17 March 1932 by the Royal Air Force.* 1 *The Great Palace, across the road, has, at the time of the photograph, not yet been dug by the EES expedition of the 1930s;* 2 *The site of the Great Aten Temple, likewise not yet excavated in 1932, occupies ground in front of the modern cemetery;* 3 *The Small Aten Temple ('Mansion of the Aten') lies newly excavated in the foreground.*

From buildings, Akhenaten's agenda moved to tombs in the eastern mountain, a high plateau of limestone beds cut by steep-sided wadis (desert valleys) and ending in the cliffs and escarpments that form the backdrop to Amarna [1.11]. The tomb for himself was cut into the rock in a narrow side valley leading off from one of the main wadis, which represented a walk of 6 km (3.7 miles) from its mouth, with another 4 km (2.5 miles) to reach that point from the edge of the city [1.12; **Pls VII, XLIII**]. The same tomb contained a burial chamber for his daughter Meketaten and an unfinished subsidiary tomb of royal type. According to the boundary stelae, it might have been for Meryetaten, but Nefertiti is another candidate. Three more rock tombs were begun in the area, so marking the start of a new Valley of the Kings. They bear not a single hieroglyph, leaving the identity of their intended occupants open to speculation.The agenda next mentions a tomb for the Mnevis bull, an

1.9 *Aerial view, looking towards the west, of the Central City at Amarna, taken in 1993. The Great Palace lies just in front of the trees in the distance. The Small Aten Temple is in the left of the middle distance. Below it, and a little to the right, is the building where the Amarna Letters were found (the Records Office).*

animal sacred to Ra of Heliopolis and given burial in a chambered tomb there. Nothing identifies such a tomb at Amarna, unless it was intended to be one of the unfinished tombs at the royal valley site. But then, there is no sign that the sacred Mnevis bull itself was brought to live at Amarna. This looks like an intention that was abandoned. The distant location of the royal tombs placed

1.10 *Plan of the Central City. The boundaries of the modern fields and of the modern cemetery are as they were in 1977–78. The grid is made up of 200-m (656-ft) squares.*

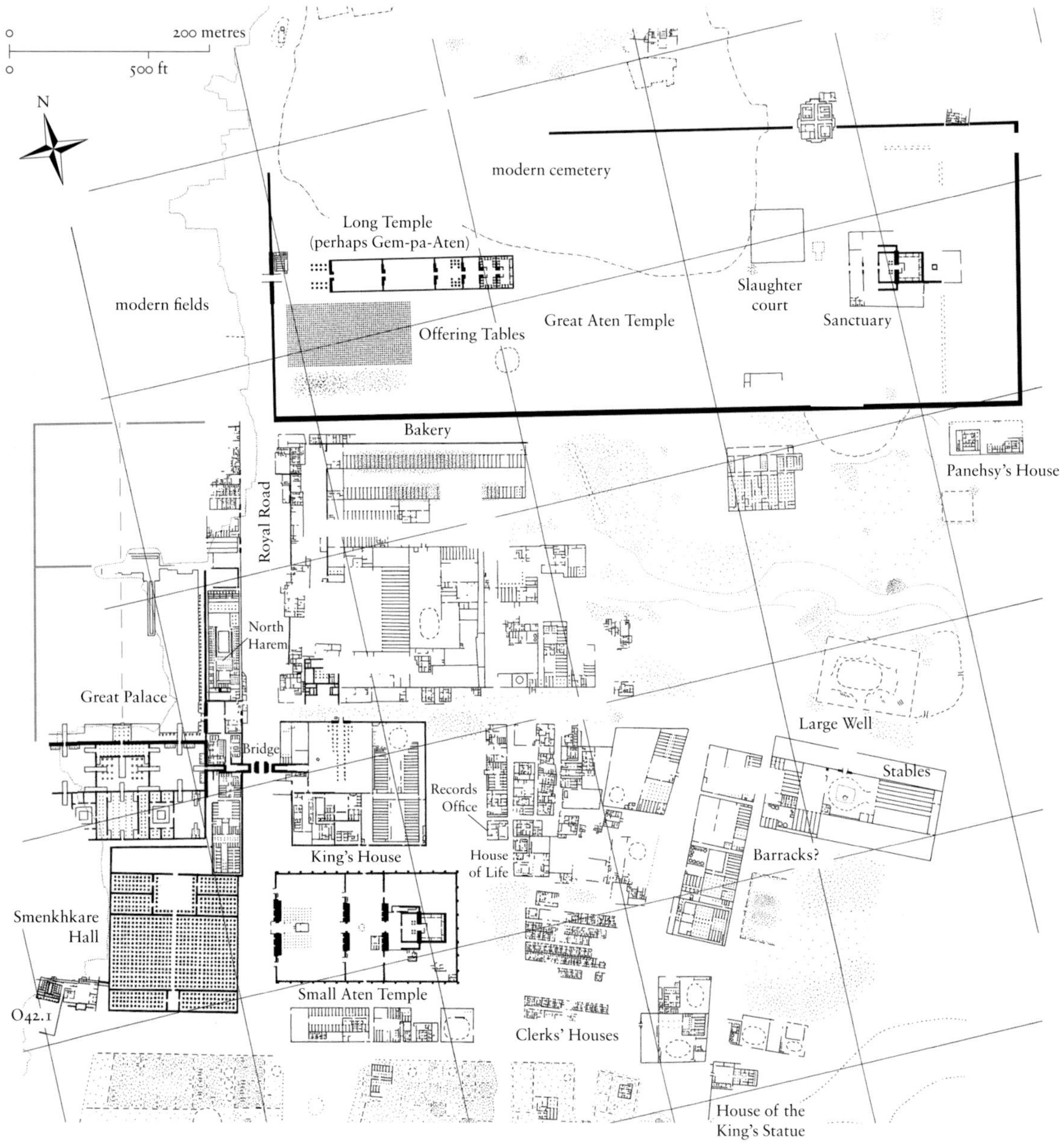

1.11 *The 'eastern mountain' of Akhetaten, which defined the 'horizon'; shown here is the portion into which the North Tombs were cut, taken in 1993. View towards the north.*

them deeply within the Aten's 'horizon', yet they are also a significant distance beyond the limits of Akhetaten, as defined with such care by the boundary stelae. This is a topography more flexible than one made by people with a modern mapping perspective.

Finally come the tombs for the various 'priests' of the Aten. As the actual ownership of the tombs reveals, this is a euphemism for people who served Akhenaten in various ways, as priests, stewards, military officers, policemen and scribes. Their tombs were cut into the rock facing towards Amarna, in two groups: a northern group that took advantage of the high cliff [1.11], and a southern group that used a low escarpment of soft rock that is actually part of the floor of a rift valley running southeastwards from the Amarna plain and representing a major break in the continuity of the high desert that fringes Amarna. The tombs, along with the cemeteries of lesser people that were made in their vicinity, will be included in Chapter 7. For the present, it should be noted that such of the decoration as there was time to complete in the rock tombs mostly comprises prayers to the Aten and scenes of the royal family living out their lives touched by the Aten's rays. It is a distinctive feature of the scenes – and one immeasurably valuable to us – that they contain much

1.12 *The entrance to the Royal Tomb, in a remote desert valley in the 'eastern mountain'. The photograph was taken during the excavation of 1935.*

incidental detail on the architecture of the temples and palaces, and on the activities of people, great and small, who accompanied the royal family.

The boundary stelae come to an end without mentioning the fact that several tens of thousands of people were going to build their houses and live at Amarna. Akhenaten does not use the word 'city' at all. The place Akhetaten was primarily the Aten's piece of desert below the cliffs. The city, with its houses, temples and palaces, was a necessary adjunct that lay on its edge. Akhenaten was no recluse. He needed a population towards whom he could direct the beneficence that flowed from the Aten, and whose time was largely taken up by serving and making things for his court.

In the year following Akhenaten's initial decree, the essence of Akhetaten, as defined by the first group of stelae, was compromised. A second group of stelae was carved, not only along the eastern cliff, but also along the western desert edge, so embracing a broad tract of agricultural land. The text explicitly admits this. Akhetaten now includes 'hills, uplands, marshes, new lands, basin lands, fresh lands, fields, waters, towns, river banks, people, herds, groves...'. This land lay adjacent to the city of Hermopolis (El-Ashmunein) and its temples, and must have belonged to the usual mixture of private owners and temples. Was it sequestrated from its original owners? The last words of the renewal of the oath in year 8 also ignore the inconsistency contained within this fundamental alteration to the character of Akhetaten. All the land between the western and eastern horizons 'belongs to my father, the living Aten, to be the House of the Aten continually and forever. Their entirety is offered to his spirit (*ka*), and his brilliant rays receive them.' (Note how the 'House of the Aten' is here a metaphor for the whole of Akhetaten, east and west.) What prompted the change is unknown.

The Coming of the Crowds

The creation of Amarna led to the uprooting and migration of thousands of people. Did they go by choice? We have no written records to tell us how they viewed the experience. However, we do know in general the way that ancient Egyptian society worked, and this can help us to understand how Amarna acquired its population.

The process involved chains of obligation. Akhenaten, like kings generally, had to rely upon a group of people who were loyal to him and who formed his court and his circle of senior officials. Some, perhaps many, were men newly chosen to be close to the king. They might have been brought up with him, at a time before it was realized that he would become a king, the chosen heir being a Thutmose, who predeceased his father. This is perhaps what the cup-bearer, Parennefer means when he states that he was 'the king's server when he [i.e. the king] was a youth'.[15] Parennefer made a rock tomb at Thebes and then, having moved with his king to Amarna, made another in the southern group at Amarna (no. 7). Especially because of Akhenaten's ambition to bring in changes that would provoke opposition, it is to be expected that, more than ever, the circle of those loyal to him contained men new to the court, outsiders.

The texts that we work from, mostly carved in the rock tombs at Amarna, are written in a style of hyperbolic praise and gratitude to the king and the Aten. Their consistent theme is total dependency upon a generous sovereign, who also offers guidance in distinguishing right from wrong. He is the fount of material rewards and, as already noted, moral instruction – a powerful combination.

> O living sun for everybody.... There is no poverty for the one who places you in his heart. He does not say 'If only I had something', but is continually on a good path until he reaches the state of reverence [i.e. death]. Let me give you adoration millions of times, let me adore you when you appear. I am an official of the ruler's making.
>
> General, Ramose[16]

One reason for expressing deep gratitude to the king was promotion from a humble station. 'I was a poor man on both my father's and my mother's side; but the ruler built me up, he developed me, he fed me by means of his spirit (*ka*)' says the king's fan-bearer, May.[17] This did not go against social norms in ancient Egypt. People had boasted about this for centuries and held it up as one of the marvels that a king could perform.

High status was publicly marked by ceremonial presentations of costly gifts. They could be in the form of golden objects and extra foodstuffs. In the decoration of the Amarna tombs, the ceremony – at the 'Window of Appearance' (an ancient Egyptian term) – was shown as one of the defining duties of the king, and it probably symbolized the king's broader role of provider to his people [1.13]. This, in turn, is part of the key to understanding how the city worked, the two-way flow of patronage and obligation, here at the uppermost level.

1.13 *Akhenaten, leaning out from the palace's 'Window of Appearance', showers gifts on his loyal courtier, the god's father Ay, here accompanied by his wife, Tey. Among the pile of gifts heaped on the ground are gloves (presumably of leather), collars, vessels and signet rings. The last three categories are likely to have been of gold. Tomb of Ay (no. 25). Compare figure 1.1.*

In maintaining a supply of gifts, instead of constantly dipping into a private treasure house, the king could make use of his power to exact levies on others. In order to benefit his chamberlain, Tutu, Akhenaten addresses his officials and chief men of the army: 'Pharaoh ordains that all the officials and chief men of the entire land be obliged to give him [i.e. Tutu] silver, gold, [cattle], clothing and bronze vessels – they being imposed upon you like taxes.' The words are then repeated, with the addition of 'every year'.[18] The custom of a national donation to the king, on New Year's Day, will feature in Chapter 8 (p. 296). It, too, is part of the key to understanding how the city worked.

The costly gifts could be people to swell one's extended household. One aspect of being an 'official' at Amarna – and there is no reason to think that this was in any way unusual for ancient Egypt – was to be the patrimonial head of many dependants. Huya, the chief official of the household of Akhenaten's mother (Queen Tiye), records in his tomb (no. 1) his appointment to be in charge of eight separate groups of men and boys organized into named groups, as if units in the army. They carry standards, but are not armed. One of them, entitled 'the company of bearers of the House of the Aten', are stated to be 'the people of' Huya.[19] These must be the kind of people who appear in the scenes that show a particular official being rewarded by the king at the palace. The reward takes place in the presence of the official's own celebratory audience, who cheer at the success of their master [1.14]. In the tomb of the god's father Ay (no. 25), little hieroglyphic texts quote the words of bodyguards and servants who stand and admire at the reward scene: 'For whom is this shouting being made, my boy?' cries one. 'The shouting is being made for the god's father, Ay, and Tey (his wife): they have become people of gold', comes the answer. 'Look at that stool and that bag!'[20] Through having his own crowd of followers, the rewarded official is a celebrity.

Another of Huya's rewards was of a set of craftsmen who included metal-workers, jewelry- and furniture-makers, and sculptors, one of them sufficiently important in Huya's eyes to be named: 'the chief sculptor of Queen Tiye, Iuty' [**8.16, 8.17**]. This scene is of particular importance when considering the basis of craft manufacture in the city and will be taken up again in Chapter 8, pp. 292–96. Presumably these craftsmen remained 'his' for as long as he remained in favour, his own hope probably to petition the king successfully for his eldest son to inherit both his job and the property (including craftsmen) that had come with it.

The king's fan-bearer, May, shows another side to this acquisition of followers. In giving thanks in his tomb for the king's generosity in promoting him, despite humble beginnings, he states how the king 'caused me to acquire people in numbers, caused my brothers and sisters to be many, caused all my

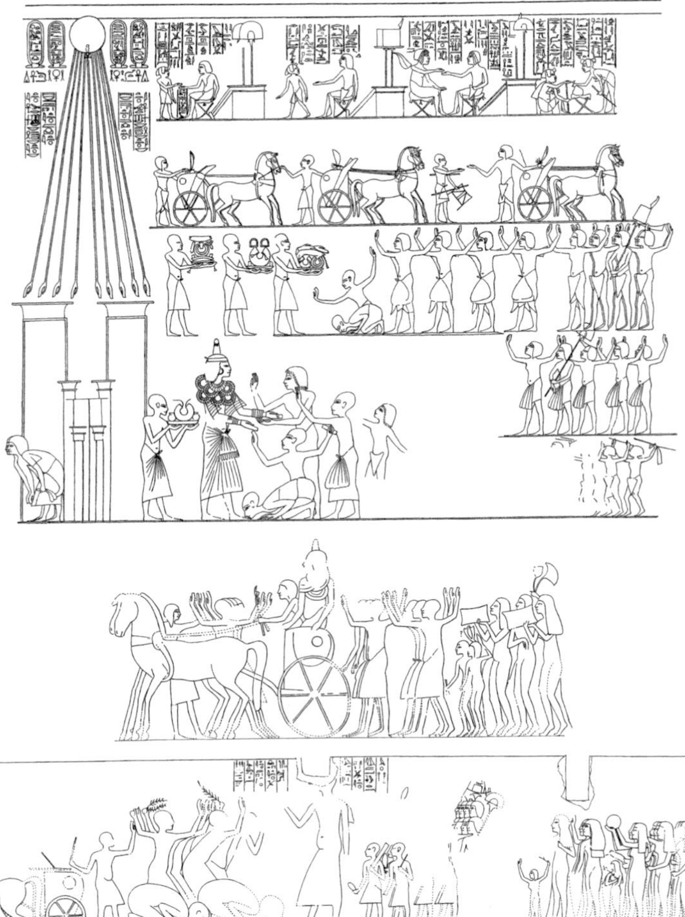

1.14 *Local celebrities. Important people measured their status, in part, by the number of their followers. (top) The god's father Ay (wearing his new gloves and collars) emerges from the Window of Appearance ceremony to acclamation from his followers. (middle) The steward Meryre (II) arrives home after a similar ceremony. (bottom) The high priest Panehsy seen doing likewise.*

people to assemble for me when I became master of my town'.[21] The high priest Panehsy, in referring to how the king 'caused me to be powerful when I had been poor', adds: 'My town comes to me at every season now that I am promoted on account of it.'[22]

May presumably, and Panehsy definitely, lived at Amarna. Panehsy has been identified as the owner of two houses. One was more of an office and lay near the Great Aten Temple [4.5]; the other was one of the larger private houses in its own estate in the Main City. Both men seem to be saying that they came from provincial towns where their favour with Akhenaten – gained presumably after migration to the court at Thebes or Memphis – made them leading figures. At this point, the interdependence between success and obligation would have made itself felt. Their growing status demanded that they had followers. The people from their community, with whom they would already have had ties of kinship, or at least prior acquaintance strengthened by a shared loyalty to a common place of origin, would have provided an obvious pool from which to draw. They are the ones who most likely accompanied their patron to the new city in the expectation of sharing in his success.

Beside Panehsy's house in the Main City, though separated from it by an open space, was a group of around forty small houses. It forms, in effect, a small village, isolated from the rest of the city by an adjacent administrative compound [1.15, 1.16]. I would interpret this as Panehsy's 'town' or village of dependants and loyalists who have accompanied him to Amarna and, in return, expect to share in his prosperity. Given Panehsy's high status at Amarna, the numbers look quite modest. But we need to remember a general rule in dealing with the ancient past: rarities like monumental buildings excepted, things were often less grand than we are tempted to imagine. Amarna illustrates this time and again. Other 'villages' that can be isolated within the city are even smaller (see 5.8–5.13).

Life in ancient Egypt (and the same was true for large parts of the ancient world) was very much a collective experience, centred on one's patron. Many people were clients. For every official who moved to Amarna, a crowd of dependants who extended beyond relatives by birth and marriage, followed at the same time. I imagine them arriving in a mass at an almost empty site, a virtual river-borne invasion fleet reaching the long curving river bank at almost the same time. From groups of boats, entire small communities emerge, disembark with their belongings and swarm across the desert to make a rapid camp and get the first fires going. Perhaps agents of their masters had gone ahead by a few days, to mark out positions for the big houses onto which the individual communities now converge. Even this may not have happened generally, however, since the layouts of some of the larger houses also look as though they came about during a scramble for plots of land. Next day, the brick-making starts, wall lines are marked out amidst communal discussion and argument. Within a matter of days, whole neighbourhoods appear, straggly and with gaps that will be filled more slowly by latecomers and by family expansion.

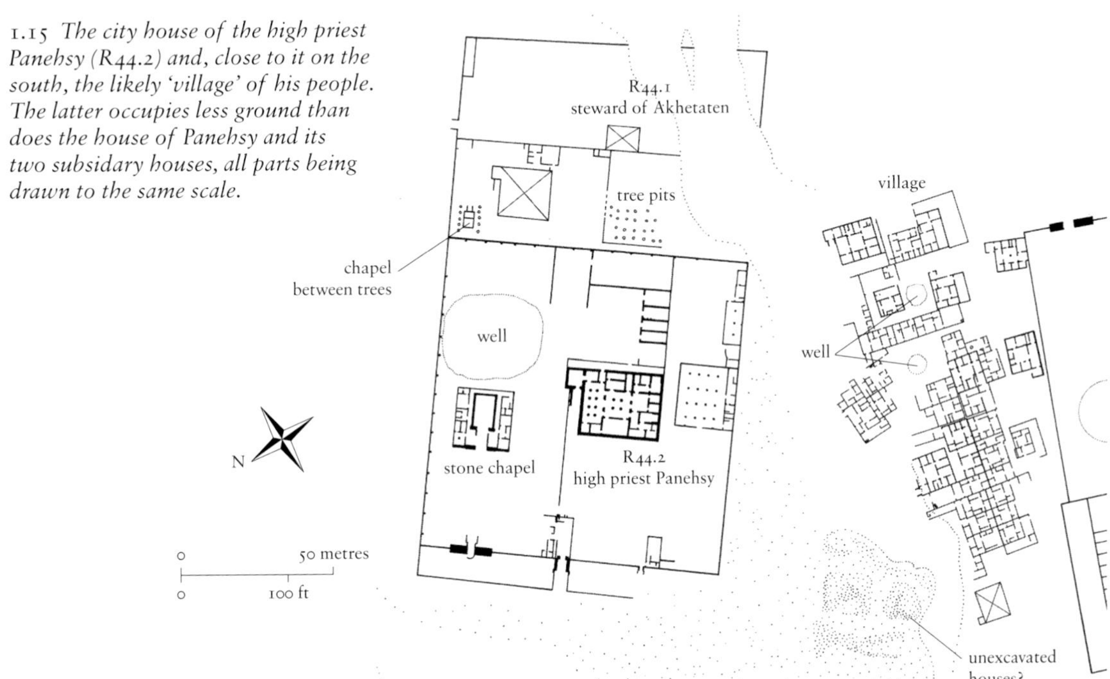

1.15 *The city house of the high priest Panehsy (R44.2) and, close to it on the south, the likely 'village' of his people. The latter occupies less ground than does the house of Panehsy and its two subsidary houses, all parts being drawn to the same scale.*

Akhenaten's great idea was to create a new home for the Aten, and this he accomplished. Here the Aten could be honoured in the way that Akhenaten thought was most appropriate: through extensive food-offerings laid out in unroofed temples built on a clean piece of desert. For the rest, his 'city' spontaneously took shape on the ground through the decisions of hundreds of ordinary people, becoming the centre of a network of social ties that reached back into the provinces of Egypt, representing the 'small-world' phenomenon about which more will be said in Chapter 8. In following this process of self-organization – it is one of the main themes of this book – we are reliving a piece of quintessentially human experience.

1.16 *The Panehsy house and village under attack from archaeologists in 1924.*

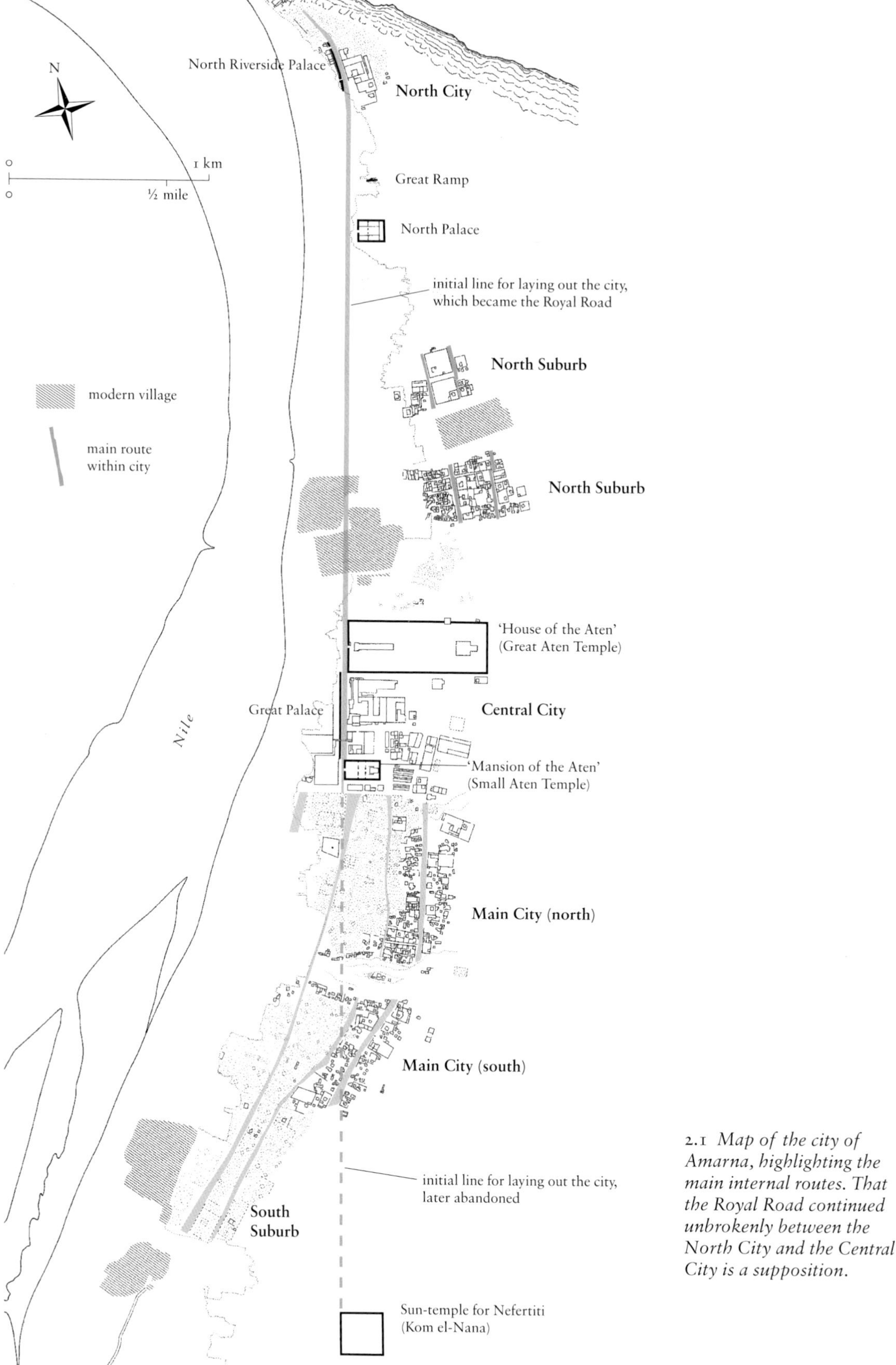

2.1 *Map of the city of Amarna, highlighting the main internal routes. That the Royal Road continued unbrokenly between the North City and the Central City is a supposition.*

CHAPTER TWO

AKHENATEN'S RESOURCES

The shape that Akhetaten–Amarna took was determined only in part by the king's vision. The resources at his disposal imposed limits. In modern terms, Akhenaten undertook a major capital project paid for from revenue. The ancient Egyptian economy does not seem to have offered scope for the raising of loans, although, in their place, came a much greater opportunity than is usually present today to draw upon obligations towards authority. High among those obligations was the donation of one's labour. Even so, the limitations are abundantly obvious if our standards and scale of measurement are those that later societies followed when undertaking grand building schemes.

The accomplishment of isolated marvels creates for modern audiences an expectation that everything ancient Egyptian was gigantic and wonderful. It was not. What we admire – and what they admired – were the exceptional creations of a society that for the most part maintained a village horizon. At Amarna, we have what is essentially a replicated mud village containing a few isolated monuments built with little thought as to their contribution to the overall urban effect. The limitations visible at Amarna were as much perceptual as they were economic. The Egyptians seem to have remained throughout their history comfortable with a modest unassuming style for towns and cities, and for much of the lifestyle that went with them.

The Landscape

The positions of the boundary stelae make it clear that the term Akhetaten was rapidly expanded to apply to the whole area enclosed by the stelae, although initially it meant only the desert part on the east bank where the city was built. Thus the largest part of Akhetaten lay across the river from Amarna and, as the stelae tell us, included fields and settlements. Preliminary archaeological survey has so far revealed no correspondence between detectable ancient sites – which are all centuries later – and anything of the New Kingdom. The level of the floodplain has risen substantially since then, and the locations of settlements might also have changed. If there is a buried landscape of Akhenaten's time beneath the modern fields it has not so far revealed itself.

The inclusion of fields and villages within the territory of Akhetaten gave the city agricultural resources, but what this meant in practical terms is not recorded. Was the land sequestrated for the benefit of the Aten temples? Nothing as dramatic need have happened. By long-established administrative processes, agricultural income was often shared out among institutions, and from time to time revisions were made to the list of those that benefited. Only written sources give answers to subjects like this and none have been found that relate to Amarna (although the Karnak 'tax' list, mentioned in the last chapter, p. 300, shows Akhenaten's mind working along these lines).

Rivers that flood across alluvial plains, like the Nile, are inclined to change their course over time. How do we know where the Nile was in Akhenaten's time? From direct archaeological evidence, we know that it followed a course not far from its present one as far back as the early centuries AD, a record of 2,000 years of a stable line of flow.[1] For Akhenaten's time, we have only artistic evidence, but that is fairly convincing. A scene of a palace – perhaps the Great Palace – in the tomb of May (no. 14) at Amarna shows, in front of a colonnade, a stretch of riverbank with vegetation and a line of boats drawn up, with mooring posts and gangways [**2.2**]. A scene in the tomb of the high priest Meryre (no. 4) is almost as explicit in juxtaposing moored boats with pictures of the temple, storerooms, gardens and other features that are clearly parts of the city.

Nowadays a strip of cultivated land, of narrow fields and many palm trees, separates the ancient city from the riverbank. Was that also the case in Akhenaten's time? Probably it was not, although direct evidence is slight. An archaeological trench dug to the west of the North Palace points to the alluvial deposits there having commenced only in the Late Roman period, almost two millennia after Akhenaten.[2] Part of the modern village of El-Till, close beside

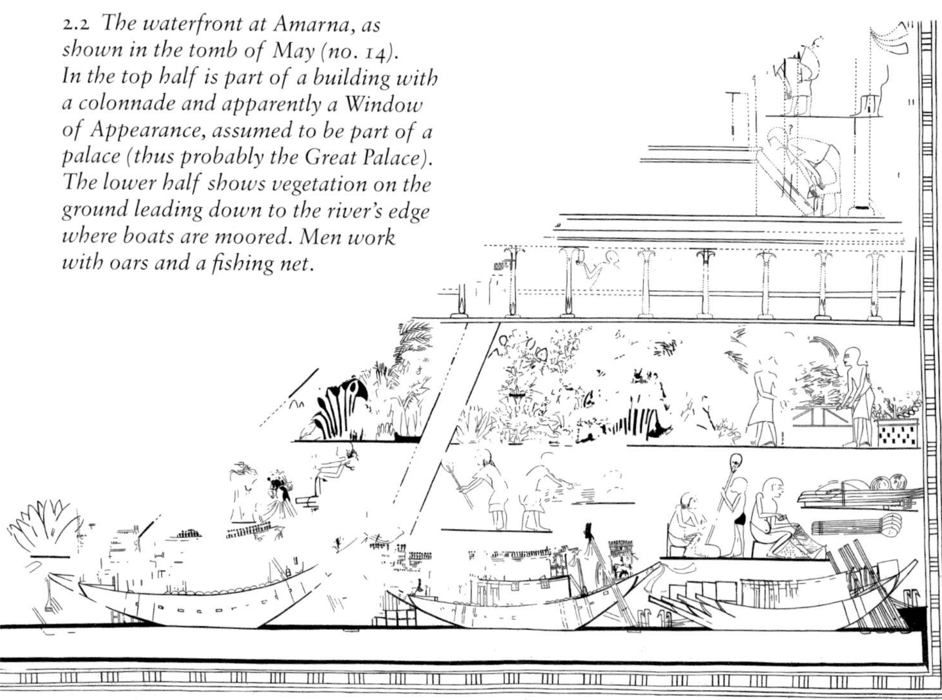

2.2 *The waterfront at Amarna, as shown in the tomb of May (no. 14). In the top half is part of a building with a colonnade and apparently a Window of Appearance, assumed to be part of a palace (thus probably the Great Palace). The lower half shows vegetation on the ground leading down to the river's edge where boats are moored. Men work with oars and a fishing net.*

the river, is built on a low natural rise in the desert, and a stony desert layer emerges from beneath the fields in front of the line of the Great Aten Temple and forms the present edge to the river.[3] Given that the river levels will have been lower in ancient times, it seems likely that the desert ran to the water's edge all the way along where the city was built. Moreover, the general trend of the streets of the main housing area of the ancient city follows a curve that is similar to that of the present riverbank [**2.1**, **2.3**].

Behind the riverbank, the chosen piece of desert was a rough semi-circle of yellow-to-orange sand and gravel, 10 km (6.2 miles) from one end to the other, hemmed in by limestone cliffs that curved out to a maximum distance from the Nile of 5 km (3.1 miles). It was not, however, a symmetrical site. Just past the halfway mark, as the cliffs curve southwards, they suddenly recede where a block of desert plateau has dropped down into a rift valley, the floor of which is just above the level of the adjacent desert plain. This gives a far more open feel to the southern half of Amarna. Akhenaten avoided it, siting his main buildings, and hence the bulk of the city, in the northern sector. This created a greater sense of enclosure, especially visible at the northern end where a part of the city rises onto the lower slopes of the cliffs as they approach the river. The boundary stelae nonetheless incorporate the southern half of the plain into Akhetaten. They mark a line across the rift valley that is about 4 km (2.5 miles) behind where the line of cliffs ought to have been and prompt the thought that this block of desert was intended to have a purpose for which no evidence has so far come to light.

2.3 *The same waterfront at Amarna as in figure 2.2, recreated as part of the Boston model. In the foreground on the right is the southern end of the Great Palace, as it was in Akhenaten's reign. After his death, a large brick-pillared hall was added to the south end. In its place in the model comes a large walled area planted with trees, to some extent a piece of conjecture.*

It might seem natural, when setting out to create a new town or city, to fix its perimeter at an early stage. In past societies, the perimeter frequently took the form of a surrounding wall, perhaps built with defence in mind, and therefore required gateways. With the perimeter fixed, the street plan followed, often coordinated with the positions of the gateways. The built city of Amarna had no surrounding wall, although, as argued below (pp. 155–61), there was probably a prohibition on unlimited expansion into the desert. The king did not, however, conceive of Akhetaten as a city, but as a tract of sacred land. The cliffs and escarpments were its perimeter, marked at intervals by the boundary stelae.

The Greening of Amarna

The modern visitor to Amarna will see fields surrounding the archaeological remains on the desert side. These post-date the mid-twentieth century and are possible only because of modern irrigation technology. In the 1960s, the Egyptian government initiated a scheme to extend farmland deep into the southern desert plain at Amarna. For many years its canals remained dry, its marked-out fields devoid of vegetation. The success of the scheme depended upon huge pumps that were to be driven by electricity. It was only in the 1980s that electricity was finally brought across the river and the pumps connected to the supply. Thirty years later, the desert that for a time bore only a sketch of an irrigation scheme is now farmland, with trees, houses and roads. It is a local testament to the fact that life depends not only upon sunlight, but also upon water, and a sufficient supply of water to the desert needs, in turn, a great input of human-derived energy.

Although a desert horizon was the proper place for a sunrise, and by extension birth and rebirth, the ancient Egyptians regarded the natural home for themselves to be one where plants grew from fertile soil, and birds and animals flourished. At the back of their minds lay a mythical primitive landscape of water and lush vegetation supporting creatures that typified animal life, primarily waterfowl. It was within this milieu that certain of the gods had once lived and humankind had come into being. A sun-temple at Abu Ghurab, north of Saqqara and dated to the reign of King Neuserra of the 5th Dynasty (*c.* 2392–2282 BC), celebrated the life-giving power of the sun with detailed depictions of the plant and animal life of the Nile valley and the seasonal cycle of the countryside. Hymns to the Aten at Amarna likewise portrayed the Aten as the source of all life in nature. The chosen home of the Aten was, however, a piece of lifeless desert that lay above the height reached by the annual inundation of the Nile in ancient times, and only limited measures to ameliorate the harshness were available.

All the evidence we have suggests that, at the time of Akhenaten, the Egyptians' ability to raise water from the Nile was very limited. The first ancient picture of the labour-intensive shaduf (a pivoted pole that raised a container of water from the ground up to shoulder height with the help of a counterweight) is actually to be found in one of the rock tombs at Amarna, that of the

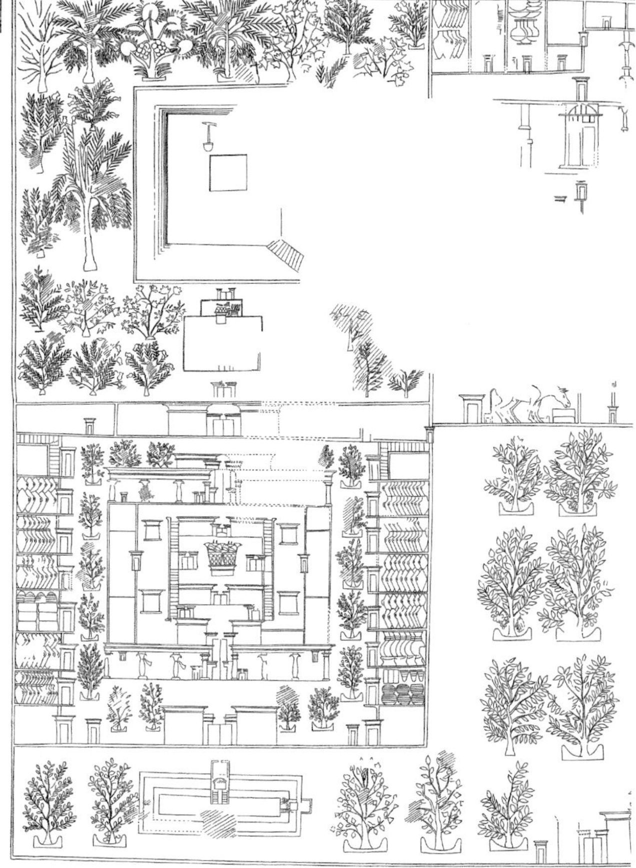

2.4, 2.5 *Scene in the tomb of Meryre (no. 4). (right) Gardens planted in the desert, the trees growing in man-made beds of alluvial soil. In the centre of the top part (and partly damaged) is a square, double-level well and the end of a shaduf (water-hoist), the first attested example from Egypt. Note the feeding horses, middle right side. (above) A photograph of part of the same scene showing the well and shaduf. The arrow points to the top end of the shaduf.*

high priest Meryre (no. 4, figures **2.4, 2.5**). Akhenaten's people will have had no more efficient way of raising water. Much of it came from wells, with which the city was abundantly supplied.[4] Many wells were in 'public' places, supplying groups of small houses that huddled around them. The larger house owners had their own, within the walled compound that surrounded their home. Some of the royal administrative areas were similarly served. The wells were dug in two stages at different levels [**2.6**]. The upper was a wide pit descending into the desert and, if necessary, lined with mud brick. The pits could be circular or, in larger cases, rectangular. The lower level was reached by a staircase cut or made in the side, rendered stable, like everything else, with mud brick and not stone. From the base of the pit a narrower circular shaft descended to the water table, which must have varied according to the season. The shafts were not lined, making them liable to the collapse of the sides. Drawing water was physically demanding: for a good part of the vertical distance, it was carried up a spiral staircase in containers that were often pottery jars.

The damaged scene in the tomb of the high priest Meryre (no. 4) preserves the top of a shaduf in the corner of a rectangular basin set within a garden. A shaduf can lift water to a height that is determined by the length of the pole and, in turn, the height of its pivot above the ground. In the recent past this was often no more than the distance that a man could comfortably raise his arms from the ground, thus around 1.3 m (4.3 ft). For use in a well of this design, therefore, either a very large and tall shaduf needing robust foundations was required, or else a vertical chain of more than one shaduf that would have platforms stepped down the side of the basin. Such stepped chains of shadufs were a common sight at the Nile riverbank a century ago. No trace of such constructions has survived, but the sides of wells were prone to erosion after they were abandoned. The most likely place to have found one would be the huge well that occupied the inner court of the North Palace [**4.22, Pl. XXXVIII**]. From its northeast corner a limestone conduit ran beneath floors and walls to supply water to the sunken garden in the northeast corner of the palace. The sides of the well have, however, collapsed and eroded, preserving no trace of how the water was raised to the conduit head. The conduit itself was exceptional.

2.6 *The well in the courtyard of the house of the chariot-officer Ranefer (N49.18), showing the steps leading down to the second level, from where the vertical shaft of the well descended. The circular granaries belong to a later stage in the house's development, by which time the well had been deliberately filled in. View to the northeast.*

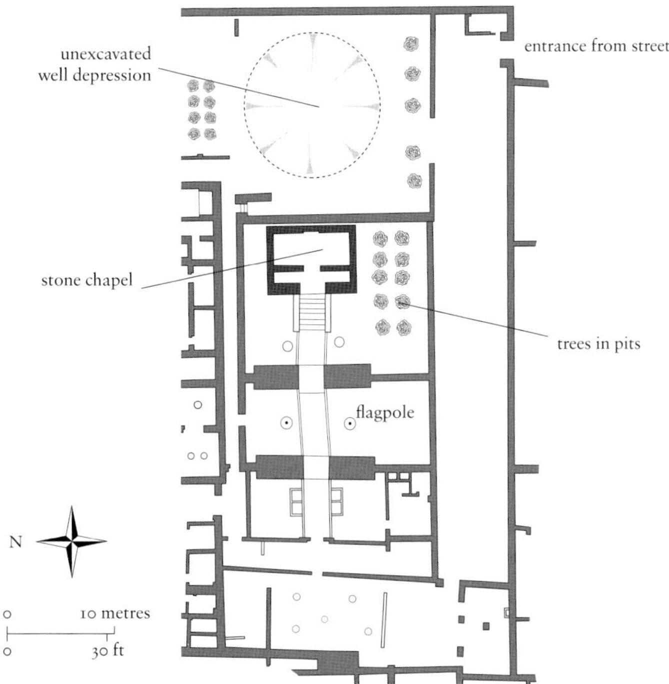

2.7 The large house U25.7 in the North City possessed its own enclosed garden largely filled with a small temple complete with pylons. Rows of trees had been planted in pits filled with alluvial soil. No trace was found of any means of channelling water from the well to the trees and garden.

No other gardens show traces of anything similar (although one cannot rule out the possibility that, in place of limestone channels, wood was used, a substance that does not survive well in open desert).

The initial making of mud bricks and mud mortar, and building them into walls that were plastered, rapidly coated the occupied areas of the city with a layer of mud that is the common surface found when the site is excavated, in addition to deliberate floors and pavements made of mud bricks or layers of mud. The constant carrying of water from the wells will have also created, especially in the winter months, a residual dampness in the ground. For trees to grow, however, they needed to be planted in pits filled with alluvial soil. Rows of tree pits have been found at the Sanctuaries of both Aten temples, in the north court of the King's House, beside the deep well at the North Palace and in gardens attached to some of the large private estates [**2.7**]. A long-standing practice in ancient Egypt was to lay out gardens, whether intended for flowers or vegetables, in the form of a grid of low mud ridges, each grid-square one cubit (52 cm, 20.5 in.) across. Each square contained a bed of fertile soil, and some of the larger examples were furnished with narrow paths and water runnels. Examples have been found at royal buildings (e.g. at the Amarna site of Kom el-Nana, a building ensemble that might have been Nefertiti's sun-temple, and at the North Palace), at the Workmen's Village and in private estates in the city [**2.8–2.10**].

The places that would have most needed irrigation were the walled garden sun-temples ('sunshades' is the ancient term) that were built out on the desert

2.8 *The garden of house R44.1, belonging to an unnamed 'Steward of Akhetaten'. The circles of dark mud are the tops of tree pits. View to the northeast, with the house in the background.*

2.9 *(left) A sunken garden at the South Pavilion at Kom el-Nana. Vegetation had grown in beds of dark fertile soil contained within the cubit-sized grid of mud ridges (1 cubit = c. 52 cm, 20.5 in.). Watering must have been done by hand.*

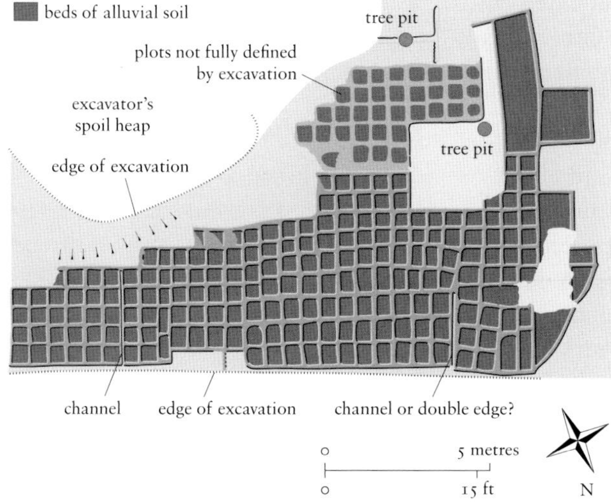

2.10 *(below) A garden laid out in a private estate in the Main City (house and garden L50.9/9a).*

plain. One of them, Maru-Aten, represents an ambitious attempt to create a veritable oasis complete with water garden [**Pl. XXXVII**] Excavations here and at the similar site of Kom el-Nana have failed to find signs of an irrigation system that brought water in from the river. The only sources were deep and large wells within the enclosures. In the fierce heat of summer, it would have been an arduous task to lift by hand sufficient water to enable these places to flourish as their makers hoped. In lacking the technology to irrigate land successfully for very far beyond the zone of natural dampness, Akhenaten had no prospect of making the desert at Amarna blossom. There could be no Hanging Gardens of Akhetaten. This part of his vision was not very practical.

When I first began to live at Amarna, the dig house had its own water supply, provided by a hand-pump at the top of an iron pipe that descended through the centre of an ancient well. The water was brackish in taste on account of the naturally high salt content of the desert. The water we drank was brought to the house in big pottery jars filled from the village tap that, in turn, drew its water from a far deeper source that would not have been accessible to Akhenaten's people. It is therefore likely that the inhabitants of ancient Amarna had to draw their drinking water from the Nile, necessitating a long journey for people living on the eastern edge of the city.

The Imitation of Nature

Within the royal buildings, architecture and art helped to foster the illusion of harmony with the natural world and its fecundity. Egyptian stone architecture had, since much earlier times, drawn inspiration from the plant life of marshes: from reeds, papyrus and the lily (until recently referred to as the lotus). To this set of motifs the date-palm tree was added. Akhenaten developed this tradition. At least three types of column can be recognized at Amarna. On one the top of the column was surrounded by curving fronds with bulbous tips, inspired by date-palm leaves. The undersides of the leaves could be decorated with inlays in bright colours (red, blue and yellow) that continued onto the shaft of the column; the same effect could also be achieved using paint [**Pl. XV**]. In the Great Palace, gilding was used on such capitals. A second type was based on the concept of many bundles of papyrus stalks placed together and held by bindings at set heights [**3.7, 3.8**]. Towards the top, the ends sloped inwards, for the plant was not yet in flower. In the third style, the stalks supported an outward-curving capital that represented the papyrus in flower, with details of the leaves and sprays of filaments carved across it. Long stems ending in lily blossoms, painted green, could be added to the column shafts, with the incongruous embellishment of a row of red-painted grape bunches. Another motif was of a group of stylized waterfowl representing the wildlife of the marshes, seemingly dead and displayed hanging upside down [**2.11**].

Some column fragments found in the Great Palace brought forth from their excavator (Flinders Petrie) an almost rapturous description:

> The form was as strange as the decoration, many of the fragments not belonging to circles, but shewing irregular flattened sections, as if even the cylindrical column had been abandoned, and variety and naturalism sought by copying the curves of tree trunks. The surface decoration is unique in Egypt, and can only be paralleled in mediæval art. Winding branches of a climbing vine twist around the column in wild confusion, their leaves turning in all directions and overlapping, with a pointed disregard of any symmetry or pattern.[5]

Another find, from the Great Aten Temple, was a block [**2.12**] that exhibited, as if hanging over the top of a scene of the royal family:

> ... a mass of trailing vine (using the word in its wide sense, as a climber) which seems to be the convolvulus or woodbine, covering over all the blank spaces of the tablet.[6]

The rounded mouldings that the Egyptians liked to set along the edges of temple walls provided the sculptor with further surfaces that he could cover with plant details [**2.13**]. Closely set reeds, in which each reed shaft was marked by subdivisions, sometimes containing the point of a new leaf just beginning to sprout, were the inspiration for stone pilasters. At the Great Palace, green-glazed tiles fluted to imitate reeds formed the surface of some columns [**4.15**].

A regular find of excavations across the city is a small bunch of grapes modelled in faience (a synthetic glazed material, more correctly called glazed frit) and with a hole for suspension [**2.15**]. Sometimes the top has a stepped profile, the easier for attaching snugly to the underside of a wooden beam. A picture

2.11 *Column shaped as a clump of young papyrus stems bound together, but with the surface decorated using a variety of other motifs, among them groups of pendant waterfowl. From the tomb of Tutu (no. 8). Inset is a photograph of a limestone block (obj. S-7086) from a similar but much larger column, probably originally from Maru-Aten. Width of fragment, 68 cm (26.8 in.); height 29 cm (11.4 in.). Estimated diameter of column at this level: 2.0 m (6.6 ft), giving an original column height of around 5.5 m (18 ft). For another example of the motif, painted on a house wall, see plate XXVII.*

2.12 *(below) Limestone* talatat-*block from the Great Aten Temple, from a scene depicting the royal family, with only the titles of two of the daughters preserved. Size 53.3 by 21.6 cm (21 by 8.5 in.).*

2.13 Wall plants. Stone engaged columns (pilasters) and rounded corner mouldings offered surfaces on which plant designs could be carved. These pieces all come from Maru-Aten. (left to right) Papyrus plants on a sandstone pilaster surface (22/249A, width 53 cm (1 ft 8.7 in.); plants carved on the underside of the spreading edge of a column capital (obj. S-7097); reeded architectural element (obj. S-7112); cylindrical corner mouldings with carved leaf designs (objs S-7121 = 22/253B, S-7113 = 22/253C).

2.14, 2.15 Architectural grape decoration. (right) A shrine or royal kiosk depicted in the tomb of Meryre (no. 4). The pendant triangles beneath the canopy are probably bunches of grapes made of faience. (below) Faience architectural ornament in the shape of a bunch of grapes made to fit to a beam.

in the tomb of Meryre (no. 4) at Amarna seems to show them suspended at regular intervals beneath the wooden canopy of a shrine or pavilion adorned along the top with cobras. Some of those found in the housing areas could be all that remains of small wooden shrines used, perhaps, to contain small statues, of the house owner, of the king or of a domestic deity.

The theme of nature was deployed on a large scale in the wall and floor paintings of the mud-brick palaces. Wall painting is best documented at the North Palace, where large areas were found still in place [**Pls XVIII, XIX**]. A common theme, painted on both interior and exterior walls, was papyrus plants growing thickly from a swampy base and providing a home for birds and butterflies. One version added more open pools of water in which fish and fowl swam. Another theme showed birds, including geese, feeding under the supervision of white-clad men [**Pls XXXI–XXXIII**]. Within some of the rooms, ceilings were painted with a grapevine pattern. At the Great Palace, the eastern mud-brick

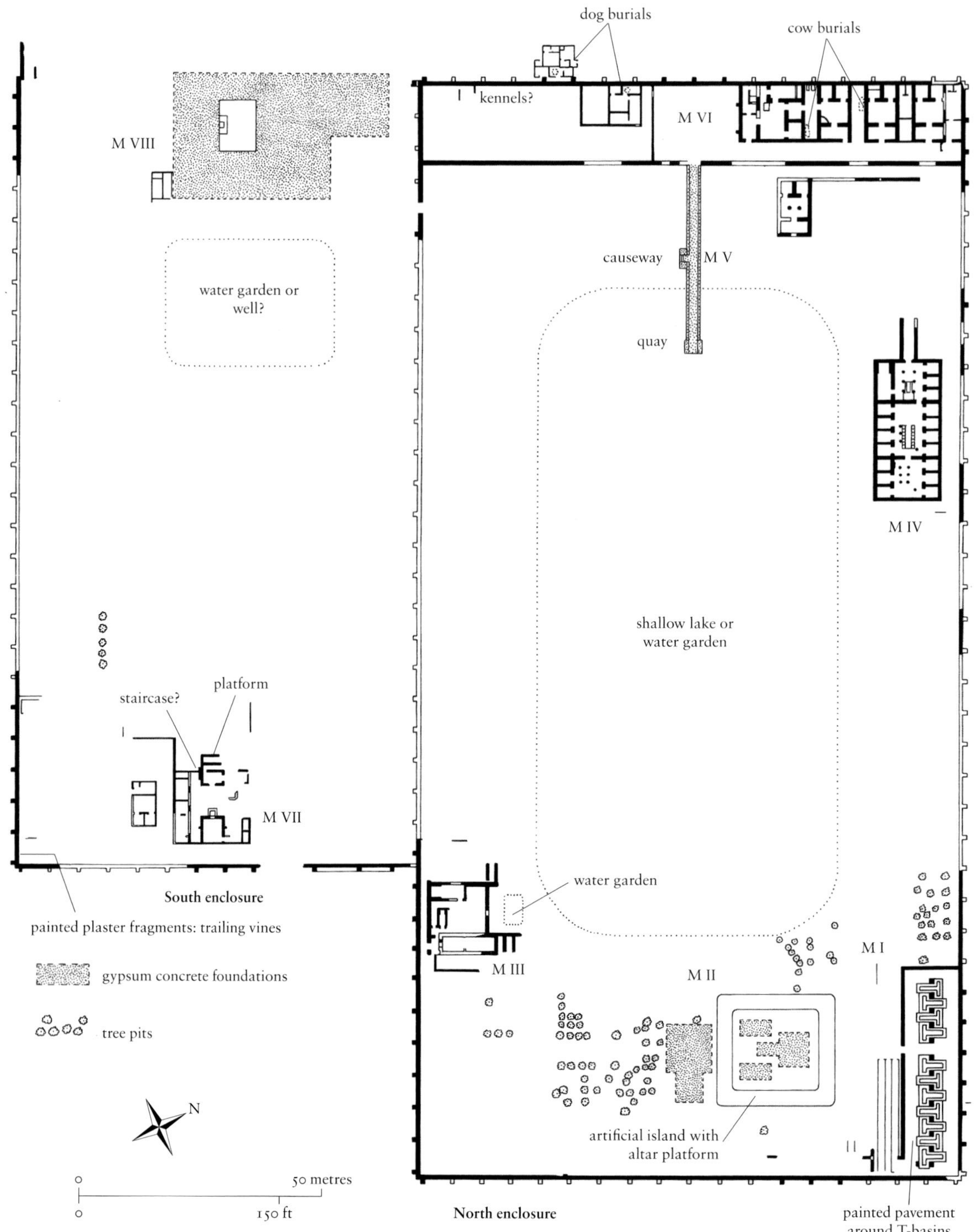

2.16 *Plan of the Maru-Aten sun-temple, destroyed by agricultural development in the 1960s. Plate XXXVII is a model of Maru-Aten.*

wing included a sunken garden surrounded by a windowed wall at the foot of which was painted a long scene showing 'a lake, lotus plants, an overseer and servants with cattle, a winding canal and boats sailing on it' [**Pl. XVII**].[7]

The principal painted floors to have survived were at the Great Palace and the Maru-Aten sun-temple. A thick hard gypsum backing brought out the intensity of the colours. Tufts of individual plants, from which birds rose into the air and through which calves scampered (one of them savaged by a lion), surrounded pools of water. In the Great Palace, the pools were painted with zig-zag water lines interrupted by lily flowers, fish and ducks [**4.17**]. At Maru-Aten, the water was real, contained in small T-shaped tanks [**2.16, Pl. XII**].

Another form of decoration used faience tiles. Many were rectangular, with a green background inset with white daisies and painted with thistles and insects [**Pl. XIII**] or showed other scenes from nature [**Pl. XLVI**]. Others, of different shapes, showed plants, water, fish and fowl, the subject matter of the gypsum floor paintings. None has been found in its original location. The subject matter implies that they were laid as areas of floor, perhaps only in small and special places.

Building in Stone

The most important parts of Amarna were built from stone. Sometimes they were whole buildings, sometimes they were individual elements in buildings that were otherwise of sun-dried mud bricks. Shortly after the end of the Amarna period, the stonework was systematically removed. Although Akhenaten's buildings were in this way destroyed, the stones themselves were re-used by later kings as a cheap source of foundation and filling material. As a consequence, many thousands of Amarna blocks have been recovered in modern times at other sites, often undamaged and retaining much of their paintwork. The greatest number comes from the site of Hermopolis (the modern El-Ashmunein), across the river from Amarna. A few of them were used in the foundations of a building project undertaken by King Horemheb, which could have been started, at the earliest, around seventeen years after Akhenaten's death.

The re-used blocks are important for showing the nature of the wall decoration in the royal buildings at Amarna where stone was used. The style and the themes seem to have been generally mirrored in the private rock tombs. The blocks contribute little, however, to the task of reconstructing the appearance of the stone buildings on paper. With only an occasional (and somewhat dubious) exception, it is impossible to tell to which particular Amarna building any set of re-used blocks belongs. The demolition was thorough, but not perfect: breakage left many fragments in the piles of rubble that stayed behind, and these have been recovered through excavation (e.g. **4.16**), though a full assessment of how they contribute to our understanding of the decorative programme of these buildings still remains to be completed.

A thousand years before Akhenaten, kings had commanded sufficient resources for the building of their pyramid tombs. Each pyramid was, however, a single great project to which maximum attention could be given. By the reign of Akhenaten, building in stone had become more widespread, though it was still largely reserved for temples, imparting to them a greater sense of permanence, a future that was 'eternity'. Each building scheme was far less gargantuan than a pyramid and, with many progressing at the same time and in widely separated places, there may have been less of a sense of central direction to force the pace and maintain consistency of construction.

Although building-stone occurs widely along the desert edges of the Nile valley, in order to complete a project of a significant size it still required a greater amount of labour for cutting and transportation than most private individuals could muster. This natural restriction created an effectual royal monopoly. Normally, stone arrived at a building site in only roughly compatible block shapes that still required skilled dressing and manoeuvring to turn them into the material for stone walls. The particular way the Egyptians built in stone required much time and labour. The idea that, in carrying out his plan to create at Akhetaten a new ceremonial centre with impressive stone buildings of its own, Akhenaten was pushing against the limits of the resources he thought were available, helps to explain several features of his building programme.

One of these was a simple innovation. Akhenaten's quarries were made to supply blocks of modest and identical size that could be carried and laid by one reasonably strong man. Only with exceptional pieces – including granite statues and large sandstone doorframe elements, all imported from distant quarries – would it have been necessary to resort to the dragging of stones on sledges. Building Amarna was not like building the pyramids. Egypt had moved on. The size of the new standardized blocks was set at one cubit in length (52 cm, 20.5 in.), by (ideally) half that in width, and a height of roughly 23 cm (9 in.). The modern term for one of these blocks is the Arabic word '*talatat*', derived from the word for 'three', probably expressing the fact that each block is three hand-spans long. Akhenaten's quarries produced tens of thousands of *talatat*-blocks.

Early in his reign, Akhenaten had a new section of a sandstone quarry opened at Gebel el-Silsila, south of Luxor, to provide stone for his scheme to overshadow the temple of Amun-Ra at Thebes (Karnak) with a series of buildings of his own. A small number of sandstone blocks were later sent to Amarna, as well as larger slabs and blocks for huge doorframes and column drums (they were used in the Small Aten Temple [3.7, 3.8], for example, and at Kom el-Nana [2.33]). Quantities of sandstone quarry chippings were also sent, to serve as solid filler in making the concrete foundations for the stone buildings. More will be said about this system later. These sandstone imports must have come by boat, floating downstream for the 450 km (280 miles) from Gebel el-Silsila.

Most of the stone used at Amarna was limestone. This is the rock, of very varying quality, that is local to Middle Egypt and is readily available in the cliffs that border the river valley. Several of the sources that Akhenaten used have been located and in themselves they shed light upon how the sudden very

2.17 *View of the entrances to the Queen Tiye quarry at Amarna, viewed to the northeast.*

large demand for building-stone was met. In part, it was by the conventional practice of opening managed quarries. Some lay outside Amarna (located, for example, behind El-Bersheh, a short distance downstream), but one was in the side of a long wadi that runs into the Amarna plain [**2.17**]. It is an underground gallery that, when first found, bore the name of Akhenaten's mother, Queen Tiye, perhaps because the skilled men who ran it were part of her extended household.[8] *Talatat*-blocks were removed in layers, leaving a space that represents many thousands of blocks.

Queen Tiye's quarry stands on the edge of a large expanse of high desert plain that is covered with shallow open quarries. Often a natural slope has been cut back by the removal of several layers of *talatat*-blocks. The most extensive gallery quarry lies just beneath the edge of the cliff that overlooks the north end of the Amarna plain. It was served by a narrow path that separates it from an almost sheer drop down the mountain side, a path that could nevertheless have served humans or donkeys, who would have carried the blocks down either by this still-visible descending track or by a longer route back over the top of the cliff and across to a gentler descent by the wadi system.

2.18 *One of the innumerable small open quarries on the surface above the Queen Tiye quarry, where the extraction of* talatat-*blocks has been abandoned.*

Other quarries existed ranging all the way down from these larger open sites to the most modest of all: places where a start has been made on outlining a few blocks on the flat or sloping rock surface [2.18]. It is common to find blocks in every stage of being outlined and removed, which have then been abandoned. One can imagine scores of small teams, or even individuals, choosing almost at random a patch of desert and settling down to hack out a small number of blocks, having brought with them only a long bronze chisel and

2.19 *In the course of cutting the entranceway to tomb no. 21, the quarrymen took the opportunity to cut column bases, perhaps as a profitable sideline. The marks left by metal chisel strokes are visible.*

perhaps a mallet. The rock is quite soft when first exposed, almost chalky, so no particular skill is needed for extraction. Here and there one finds unfinished pieces that are not *talatat*-sized: longer narrow slabs that could have been worked into door jambs, and circles outlined by a trench that were going to be column bases. The demand for cut stone created opportunities for enterprise: the workmen who hollowed out the rock tombs did so by removing the stone, where they could, as blocks or even as column bases [**2.19**].

There is a contrast of organization here, between the managed operation of, on the one hand, the Queen Tiye quarry and perhaps the larger gallery quarries and, on the other, the almost uncountable small extraction sites, which look as though they are self-organized. One explanation for the latter is that, in order to increase the supply of building blocks, the city population as a whole was made the subject of a levy. Each household had to supply the king's officials with a set number of blocks. Many – perhaps the population of whole neighbourhoods – combined to work together to open larger quarries, but some worked almost alone. There are no written sources to prove it, but the theory matches the spread of evidence in the desert and also the way that ancient Egypt functioned generally, with greater autonomy given to the individual than we might expect. It also fits the picture derived from the archaeology of the city as a whole, in that one of its basic roles was to supply the palace, the king's circle, with commodities of all kinds. It is the method that Akhenaten used at the beginning of his reign for the supply of sandstone blocks for his buildings at Karnak, as recorded in a text at his quarry at Gebel el-Silsila: the responsibility for providing these blocks was laid on a high official and on 'the leaders of the army to perform a great forced-labour duty of quarrying sandstone'.[9]

There was a demand, too, for harder stones: red granite and black speckled granodiorite from Aswan, and quartzite in a variety of warm brown to purple hues from Gebel Ahmar near Cairo and from Aswan. Their most prestigious use was for statues, but these harder stones were also needed by individual households for querns for the grinding of cereals, and are a frequent find. Basalt and dolerite (the nearest source for both is Gebel el-Teir, 60 km (37 miles) downstream from Amarna, though it is not clear if it was exploited at this time) were the raw materials for stone-working tools: pounders and smaller hammerstones. In the case of querns and stone tools, it looks as though the quarries supplied quantities of rough pieces, sometimes natural small boulders, which served as blanks from which a finished tool would be produced at Amarna itself. It is less easy to assess the state of readiness in which the stones that would become statues were received at Amarna from the distant quarries.

Another stone much liked by the Egyptians was soft, banded, white and crystalline: in the past called alabaster by Egyptologists, but, so geologists now say, more correctly called travertine. Its most famous source, Hatnub, lay close to Amarna, in the desert and due east, at a distance of 16 km (10 miles) from the city. It was used in the Great Palace, most notably for carved balustrades that bordered the ramps leading to and from important doorways.

Gypsum

The Egyptians generally, and those of the Amarna period especially, made great use of gypsum, a white sedimentary rock that occurs in layers and veins in many parts of Egypt. When heated to a relatively low temperature (100–200 °C) it is reduced to a powder that, when mixed with water, sets into a plaster often known as plaster of Paris. It is not as hard and durable as lime plaster, but that has to be produced by heating lumps of limestone in a kiln at a higher temperature (900 °C).

Gypsum mostly had to be brought to Amarna from outside, though from where exactly remains unknown (it is actually present in the higher desert at Amarna though it has not been definitely established that it was dug out during the Amarna period). A number of cones of gypsum have been found in the Central City. On the flat base of each has been written in ink the day and the month, and the notation 'gypsum of Akhetaten'. The main concentrations of these objects are in the King's House and the small offices that lay behind it to the east. These are all buildings of mud brick. The principal use of gypsum would have been to create the gypsum foundations for stone buildings (see below) but only a single example of one of these cones has been found in such a place (hieratic register no. 35/227 from the central halls of the Great Palace). It has been suggested that the cones are samples of deliveries that were subject to an inspection for quality, and it could be that some of the deliveries themselves were stored in these buildings. One group, which included many that were not inscribed, was found in pits and so perhaps was the remains of deliveries made in the city's early days.[10]

Where stone buildings were to be erected, we meet an innovation in preparing the site that complemented the delivery of stone as standardized blocks, and was presumably intended to hasten the building process [**2.20**]. It is an important example of rationalization, and thus of the capacity of the ancient Egyptians to innovate. Akhenaten wanted shrines and temples to designs that were his own. Egyptian builders did not make detailed scaled drawings of buildings beforehand. They sketched outlines and annotated them with dimensions expressed in cubits. No sketches of this kind have survived for Amarna stone buildings, but the fact that *talatat*-blocks were one cubit long implies that Akhenaten and his builders thought out their architecture in the same way, as a series of cubit lengths.

The first stage in laying out a stone building at Amarna was to remove the sandy topsoil and to dig out a foundation pit that covered the entire area of the intended building. This could be quite shallow. Sand and gravel do not compress much, so deeper foundations would not necessarily have improved the stability of the building. A thick layer of concrete was then spread over the floor of the pit. It was made from gypsum paste mixed with sand grains, which increased its hardness and workability, and was reinforced with chippings of sandstone and limestone. The surface was carefully worked and smoothed so that the chippings generally did not show. The workers responsible used a

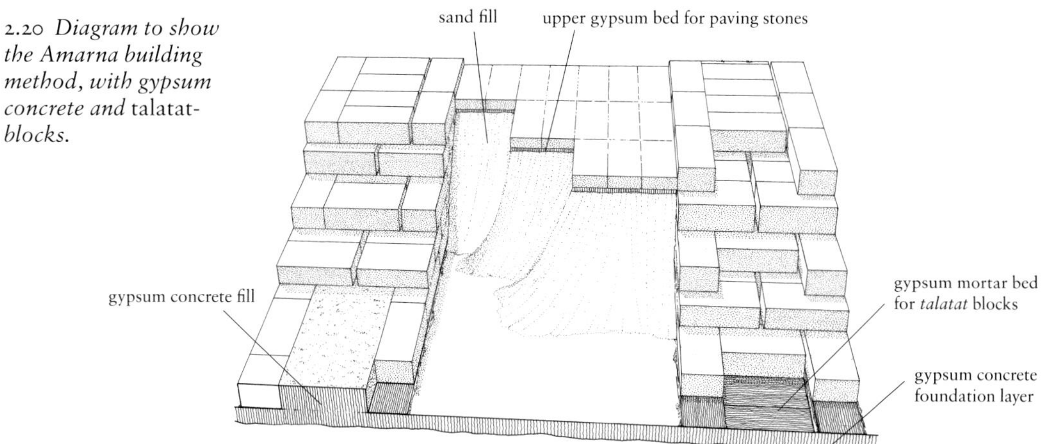

2.20 *Diagram to show the Amarna building method, with gypsum concrete and* talatat-*blocks.*

mix that did not shrink and crack, but set in a smooth even surface that could extend over large areas. For example, the foundation layer for the Long Temple in the Great Aten Temple enclosure included, towards the rear, an originally unbroken area of over 2,000 sq m (65 by 32.5 m; nearly 23,000 sq ft, 213.3 by 106.6 ft).

Sometimes the use of gypsum was sparing, as where gaps were left to correspond with open spaces in the intended building. A clear instance is at the Long Temple. Across the unusually long open courts in the front and middle sections, only the strips where the offering-tables were to go were spread with gypsum. Empty strips of space down the centre and around the edges were marked off with mud-brick walls and filled with desert sand and gravel. On top of this a thin and rough layer of gypsum mortar was laid to receive the paving blocks. In some of the columned pavilions, the pattern of square foundations for columns with linking walls was picked out individually with gypsum concrete, the intervening spaces remaining unfilled (**3.30** is an example).

The gypsum bed created the equivalent of a drawing board at full size. Working sometimes with ink lines and sometimes with grooves scratched into the surface, the builders laid out their design, measuring the parts to the nearest cubit or half cubit. There are no signs that triangulation was used or that special orientation lines were set up. The laying out was probably done by a combination of linear measurement, a set-square for right angles and a good and experienced eye. The Great Pyramid at Giza is famous for its eerily exact dimensions and orientation. It was, however, quite exceptional. Most kings and builders approximated, and Akhenaten was no exception.

With the plan covering the ground at full size, the next step was to spread a thinner layer of mortar, also made of gypsum, along the lines of the walls and other features, and this became the bed for the first layer of blocks. These were laid into it, tightly packed together and usually without mortar between the vertical joints, thus automatically creating walls to a cubit scale (or approximately so).

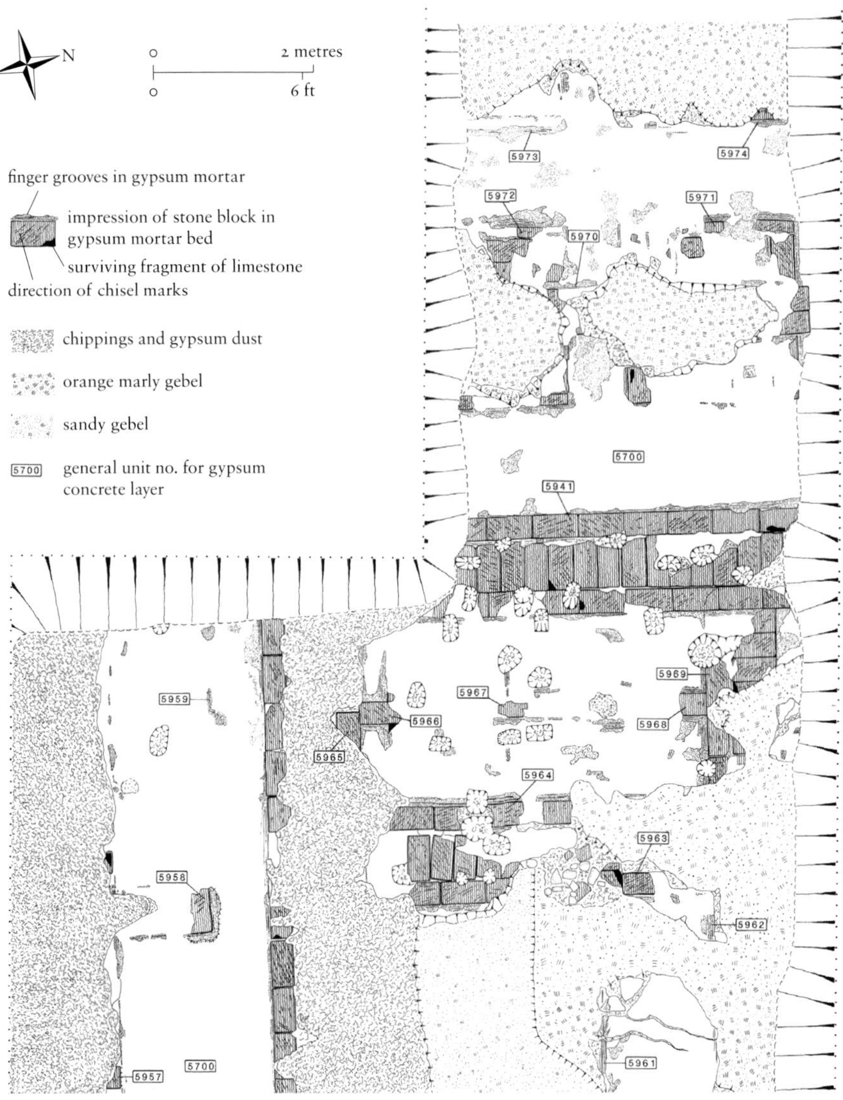

In the aftermath of the Amarna period, every stone building at Amarna was systematically demolished. The gypsum concrete foundation layers were, however, left behind, although often much damaged [**2.23**]. They preserve many traces of what had been built upon them. Often the actual beds of mortar of the first layer of blocks remain, stuck firmly to the concrete foundation layer. Even if the mortar bed had come off, adhering to the bottom of the block as it was levered out of place, a line of roughly parallel impressions might be left where the builder had run his fingers along the surplus mortar squeezed out along the lower edge of the blocks. Sometimes what survives are the ink or scored lines that the architect had first laid out.

When these various traces are recorded on the archaeologists' plans, they become the clues for making a reconstruction of what the building actually

2.21 (opposite) Part of the detailed excavation plan of the remains of the South Shrine at Kom el-Nana. For ease of identification, the key elements are given individual 'unit' (or 'context') numbers.

2.22 An interpretation of figure 2.21, in which the foundation layer of talatat*-blocks has been restored as well as the outlines of column bases on their square foundations.*

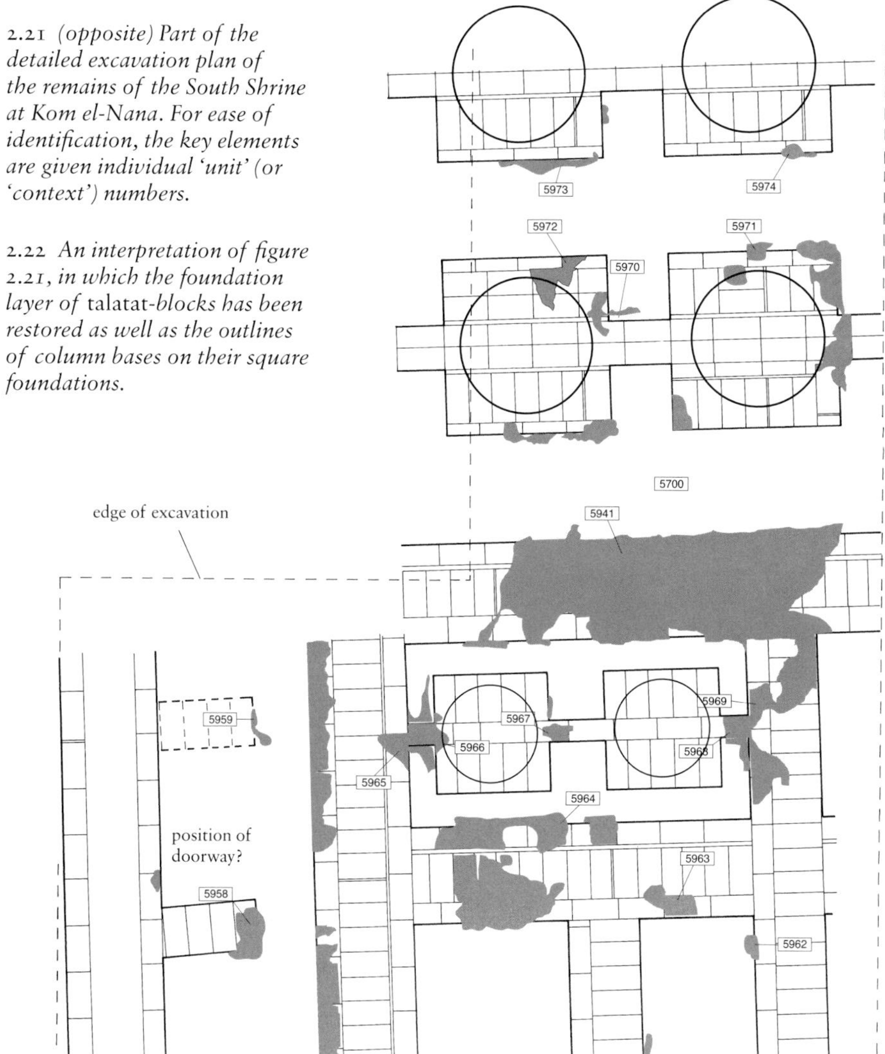

looked like above the foundation level [**2.21**, **2.22**]. Thus, where columns were to stand, a square foundation was made for each one, linked to its neighbour in one direction by a short narrow wall that would not have appeared at ground level (but would have stabilized the sand fill). However, the places where doorways were to be inserted in walls were often not marked at foundation level, unless they were to have ramps running up on either side (the main example is the Great Palace, **4.12**). We are obliged, if we reconstruct the plan, to estimate their positions and widths, and the same is true for other features, such as screen walls between columns, stone statues and daises or platforms.

Once the foundation courses of blocks were in place, the intervening spaces were filled with sand, gravel and stone chippings to create a level surface flush with the tops of the blocks. The builders then raised the walls and columns to roof level. The open spaces were paved with *talatat*-sized slabs. At the Long Temple, some of the altar foundation blocks were left behind when it was demolished [**2.24**]. Two courses remain, very roughly mortared together with gypsum. This provides an indication of the depth of the foundations, which probably raised the floor level to slightly above that of the surrounding ground.

Although gypsum was a commodity to use carefully, it seems also to have served as a substitute for stone, mainly above the foundation course, for thicker walls and pylons. A mixture of gypsum with stone chippings was packed between the lines of facing stones. Lacking the strength of proper lime concrete, however, when the stonework for the temples was removed after the end of the Amarna period, the gypsum concrete filler was reduced to a mixture

2.23 *An area of gypsum concrete foundations for the South Shrine at Kom el-Nana, viewed to the south. The line of block impressions on the left is marked as unit 5941 in figure 2.21.*

2.24 *Foundations for a court full of offering-tables at the Great Aten Temple, as revealed by the EES excavations of 1932.* 1 *Gypsum foundation layer;* 2 *Sand fill;* 3 *Floor level.*

of powder and chippings that is still a conspicuous feature of the sites of Amarna's principal stone buildings. At Maru-Aten (building M VIII), the excavator remarked on 'the use in the foundations of large blocks of concrete cast in moulds and measuring 1.50 m by 0.60 m by 0.35 m[4.9 ft by 2 ft by 1.15 ft]'[11] These had departed from the *talatat* norm.

Brick

Part of the experience of living in ancient Egypt was contact with mud, not just through working – or seeing others work – the ploughlands along the Nile where almost everybody lived, but because it was the material of the walls, floors and ceilings of everybody's dwelling, from a herdsman's hut to the palace of the king.

Most bricks in ancient Egypt were made from a wet mixture of mud and fragments of plant material, pressed out from rectangular open wooden moulds and left to dry in the sun. Amarna, however, was a desert site. The floodplain and its muddy fields lay across the river. Some of the royal buildings did use bricks made from Nile mud and plant fragments; however, most of the bricks that built Amarna represent another compromise over traditional practice. They consist of desert materials. This is visible now in the gravel that was used as a binder (a very effective one) instead of straw [**2.25**].

The desert is also visible in the colours of the bricks. That part of it at Amarna that extends below the cliffs is not composed of solid limestone rock, as is the high desert above. Instead, it is a mixture of beds of gravel, sand and crumbly marl, displaying a range of colours from yellow through orange to a browny-purple. Some of these materials, alone or in combination, make perfectly good bricks (as has been established experimentally). Various pits found beneath the floors and walls of houses at Amarna might have been dug for brick-making materials. The most conspicuous case is at the Workmen's Village. The largest pit, dug into a marl deposit of a similar colour to many of the bricks used in adjacent constructions, was really a small quarry, roughly 25 m (82 ft) across and 2 m (6.5 ft) deep [**5.30**]. To judge from the colours of bricks, however, it was also common to mix in some of the grey-brown alluvial clay from the river banks as well.

The moulds that made the bricks were rectangular, usually with a length of around 32 cm (12.6 in.). Moulds could be made in other shapes, however. The owner of house Q44.1, for example, built his domed granaries using bricks made in a curved mould [**2.26**]. Cylindrical columns made from prefabricated mud sections illustrate just how versatile mud could be [**2.28**].

The softness of mud bricks and of the mud plaster that covered them will have had quite an effect on the general appearance of buildings, both inside and out. Mud is very malleable and could be spread to fill corners and cover irregularities, and generally to merge surfaces into an unbroken, though far from flat, plane. In time, corners became worn and rounded, surfaces were easily scratched, but also easily re-plastered. Networks of cracks developed, especially towards the ceilings. Crumbly patches appeared where walls met floors, most often in the corners. Mud-brick walls are also full of cavities and develop a largely invisible 'creepy-crawly' fauna (which includes scorpions). In some small storerooms, shelves were fitted, stretching between walls or with intermediate brick supports, but otherwise nothing was fixed to the walls apart from short wooden pegs, for mud brick is too soft to hold anything with a significant weight.

2.25, 2.26 *(left) Section through a brick made from a mixture of desert marl and gravel, from the Workmen's Village. Length of brick, as shown, 30 cm (11.7 in.); thickness 10 cm (3.9 in.). (right) Brick for a circular granary made in a curving mould, from house Q44.1. Length of brick, along middle line, 39 cm (15.4 in.); width 16 cm (6.3 in.).*

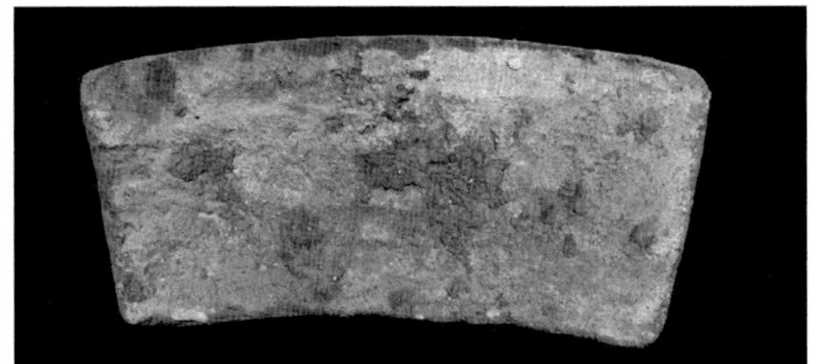

2.27, 2.28, 2.29 *(right) Column made from prefabricated mud sections, found in building R41.5. (below) Diagram to show how mud-brick walls were constructed for important buildings. (bottom) Part of the enclosure wall of the North Riverside Palace, showing the pattern of inserted wooden beams.*

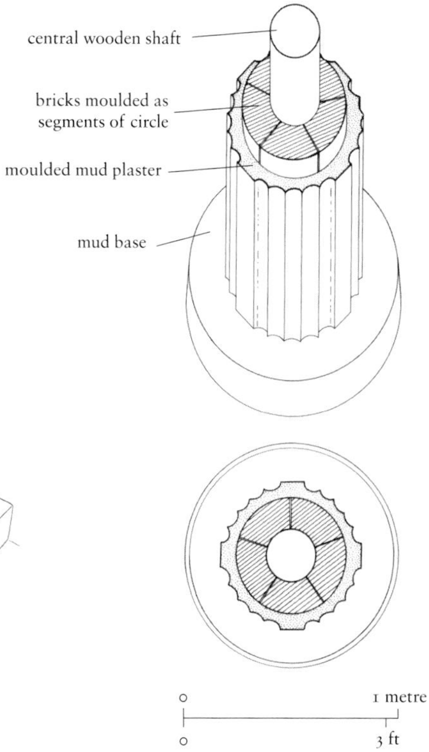

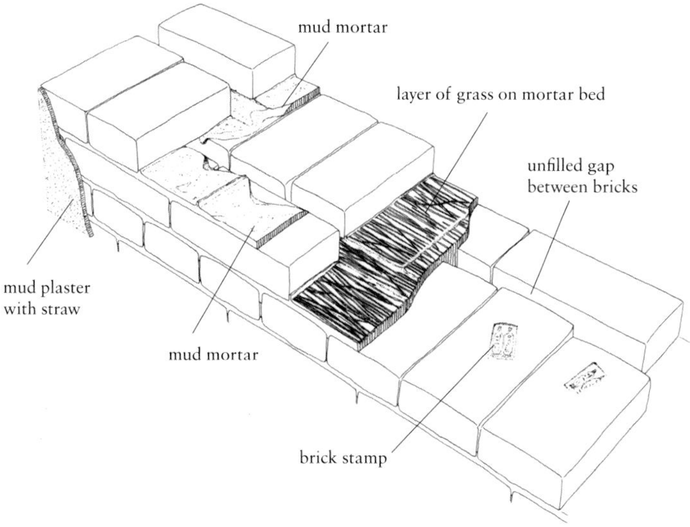

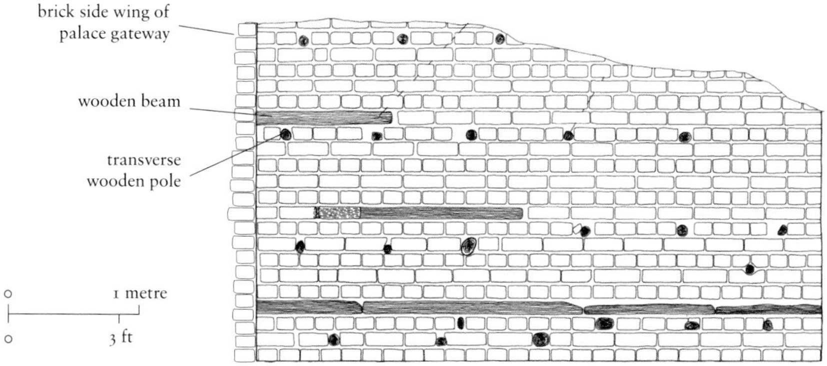

Externally, mud-brick buildings would not long have kept their original appearance. From time to time in Egypt, rain falls, in a light shower or as a torrential downpour, though the latter only every few years (in current conditions). Even without rain, exterior surfaces that have been whitewashed quite quickly lose their freshness and become off-white. Rain adds muddy streaks, as little gullies form on the top edges of walls to release rain trapped on roofs. Mud roofs do not, of course, trap rain very effectively. It readily seeps through cracks, runs in muddy trickles down interior walls and loosens ceiling plaster, which falls in irregular flakes and slabs, staining whatever it lands on.

Mud brick buildings decay rapidly. Although occasional well-preserved patches of plastered walls show that repainting was undertaken, a fair degree

2.30 *Male cleaners in the palace, from a wall-painting within the Great Palace.*

of tolerance of wear and tear on buildings is very likely, and should be borne in mind as a corrective to modern reconstructions that show buildings in pristine conditions. This is especially so for the outer pylons of the two main temples. They were built wholly of mud brick, on a scale to rival some of the larger stone temples of Thebes. Weathering of the upper parts must have been very rapid, and it remains unclear to what extent the surfaces were ever decorated. Akhenaten's new city must, very quickly, have taken on a worn and lived-in appearance.

And then there is the dust. Windows in the Amarna houses seem to have been provided with shutters, but when the wind blows, the dust it raises filters through every tiny crack, the heavier particles forming little drifts not far inside, the lighter particles hanging suspended in the air and dispersing through the rooms. Mud wall plaster, whether whitewashed or painted with bright colours, has a matte surface. Dust finds innumerable places where it can cling and form a fine but still visible surface of its own, turning white to grey-brown, and dulling colours. Old dust, gathered into the fabric of cloth, gives off a slight smell, which can only be described as that of old dust.

Amarna people, nonetheless, at least tried to keep their floors clean. When the interior rooms of their houses are exposed (if they have not been previously dug up) little in the way of layered waste-matter is found; indeed, often little of anything lies on the floor beneath the rubble from the subsequent decay of the building. Scenes of palace life depict men sprinkling the floors with water flicked from a jug and sweeping with brushes that look like tied bundles of long reeds [**2.30**, **4.18**, **4.19**]. Even in the palaces, however, most of the floors were of mud bricks covered with a layer of mud plaster. The effect of sprinkling with water would be not only to reduce the amount of dust dispersed again into the air by brushing, but also to create a slight temporary mulch into which the latest dust would be incorporated, soon to be trampled flat.

Despite failing to be a complete barrier against the elements, mud brick does provide insulation against the outside temperature, though its benefits are limited. Mud bricks resemble the materials used in modern storage heaters, and have the same effect. In the summer, they slowly absorb the peak temperatures of midday and then radiate the trapped heat back at night, so it is more pleasant to sleep outside. In winter, the reverse happens and the house remains a reservoir of cold air during the daytime.

Timber

The city needed constructional timber: for roofs, columns in houses, doors, windows and for the less obvious task of reinforcing the brickwork of thicker walls [**2.29**]. In the piers of the bridge across the main road in the Central City (described in Chapter 4, and see **4.7**), the insertion of beams reached the point where, across the face, they replaced every other course, helping to prevent cracking beneath the immense weight of the bridge itself. There was also a permanent demand for fuel for fires. The central palace area consumed huge quantities to meet the demands of a major centralized food-rationing system channelled through the Aten temples; every household needed fires for cooking and the cold nights of winter; and many of the same people manufactured objects in backyard workshops or little factories that required sources of heat. The relic of this demand is charcoal. It occurs in more or less every bucketful of spoil that is removed during archaeological excavation, whether sand, rubble or ashy layers beside ovens and fireplaces. The grey stain of wood ash must have been one of Amarna's colours once the city was established.

Charcoal is a source of information. Experts can identify the wood species. A long-running study of charcoal samples from thirty-two years of excavation has established a fairly consistent pattern of the wood consumed for fuel. Many species are represented, including fruit trees and the imported cedars of Lebanon. These charcoal pieces were presumably from off-cuts and waste for which people would have constantly kept an eye open. Overwhelmingly, however, people were burning wood from the acacia tree and, to a lesser extent, from the tamarisk. This was a sensible choice. Acacia has a heavy and durable heartwood, which burns steadily with high calorific value and also was an important source of prefabricated charcoal needed for achieving high temperatures in kilns. The robust and thorny tree is easy to recognize by its compact rounded crown, the rough dark stem, bright yellow flowers in round heads, the sharp projecting spines and the long wavy green seed pods. It grows along the Nile and channel banks, in the oases and on moist ground in the western desert. It was the dominant wood element in the local vegetation.

We will never have proper figures, but Amarna must have consumed many tons of firewood every year. A thousand years before, a high official named Uni was sent by his king to fetch great blocks of travertine (alabaster) from Hatnub in the desert east of Amarna. He records that, while the blocks were being fetched, his men built a transport barge of acacia wood.[12] The trees could have been growing on the west bank, but they could also have been on the shallow wadi floors behind the place where Amarna was later built. These faint watercourses are not devoid of vegetation now, but anything that reaches a size that is useful is quickly scavenged by villagers, and so the wadi floors look more arid than they might be in their natural state. But however much vegetation was to be found in the wadis in Akhenaten's time, it would have been quite insufficient to support a city. Amarna must have relied upon constant importation, from across the river and from further afield. Administrative records from a slightly later period, from the state-supported village of tomb-makers at Deir el-Medina (western Thebes), show that that village received regular deliveries of firewood, supplied under the authority of the vizier. The scale of demand and the consistency of the species supplied at Amarna points to a similar system, which included the management of the growing and cutting of trees, in this case deployed across a whole city.[13]

In the desert, all timber, whether structural or in furniture, is at risk from termites. Their colonies, which are quite small and live inconspicuously under the ground, seek out wood and consume the cellulose, eventually leaving nothing but a network of tunnels made from grains of sand cemented together. Amarna's reinforcing timbers and roofing beams were doomed to become powder. To judge from modern experience, within ten years the problem would have become quite noticeable and people would have had to start replacing wood. Termite preference also extended to the straw used in the mud plaster on walls, so the painted walls of palaces would have started to flake when touched.

Human Resources

Who actually built Amarna? Where did most of the labour come from? In ancient Egypt, royal projects could draw upon a pool of permanently employed labour. The best-documented example is provided by the village of Deir el-Medina at western Thebes, which housed, throughout the New Kingdom and within sixty-six little dwellings, the labour and craftsmen needed to cut and decorate each royal tomb in the Valley of the Kings. Amarna had a very similar village, known as the Workmen's Village, also isolated in the desert, and occupied until the very end of the Amarna period. Given that it took the whole of the Deir el-Medina village to make one royal tomb at a time, the Amarna equivalent could not have made a significant contribution to the initial city-building programme, which seems to have been pursued quite speedily.

The state also maintained, however, a much larger and more mobile labour force. There were communities of foreign prisoners from the wars of the 18th Dynasty, as well as the Egyptian army (itself the result, at least in part, of conscription and of the involvement of foreign captives or mercenaries). Several sources from the New Kingdom show the army being used on construction projects. In a school exercise of the 19th Dynasty, for example, a scribe has to calculate the number of bricks needed for a huge construction ramp that is under the control of an army commander, and to organize the soldiers who are to erect a colossal statue.[14] Closer to Amarna, the Gebel el-Silsila text mentioned above (p. 63) records how the quarrying of thousands of blocks for the Karnak Aten temples was organized by army officers through conscription.[15] Amarna had its army units and officers, who paraded wherever the royal family went, and who could have contributed to the initial pool of labour.

The same power of conscription that was used to maintain the army was also exercised over the Egyptian population as a whole. In theory, Amarna could have been built by people drafted in for the purpose from all over the country. Nothing has been excavated at Amarna that looks as though it might have been a temporary workers' encampment. But a temporary population at a riverside site might not have required one. They could, for example, have based themselves on a line of large house-boats kept moored at the bank for the duration of the main construction phase. A floating encampment would leave no archaeology.

But why should the people who were about to move to Amarna have been exempt? Would it not have made sense to conscript temporarily a substantial portion of the incoming population to supply some of the labour for the royal projects, perhaps with army units added? The means of controlling this potential workforce, the patron–officials who were also in the process of moving, were ideally placed and available. The quarrying of stone blocks at Amarna can be explained in this way, as having been done by a mixture of professional quarry teams and numerous groups and individuals temporarily assigned to the task from the civil population (see above p. 157). Among the small number of house owners at Amarna whose names we know are two, Hatiay and Maanakhtuef, whose titles (respectively Overseer of Works and Overseer of Builders) point to their involvement in construction, most likely for the major stone buildings, especially the Great Palace that was Akhenaten's extraordinary showpiece (see Chapter 4).

Most of the city consisted of areas where housing predominated. When looking at these parts, a case can be made that it is the result of self-building, in the way that modern squatter settlements come into existence (see Chapter 5). The intricate interlocking nature of much of the city reflects innumerable personal decisions by those who were to live in its houses. Amarna arose with little in the way of a predetermined plan. It is not likely, therefore, to have been built by a separate external workforce drafted in for the purpose. The larger houses and especially the brick palaces were built with the regularity of layout and construction method that one expects from professional builders. Basic building skills, sufficient to put up smaller houses, are likely to have been widespread, however. People who have to live without the safety nets of modern society, who live much closer to the edge of survival, have to learn to do these things themselves. My impression of villagers in modern rural Egypt is that, if suddenly transported to a new location, most of them would, with great speed, create a place to live in from whatever materials were to hand, and turn it into a home. An example of rapid self-build is illustrated in Chapter 5 [5.14].

Quality Control

Rapid building, self-building, a mindset comfortable with inconsistency, approximation and the rusticity of mud-brick architecture: how does this fit the popular modern image of the Egypt of superlative craftsmanship? In the Aten temples (including the garden sun-temples) and the Great Palace, huge areas of wall made from *talatat*-blocks were covered with carved and painted scenes. Books on the art of the Amarna period select some of the best work that has survived, and thus impress the reader. It is as yet impossible to quantify, but one can form the impression, when faced with a mass of pieces from the same building, that the finely carved scenes were in the minority. Much was less than skilful, the individual subjects outlined irregularly on a surface only roughly smoothed, the whole then covered with thick paint hastily applied [2.31–2.33]. These were buildings designed to impress from a distance. The frequent lack of fine detail discouraged the viewer from making a close inspection.

The variable quality of work is well evaluated in a comment made (in 1922) on the results of excavation at Maru-Aten:

> The column-capitals were in limestone, of the palm-leaf type, the surface of the leaves being cut into cloisons (as if to give the veining) which were filled with coloured paste. This is a cheap imitation of the splendid capitals which adorned the northern palace [now called the Great Palace], where the inlay was in faience and the edges of the stone cloisons were gilded; here a soft paste was used and the stone was but painted yellow. All through this building there was a lavish employment of paint to conceal a real poverty of material and slovenly workmanship; apart from one fragment of a red granite statue, all the rest was of limestone or the poorest quality of sandstone, and nowhere did we find traces of the elaborate inlay which enriched the sculptures and inscriptions of the little temple in the northern enclosure; only bright colour redeemed the rough cutting of hieroglyphs and uraeus cornices.[16]

When we consider the full range of royal buildings that were scattered across the Amarna plain, we can conclude that, for Akhenaten and his family, quantity was at least as important as quality.

The royal buildings also housed statues of the royal family. Some were in granite, but many used the particularly hard, granular stone commonly called quartzite that came in various warm natural colours, from creamy-brown to purple. The statues were systematically smashed after the end of the Amarna period, so we have to form our impression from fragments, of which many thousands have survived (mainly, it would seem, from the Great Palace). In them, the bodily exaggerations of the royal family were combined with astonishing technical virtuosity in carving, and the same high level seems to be uniform [2.31–33]. The second-rate carving so often visible on the wall blocks does not appear in the statues. The explanation for the difference could be that, in the making of statues, it is probably easier to 'lose' the work of apprentices and those whose skill level will remain mediocre, because there was more rough stone-cutting to be done before the final finish by the master sculptors. The amount of stone removed on wall blocks was, by contrast, much less.

We can see the effects of a building programme running ahead of the supply of properly trained and experienced craftsmen in the condition in which several of the rock tombs of Akhenaten's officials were left.[17] A set sequence of craftsmen was needed: stone-cutters to carve out the halls and columns, gypsum plasterers to render the surfaces smooth, outline draughtsmen to lay

2.31, 2.32, 2.33 *The variable quality of stone-working. (left) Part of a greywacke statue of Akhenaten (obj. S-5285), showing the fine modelling of the kilt of creased or pleated cloth. Perhaps from the house of Thutmose. Height, 25.7 cm (10.1 in.). (centre) Limestone trial piece showing the face of Akhenaten (obj. 34931), from a spoil heap opposite the front of the Small Aten Temple. Maximum width, 15.2 cm (6 in.). It illustrates the deftness of a practised sculptor. (right) Sandstone block from an architrave, Kom el-Nana. The cartouches of Akhenaten are intact, but that of Nefertiti, right, has been hacked out. Width of base, 78 cm (30.7 in.); height 40 cm (15.7 in.). The quality of the carving is poor.*

out the decoration, sculptors to carve the scenes, painters to apply the colours. The tomb owners found it impossible to phase the work so that each stage followed the completion of the previous one. When perhaps part of one wall was dressed flat (even though the rest of the tomb was being quarried out) the decorators put in a few days to get the wall scenes started, the outline draughtsman only a short distance ahead of the sculptor. The impression left is of craftsmen working for a few days here and then a few days there, trying to balance the competing claims of clients. The high priest Meryre succeeded in getting the front hall of his tomb (no. 4) completely finished. By contrast, the god's father Ay, starting his tomb (no. 25) early (to judge from the use of the earlier form of the name of the Aten) managed some fine scenes close to the entrance, but on a section of wall smoothed at a time when the quarrying of the front hall was still not finished (as it remains to this day). Ay must have been a powerful figure at court, becoming king for a short time after the death of Tutankhamun, but this still did not gain him the share of the skilled work force that his grandly designed tomb demanded.

Histories of Akhenaten see him occupied in a personal struggle, part spiritual and part political. His whole city, however, must also have been the scene of innumerable individual struggles: by people forced to start a city from scratch, relying as much upon their innate capacity to pull together as upon the country's administrative system. That they went through a time of hardship is suggested by the condition of the bodies excavated in one of their main cemeteries, where dietary deficiency and back injury are common (see Chapter 6).

3.1 *The Boston model of the Central City of Amarna, viewed as if to the south. Some parts, especially along the river bank, are restorations, as can be seen by comparing the outline plan, figure 1.10. For aerial photographs, see figures 1.8, 1.9.*

CHAPTER THREE

THE CITY OF THE SUN-GOD

Akhenaten moved to Amarna with a plan in his mind and a clean expanse of desert on which to develop it. Amarna thus offers a rare example of religious innovation on the scale of a major state, captured through archaeology at its inception. The modern world is used to religion being expressed primarily in words. In the ancient world, buildings and images counted for much more. How the Aten was to be conceived was, in large part, defined by its temples and the landscape in which they were set.

The modern mind might sense a paradox. If the solar god was to be experienced through the disc of the Aten, visibly in the sky, why a need for temples at all? In particular, why fill them with tables to support gargantuan quantities of food-offerings? Akhenaten's escape from the traditions of his culture was only partial. The enchantment of architecture, the allure of grand performance within it, and of beneficence through overseeing the inward and outward flow of the god's food, remained as prominent in his mind as in the minds of his predecessors. The austerity of his conception of god was not matched by a rejection of materialism in the expression of piety.

The Object of Devotion

Although Amarna can scarcely be said to have followed a predetermined city plan, it reflects a simple ordering scheme that was already well established in Egypt. This gave primacy in the orientation of temples to the course of the river Nile (regarded as flowing in a south to north direction, even when curving around a bend). The axis of a major temple was then frequently laid out perpendicular to this line. At Thebes, the city lay on the east bank and the major temple, dedicated to Amun-Ra at Karnak, faced the river and hence ran back towards the notional east (in reality the southeast). Amarna followed this plan. At its heart lay three large buildings at right angles to one another, as if along the sides of a rectangle [2.1, 3.1]. The building parallel to the riverbank seems to have used a greater volume of architectural stone and to have contained more statues than any other at Amarna, but may have served the ceremonial needs of the king more than the cult of the Aten. Its modern name is the Great Palace and it is described in the chapter devoted to palaces (Chapter 4).

The other two buildings have much in common with each other and are clearly temples to the Aten. Their modern names are the Great and Small Aten Temple, respectively to the north and to the south. Both of them ran back from the line of the river, appropriately towards the east. The Small Aten Temple is aligned almost (but not quite) towards the entrance to the valley that leads to the Royal Tomb. If one prolongs its axis eastwards across the high desert plateau, the line passes across the location of the Royal Tomb itself. To what extent the temples communicated with the Nile by means of a ceremonial pathway has not been directly established, although with the Great Aten Temple the proximity of the riverbank makes it likely [**3.1**]. In the case of the Small Aten Temple, the ground in front was later covered by the huge brick hall of Smenkhkare, seemingly his only significant contribution to the city during his brief reign. It is still possible, however, that the ground here remained open during Akhenaten's reign, providing direct access to the river (as in **2.3**).

Conventional temples were designed to sweep the imagination in a straight line from river frontage to a concealed sanctuary at the back of the temple. The two main Aten temples did this even more overtly by having doorways to their outer pylons so wide that they cannot have been closed by doors. In the case of the Small Aten Temple, this openness continued as far as a point deep within the sanctuary, which was finally screened off by a pair of overlapping walls that crossed the temple axis.

It seems to be widely true that the act of devotion becomes more satisfying if people are given a sense of direction or a focus. Churches have their high

3.2 *As his act of worship, the king concentrates on tending the food-offerings, the scale of which are the measure of his piety. The Aten, self-sufficient and without an intermediary image in human form able to absorb the food, hangs in the sky above, outside the range of the king's gaze. Behind him, Nefertiti clasps a sceptre, and behind her stands the tiny figure of their heiress, Princes Meryetaten, shaking a sistrum (metal rattle). From the tomb of Mahu (no. 9).*

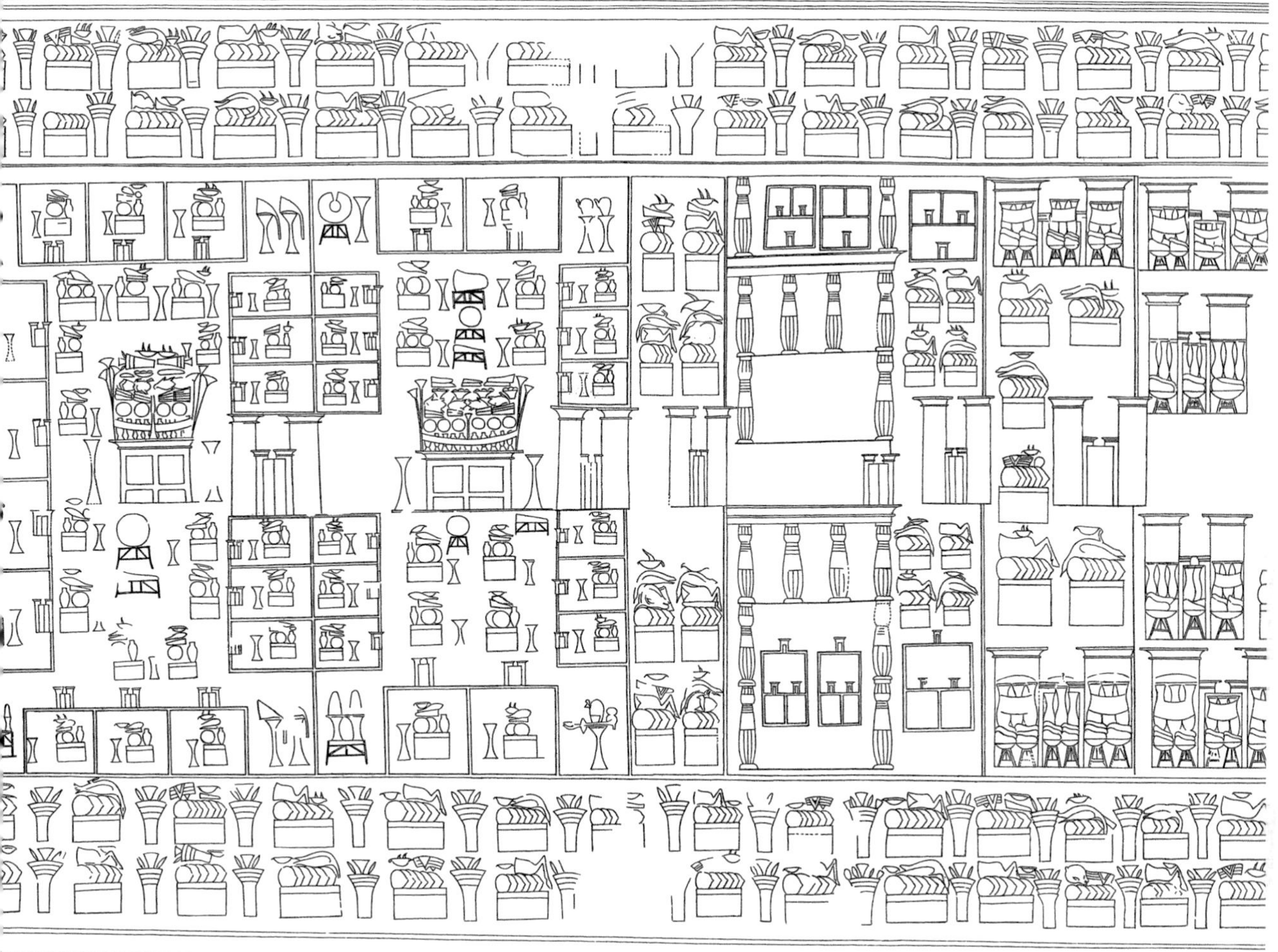

3.3 *The rear of the temple as shown in the tomb of Meryre (no. 4). The profusion of offering-tables leads one to the centre of attention: a pair of bigger offering-tables (towards the left side of the picture, thus at the back of the temple).*

altars at the east end, mosques their prayer-niches that face towards Mecca, both have pulpits from which the spiritual leader addresses the faithful. Scenes of Aten worship show the king, with members of his family, facing the sun, a table of food-offerings in front of them [**3.2**]. In the temple sanctuaries, in the place where one most expects there to have been a major symbol, the artistic and archaeological evidence agrees that one or a pair of large, but not particularly tall, tables of offerings occupied the crucial space [**3.3**]. According to the scenes, these tables were the necessary adjunct to the act of worship when the king stood in front of one of them facing towards, but not looking directly at, the sun's disc, which was the real focus of attention.

The incorporation of sun, moon or stars into the cult and ritual of sacred places excites the search for significant alignments that join up landscape features or the parts of buildings. This is claimed to be the case at Amarna.[1] Sceptics (myself among them) see the coincidences as accidental rather than as evidence for a predetermined geometric design. The closest that anyone seems to have come to finding an alignment that invokes the passage of the sun and surpasses accidental coincidence is the demonstration that the axis of the Small Aten Temple points to sunrise (and simultaneously to the Royal Tomb) at the time of year when the spring equinox occurred in Akhenaten's time [**Pl. VI**].[2]

Several other buildings or parts of buildings at Amarna look like places that called forth acts of devotion to the sun or perhaps homage to the king (it is not always clear from the building foundations whether an 'altar' to the Aten or a 'pavilion' where the king sat was originally present). They do not follow a common alignment and collectively suggest that Akhenaten generally did not think in this way. With unlimited choice as to the direction in which to cut his own tomb, the axis of the Royal Tomb runs southeast to northwest (although, as we have seen, it lies on an invisible extension of the axis of the Small Aten Temple). In their tombs, his courtiers worship the rising sun, kneeling in adoration and speaking the words of hymns, but geology dictated that they faced (approximately and with variations) to the west (while tomb no. 16, one of the finest, faces northeast). When viewed at ground level, the sun rises at Amarna above the sharp horizon line of the desert cliffs, and sets amidst the trees of the western floodplain, the western desert edge being too distant to be visible. The general intention to direct prayers and offerings to the sun was sufficient, and outweighed the need for the considerable extra labour required to orientate a tomb at other than right-angles to the desert slope that had been chosen for its location.

The proper name for the Great Aten Temple was the 'House of the Aten'; but it was also sometimes called 'The Mansion of the Benben'. The original Benben was a standing-stone of distinctive profile in the temple of the sun-god Ra (or Ra-Horakhty, 'Ra-Horus of the Horizon') at Heliopolis, its pointed top the place where the sun-god alighted each day. The Egyptians (including Akhenaten) manufactured replica Benben-stones, often giving them the shape of an obelisk. In the reign of Thutmose IV (Amenhotep III's predecessor), a single large granite obelisk was set up on the axis of the temple at Karnak, where it formed a focus of attention for those approaching the temple from the east side, where the city of Thebes was situated.[3] Akhenaten's first recorded act is the opening of a sandstone quarry at Gebel el-Silsila for the extraction of blocks for the 'great Benben of Ra-Horus of the Horizon in his name of "Shu who is the Aten", in Karnak',[4] which probably points to the building of a temple that gave even greater attention to this existing obelisk.

At Amarna, the name 'The Mansion of the Benben' was mostly written with the hieroglyphic determinative of an obelisk. None of the pictures carved in the tombs at Amarna show an obelisk, however, even though some of them

3.4 *Objects on which to focus the attention when in the 'House of the Aten': statues of Akhenaten and Nefertiti, solid tables and hollow offering-stands on which are perched food-offerings, and (at the right side of the picture) a seated statue of Akhenaten beside a round-topped stela that probably listed the offerings. Part of the picture of the Aten temple carved in the tomb of the high priest Meryre (no. 4).*

include detailed renderings of Aten temples. Obelisks require a square pedestal on which to stand. A square pedestal stood behind the Sanctuary of the Great Aten Temple, on the main axis. It has the right location for an obelisk, but, in being a mud-brick box filled with sand and in lacking a gypsum foundation layer, does not have the right characteristics. Massive concrete foundations for the support of something square and heavy are to be found in the Great Palace (see Chapter 4, p. 140), but this was not the 'Mansion of the Benben'.

In one hieroglyphic text at Amarna, a round-topped outline shape replaced the obelisk as the determinative for the name, 'The Mansion of the Benben'. Pictures of the temple do show a round-topped stela standing on a pedestal, accompanied by a seated statue of the king [3.4], but not located in a position of prominence. It was probably a stela listing the regular offerings in the temple. We are left with the explanation that the term 'Mansion of the Benben' was a poetic variant of 'House of the Aten', and did not refer to a specific fixture within the building, though it gave it an air of antiquity (there being a strong association between the Benben-stone and the place of the world's original creation) and thus legitimacy. It illustrates a recurrent difficulty that we have in trying to match pictures and texts from Amarna with what was actually built and done on the ground. They are not quite two sides of the same coin.

The Temples of the Aten

Because they were never further developed, or built over in later periods, the two Aten temples give us a much clearer picture of their full layouts and of what occupied the neighbouring ground than do most other temples of the New Kingdom.

By the time Amarna was founded, large stone buildings in the new Atenist style, employing several tens of thousands of stone blocks, had already been constructed at Karnak. Despite this trial run, the first attempts to lay out the main Aten temples at Amarna were in some way unsatisfactory and had to be abandoned in favour of altered designs. In the case of the Small Aten Temple, this early phase was in mud brick and can be interpreted as a hasty scheme to create, perhaps within a matter of weeks, a place where the cult of the Aten could be started. The first set of boundary stelae record how, on Akhenaten's first visit to Akhetaten, a huge food-offering was made. It is perhaps not a coincidence that the most prominent feature of this first phase was a large offering-platform reached by steps. At the Great Aten Temple, however, the first phase, being of stone, has the look of something more permanent [3.5, 3.6], though it can have lasted for only a few years before being replaced by something larger.

Given the limits to the king's resources, why were there two temples and not one? Akhenaten's list of promised constructions recorded on the boundary stelae begins with the 'House of the Aten' and the 'Mansion of the Aten'. Stamped bricks containing the latter name occur in the walls of the Small Aten Temple and so identify this as the second of the two. This leaves little room for doubt that the Great Aten Temple to the north is the 'House of the Aten'. The idea of two temples was thus in the king's mind at the outset, but we have no explanation why. The tomb pictures, in depicting an idealized Aten temple in use, do not clearly recognize that there were two of them, and so offer no guidance, and the nuances of meaning that separate 'house' from 'mansion' also fail to provide an answer.

An explanation sometimes put forward is that the 'Mansion of the Aten' had a role equivalent to the royal mortuary temples at Thebes. It does, literally, point towards Akhenaten's tomb. Conventional mortuary temples included separate chapels for statues of the king who built it, and for his father, but nothing equivalent can be identified at the Small Aten Temple, and so the explanation remains speculative.

The Aten temples were completely (and rapidly) excavated in the 1920s and '30s. The most valuable results are to be found in the plans of building traces that remained on the huge areas of gypsum concrete foundation platforms (of the kind described in the last chapter, pp. 64–69). They provide direct evidence for size and layout, but are virtually two-dimensional. In trying to visualize the appearance of the masonry that rose upwards, we are, to some extent, guided by the general traditions of ancient Egyptian architecture, but there are also remarkably detailed pictures of Aten temples carved on the walls of some of the rock tombs at Amarna. The pictures do not coincide exactly with the excavated plans and differ from one version to another. A degree of personal interpretation is therefore inevitable.

There were also, in reality, three temples to the Aten rather than two. The enclosure of the Great Aten Temple embraced two substantial stone buildings, the Long Temple (the original name of which might have been Gem-pa-Aten, 'The Finding of the Aten') at the front and the Sanctuary at the back, separated by 340 m (1,115 ft). Both of them, and the Sanctuary of the Small Aten Temple, shared an overall similarity of design. One characteristic was to give enhanced emphasis to the main front entrance, by adding a pair of deep columned porches to the front of the pylons, separated by a wide gap that fell on the temple axis. The effect was to contrast the bright pathway into the roofless interior with the deep shade of the towering columns and their heavy roofs.

How tall were these parts? Some individual blocks, from columns and doorways, provide a basis for estimation that gives a height of 8.5 m (28 ft) for

3.5, 3.6 The remains of the first cult layout at the Great Aten Temple. Rows of stone offering-tables, each one on its own gypsum foundation, probably led to a shrine that was later covered by the larger scheme that replaced it. Here the southern two rows of offering-tables can be seen disappearing beneath a brick construction wall of the later temple.

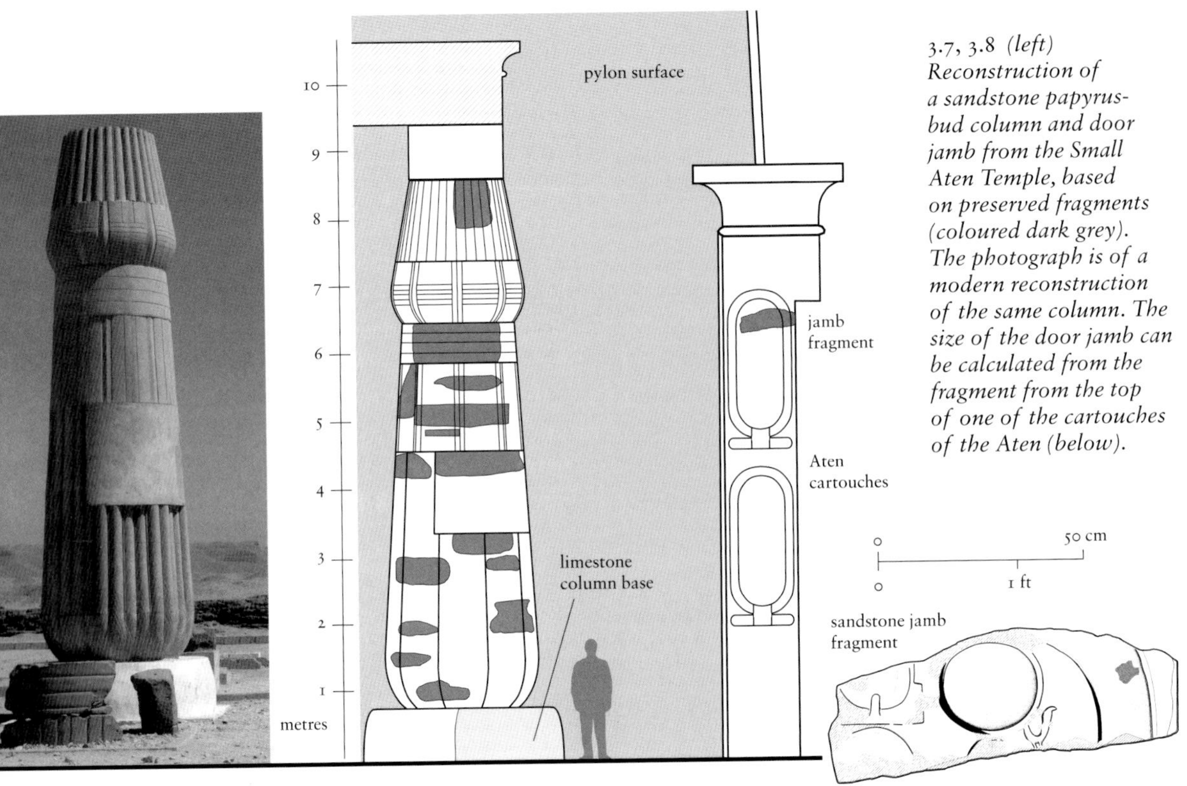

3.7, 3.8 *(left)* *Reconstruction of a sandstone papyrus-bud column and door jamb from the Small Aten Temple, based on preserved fragments (coloured dark grey). The photograph is of a modern reconstruction of the same column. The size of the door jamb can be calculated from the fragment from the top of one of the cartouches of the Aten (below).*

the sandstone columns at the Small Aten Temple Sanctuary, with a further 2 m (6.6 ft) to add for the architraves and roof [3.7, 3.8]. The pylons will have overtopped them (the tomb pictures show this), taking one up to perhaps 12 or 13 m (39 or 43 ft) for the tops of the stone pylons, and creating landmarks visible from far away.

The following descriptions cover the main elements as they stood towards the end of the Amarna period.

The Small Aten Temple

Of the two main temples, the smaller is the easier to comprehend. It was designed as a single, subdivided building whereas the enclosure wall of the Great Aten Temple surrounded a space containing several parts that were physically unconnected. The mud-brick enclosure wall of the Small Aten Temple (its outside dimensions 192 by 111 m, 630 by 364 ft) was provided on the outside with regularly spaced rectangular buttresses, which were seemingly not structurally necessary, since the much more extensive enclosure wall of the Great Aten Temple lacked them. Artistic and architectural evidence from other sites of the New Kingdom shows that buttressed temple-enclosure walls were rendered to look like fortresses by the addition of crenellated battlements around the top. Scenes of Pharaoh's victory over Egypt's enemies carved on the outer walls and pylons of the stone temples that stood within continued the theme that these temples were the strongholds of the gods. We do not know whether the decoration of the outside walls of the stone sanctuary within the Small Aten Temple included scenes of warfare (though the probability is that they did not), but a battlemented external appearance for the Small Aten Temple is a distinct possibility and would have conveyed to the outside world the same sense of impregnability.

The enclosure was divided into three unequal parts by cross walls. Passage through them was across broad stone thresholds that marked the rising slope of the ground on which the temple was built. They were flanked by large rectangular mud-brick pylons each provided with four tall wooden masts, to which coloured streamers were tied at the top, set into niches in the brickwork. The first two courts contained relatively little: a set of 106 mud-brick offering-tables at the front, and a small mud-brick building of uncertain purpose facing the axis in the middle court. The third court, by contrast, was largely filled by a monumental sanctuary constructed of stone, described below.

The Great Aten Temple and its Parts

The Great Aten Temple is a terribly wrecked site that suffers from being next door to one of the modern villages whose cemetery covers a large part. Visitors to Amarna drive past it without realizing it is there. Its original excavation also produced reports that were brief even by the parsimonious standards of their time. The precinct was defined by a mud-brick wall that enclosed an area measuring 800 by 300 m (2,624 by 984 ft). Most of this space was, however, left empty, such that the individual buildings (notably the Long Temple and the Sanctuary) seem lost within it. This aspect needs to be accounted for in explaining the whole complex.

The main entrance was in the centre of the west wall and took the form of a pair of brick pylons, each 22 by 5 m (72 by 16.4 ft). As just noted, at the Small Aten Temple, where the brickwork is better preserved, the façade of each of the pylons was indented with four deep rectangular slots to hold tall wooden flagpoles. The tomb pictures of Aten temples (which most probably concentrate on the Great Aten Temple) show sets of five flagpoles clamped to the façade and rising higher than the pylons, with long cloth streamers attached at the tops [3.9, 3.10]. The plan of the Great Aten Temple pylons shows no sign of grooves for flagpoles, but this could be because the pylons had been eroded too badly to enable detection of grooves. In the tomb pictures, however, the pylons stand inside an outer courtyard with its own entrance that lacks flagpoles. No trace of this has been found. A solution is to move the flagpoles back and to place them on the façade of the first building approached after entering the enclosure, the Long Temple, which was built of stone [3.11]. This is but one example of the choices that constantly have to be made when trying to reconstruct the appearance of Aten temples.

The gateway between the pylons, at a width of 6 m (19.7 ft), was wide enough to take a major procession, even chariots, and probably too wide

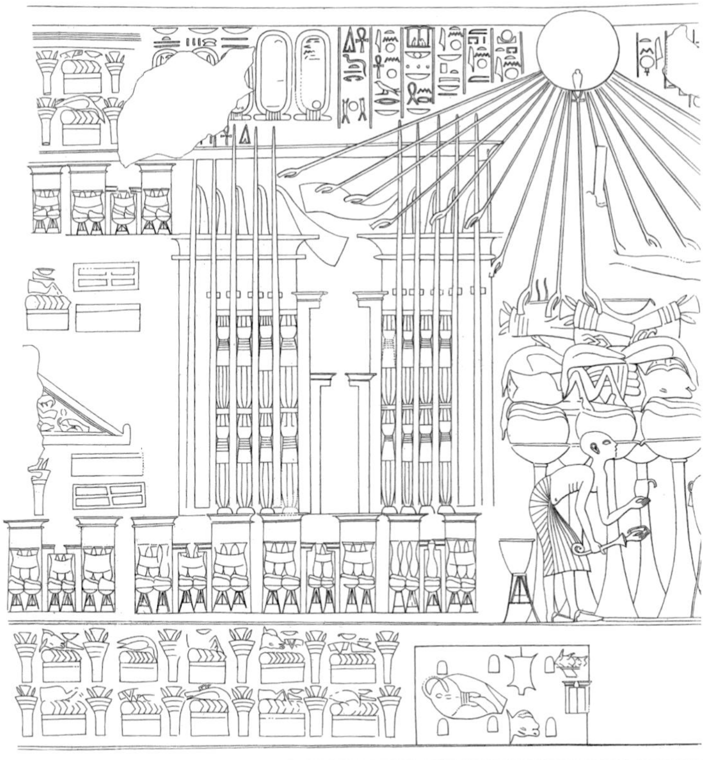

3.9, 3.10 *Pictures of the pylon entrance to the 'House of the Aten', the Great Aten Temple. (above) In the tomb of Meryre (no. 4), the direction of entrance being from the right. (left) In the tomb of Panehsy (no. 6), the direction of entrance being from the left.*

3.11 *(opposite) Restored elevations of the front of the Long Temple (the letters refer to points marked on figure 3.13). (above) Along line AA. (below) Across the façade, along line BB. On the left, the restoration is without flagpoles; flagpoles have been arranged along the face of the right-hand pylon, as suggested by some of the tomb pictures, including that in the tomb of Meryre (no. 4), (figure 3.9), but fitting awkwardly behind the colonnade. In the model (plate XXXVI) they stand in front of the outermost, mud-brick pylons.*

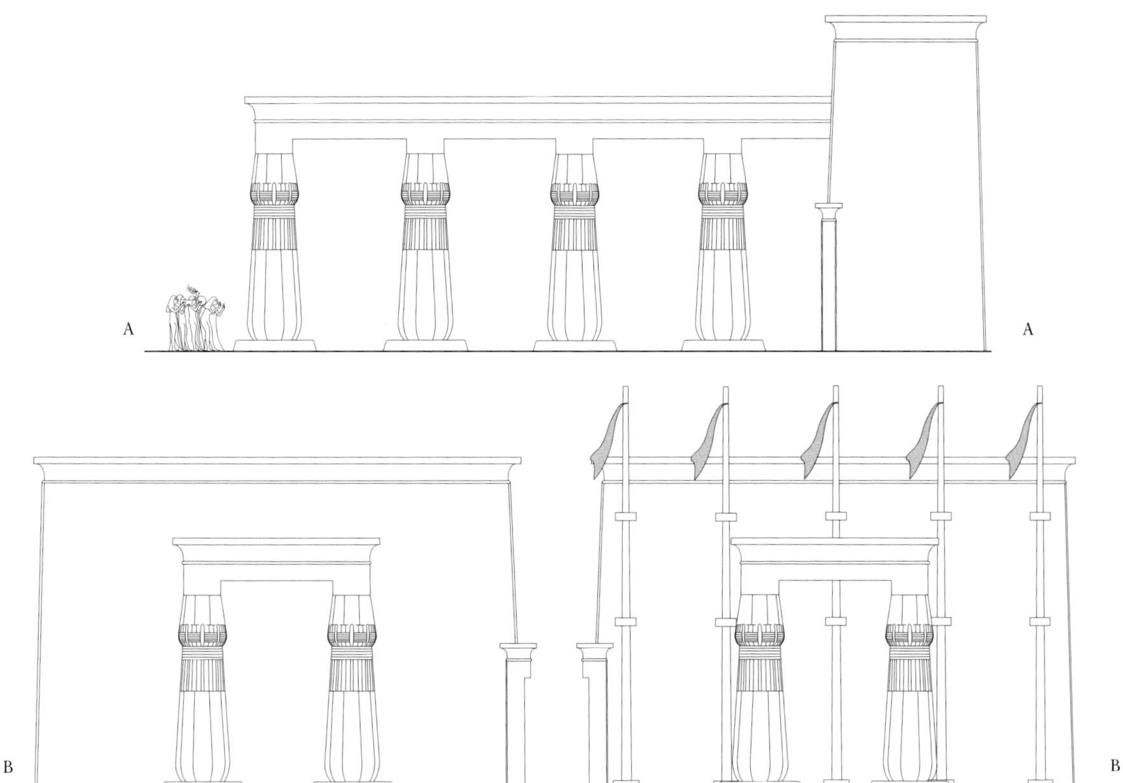

to be closed by doors [**Pl. XXXVI**]. Although the ground was flat on either side and at the same level, the pavement of the gateway had been raised, such that to pass through the gateway one ascended and descended a low ramp of sand (presumably coated with mud plaster to stabilize the surface) held in place with side walls of brick. This was a feature of major gateways in the Small Aten Temple and Great Palace, too, and seems to have been a device to heighten the sense of occasion when passing from one space to another, as much as to accommodate changes in ground level. On the left (north) side of the axis stood a stone building that, to judge from the foundations, mostly consisted of a columned hall (partly visible in figure **3.12**). It was the principal part of the whole complex that was enclosed and roofed, offering privacy and security. There was certainly a need for a 'treasury' to store valuable temple equipment, but whether it was used for this purpose is not known.

The Long Temple and the Field of Offering-tables

At a distance of 32 m (105 ft) beyond the pylons stood the façade of a long and narrow building of stone. The excavators identified it with the place known to Akhenaten as 'Gem-pa-Aten', thus 'The Finding of the Aten', but the grounds for this are weak, and to apply such a name prejudges the difficult question of the extent to which there was a close correspondence between individual buildings and the various building names that are found in the texts. Here I call it simply the Long Temple.

Everything that the excavation uncovered was originally below the floor. The key to its design is preserved in the gypsum concrete foundation, which is a particularly impressive specimen [3.12; also 2.24]. At the very front, the foundations are unusually thick and solid (visible in the background of 3.5). The block impressions belong to a set of large columns that formed an open colonnade in front of the temple and gave its façade depth through shadow. Behind them is one option for where the flagpoles may have been set up [3.11].

Behind the front of the temple, the block impressions left by the outside wall on the gypsum bed define a rectangle measuring about 190 by 33 m (358 by 108 ft), and further block impressions mark cross walls that subdivided it into six sections. All but one of the cross walls thicken in the middle, suggestive of pylons, with rear extensions that made the gateways even deeper (the exception, running across the middle of the third court, I have interpreted as the foundations for a line of columns connected by screen walls). Long narrow areas of raised ground (of sand topped with gypsum plaster) now run through

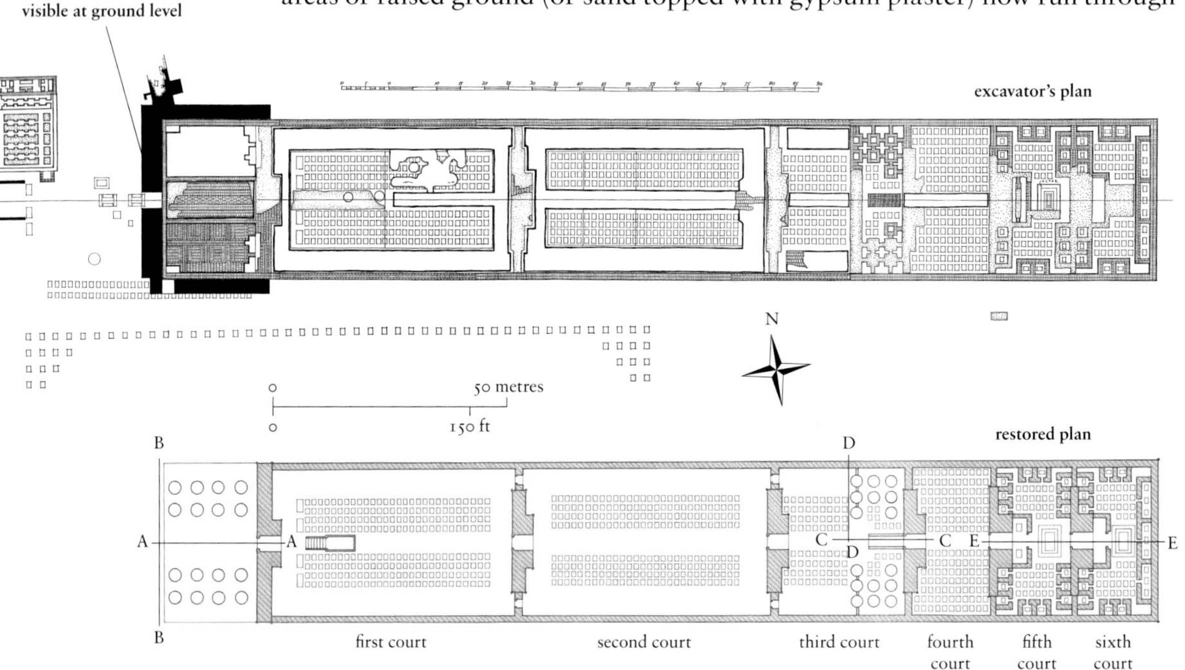

3.12, 3.13 *The Long Temple, the main building within the huge enclosure of the Great Aten Temple. (above) The plan of foundations made by the architect Ralph Lavers following the excavation of 1932. (below) An interpretation of how the foundation traces should be understood. The lines and capital letters refer to the elevation drawings (figures 3.11, 3.14).*

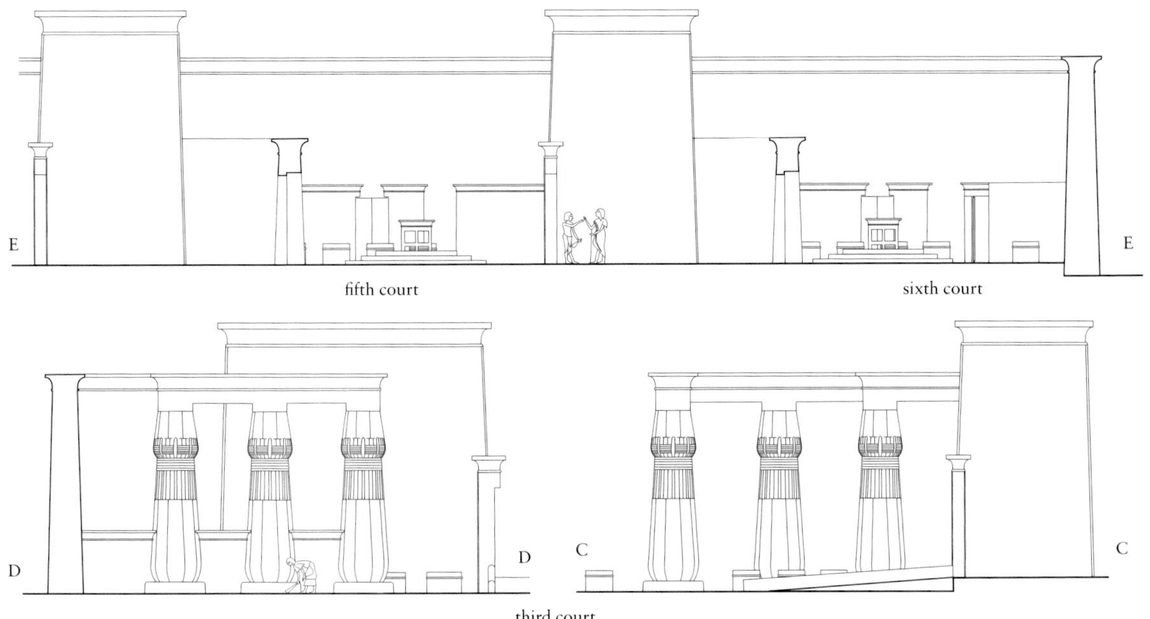

3.14 *Further restored elevations within the Long Temple. The letters refer to the plan opposite.*

the subdivisions and give the impression of having served as raised causeways (they are marked as 'platforms' on the 1932 plan, **3.12**). But this is an illusion: they were simply a way of economizing on the gypsum, and were originally invisible below an even floor level. The Long Temple was basically a string of courts open to the sky, though with a second colonnade separating the third and fourth courts [**3.14**]. From fragments found in the debris, we know that the columns of that part were of the clustered papyrus-bud form (as at the Small Aten Temple, see **3.7**, **3.8**).

In the fifth court, an area of gypsum was marked with concentric rectangles, the outer measuring about 7 by 5 m (23 by 16 ft). An empty space in the gypsum in an equivalent position in the sixth court, close to the rear wall of the building, could have been the site of another such area. They occupy the commanding position in the temple, the place where one would expect the principal focus of attention to have been. The tomb pictures agree in showing the culmination of the temple to have been a table, with legs and open sides (was it made of wood covered with gold?), heaped with offerings [**3.3**]. A second table is shown behind, a duplication that seems to match the traces on the gypsum foundations just described. The tomb pictures also magnify a stepped platform near the front of the temple (the sloping balustrade is at the left edge of **3.9**), which the royal family ascend for a presentation of offerings. At its expected location in the first court, the gypsum foundation layer has a large gap, the result of later destruction [**3.12**]. The shape of the stepped platform has been added to the restored plan [**3.13**].

From the front to the back of the Long Temple, the gypsum foundations beneath the courts were marked with numerous small rectangles, each one measuring 90 by 110 cm (35.4 by 43.3 in.), and separated from its neighbour by a gap of 50 cm (19.7 in.). The total reached at least 791. In the rear parts, many of them were enclosed with marks indicating the presence of walls. In the first court, foundation layers of limestone *talatat*-blocks were found, still standing on a few of the rectangles when the site was excavated in 1932, proving that each of the rectangles had been individually built up [**2.24**]. We do not have to guess what they were; the tomb scenes leave no doubt. They were tables or benches on which offerings to the sun, of food and incense, were heaped. Those towards the rear are depicted standing within their own walled courts, just as is indicated by the foundations.

It might not be an invariable rule, but people who fix their minds on quests tend to become obsessive. Akhenaten's multiplication of offering-tables is surely a symptom of obsession. It becomes even more obvious when the frame of reference is widened: over an area of the enclosure beside the Long Temple on the south, a further 920 offering-tables, this time of mud brick, were constructed (shown to the right of the temple in plate XXXVI). The excavators of the '30s claimed to have found traces of a matching set on the north side, but provided insufficient verification. Even without the northern set, the number of offering-tables in and beside the Long Temple amounted to more than 1,700.

Ancient Egyptian temples of other periods offer no parallels. It is not a relic of past practice that Akhenaten has kept. The intentionality of this multiplication of offering-tables, which the tomb scenes show piled high with offerings, implies that this is an innovation that we should not dismiss as a symbolic

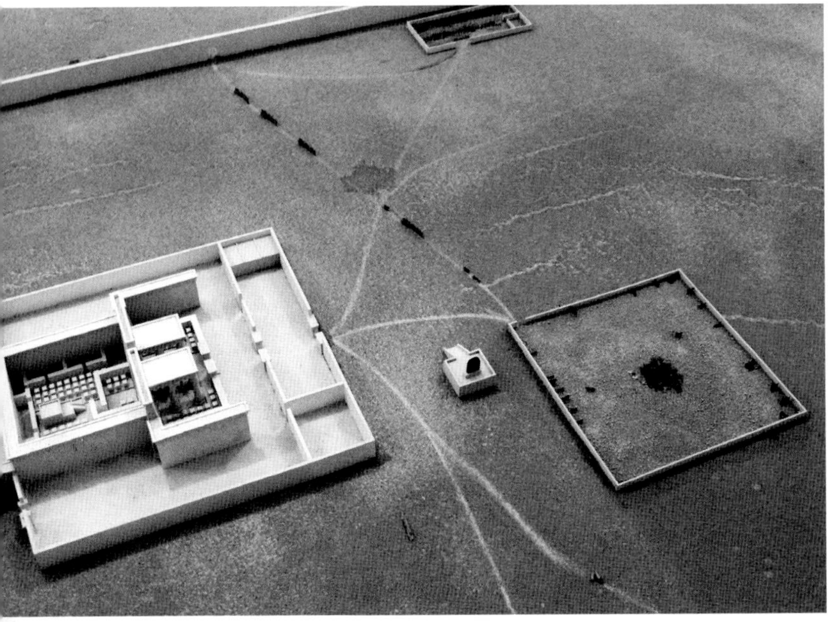

3.15 *Model of the Sanctuary at the rear of the Great Aten Temple enclosure. To the right are the platform for the round-topped stela and the square enclosure where cattle were slaughtered. The banked-up sides of the Sanctuary (figure 3.17) have been omitted in this model and the offering-platform at the back should be replaced by a large openwork offering-table. A part of the Boston model.*

gesture. Traditional temples owned extensive estates that produced foodstuffs, and some had access to mineral resources and owned trading ships. All temple income was classed as 'offerings', but only a token was ever presented before the gods. Akhenaten seems to have been following a more literal interpretation of the practice, setting out quantities that might have approached a more realistic representation of the full temple income. What you saw was what existed.

The Sanctuary

The largest element in the Great Aten Temple enclosure was a huge central space almost devoid of features. If it had been intended for gardens or plantations of trees then we would have expected traces of irrigation installations, particularly a depression marking the site of a large well (the Maru-Aten enclosure offers an instructive parallel). Previous excavators discovered nothing of the kind, nor are traces visible on the ground or in aerial photographs. It seems to have always been a flat piece of desert.

Located beyond this area, at a distance of 340 m (1,115 ft) behind the Long Temple, the Sanctuary was the second major stone building within the temple enclosure [3.15]. Its relative remoteness and the fact that it stood close to a number of ancillary structures made it, in effect, a separate place of cult. It stood within its own perimeter wall of brick only about 60 cm (23.6 in.) thick, built without buttresses, implying a height of perhaps not much more than 2 m (6.6 ft), such that the Sanctuary itself would have been easily visible from no great distance. Its damaged gypsum foundation had a size and shape very similar to the better-preserved Sanctuary at the Small Aten Temple [3.16]. Both were essentially rectangular buildings, 30 by 47 m (98 by 154 ft) in extent,

3.16 *Aerial view of the Sanctuary of the Small Aten Temple. The outlines of walls and positions of columns have been laid out with new stone blocks, along the lines preserved on the now-buried gypsum foundation layer. Near the bottom of the picture, part of the entrance to the Sanctuary court is visible, set between a pair of thick mud-brick pylons.*

divided into inner and outer parts probably by a large stone pylon. Immediately in front of where the pylon for the Sanctuary of the Great Temple would have been, there survived stone foundations for a pair of tall objects that were sufficiently heavy to have stood on a granite base, were 30 cm (11.8 in.) across, had been sheathed in bronze and were 6 m (19.7 ft) apart. Rather than having supported pivots for very large doors, the design of the foundations suggests that tall masts for streamers stood there.

The Sanctuaries at both the large and small temples were essentially compressed versions of the Long Temple, filled with stone offering-tables. Whether either of them had a central focus of attention towards the rear, equivalent to the openwork tables of offerings in the Long Temple, is not possible to assess from the severely damaged remains. Another odd feature is the pair of L-shaped walls that run out from the ends of the pylons. At the Small Aten Temple Sanctuary, the space created within the L shape was partially occupied with mud-brick chambers, but this was surely a conversion into something useful of an architectural feature intended to stand alone (a scene in the tomb of Ahmose (no. 3) seems to show one of the side wings fitted out as a throne-room[5]).

It is natural to seek a single all-embracing explanation for the whole ensemble of the Great Aten Temple, which was Akhenaten's principal tribute to the Aten. One way of looking at it is to see it as a miniaturized rendering of Akhetaten itself, reduced to a set of architectural symbols. An example of the Egyptians thinking in this way comes from the temple of Seti I at Abydos, built 50 years after Akhenaten's death. Its enclosure wall surrounded not only a monumental stone temple (and its brick storerooms), but also, behind it, an elaborate simulacrum of the tomb of the god Osiris (the Osireion). His actual tomb (so the Egyptians believed) lay about 1.5 km (0.9 miles) back in the desert, much closer to the cliffs that partly embraced the site, much in the same way as they do at Amarna. At Amarna, there was no tomb for the Aten. The Aten's special place was the desert and especially his place of sunrise in the 'eastern mountain'. The Sanctuary at the back of the Great Aten Temple thus represented (so one can argue) the eastern mountain. The strange stone wings that ran outwards and forwards from beside the pylons are a simplified rendering of the desert cliffs that, having formed the horizon for Amarna, turn and run towards the river.

Moreover, the idea that the Sanctuary stood for the Horizon of the Aten, the distant line of cliffs and thus a plane elevated above the desert in front, was given material form by making it seem to stand on a white hill. There still survives around the rear edge of the site where the Sanctuary stood an embankment of stone fragments cemented by gypsum and sealed beneath a hard surface of the same material. This surface slopes evenly downwards and away from the building, which would have appeared as if rising from a low white mound [3.17]. In this explanation, the big flat open space in front represents the desert of the Amarna plain, and the Long Temple the place in the city where people gathered to greet and celebrate the sunrise.

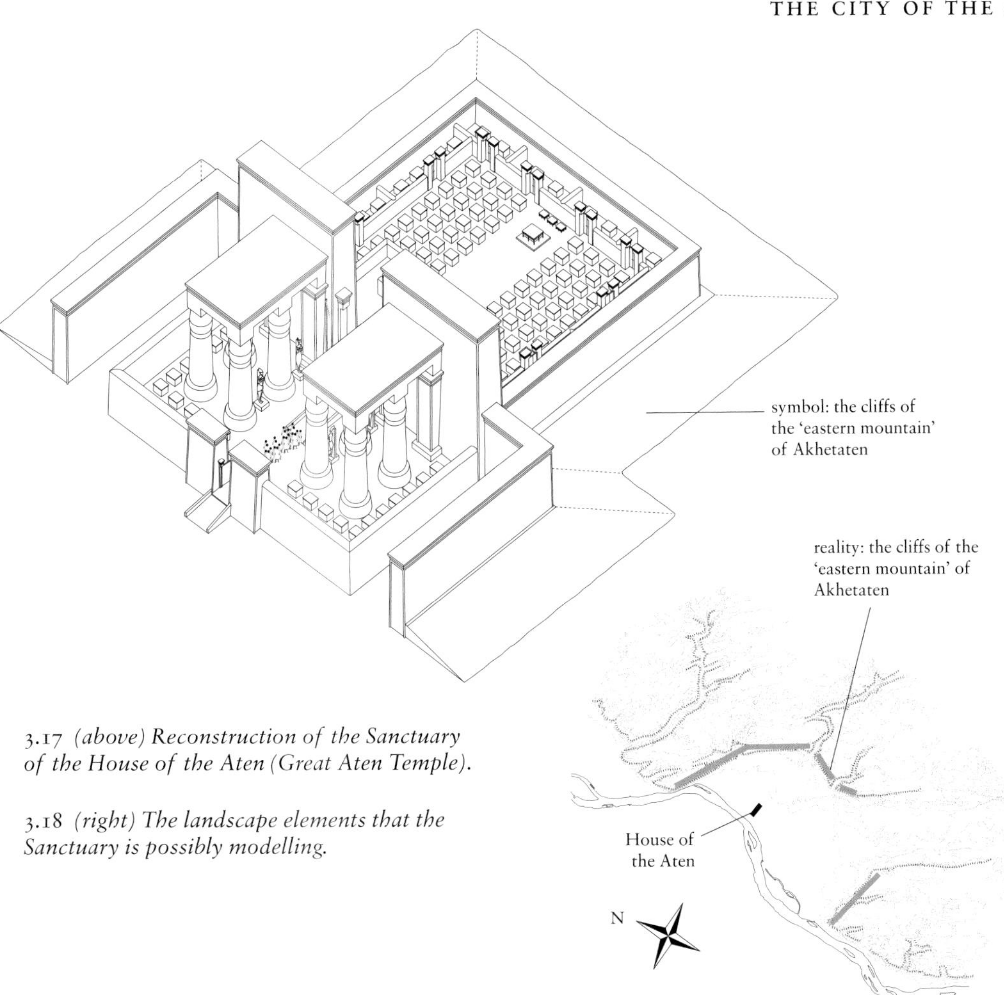

3.17 *(above) Reconstruction of the Sanctuary of the House of the Aten (Great Aten Temple).*

3.18 *(right) The landscape elements that the Sanctuary is possibly modelling.*

Ideas like this, built on the mental substitution of one thing for another, are particularly difficult to prove in the absence of eyewitness evidence, if not impossible. And it is perhaps unnecessary to think of an either/or choice, between a pragmatic and a symbolic explanation, especially given the Egyptians' tolerance for alternative ways of looking at things.

Ancient Views of the Temples

Several of the Amarna rock tombs include pictures of Aten temples in their schemes of wall decoration. They combine elements of plan and elevation in the same view. Two of the tombs belonged to men with titles that suggest they were the priests in charge: Meryre (tomb no. 4), who was 'Chief of Seers of the Aten in the House of Aten in Akhetaten', and Panehsy (tomb no. 6), who was 'Chief Servitor of the Aten in the House of Aten in Akhetaten'. Panehsy was also the owner of an official residence just outside the rear of the Great Aten Temple (his private house lay separately in the Main City). We should expect their pictures of temples to be particularly faithful.

The pictures show closely subdivided spaces and their doorways [3.3, 3.4]. Very few columns appear and, when they do, they can be explained as supporting an open colonnade. This agrees with the excavated plans, indicating that the temples were essentially open to the sky. Spaces large and small are filled with offering-tables, sometimes accompanied by narrow offering-stands, all piled with food (joints of meat, poultry, vegetables, loaves of bread) and flowers, which also stand or lie in separate bouquets. Bowls of smoking incense are perched on top. Other objects, including broad bead collars, lie on wooden tables; tall jars that might be of bronze or pottery are supported within wooden stands and could have contained water or beer. The impression is of overwhelming material abundance. Even the focus of attention at the back of the temple is an offering-table, although one larger in size than the others.

We see flagpoles with streamers in front of pylons, and statues of Akhenaten and Nefertiti between columns. The wings that project from the sides of the Sanctuaries are shown. Some components are rendered as if close beside the temple: rectangular basins, a round-topped stela on a pedestal beside which is a seated statue of Akhenaten, a slaughtering-court for cattle, complete with tethering-stones, and what is shown as a small house-like building with an ornate window. Over the whole scene is the standard representation of the Aten and its downward-reaching rays. The accompanying legend calls the building simply 'The House of the Aten in Akhetaten'.

We are also shown the drama of the cult itself, performed by the king, queen and daughters, scaled according to their importance [3.2]. It appears to follow a traditional form, with the necessary omissions of those acts that required the presence of a statue of the god (though whether these were maintained for the cult of the king's own statues we cannot tell). The royal couple present to the Aten a token of the food- and drink-offerings that otherwise fill the whole temple, sometimes brandishing a sceptre in the shape of the hieroglyph for 'power' (*kherep*), another example of the acceptance of tradition. Sometimes they raise aloft a tray bearing offerings. Behind them, their daughters shake metal rattles (sistra). A group of men sing or chant, clapping their hands as they do so; a company of male musicians and vocalists perform sitting down (but what kind of words are they singing?); groups of women sing to the accompaniment of hand-clapping, the waving of palm-branches and the playing of drums. In one version of a hymn to the Aten, sunrise is said to be celebrated by 'singing, chanting and joyful shouting in the courtyard of the Mansion of the Benben and [in] every temple in Akhetaten'.[6] Courtiers throw themselves to their hands and knees in a gesture of respect; military escorts and even distinctively attired foreigners are in attendance as well.

The people present are shown as if they are small groups allowed the privilege of observing the royal family at worship. But might the statement about 'singing, chanting and joyful shouting' point to the presence of real crowds as distinct from a hand-picked entourage? There was certainly space for crowds in front of the Long Temple and especially in the succession of courtyards at

I (previous page) Upper part of a colossal statue of Akhenaten, sandstone, from Karnak. Traces of paint (including blue beard and red lips) remain. Height 2.05 m (6 ft 8 in.).

II (opposite) Painted head of Nefertiti, found in the house of the sculptor Thutmose at Amarna in 1912. Limestone and gypsum. Height 50 cm (19.5 in.).

III (above) Head of a princess, found in the house of the sculptor Thutmose at Amarna. Yellow-brown quartzite, with red and black pigment applied. Beneath the neck is a long tenon (mostly invisible in the photograph) that would have been used to attach the head to a separately made body. The head had been broken from the neck and rejoined in ancient times. Height 19 cm (7.5 in.).

IV (right) Statue, restored from fragments, and thought to be of Akhenaten. Originally a seated statue of a female was against his right side, arm behind his back. Unidentified yellow stone. Provenance unknown. Height 64 cm (25 in.).

V (below) Piece of balustrade from an entrance ramp at the Great Palace, made from indurated limestone. It depicts Akhenaten and Nefertiti offering libations to the Aten. Behind them a daughter shakes a sistrum. Height 1.05 m (4 ft 2 in.).

VI Sunrise at the Small Aten Temple, 19 February 2005.

VII (below) The centre point of Akhetaten: the entrance to the valley or wadi that leads to the Royal Tomb in 'the mountain of Akhetaten, the place of truth (*Maat*)'.

VIII View eastwards across the full extent of Akhetaten from boundary stela A. The remains of the track in front of it are of the Amarna period (and are now obliterated beneath a modern access stairway). The location of boundary stela X, on the far side, is well to the left of the white patch on the cliffs (caused by modern quarrying, now discontinued). The photograph was taken in 1975.

IX (opposite above) The Amarna plain in 2000, looking south from the northern headland.

X (opposite below) View of the rear part of the North Palace, taken in 2011, towards the south. In the foreground is the garden court. See also Pl. XVIII.

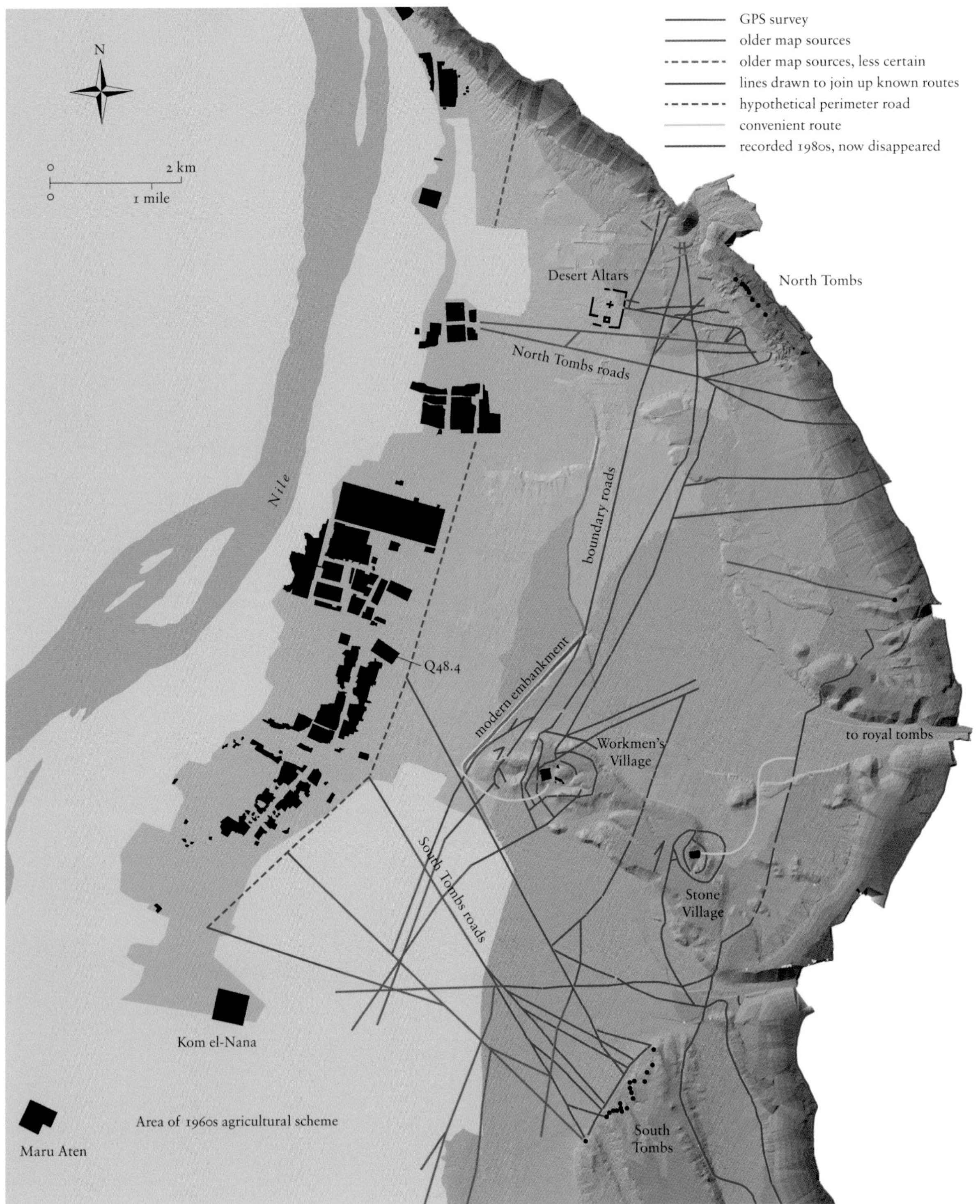

XI Draft map of the desert road system laid over a provisional topographic model. It represents an early stage in the production of a map of the Amarna plain by Helen Fenwick. The southernmost part of the Amarna plain is not included. The yellow broken lines near the Workmen's Village and Stone Village mark naturally convenient routes.

the Small Aten Temple. These can be interpreted as providing, in the front court, a place for assembly, followed by a narrower court that buffered the Sanctuary, standing within its own court, from the public area. A point to note is the unusual width of the doorways between the brick pylons, both at the main entrance to the Great Aten Temple and at the three entrances leading through the courts of the Small Aten Temple. None is less than 6 m (19.7 ft) wide (those at the smaller temple closer to 8 m, 26 ft) and so could not have been closed by wooden pivoting doorways, as was the usual practice in Egyptian temples. As if to emphasize that much of the temple was open to inspection from outside, the final, rear part of the Sanctuary was closed off by a pair of overlapping screen walls that shut it off from outside gaze.

There is no compelling evidence for deciding between two contrasting images of Akhenaten and the cult of the Aten. One image is exclusive. It is of Akhenaten, with only essential supporters, leading the worship of the Aten (and dwarfed by the scale of the architecture) on behalf of a population kept well away from his presence and from the interiors of the temples. The other is inclusive, of Akhenaten suitably distanced, but still at the head of a portion of the citizenry who periodically entered the temples, drawn by the attraction of celebration and the distribution of food. It should be borne in mind that the absence at Amarna of traditional temples dedicated to the long-established gods removed from Amarna's society a rich calendar of festivals that otherwise featured prominently in the lives of Egyptians. To accept this second image, of a cult that filled the vacuum left by the lack of a traditional cycle of festivals, is to credit Akhenaten with a populism that many people who study the Amarna period do not accept. From a modern perspective, it would have been a wise political decision, deflecting potential discontent among a population dragged to an arid, rootless and curiously disease-ridden building site.

Not Just Architecture

The tomb pictures that show the temples, not to mention the general run of modern reconstructions, concentrate on architectural shapes that leave a monochrome impression. The reality for anyone who was actually present, at least within the stone parts, was an assault on the eyes by harsh colour. The stone walls were covered with carved scenes in which each shape and hieroglyph was filled with a single colour from a very limited palette of thick mineral pigments, standing out from a white background. On some of the reliefs of the royal family their ornaments had been covered with gold leaf.[7] A small number of faience tiles and inlays point to the use of this additional form of decoration.[8]

The most obvious foils to the uncompromising flatness of the architectural planes were the columns, though these were used sparingly and were also brightly painted. Of softer and more interesting effect were the statues. According to the tomb pictures, they primarily stood between the columns, but only fragments have been found and none necessarily close to where they had originally stood. The most important group was found by Howard Carter in 1892. He wrote: 'in a sort of fosse, just outside its temenos [sacred precinct] wall, I discovered portions of seventeen statues of the king and queen. These had been ruthlessly destroyed by the victorious sectarians when the reaction in favour of Amun triumphed. These were wrought of a pure white semi-crystalline limestone and were of the finest workmanship.'[9]

Petrie, who supervised Carter's work, added:

> Beside these life-size statues in the temple, there were also colossal standing figures of Akhenaten, in soft limestone, of which an ear, a toe, and a piece of the chest were found. The attitude seems to have been with crossed arms holding the crook and flail....
>
> Among the fragments of the statues were also pieces of tablets, inscribed on the front with the cartouches of the Aten, and on the sides with those of the king. On one of these the position of the hands carved below it points out that it was held by a kneeling figure, presenting it in the usual posture of offering: the tablet resting on one hand, and being steadied by the other hand behind it.
>
> Other similar tablets, made of blue-glazed pottery in high relief, were perhaps placed in the hands of other statues.[10]

Forty-four years later, Pendlebury found yet more statue fragments, some from colossi in 'bad local limestone'.[11] The extensive dumps south of the temple enclosure remain a source of statue fragments for a current project to catalogue and elucidate the extent and nature of Akhenaten's statue programme at Amarna.

Traditional temples in New Kingdom Egypt received pious gifts of equipment and furnishings that are well documented in contemporary illustrations, but of which relatively few examples have survived. They came not only as gifts commissioned by the king, but also from a custom according to which people throughout the country were expected to demonstrate their loyalty by having items made that they would then send to the palace for a New Year ceremony, the king subsequently passing at least some of the objects to the temples.[12] Two prominent categories of temple treasures were vessels made from metal (bronze, silver and gold) and wooden objects overlaid with gold leaf, principally statues and the shrines that housed them. A few examples of the latter (shrines and statues) were discovered in Tutankhamun's tomb, and a shrine in the Amarna style in the contemporary tomb KV55 in the Valley of the Kings.

Examples of both categories have been found in the ruins of Amarna's temples, pointing to the likelihood that the custom of lavishing some of the choicest products of the country's craftsmen on the leading temples was maintained at Amarna. Metal vessels are represented by a group of seven in bronze found buried beneath the foundations of the Sanctuary of the Great Aten Temple [**3.19–3.21**]. One of them was an offering-stand, a shallow bowl on a slender stem, the whole 35 cm (13.8 in.) tall. The remainder were deep, wide-mouthed vessels suitable for containing liquid. The royal names had

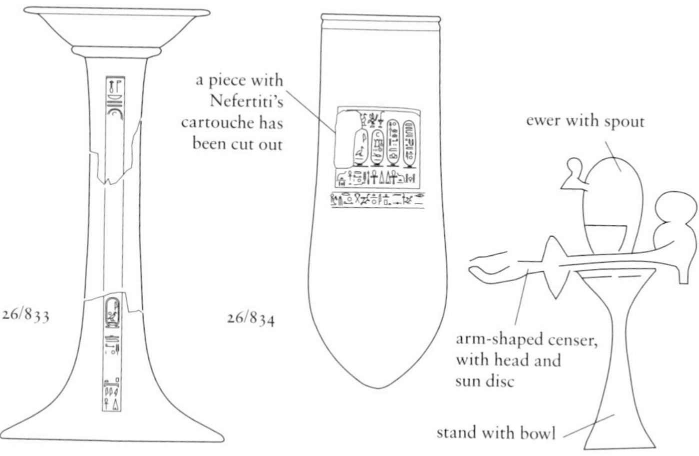

3.19, 3.20, 3.21 *(left and centre) Two bronze vessels from the Sanctuary of the Great Aten Temple. On the left (26/833) is a stand supporting a bowl perhaps for incense, with a vertical column of lightly incised hieroglyphs giving Akhenaten's names and titles (present whereabouts unknown; it is not certain if both parts belong to the same object). The restored height is said to be 35 cm (13.8 in.). The central vessel (26/834) has a panel giving the names of the Aten and the names of Akhenaten and Nefertiti. Her cartouche has been cut out, presumably when the vessel was buried along with others. Height 30.5 cm (12 in.) (JdE 50940, Egyptian Museum, Cairo, where the cut-out fragment is said to be). (right) A set of vessels, presumed to be of metal, shown in the picture of the Great Aten Temple in the tomb of Meryre (no. 4) (see figure 3.3).*

been lightly incised in hieroglyphs on most of them. It is of special interest that one [**3.20**) bore a private dedication: 'Made by the standard-bearer of the regiment of Sehetep-Aten ["pleasure to the Aten", perhaps an epithet of Akhenaten], Ramose'.[13] Here we have a documented case of private donation. The tomb pictures also show, here and there amidst the offering-tables, ritual objects, such as arm-shaped censers (one visible in **3.2**, lower middle, on a narrow stand; also **3.21**).

Fragments of furniture covered with gold leaf have also been recovered from the Great Aten Temple, one group from beside the north enclosure wall and consisting of 'seven wooden uraei and fragments of the bar to which they were attached. Gilt disk, blue head, bodies blue, red, and green picked out with gilt, 15 cm (5.9 in.) high';[14] the other, a 'Fragment of painted and gilt wood and some gold leaf',[15] was found in the Sanctuary and considered at the time to have been perhaps a 'foundation deposit', presumably because it was found in one of a line of four pits towards the front of the building. The employment of wood for sacred objects is also illustrated by pieces from a shrine and statues, one of them a sphinx [**3.22**], although these are not from one of the stone temples, but from a mud-brick building in the Central City. A panel from the shrine refers to 'the great statue that the king caused to be made' [**3.24**; also **3.25**].[16] In addition, if we accept as true the ancient depictions of the temples, the equipment would have included numerous wooden latticework stands for holding vessels.

Conventional temples, roofed, windowless and with doors that could be bolted, were naturally secure places for the storage of sacred and costly temple equipment. From documents covering a long period of time we know that those responsible for temples feared theft of temple treasures and employed various means to safeguard them, developing a security culture of paperwork and punishments. One might expect that the upheavals that accompanied the creation of Amarna only increased the risks. The front part of the Great Aten Temple, which included the Long Temple, shows no sign of places for secure storage other than the separate roofed building just inside the enclosure on the north side of the axis. Did this serve as a 'treasury'? In the case of the Sanctuary at the back of the Small Aten Temple (and by implication the Sanctuary of the Great Aten Temple) the spaces created by the 'wings' on either side seem to have been subsequently roofed over in brick and so could have served this purpose, but they look like afterthoughts. All parts of both temples were also designed to

3.22, 3.23 *House of the King's Statue (building R43.2) on the edge of the Central City, showing the plan and some of the principal objects (for its location, see figure 1.10).* a *36/179, wooden sphinx bearing traces of blue paint, length 26 cm (10.2 in.);* b *36/161, wooden plumes from a statue (Queen Tiye or Nefertiti?), faint traces of a design in red on yellow, height 16 cm (6.3 in.);* c *36/172, wooden forearm and hand from a statue, length 13.5 cm (5.3 in.);* d *36/165, blue faience helmet from a composite statue of Akhenaten, height 12 cm (4.7 in.);* e *36/162, bronze tongs ending in hands, length 38 cm (15 in.).*

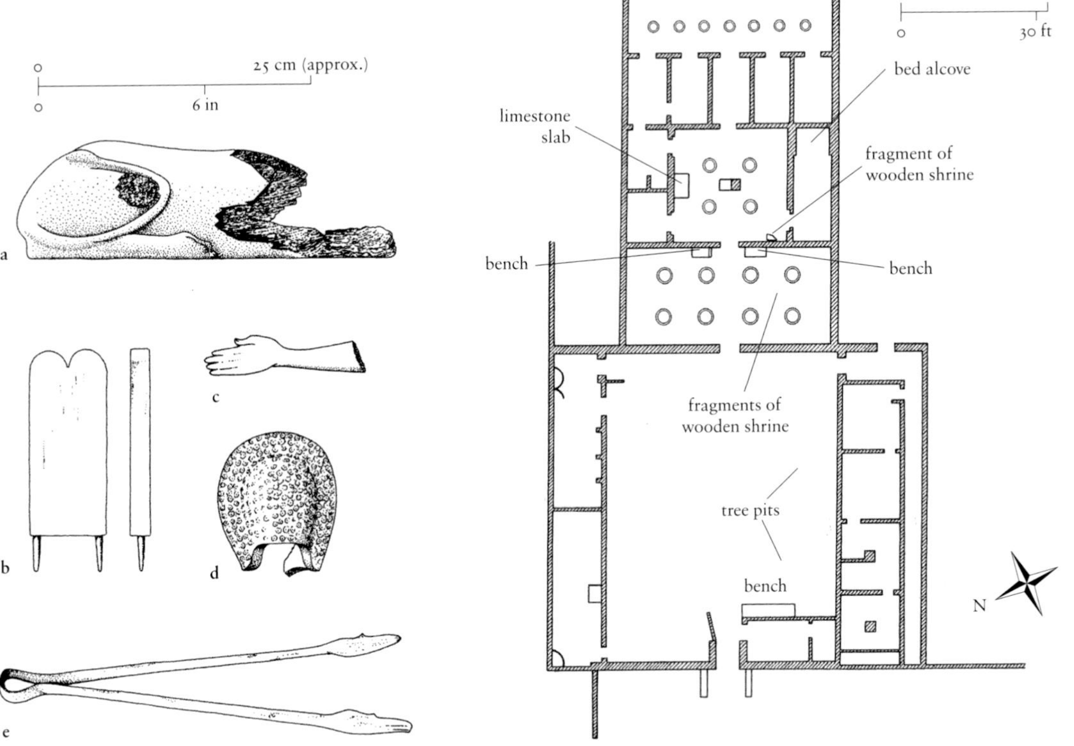

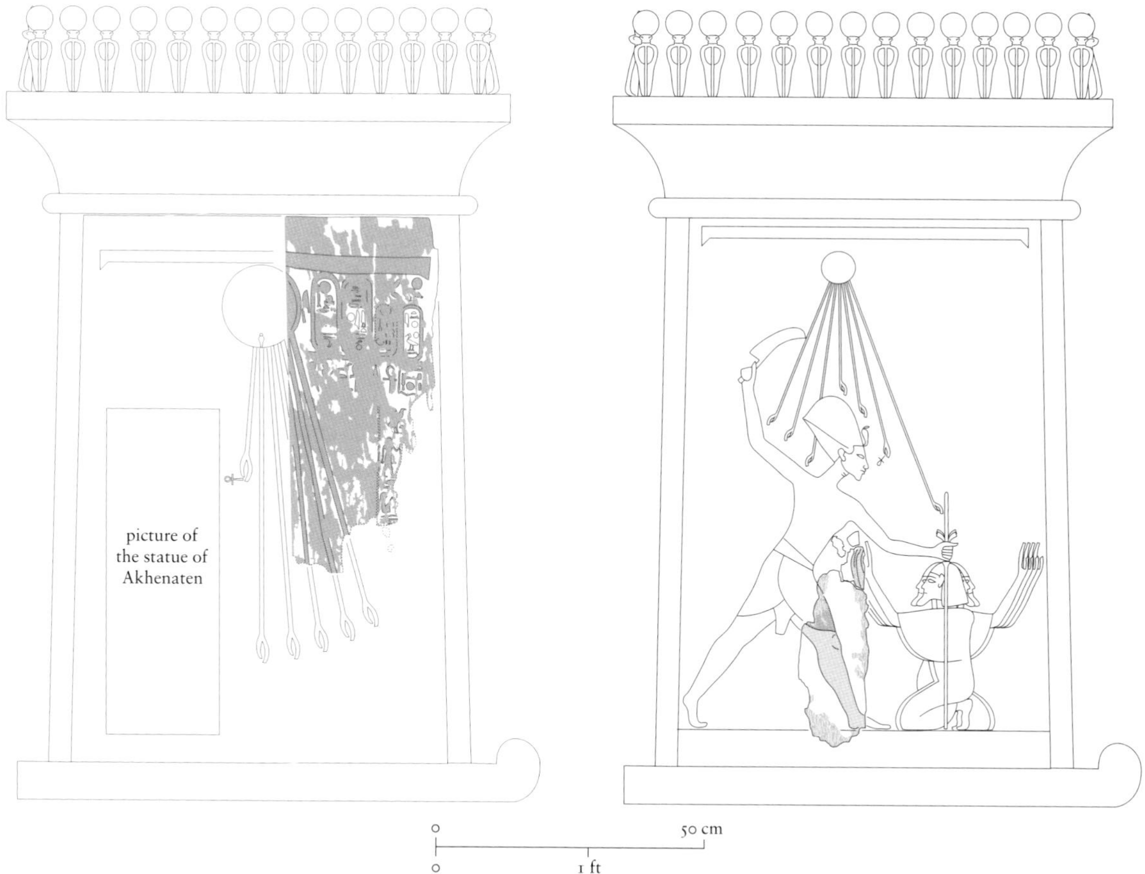

3.24 *(above left) Part of a wooden panel from a small shrine from building R43.2, based on excavation photographs. Under the cartouches of the Aten and of Akhenaten one can read the word 'statue', which has the normal determinative for a statue of a standing figure holding a staff. The size of the panel was* c. *27 cm (10.6 in.) wide and 63 cm (24.8 in.) tall. The original width must have been* c. *65 cm (25.6 in.). This is approximately the width of a brick pedestal found in the central room of the building. The white surface of the panel suggests a coating of gypsum, the normal underlay for gold leaf. The row of wooden cobras on the top is a reconstruction based on some that were found, obj. 36/171, as drawn on the EES record card.*

3.25 *(above right) Another wooden panel from building R43.2 (cf. figure 3.24), which preserved part of a leg of a king striding and smiting a group of enemies who kneel with arms upraised begging for mercy. From these traces the full figure can be reconstructed.*

expose as much as possible of the temple interior to the elements, thus to dust, punishing sunlight and occasional rain – a combination that would warp and split any wooden furnishings left out for long periods.

The near-absence of secure storage is, however, only part of a wider issue concerning the way the Great Aten Temple was used. It seems it was also regularly filled up with offerings. The practicalities of this both strain our capacity to understand ancient evidence and go to the heart of what Akhenaten had in mind.

Fixation with Food

The two Aten temples acted as giant food displays. The art of the Amarna period exhibits something of an obsession with victuals. Pictures of abundance in the form of food and drink, accompanied by incense and floral bouquets, are indispensable adjuncts to the life of the king and to the adoration of the Aten. In pictures of the palace and other buildings, wooden tables and stands are loaded with such offerings; in images of the Aten temples they are joined by a profusion of offering-tables also piled high and accompanied by bowls of smoking incense. According to the pictures, the food that was laid out required the minimum of preparation: whole loaves, large joints of meat, complete geese. These are, of course, the raw materials for meals that were presumably prepared elsewhere. The offering-tables were not picnic tables.

At this point we need to step back and observe the setting of the Great Aten Temple. It forms part of a collection of buildings that, in modern times, has been called the Central City. This district housed the smaller temple, the Great Palace and offices that served the king's administration. Although it was not enclosed within its own wall, the totality of the Central City was the king's palace (see Chapter 4). At its centre, and evidently serving all its parts and, in a way, binding the whole royal quarter together, was a giant food depot [**Pl. XXXV**]. Its most obvious component was a huge bank of ovens where bread was baked, but in other parts grain was stored and processed, cattle were kept and meat was stored in pottery jars. Both Aten temples must have drawn upon this resource for their offerings, and so must the palace for its sustenance.

Sacred Cattle

Cattle had long held a special place in temple ceremony, joints of meat (real or models) being buried in foundation deposits. At Amarna, pictures show the cattle being led to slaughter in the cult of the Aten, garlanded with flowers. Although slaughtering is a noisy, smelly, messy business, the Great Aten Temple was laid out to accommodate it. The tomb-pictures of the temple regularly show a slaughtering and butchering court on one side of the enclosure, identifiable from its tethering-stones, butchered carcasses and flayed hide [3.4, bottom right). This has been identified with an area of desert, 52 m (170.5 ft) square and enclosed with a mud-brick wall, that lay on the north side of the great enclosure, between the Long Temple and the Sanctuary [3.15]. The excavators found: 'One or two pierced tethering stones' on the surface.[17] Alongside it, a stone construction had left a T-shaped depression in the ground, floored with a gypsum foundation layer. The outline suggests a staircase leading up to a south-facing pedestal. A purple quartzite stela had been smashed to pieces here, leaving a spread of fragments over the surrounding ground, some of them carved with an extensive list of offerings that included cattle.[18]

The high priest Panehsy was also 'Superintendent of the Cattle of the Aten in Akhetaten' (as well as 'Superintendent of the Granary of the Aten'). In addition to a large house in the Main City, he possessed a second, isolated house that lay just outside a rear side entrance to the Great Aten Temple [4.5]. An adjacent building provided with stone floors and brick mangers (building S40.1) could well have acted as a series of holding pens for cattle, if not as a major byre. During the excavation of Panehsy's house, the excavator noted (in 1926) 'remains of cattle, horn and bones, cropped up everywhere',[19] and cattle bones were also found in S40.1. A sample of bone from the 1926 excavation dumps beside Panehsy's house was recovered in 2006. It proved to be overwhelmingly of cattle that had been butchered to provide a range of joints more varied than the preference for heads and forelegs shown in offering-scenes. Many of the long bones had been split, probably for marrow extraction. The bones come from large and well-fed cattle. Some grew so fat as to develop laminitis, a condition of tenderness on the underside of the hoof. The animal rests on the backs of its hooves, allowing the front parts to grow excessively, creating a slipper-like appearance. Pictures of cattle with this condition are shown in the tomb pictures (and also the stela in 3.29).

From this evidence, we have the first steps along the route of temple meat supply. Live cattle, at least some of them garlanded, were assembled outside the south wall of the temple. They were driven across the huge interior space to the slaughter court and there despatched and cut up. Now comes the difficult part. If we are to believe the tomb pictures, selected joints were then carried and laid out on the offering-tables. To achieve this, in the case of the Long Temple, the joints had to be carried for half a kilometre (a third of a mile) to the front of the building, the plan of which seems to preclude the existence of back or side entrances. This is a layout designed by a ritualist (who could take for granted abundant cheap labour) and not by someone with user convenience in mind.

Food animals provide more than chunky joints. If efficiently used, there is a lot of offal and smaller pieces of flesh. The Egyptians also had a long tradition of dry-curing meat (turning some of it into something like biltong) and salting it, so that meat could be transported and stored, in sealed pottery jars.[20] The archaeology of the Central City documents this aspect of the meat supply, too, one that took place off-stage from the awkward formality of the Great Aten Temple. In part of the complex beside the temple, cured meat was stored in large wide-mouthed, wide-bellied pottery jars without handles [3.26]. Ink labels identified the contents, as illustrated by the following two examples:

> Regnal year 7, 3rd month of summer. The depot 'Soul of Ra lives' [an epithet of the Aten]. Preserved meat: intestines, for the daily offerings, provided by the butcher Wepet.[21]

> Regnal year 11. Preserved meat for the festival of the Aten (life, prosperity, health!), being the birthday of the Aten. The preparation-room of the Estate of the Aten (life, prosperity, health!), under the authority of the retainer Tutu.[22]

The phrase translated 'meat for the festival' could equally well be translated 'meat of the festival' (that is, 'meat from'), reflecting a grammatical ambiguity

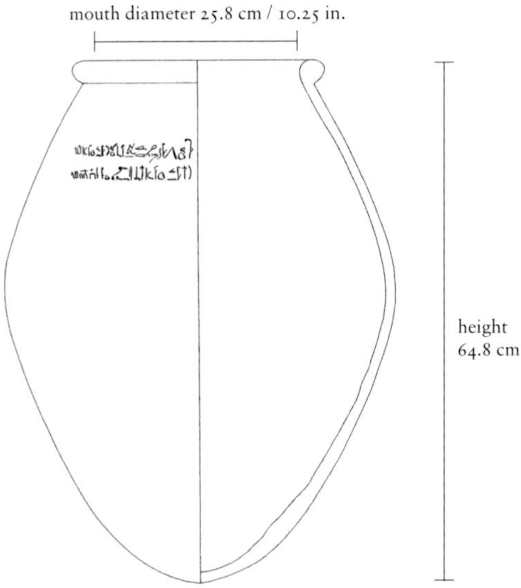

3.26 One of the uses to which this type of large pottery jar was put was to store meat products. Some of these jars bore ink labels documenting the contents. The hieratic label used in this (made-up) illustration comes from TA, Pl.XXIII.46, and p. 33. The first line reads: 'Regnal year 10, preserved meat for the Festival of the Aten....'

that would not have troubled the ancient Egyptians, who would have fully understood the context. Two other labels tell us that the meat came from 'Kush' and 'the South', helping to tilt the balance towards the translation 'meat for the festival'. The festival entitled 'birthday of the Aten' occurred at least once a month and some meat was for 'the daily service'. The labels give the names of a depot and of a preparation-room. One interpretation is that they are names of parts of the food depot in the Central City, and thus that the labels probably came from jars intended for export (and so accidentally broken or left behind when the city was abandoned). The alternative interpretation is that the jars had arrived from outside, bringing preserved meat for the temple cult from administrative centres in other parts of the country. This seems, on balance, the more likely explanation.

As for the intestines that had been packed (presumably dried and salted) in these jars, they do not match the pictures of selected major joints that were laid out on the offering-tables. In fact, packed preserved meat generally does not. Nor do quantities of 'fresh fat', often from geese, labelled as for the festival of the Aten and also stored in pottery jars.[23] It suggests a two-tier scheme of meat handling: fresh joints laid out for the Aten; preserved meats and other substances to supplement the portions that would be handed out or served for private consumption and maybe for royal banqueting.

Humbler Bread

For the provision of meat, the source – the living cattle – was paraded into the temple enclosure for slaughter. This reflects the long-standing special association that cattle had with temple cult. The process of killing and dismembering them was a piece of ritual in itself, which kept its status in Akhenaten's eyes. The same did not apply to the commodity that formed the bulk of the offerings: bread. This came as flat round loaves and as cone-shaped loaves baked in pottery bread moulds, both kinds depicted among the offerings on the offering-tables.

The source of the bread lay just outside the temple enclosure: a huge bakery, made up of rows of narrow parallel chambers. Each chamber was a single baking unit, containing one or more circular ovens of standard domestic design at the back. Various brick bins lined the walls. The total number of baking chambers amounted to more than 100. Details of what went on inside are illustrated on a relief from Amarna [**3.28**]. It depicts part of a bakery. From one side of a courtyard two chambers open. The curvature across the top of each one probably depicts a vaulted roof. In each chamber, a man tends an oven. Behind the one on the left, flat round loaves are stacked on a table. Behind the other, the table bears long cylindrical pottery bread moulds instead.

Fragments from tens of thousands of these moulds are not only heaped on the desert to the east of the bakeries, they seem largely to bury the baking chambers as well. The pottery moulds are a distinctive type, easily recognizable amidst a collection of ancient sherds. A study of the pottery recovered

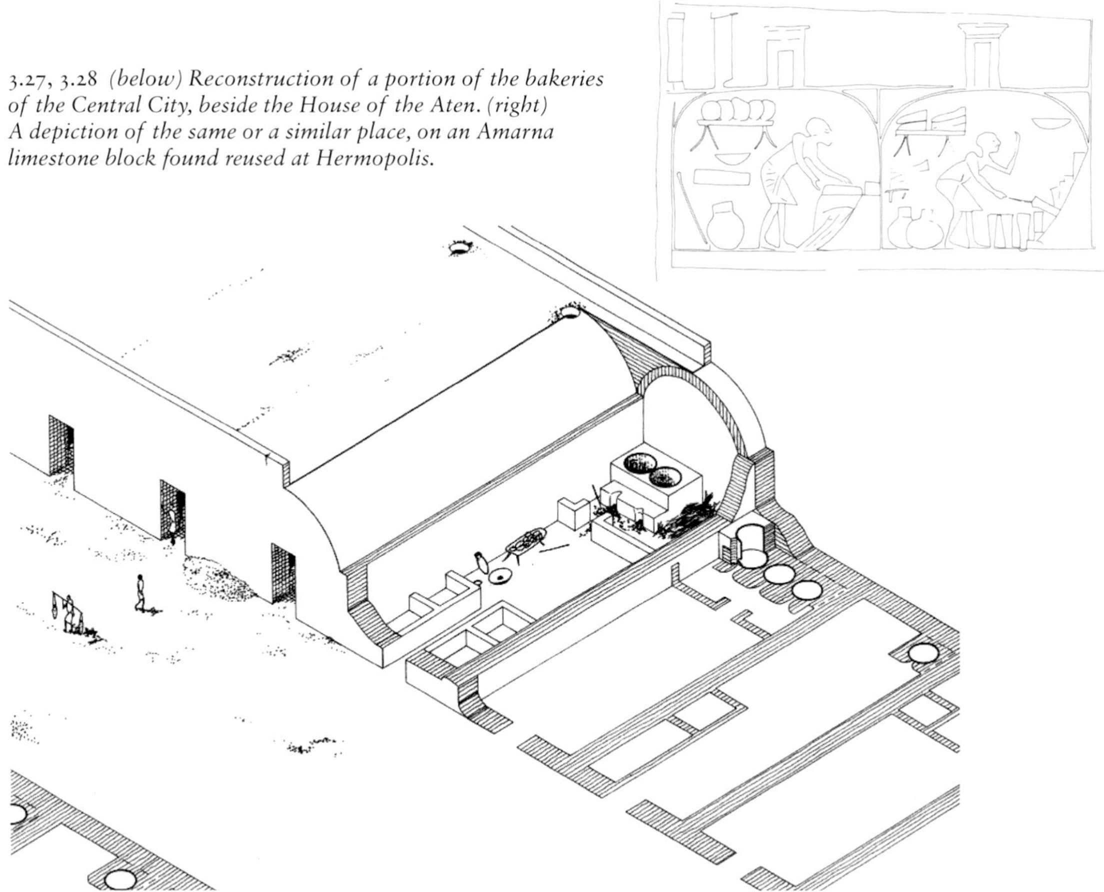

3.27, 3.28 *(below) Reconstruction of a portion of the bakeries of the Central City, beside the House of the Aten. (right) A depiction of the same or a similar place, on an Amarna limestone block found reused at Hermopolis.*

from the extensive excavations at Amarna also reveals that their distribution was very uneven. They were rare in the residential areas, but common around the central bakeries. What was so special about mould-baked loaves? By the New Kingdom they seem to have denoted a sense of occasion, in particular of ritual occasion. They were celebratory festival loaves.

Bread depends upon the prior production of flour, which, if from emmer wheat, requires that the cereal-heads be pounded first in a stone mortar. A shed of forty-eight mortars sunk into the ground formed a more distant part of this building complex (within R42.3), while a major concentration of quernstones has been found between it and the bakery blocks (both marked on pl. XXXV). The separate location of mortars, querns and ovens matches written material from the period, which shows how each stage was separately administered.[24]

In addition to the meat and bread, scenes show geese, flowers and incense heaped on the offering-tables, with jars of liquid standing alongside. One point to note is that the attempt was made to keep the huge temple enclosure reasonably clean. There is no obvious sign of organic rubbish. The ground outside the southern entrance, near the house of Panehsy, was the place where the waste was dumped: bones from cattle (and some from geese); pottery jars (many had held wine); pottery bowls, frequently showing signs of burning and incense on the interiors; tiny 'offering pots'; pieces of tall offering-stands; pierced lids with a handle, which could have been covers for incense bowls; and crudely made jars often termed 'beer jars' in modern reports.[25] Petrie had noted earlier that, 'in the heap of rubbish with the statues, were many pans of red pottery, containing resin melted in and pieces of charcoal'.[26]

How Did it All Work?

We are dealing with a complicated system, the two ends of which – the suppliers and the beneficiaries – we are still some way from understanding. Established Egyptian practices simultaneously integrated and kept separate private and institutional ownership and usage of commodities, such as cattle and land. Where we see, in Amarna tomb scenes, unidentified people entering the temple carrying fowl and bouquets of flowers, and leading cattle,[27] we cannot be sure if they are employees bearing what was, in effect, state property or private people making a gesture of loyalty by donating their own produce to be processed by a state institution, in this case the temple to the Aten (and perhaps receiving a portion of it back for their own consumption).

On the supply side, we can take for granted that the Aten temples possessed resources of their own, on the common Egyptian model. The huge expansion to the territory that comprised Akhetaten, marked by the locations and texts of the second set of boundary stelae, reflects the acquisition for the cult of the Aten of extensive agricultural lands. A tomb stela found at Saqqara belonged to an 'Overseer of Traders of the Temple of the Aten' named Huy, who probably lived at Memphis.[28] The role of 'traders' was to act as agents in the management of economies, both those of institutions and of private individuals.

At Amarna, the high priest Panehsy was in charge of the cattle and granaries of the Aten. The Aten temples themselves, however, contrary to common practice, lacked granaries within their own precincts. The only identifiable large storehouses nearby that could have accommodated grain were within the general central area, which probably served both temples and palace. It might have been piously assumed that all commodities in that area (the part we call the Central City) belonged to the Aten.

The larger houses in the city were also designed to store farm produce. Many had quite large granaries and some contained cattle stalls, where cattle were presumably fed for the last stage of their life, probably on grain [**2.6**, **5.27**]. This evidence matches literary texts from slightly later that extol the material benefits of being a 'scribe', prominent among them being an abundance of farm produce, including cattle.

It would be satisfying, for a rational understanding of how the system worked, to be able to separate the institutional from the private, but this may never be fully possible. One occasion for a banquet was the death of someone of standing in the community. A scribe named Nawawi has left a stela as a memorial to a deceased colleague, a scribe named Any [**3.29**]. Nawawi is shown leading a fat, garlanded ox, and two of his utterances are recorded. One says: 'See the ox that I was told to bring.' The other: 'Let us behold the good things that the ruler [i.e. Akhenaten] has done for his scribe of the offering-table, for whom he has ordered a good funeral in Akhetaten.'[29] Does this mean that, for Any's funeral, Nawawi, his friend, feels obliged to supply an ox for a feast, but that it is butchered as part of the offering ceremony in the Great Aten Temple

3.29 *Stela of Nebwawi. The scribe Any (owner of tomb no. 23, see figure 7.18) stands top right, facing a friend or colleague, the scribe Nebwawi. Below, the same Nebwawi leads a fat ox. The stela was one of a group set in niches at the entrance to Any's tomb and thus most likely a consequence of Any's funeral. Height of stela: 42.5 cm (16.7 in.).*

(with parts retained, tax-like, for circulation within the temple)? The overlapping of private and institutional resources, and the blurring of the language used, were normal, despite a keen sense of property ownership. In a scene of a funeral in the tomb of Huya (no. 1), three cattle are led in, promising a very grand banquet indeed [**7.22**].

Charity is an important feature of the main religions of the modern world. Pious giving by the faithful helps to support institutions that ameliorate the lot of the needy. The food handouts that were traditionally at the centre of Egyptian temples and their cults were not, however, charitably for the poor. The beneficiaries were temple employees, officials and people involved in private funerary cults. Having said that, the duty of the rich to help the poor was also part of the largely secular teachings that guided the consciences of the ancient Egyptians (who would have learned texts commending these responsibilities). As a result, commodities will have seeped out from those who formally benefited from temple distributions to those who did not.

In their tomb chapels, some of Akhenaten's senior officials recorded the food benefit from the temple, wishing for its perpetuation after death. On appointing him to be 'Chief of Seers' (that is, High Priest) the king says to Meryre: 'I give you the office specifically so that you may eat the provisions of Pharaoh, your lord, in the House of the Aten.' He says the same to the chamberlain Tutu, and similarly to the god's father Ay: 'May you be given offerings and provisions from the offering-basin of the House of the Aten.'[30] The steward Huya, and Meryre also, prays that, after death, they might continue to partake of the offerings that issue from the House of the Aten.[31] Panehsy asks to receive offering-loaves 'on every festival of the living Aten in the Mansion of the Benben'.[32] There was no state monopoly, however. In the little shrine at the back of his tomb, Huya's mortuary priest also promises a supply of 'bread and beer of your house..., water from your pool..., fruit [?] from your trees'.[33] The reality of benefits after death consisted of payments or distributions to relatives to maintain the various ways in which the deceased was remembered.

These officials were rich people; but the scale of the offering layout at the Great Aten Temple implies a system that reached far more people. In his early Karnak days, Akhenaten recorded that the towns of Egypt, through their mayors, and the royal domains were obliged to pay an extra levy to support the staff of the Aten temple at Thebes, one total giving the figure 6,800 persons.[34] If the figure referred to men who were heads of their households, it could represent the bulk of the families of a city the size of Amarna. Although we lack an equivalent statement from Amarna, the offering layout itself, to which the temple architecture is almost subordinate, speaks strongly in favour of a major system of public food benefit. Whether or not it exceeded what was done under the old system, Akhenaten wanted it to *appear* as if it exceeded. He wanted to claim credit for an exceptional scale of giving. How much his citizens did benefit is questionable, however, to judge by the evidence of bones recovered from one of their cemeteries (see Chapter 6).

Communal Feasting or Takeaway?

Was all the food meant for banquets or for consumption in private? The answer makes quite a difference to how we characterize the life of the city. I have sometimes toyed with the idea that the huge central space in the enclosure of the Great Aten Temple was a dusty picnic ground or rough stadium for the citizens, who could not wait to consume their portion of the food-offerings and cooked it on the spot (with an area of around 250 m (820 ft) square, thus 62,500 sq m (672,728 sq ft), it could have accommodated tens of thousands of people[35]). In this version of events, the king and the Aten welcome and involve the people as well as support them. But this seems too democratic, ignoring the need to preserve distinctions in status. At other times, the image of the temple enclosure as an austere symbol of the Aten's chosen piece of uncontaminated desert comes to the fore and seems to run counter to the presence of crowds and cooking (despite the regular procession across it of nervous cattle approaching their end).

The question of feasting or banqueting points us towards an artificial distinction in the way we organize knowledge, as reflected in the chapters of this book, for example, where Aten temples and palaces are treated separately. We prefer knowledge to be like a tin of neatly packed biscuits rather than a plate of spaghetti. The Central City at Amarna was, in its totality, *the* palace of the king. The two Aten temples and the Great Palace were all parts of the same complex, grouped around a single sprawling service hub. As far as we can tell, the palaces did not have their own bakeries, slaughtering court and meat-processing depot. So when we talk of feasting, and of who benefited from the 'offerings' and where they took them, we should not treat this as a topic separate from the role of royal feasting and banqueting. A continuation of the discussion is, therefore, postponed until the next chapter, which concentrates on the palace.

Not All Temples were for the Aten

The two temples to the Aten in the Central City, when taken with the scenes in the tombs, largely define the Aten cult at Amarna, its open-air nature and its celebration of food. Not all temples and shrines at Amarna were like this, however, even if one excludes the small personal versions that stood in private gardens or houses (see Chapter 7). Some were largely roofed and employed columns in central halls or at the front. One of them (O42.1) stood facing southwards down the long wide road that must have run close to the riverbank south of the Great Palace [**3.30**]. The main part was stone and probably roofed, with a wider portico at the front, looking out into a deep courtyard surrounded by a mud-brick wall entered between pylons.

A second example, badly damaged and incompletely excavated, can be found in the southern enclosure at Kom el-Nana [**2.21**, **2.23**]. A third example (R43.2) comes with evidence to explain its purpose [**3.23**].[36] Built of mud brick, it lay on the edge of the Central City, close to a scribal 'village' and what we

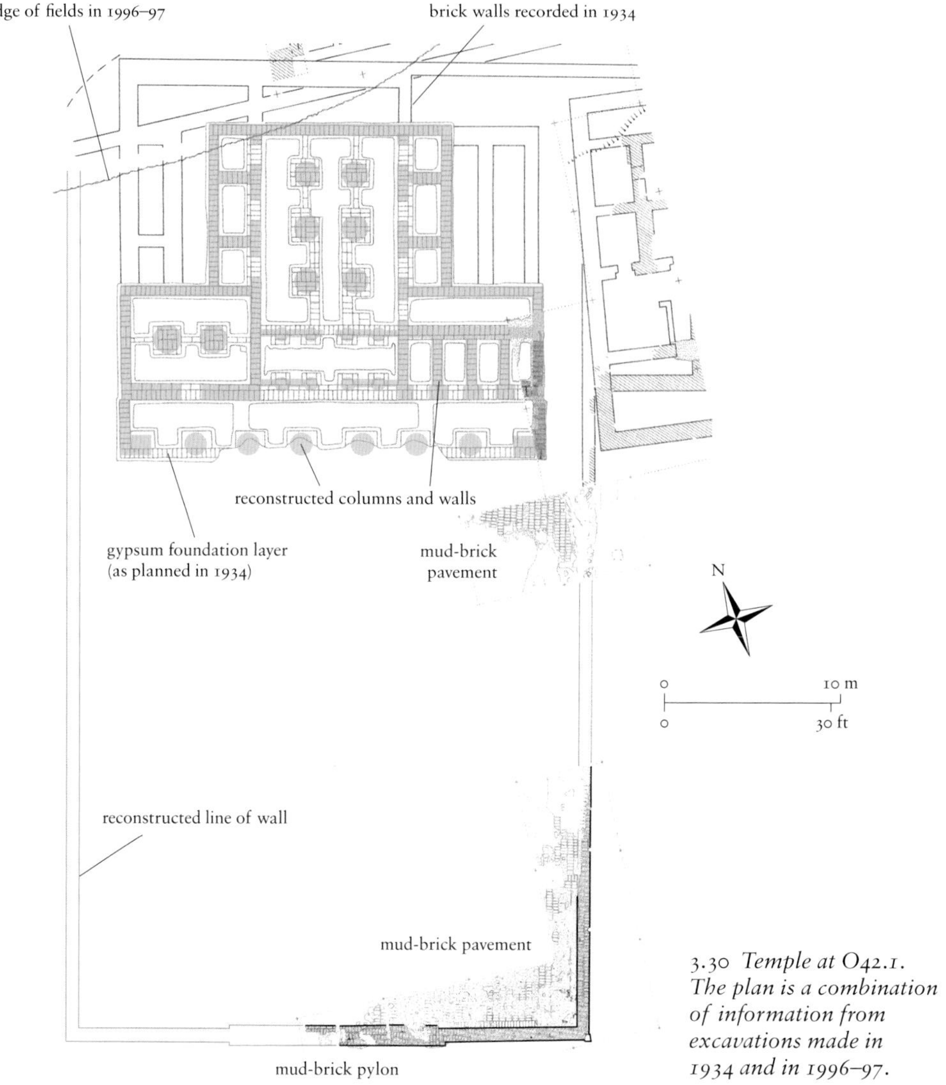

3.30 *Temple at O42.1. The plan is a combination of information from excavations made in 1934 and in 1996–97.*

presume were military barracks, and equally on the edge of the main residential area. Behind a courtyard, entered through a central doorway not thickened to create pylon towers, was a rectangular building with a wide colonnade at the front, the whole evidently roofed. Its plan is broadly comparable to that of a temple. The remains of one or more wooden shrines lay in the debris, including a decorated panel that referred to a 'statue' [**3.24**]. From a plumed headdress we can deduce that a statue of a queen (Tiye or Nefertiti) had been present as well. Another panel had depicted a king (almost certainly Akhenaten) in the traditional pose of smiting Egypt's enemies [**3.25**]. The shrines and statues were quite small. The other roofed shrines, already noted (pp. 57, 107), were perhaps also for the cult of royal statues. They are notably free of offering-tables.

'Sunshades'

In the earlier proclamation on the boundary stelae, the third construction that the king promises to build, after the 'House' and 'Mansion' of the Aten, is the 'Sun-temple' of Nefertiti. The phrase translated here as 'Sun-temple' is literally 'The sunshade of Ra'. Tomb no. 1 at Amarna belonged to a man, Huya, who was steward of the king's mother, Queen Tiye. It contains a detailed temple scene, identified in hieroglyphs as 'Her sun-temple', referring to Tiye. It looks very similar to the other temple pictures, to the extent that, before excavations had revealed the Great and Small Temples, the assumption was made that Queen Tiye's sun-temple was simply the main Aten temple given a different name in honour of a visit made by the queen. Although a sun-temple for Queen Tiye has not yet been identified on the ground, this possibility has grown less likely, in part because several buildings called 'sunshades' can now be independently identified (all belonging to royal women). Huya's picture probably demonstrates the extent to which artists conformed to stereotypes, in this case substituting a detailed but conventional picture of an Aten temple – based upon those in the Central City – for a realistic rendering of a building of a different character. Tomb no. 2 at Amarna belonged to the steward of Nefertiti, Meryre [II], but he chose not to depict her sun-temple, nor does it appear in any Amarna tomb. Nevertheless, we have direct evidence as to what buildings of this kind looked like.

The term 'sunshade' has been found on stonework at the site known always by its ancient name, Maru-Aten [**2.16, Pl. XXXVII**]. As was the case at the North Palace, the stonework recorded the name of Akhenaten's eldest daughter and heiress, Meryetaten. Her name had perhaps been carved over an earlier female royal name (the choice is between Queens Nefertiti and Kiya). Maru-Aten lay on its own, 1.5 km (0.9 miles) south of the southern limits of the city and perhaps not far from the river towards which it faced. It consisted of twin enclosures surrounded by buttressed brick walls, one of the enclosures larger than the other. Both enclosures seem to have been mainly given over to shallow pools or lakes and to gardens planted with trees, with small pavilions of various kinds set around the edges, some of brick and some of stone. A long narrow stone causeway and pier, with a decorated kiosk at the end, projected into the larger lake.

The most distinctive elements to have survived lay in the northeast corner of the larger enclosure. A square artificial island surrounded by a ditch supported a stone platform bearing an open-air offering-place. Behind it, and occupying the corner of the enclosure, was a long pillared construction that shaded a series of interlocking T-shaped water basins [**2.16**]. These were surrounded by a gypsum pavement painted with designs from nature, divided into panels. Fragments of carved stone from the buildings also celebrated nature through the use of plant motifs [**2.13**]. Maru-Aten, both in its design and in its name (which means 'Viewing-place of the Aten'), reflects the search for tranquillity to be found in sunlit gardens where shrines add a spiritual dimension.

Just over 1 km (0.6 miles) away lay a comparable pair of adjacent enclosures, now known under the modern name of Kom el-Nana. They face the line of a continuation southwards of the Royal Road [**2.1**] and are a strong candidate for being the 'sun-temple' or 'sunshade' of Nefertiti of the boundary stelae texts (the word 'sunshade' occurs on stone fragments found at the site).[37] Kom el-Nana was later the site of an early Christian monastery. That later structure, together with the incompleteness of the excavation, makes it hard to give a full assessment of the site. It had contained two stone buildings, presumed to be shrines, erected on the usual gypsum foundation layer. The plan of one of them [**2.21**, **2.22**] is of a roofed building, so the cult object is likely to have been one or more royal statues. A mud-brick pylon in the south wall led to a set of ceremonial buildings also of mud bricks, one of them a platform with perhaps a Window of Appearance [**4.13**]. The enclosure differs in many respects from Maru-Aten. It contained much open space, but so far the evidence for garden cultivation covers only a very small part of it. The northeast corner had been filled with a 'bakery' block where many pottery bread moulds had been in use. This implies a visiting population of some size, which might explain the open space, though as yet there is no sign of offering-tables.

There appear to have been at least three more stone buildings around the periphery of the city.[38] Two of them, to the south of the city, had been destroyed before a proper record could be made, although a stone block recovered from one of them, El-Mangara, does actually have the term 'sunshade' carved on it. The third, beside the Desert Altars in the north, stood on the mid-axis, towards the rear, of a rectangular enclosure surrounded by a mud-brick wall reinforced with external buttresses. Only small parts of a gypsum layer survived to modern times, together with several fragments of carved stonework. (The Desert Altars themselves will be described in Chapter 7, pp. 252–53, and see **7.24**.)

The 'sunshades' – garden temples – of Amarna draw out the ambiguous attitude that the Egyptians had (and still have) towards the desert. Although it could be a place of escape and spirituality (presumably Akhenaten himself felt this), what lay in the heart and imagination of Egyptians was the valley, with its fields and marshes, shady trees, birds and general sense of abundant life maintained by the interaction of sunlight and water. The hymns to the Aten played to this enjoyment of tamed nature. Gardens provided with small pieces of architecture were highly desirable places of relaxation and solace. Because it was imagined that the dead needed them just as much, our knowledge of the ideal garden comes as much from tomb pictures as from written descriptions and excavated evidence. A few rich men created their own garden shrines beside their houses at Amarna [**7.2**].

Perhaps other royal residence cities (Thebes, Memphis, Per-Ramesses in the years to come) had their equivalents – garden temples with cool pavilions – appropriately set among the lush countryside on the floodplain of the Nile. The location of Amarna offered uncompromising settings for such places, on bleak windswept areas of desert. Akhenaten seems to have taken as a template what could be accomplished on the floodplain and transferred it to the desert plain at Amarna. Within their enclosures, the builders did their best to recreate the parkland and marshes of the floodplain, planting shrubs and trees, digging wells and, at Maru-Aten, lining with mud a large shallow basin to create a central water feature. Dispersed around the edges were small pavilions and rest-houses, of decorated stone and brick, where the cult of the sun could be celebrated and where the royal owner could find some peace and leisure. But the best efforts of the builders could never fully ameliorate the periodic dust storms and the searingly hot winds that blow from the south in the early summer. There might be greenery and shade within the enclosures, but they stood isolated in a flat parched landscape that had to be crossed to reach the havens of the main palaces that lay close to the river. It is hard to think that they were inviting places for other than occasional visits in good weather.

The outlying enclosures at Amarna and the layouts of the Aten temples are likely to be direct expressions of Akhenaten's thoughts. Both share the same characteristic: they are not very practical. The danger of being an absolute ruler is that no one dares tell you that what you have just decreed is not a good idea.

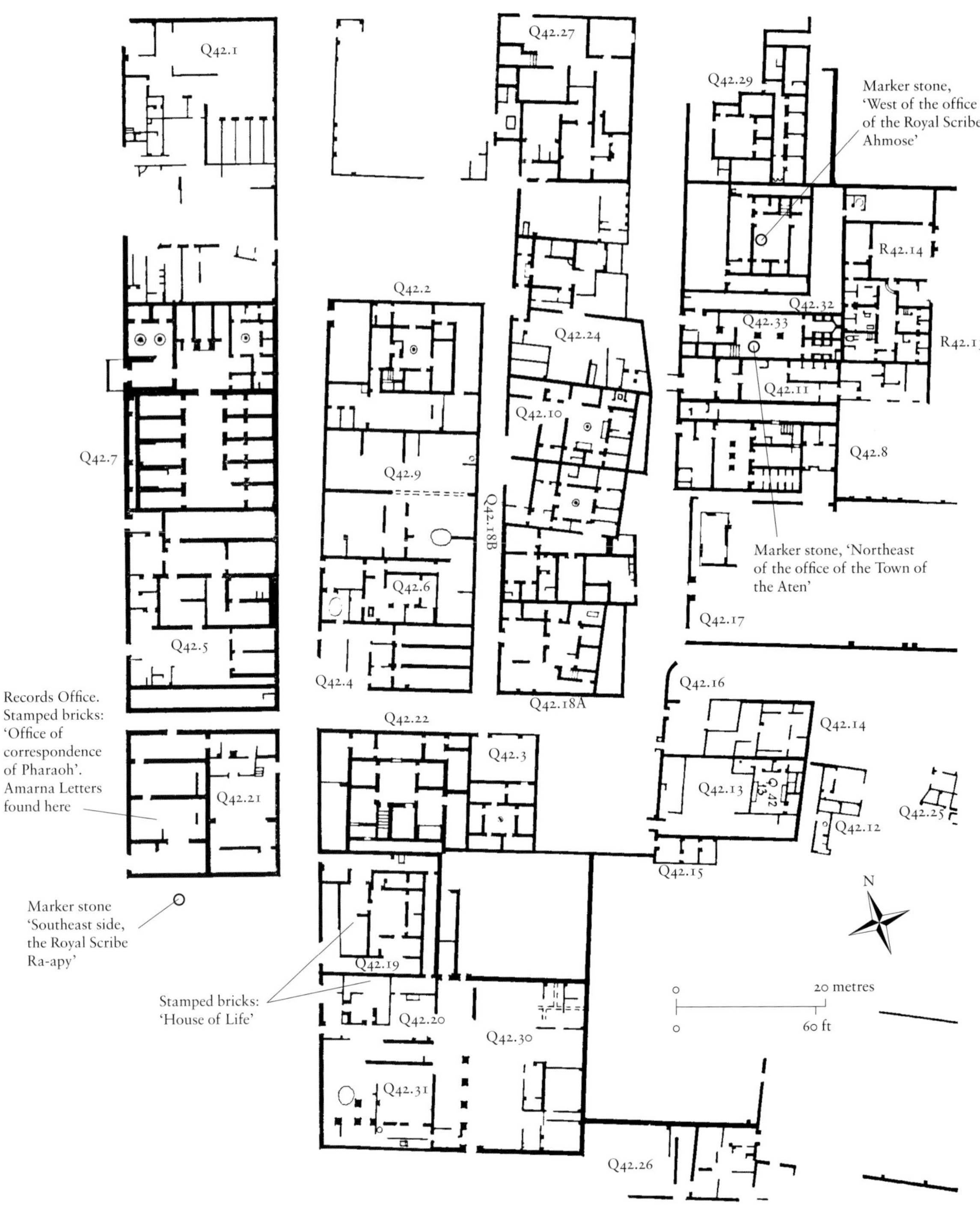

4.1 *The office buildings of the Central City. A more detailed plan of the records office is given in figure 4.3.*

CHAPTER FOUR

THE APARTMENTS OF PHARAOH

On the earlier set of boundary stelae, Akhenaten follows his promise of three temples with a further promise, to build a 'House of Rejoicing' and, seemingly as separate places, 'apartments' or 'houses' of Pharaoh (that is, himself) and of Nefertiti. The natural interpretation is that, by 'apartments' or 'houses', he means palaces, although the word he uses is a broad collective term. It is also commonly thought that the 'House of Rejoicing' refers to the Great Palace rather than being a more generic term for a place blessed by the presence of the king and the Aten (although he still might have had in mind the Great Palace rather than anywhere else; it was the largest of his constructions at Amarna).

On the ground at Amarna, at least four buildings have been identified as palaces on the basis of their size and ground plan. These are the Great Palace and the King's House in the Central City, the North Palace and the North Riverside Palace [**2.1**]. They differ considerably, and it is hard to fit them to the vague terminology of the boundary stelae.[1]

Palaces, like temples, seek to create a world apart. They reflect not only a rich diversity of function, but also a discovery of architects the world over: that spaces and their interrelationships create powerful overall effects in the minds of those who use or visit grand buildings. Palaces separate rulers from the rest of society, by being large, different and designed to set up barriers to intimacy. We should not expect every room or courtyard to have served a specific function. In part, palaces are like stage sets, there to accommodate variations in the life and schedule of the court. They existed to convey by their volume and spaciousness, and sometimes by symbolic associations, the aura of power that surrounded a ruler. Palaces take us into the realm of behavioural extremes. Although palaces are almost bound to reflect existing taste in their design, their history and the history of palace life show how they encourage megalomania.

In saying this, however, I am already assuming that a palace was a large distinctive separate building where a ruler lived and from where he (or she) exercised authority. I am readying myself to be impressed. Might I be prematurely imposing on the evidence too fixed an idea? No Egyptian text describes in detail what functions a palace performed or what a palace looked like. A somewhat earlier account of the duties of the king's vizier (see below) draws a distinction between the 'Residence' and the 'King's House', implying that the latter was a more private section of a broader entity, but how they differed on the ground we cannot tell, nor ascertain to which term the translation 'palace' is the more appropriate.

What is a Palace?

In trying to fill out a picture of Amarna palaces, it can be helpful to see what people have made of the subject in other societies where the documentation is better. It can, at the very least, give us a list of questions. Did Amarna palaces accommodate such-and-such a function that rulers in other times and places have found to be necessary or appropriate? I have chosen as my guide a scheme worked out for the palaces of Hellenistic rulers, who included among their number the Ptolemies and Cleopatras of Egypt as well as the remarkable palace builder, King Herod of Palestine.[2] The list of functions runs as follows:

- Official and ceremonial: audience hall/council hall/court room/ reception hall or area
- Social: banqueting hall(s)
- Religious: temple for the tutelary deity/dynastic sanctuary/mausoleum
- Defensive: precinct walls/citadel/barracks and arsenal
- Administrative: offices/archives/treasury
- Service: storerooms or magazines/kitchens, etc./servants' quarters
- Residential (king and family): bedrooms/bathrooms/private dining-room(s)/harem
- Residential (court/guests): apartments
- 'Public': gymnasium or palaestra/library/theatre/hippodrome
- Recreational: gardens/parks/pavilions/(swimming) pools

This list envisages the palace as an institution as much as a building, performing many functions. If each were accommodated separately, would the collective whole still count as a palace, or must a palace have an architectural unity, perhaps created by nothing more than an enclosure wall? This is an important point for Amarna.

It was noted in Chapter 3 that the central 'square' of Amarna was occupied by a sprawl of mud-brick buildings that seem to have been an extension to the role of the Great Aten Temple, serving as a food distribution centre [**Pl. XXXV**]. The next block of ground southwards, extending as far as the smaller of the two Aten temples and running behind it, was filled with a relatively dense collection of mud-brick buildings that were, with the exception of one (the so-called King's House), quite small and of no fixed plan. Several of the functions on the palace list above seem to have been served by them. Consequently, if a wall had surrounded the whole Central City – including the two temples (thus the third item on the list: 'religious') and the Great Palace (the first on the list) – we would probably see the entire enclosure as a 'palace', for it housed many of the elements that equipped Akhenaten to rule. But should an enclosure wall make such a difference? If we choose to regard a palace primarily as an institution rather than an impressive single piece of architecture, the Central City becomes, in its entirety and in its variety, Akhenaten's principal palace. The fact that it lay spread out, unwalled on open ground, is an incidental comment on the character of his society.

It is here, perhaps more than anywhere else at Amarna, that the modest scale of things makes its biggest impact. Egypt and its empire seem to have been governed from a collection of buildings that were not much more than mud huts. This disparity in scale can be taken as another illustration of the limits to Akhenaten's resources. Part of that limitation, however, was perceptual, an only partially developed sense of grandeur, or an acceptance that grandeur was appropriate only to an individual building here and there that rose from a background of the small-scale and the ordinary. The long retention of the village scale is something that one encounters frequently in ancient Egypt, as in other past societies. Most if not all of those with whom Akhenaten dealt will have shared that view. It was not necessary to impress everybody with all the components of the city, and we, too, should not feel cheated.

The Accommodation of Office

The centre of Amarna was laid out on either side of the Royal Road. On the west was the Great Palace and seemingly nothing else. On the east side, at the north and south ends, were the two main Aten Temples, their positions determined to a great extent by their perpendicular alignment to the river and the attraction of having them point towards the desert horizon. In between, a portion of the ground was filled by the mundane 'office' portion of the palace area. Its layout owed much to self-organization, although done by people wanting to maintain (though not very exactly) the north–south alignment of the main buildings that faced onto the Royal Road over to the west. The ground plan seems to be of a series of islands or blocks, each one laid out by individual command. We cannot be sure, but six or seven 'departments' seem to be present [**4.1**]. Like the houses in the residential parts of the city, the size of each block and building seems to have been determined by what was urgently needed. In the end, enough open ground remained to have accommodated each block had it been made twice as large.

Something has actually survived from the laying-out process. Several irregular limestone cobbles were found during past excavations bearing ink labels showing that they had been used to mark the boundaries of the individual offices [**4.2**]. I imagine them resting on the tops of small piles of bricks marking the corners. Three of them have been published (their approximate positions marked on **4.1**). They read: 'Southeast side, the Royal Scribe Ra-apy' (from beside the south side of Q42.21, the so-called 'Records Office); 'West of the office of the Royal Scribe Ahmose' (building Q42.32); 'Northeast of the office of the Town of the Aten' (building Q42.33).[3] 'Royal Scribes' with the names Apy and Ahmose were owners of two of the rock tombs at Amarna (nos 10 and 3, respectively). Both of these men had more exalted titles as well, however, and the names are not uncommon, so we cannot justifiably accept that they were one and the same, tempting though it is. The same is true for two pieces of stone with just the words 'the Scribe Any' (a namesake of the owner of tomb no. 23) found in the building R42.9.[4] The stones do add to the evidence, nonetheless, that these buildings were offices of the royal administration. And who would one expect to find in charge of the 'Office of the Town of the Aten'? The mayor of Akhetaten named Neferkheperu-her-sekheper, perhaps, who was the owner of rock tomb no. 13.

The word translated 'office' (literally 'place') was also part of a label found stamped into some of the mud bricks of the building nowadays often called the 'Records Office' beside which one of the stones was found [**4.3**]. The full stamp reads: 'The office [place] of the correspondence of Pharaoh: life, prosperity, health!'[5] It was here that the bulk of the clay tablets were found that together comprise the Amarna Letters [**4.4**]. Most of them had been sent to the Egyptian court from foreign rulers of the Near East; a few were copies of letters sent by pharaoh in exchange. Some seem to have been educational material (syllabaries, lists of words, and literary texts) used in a scribal school. There were even a few unused tablets.[6]

Across the narrow street lay a separate block (Q42.19, 20) where stamped mud bricks had also been used. Here the words of the label read 'House of Life', a term used for a place where texts of a serious intellectual nature ('sacred' is a somewhat misleading term) were copied and stored.[7] Together, the evidence suggests that this particular set of offices not only accommodated officials responsible for diplomatic letter-writing and interpretation, but also served as a centre for study and education, attended by foreign visitors from the north as well as by Egyptians.

Other brick stamps appear amidst the walls of this general group, spread in such a way as to suggest that no single organizing procedure was at work.[8] The 'House of Life' also used bricks with a different stamp, the design not fully recoverable, but ending in the words 'of the Aten'. The complex of tiny buildings that included Q42.25 and R42.6 incorporated into its walls bricks of 'The House of Rejoicing of the Aten'. Huge quantities of bricks bearing the simple

West of the office of the royal scribe Ahmose

Northeast of the office of the Town of the Aten

4.2 *Natural large pebbles that have been used as temporary boundary stones during the initial laying out of the city.*

4.3 *Mud brick from the Records Office bearing the official stamp: 'The office (place) of the correspondence of Pharaoh: life, prosperity, health!'*

design that reads 'Mansion' supplied material for the walls of the Small Aten Temple, the King's House, one of the small groups of offices (Q42.29) and a set of production facilities beside the Small Aten Temple (P43.1). These last had also used bricks from a separate source, stamped with a design that read '[The Storehouse] of Service to the Aten'. In many of the blocks of buildings, however, no stamped bricks have been found at all.

Such stamping of bricks gives the impression of a somewhat haphazard practice. It matches the picture of individual officials organizing the building of their own offices, making their own arrangements. Some of them, more eager than their colleagues, had a stamp made to keep their particular supplies of bricks separate and identifiable, while others had access to stocks of bricks initially ordered for another project.

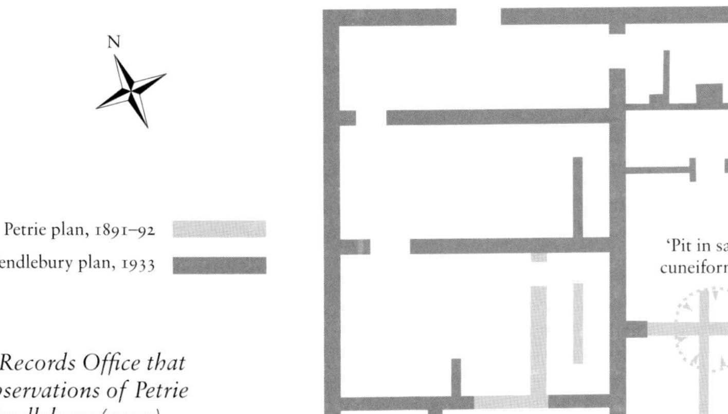

4.4 *Plan of the Records Office that combines the observations of Petrie (1891–92) and Pendlebury (1933). The quoted labels are the annotations on Petrie's plan. He commented (on p. 23) 'From the appearance of the chambers I believe the tablets were in the S.W. room.'*

The office area was not designed for the bulk storage of commodities. The only part that, from its plan, approaches the appearance of a warehouse or set of magazines is a part of Q42.7, and this is relatively small. Administration in Egypt centred on written records, mostly papyri, but also, for correspondence with parts of the Near East and eastern Mediterranean, clay tablets. It was accepted in ancient Egypt that when disputes arose, over ownership of property or ways in which individuals had behaved, it was important to refer to written documentation. Some kinds of documents were kept over several generations, so substantial space for storing them was required.

Storage in Egypt was often within wooden chests, although pottery jars were used for papyri as well. Smaller areas suitable for storage are identifiable throughout the office area although we cannot be sure in particular cases what might have been kept there. The thin partition walls in one of the rooms of Q42.8 are probably supports for shelves. At the back of Q42.33 are two sets of tiny brick benches or alcoves, each less than a metre (39.4 in.) wide, packed into two small rooms, which could have served as storage racks. This is in the vicinity of the boundary stone used for setting out the 'Office of the Town of the Aten', a place where one would expect archives to be stored.

One common method of storage at Amarna was burial beneath the floor, in brick-lined pits, sunken pots, or simply holes dug down through the floor and into the underlying desert (see Chapter 6). As a means of long-term storage it was acceptable as official practice. The bulk of the cuneiform tablets in the 'Records Office' had been found by villagers only a few years before Petrie's excavation of 1891–92, and he formed the opinion that they had come from a room in the southwest corner of the building, though he could not establish the precise context. During his own excavation, he found fragments of eighteen further tablets (and an inscribed cylinder). All but one were in two pits beneath internal walls [**4.4**], the odd one out in a room in the southwest of the building. Whether the bulk of the tablets also came from the pit in this room cannot be known, though it is likely. This implies that chests of documents (educational material as well as letters) began to arrive before the building was finished and the opportunity was taken to bury some of those thought less likely to be needed in the future. The practice is the secular counterpart to the long tradition of burying surplus statues and other votive gifts within the precincts of temples.

Scattered among the non-standardized administrative buildings of the Central City are several that, if they were found in the suburbs, would be classed as houses (examples are Q42.2, Q42.10, its neighbour in the group Q42.18B and Q42.22, see **4.1**). It is common in modern societies for institutions to rent private flats and larger dwellings to accommodate government business. For many years, the headquarters of the bureau of state security in Mallawi, the town across the river from Amarna, was the rented ground floor of a block of private apartments. This was maintained during the outbreak of local terrorism in the mid-1990s, when the private residents had to accept a fortification being added to the front. It illustrates that there is nothing unique or sacred about houses. In the end they provide shelter for people (including policemen) and are usually very adaptable. The people inside can be doing office-work or interrogating suspects as readily as bringing up a family.

We do know the identity of the owner of one of these centrally located 'houses'. He was the high priest Panehsy. This house was not within the compact Central City group, but stood on its own, beside the rear of the Great Aten Temple, its location perhaps determined by his other role, that of superintendent of the Aten's cattle, discussed in Chapter 3. Panehsy actually possessed two houses. The other lay at the northern end of the Main City (and so on a plot of ground close to the Central City), a large residence in spacious grounds, its garden chapel one of the very few private chapels to be built of stone [**1.15**]. To judge from its location, this was his domestic residence, his proper 'home'. The excavators of his house beside the temple noted variations from the expected plan of a house of this size, but nonetheless its general 'houseness' is beyond question. It shows that his duties required a house-like building in the Central City.

For an official of his prominence, we expect his duties to have been largely sedentary, as he received reports, dictated documents and issued instructions. The domestic layout of his northern house was evidently suited to its non-domestic role and must have been the layout of choice. It created the right atmosphere and accommodated whatever materials and personnel his office required. The storage of papyrus documents and space for scribes to work would have been, so one imagines, the priorities. If the plan seems too small and crowded, the house did possess a staircase that could have led to one or more upper floors. In a conventional house of this kind, we expect the upstairs to have provided an extra degree of domestic privacy. But here, it might have been security or at least inaccessibility that counted more. The excavation of his house also produced numerous animal bones, mostly of cattle (and including horn cores). Panehsy's priestly and scribal rank evidently did not buffer him from the practicalities of his role as superintendent of the Aten's cattle. His official residence became a repository for butchers' waste [**4.5**].

We know Panehsy owned both of his houses because of the lucky accident that carved stonework bearing his name survived in each case. Several other high officials had reason to conduct regular business in the Central City, for example, the 'Chamberlain, Tutu' and the 'Mayor of Akhetaten, Neferkheperu-her-sekheper'. We can suspect that several of the house-like buildings embedded within the Central City were their offices. The boundary stone for the 'office of the Royal Scribe Ahmose', mentioned above, was found at one of them. A whole village of small houses lining narrow streets behind the Small Aten Temple [**4.6**] seems to give an indication of the extent to which the common house plan was retained for offices. Though a village laid out on a regimented plan, the houses vary in size, unlike those at the Workmen's Village [**5.30, 6.1**]. They also lack ovens and other food-production equip-

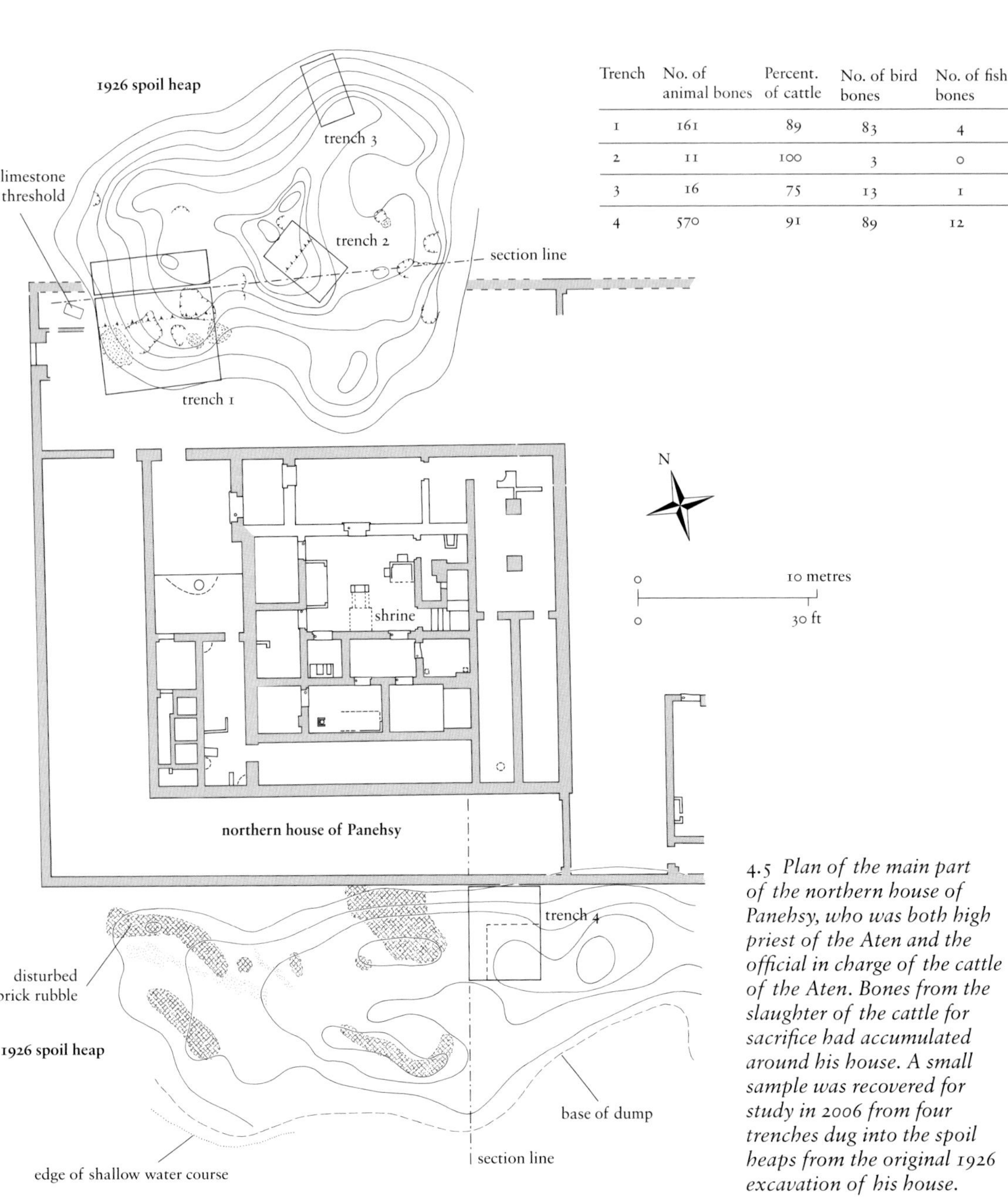

Trench	No. of animal bones	Percent. of cattle	No. of bird bones	No. of fish bones
1	161	89	83	4
2	11	100	3	0
3	16	75	13	1
4	570	91	89	12

4.5 *Plan of the main part of the northern house of Panehsy, who was both high priest of the Aten and the official in charge of the cattle of the Aten. Bones from the slaughter of the cattle for sacrifice had accumulated around his house. A small sample was recovered for study in 2006 from four trenches dug into the spoil heaps from the original 1926 excavation of his house.*

4.6 *Plan of the Clerks' Houses in the Central City.*

ment, although many possess brick-lined pits where material of value could be stored. They must have accommodated part of the secretariat of the royal administration. The widespread use of 'houses' for offices further underlines the village character of the city.

Bridging Two Worlds

The two worlds of the scribal offices and the Great Palace were separated by the wide space of the Royal Road. This was spanned by a bridge raised on massive brick piers [4.7]. Fragments of painted wall plaster fallen between the piers point to the passageway having been decorated with painted scenes. Of all the pieces of architecture at Amarna the bridge is the one that most confounds expectations. Egyptian builders employed terracing and platforms for effect, but seem generally to have been reluctant to allow different planes to cross or intersect without making contact. The bridge did this. It provided a wide passageway that allowed people to pass between two important buildings independently of the major road that it crossed. In so doing, it literally bridged the two very different worlds on either side. This imparts a particular degree of importance to the building at its far (eastern) end, the King's House, which is thereby made to appear as a protrusion of one zone (the king's) into another (the scribes').

4.7 *View of the mud-brick supports for the bridge that linked the King's House (right) with the Great Palace (left), photographed after excavation in 1931 and 1933, and viewed to the northeast.*

4.8 *Plan of the King's House in the Central City.*

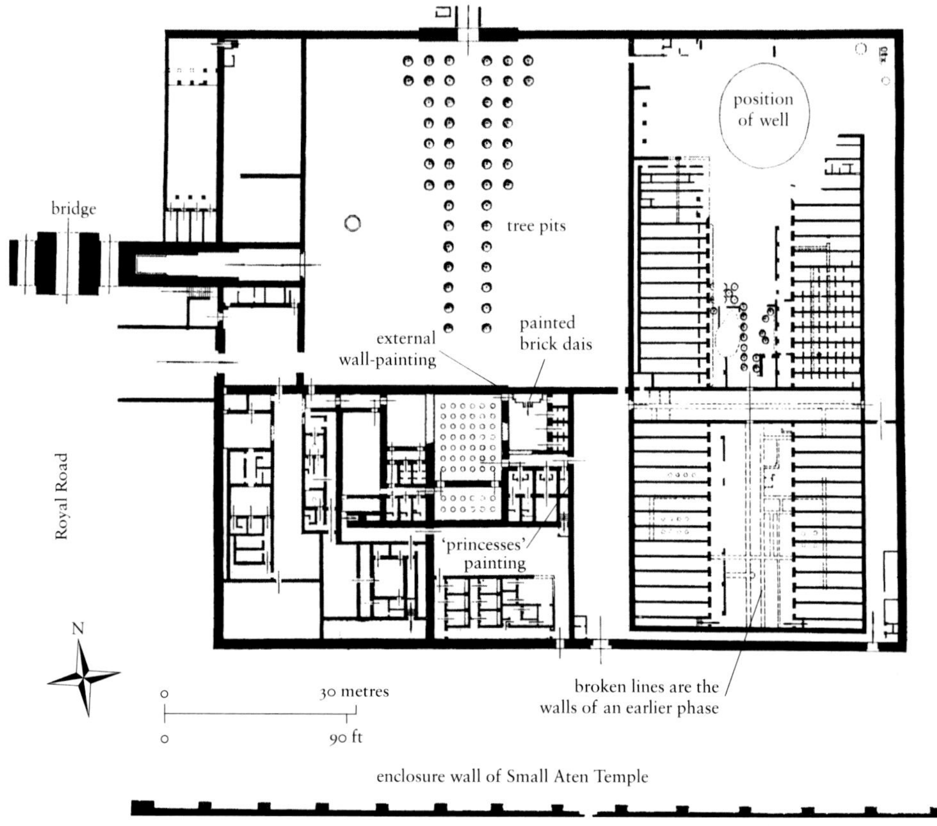

The King's House has for a long time been classed as a palace despite its relatively small size [**4.8**]. It stands out for having had painted wall scenes, one of the subjects being the royal family relaxing on cushions along with their daughters [**Pl. XX**]. It also possessed a dais decorated with kneeling foreigners, a motif appropriate to kings. Unusually, an area of the outside wall was painted, apparently also with figures of kneeling captives. A scene of this kind is shown in several of the rock tombs as the decoration of the wall beneath the Window of Appearance from where Akhenaten dispenses rewards, evidence perhaps that such a window (though not necessarily the main one) was inserted into this wall.[9]

Much of the oversight of royal administration in the New Kingdom lay in the hands of the king's chief ministers, the viziers, who often numbered two, one each for the south and north (with the Viceroy of Kush acting the part of a virtual third for the annexed territories of Nubia in the far south, modern Sudan). At least one of Akhenaten's viziers (Nakht[paaten]) maintained a large house at Amarna and intended to have one of the rock tombs (no. 12). He is the most prominent official whose administrative residence we should attempt to locate in the Central City. To achieve this, it is helpful to understand the vizier's role in the city.

Descriptions of the duties of a vizier, dating from a century beforehand, inform us that he maintained a regular daily routine of consultation with his officials over the state of the country and its resources. By means of messengers, he also kept in close contact with the leading officials of the provinces. He presided over his own court in which a strict protocol was observed among a group of senior officials, who gathered to hear petitions from aggrieved members of the public. The vizier, when hearing cases had to:

> sit on the throne of office, the reed-covered dais beneath, the robe of office on him, a leather cushion at his back, a leather cushion under his feet ... the sceptre of authority beside him, the forty leather rods spread out in front of him, the magnates of the 'Ten of Upper Egypt' in two rows in front of him, the chamberlain on his right-hand side, the controller of access on his left-hand side, the scribes of the vizier beside him.[10]

From his court, the vizier sent for documents held in other departments and, when they were brought, they were opened, read and then sealed again with the vizier's seal. The documents, it seems, were frequently at the heart of disputes over land boundaries and ownership throughout the whole territory under the vizier's jurisdiction. Moreover, the vizier controlled access to the palace and supervised the security forces who protected the king. His office was the real hub of the kingdom.

In his tomb at Amarna (no. 9) the chief of police of Akhetaten, his name Mahu, is shown reporting a case of suspicious transgression in the desert to the vizier and his colleagues [5.3]. The colleagues, who are dressed as if they are officials, are actually described as 'The great officials of pharaoh (life, prosperity, health!) and the leaders of the army who stand in the presence of His Majesty.'[11] It is never made clear in Egyptian texts of the period just how the vizier and the army shared their powers. The extent of the latter's authority was realized not long after Akhenaten's death, when Egypt passed under the control of a succession of army leaders, beginning with Horemheb. In the Central City they appear to be represented by buildings on the eastern fringe, one of which seems to have been a set of stables [1.10].

The vizier's duties culminated in a daily meeting with the king.

> Now he shall enter and greet the Lord each day when the affairs of the two lands have been reported to him in his residence. He shall enter the Great House when the overseer of the treasury has drawn up his position at the northern flagstaff. Then the vizier shall move in from the east in the doorway of the great double-gate....[12]

No written version of the vizier's duties dates from the Amarna period. Akhenaten, however, maintained the same, or a closely similar set of, officials as his predecessors. Many of them appear, identified by their titles, on the walls of one of his stone buildings at Karnak and similar people owned the rock tombs at Amarna. The sense of hierarchy and formality in which the vizier conducted his working life is likely to have been transferred to Amarna and provided for in its architecture. Akhenaten's main palace, in its stone layout, seems to have taken formality to an extreme. The texts of the vizier's instructions are an important reminder of the highly structured life that went on around the king.

The vizier Nakht's large private house in the Main City (K50.1) was, unlike the high priest Panehsy's, located towards the far southern limit. He lived just about as far as he could from the palace and its offices. To fulfil his duties, Nakht must have journeyed daily into the Central City and taken his place in a building that served as a daytime residence and as the supreme court, and also a place of contact with the king.

In the set of written duties, the 'office' of the vizier seems to be part of a larger 'house of the vizier', which, in turn, is part of the 'house of the king'. The King's House at Amarna seems better fitted to the role of 'house of the vizier' than any other. It has sufficient size and dignity for the holding of a court. As befitted the general custodial role of the vizier, it was also, through the bridge, designed like a funnel into the Great Palace for the activities carried out in the myriad scribal buildings that lay on the east side of the main road. The King's House was both a seat of authority and a superior porter's lodge. Its painted decoration of palace scenes also fitted it for occasions when the flow of authority was reversed and the king made his way to the vizier's court. It thus remains a palace, at least for the purposes of modern classifications, but one not exclusively for the king.

The King' House had a further function. Roughly one third of the building consisted of storerooms. A scene in the tomb of Meryre (no. 4) shows

4.9 A well-stocked magazine, as carved on the wall of the tomb of Meryre (no. 4). In the second row, the objects with incurving sides are 'ox-hide' ingots, probably of bronze or tin, a shape widely used in the ancient Near East for this purpose. For a line drawing, see RT I, *Pl.* XXXI.

a similar set of storerooms filled with all manner of commodities: grain in heaps, fish, fruit, metal ingots, elaborate vessels (almost certainly of metal), sacks and pottery amphorae – a veritable treasury of necessities and luxuries [**4.9**]. Whoever was in charge of the King's House controlled an important part of the king's wealth.

Stage Management

It has long been recognized that the layouts of Egyptian palaces and temples have much in common. They were both designed to stage-manage a divine being (whether god or king), and to create a degree of dramatic tension between a hidden and a revealed figure, between concealment and adulation, between a world of shadow behind doors and the bright Egyptian sunlight. Thus we find, at least in some palaces, that the throne room was small and at the end of a central line of approach through successive doorways. The best-preserved example at Amarna is in the North Palace, intended for a queen, where the throne dais, in a room measuring 6 by 5 m (19.7 by 16.4 ft), was a brick plinth, one course high, 90 cm (35.4 in.) deep and 80 cm (31.5 in.) wide. It would neatly take one of the thrones from the tomb of Tutankhamun [**4.10**]. In this room, located as if it were a sanctuary in a temple, there was no room for a crowd to cluster around the throne. The North Palace provides a valuable model for interpreting other palaces where the remains are less well preserved.

An important term in the ancient Egyptian vocabulary of kingship was 'to appear'. This was the charged moment when the king revealed himself to the outside world. Akhenaten, like his predecessors, was 'Lord of Appearances'. To judge from the subject matter in the tombs of Akhenaten's officials, a defining moment in their lives was to be summoned for a reward ceremony at a Window of Appearance (an ancient Egyptian term).[13] From an ornate architectural frame, and leaning across a patterned cushion, Akhenaten 'appeared' and distributed gifts and announced promotions [**1.13**]. If the largely hidden

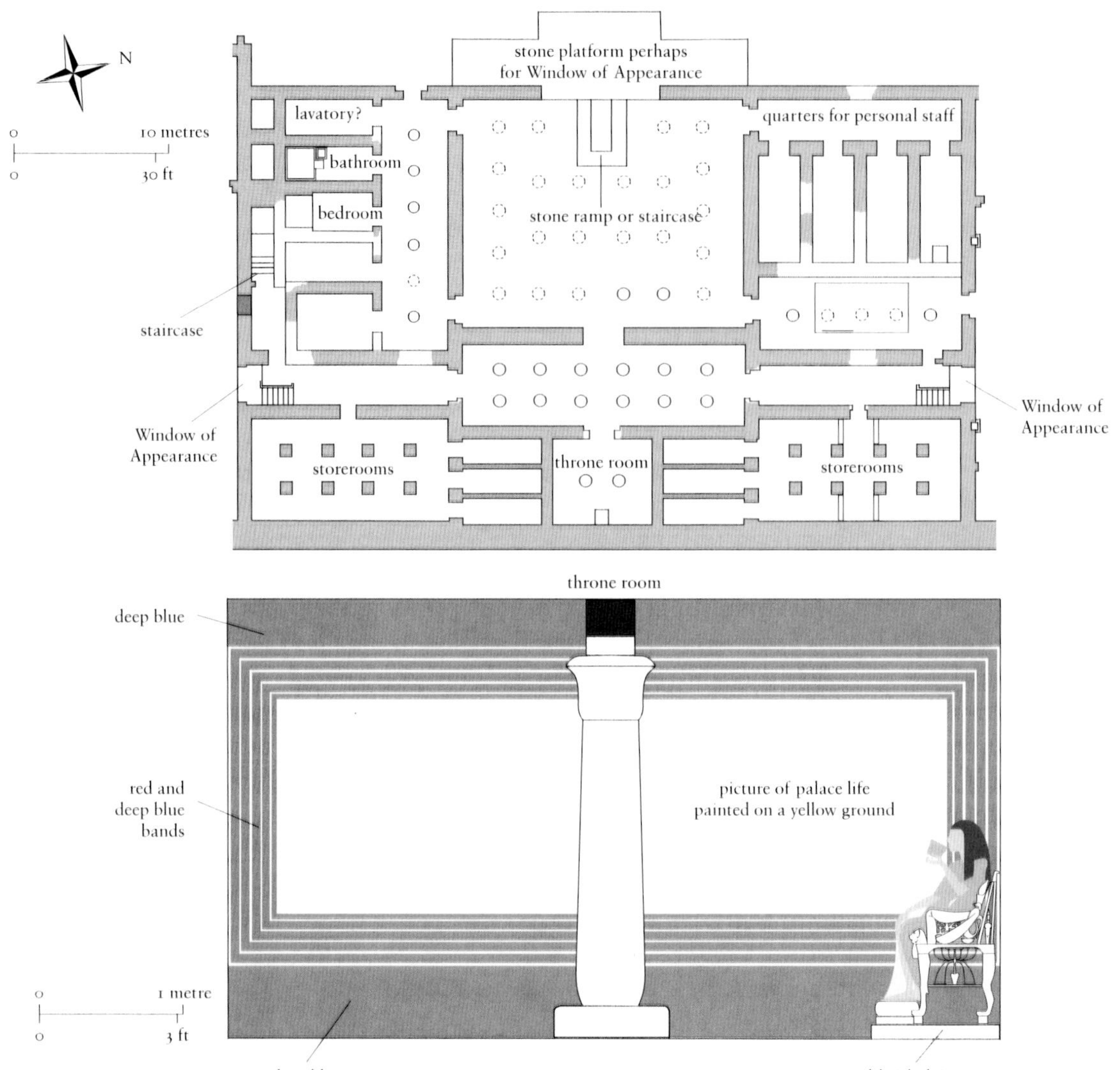

4.10 *(above) Plan of the rear part of the North Palace, showing the location of the queen's throne room. (below) Elevation of the throne room, showing the original tiny throne dais and an outline of the scheme of decoration. Fragments of a painted scene suggest that the original picture resembled that of the 'Princesses Panel', see plate XX; see also Weatherhead,* Paintings, *199–200, Fig. 111a. The throne is based on that from the tomb of Tutankhamun.*

throne room represented one pole of the axis of the king's symbolic life, then the Window of Appearance was the other, designed to attract attention rather than to deflect it. The favoured officials are shown accompanied by a crowd, evidently including their personal retinue of family and dependants, who both acted as audience and helped to carry the rewards away. Soldiers (or private bodyguards) with their chariots waited outside.

Some of the scenes add pictures of the interior of the palace that evidently lay behind the window. Here then is another key feature to look for in the ground plans of Amarna palaces. At the North Palace, a pair of unmistakable Windows of Appearance, built on a very modest scale, lay at the ends of a cross-axis that passed in front of the throne room [**4.10, 4.22, Pl. XVIII**]. The direct axis of the palace led, however, to a stone-built ramp or staircase before a platform that faced a large open space. Was this the foundation for the main Window of Appearance? Another candidate is even further to the west, where a broad span of gypsum foundation interrupts the brickwork that divides the open space of the North Palace into two separate courts [**4.22, Pl. XXXVIII**].

The Great Palace

The Great Palace is the largest building we can identify at Amarna. It ran for much of the length of the Central City, along the west side of the Royal Road. A portion is now buried beneath fields or lost altogether. The central part was constructed from stone on a foundation platform of gypsum concrete, its parts arranged symmetrically about an axis that ran parallel to the river, with the back of the building to the south. If we ignore the large brick extension that was added to the south after Akhenaten's death, we are probably looking at a rectangular building measuring at least 440 m (1,443 ft) from north to south, 250 m (820 ft) from west to east, with at its heart a stone construction of some 282 m (925 ft) in length and 174 m (571 ft) in width. It was designed to impress, although primarily through its interior. Its great stone court, a setting for statues of the royal family, and its stone halls and inner courts were screened from the landward side by a mud-brick wing [**4.11**] that included a separate throne-room complex (the North Harem, a misleading modern term).

4.11 *Part of the Boston model of the Central City, showing the Great Palace in the foreground. Behind is the bridge leading to the King's House. The huge courtyard (in the bottom left corner), surrounded by statues of the king and queen, offered space for banqueting, complete with raised dais, partially roofed, for the royal family.*

It is to be expected that a building of this size would have a grand entrance façade, and this would have been at the north end. The foundations at this point are especially hard to interpret, however. They were dug more deeply than usual, and the trenches filled with layers of stone that included unwanted column bases. Tall pylons are an obvious reconstruction (as in **3.1**). What lay in front of the façade is now lost beneath the modern fields, but from the way the brick buildings that separated the stone palace from the Royal Road continued northwards for at least another 150 m (492 ft), we can reconstruct the presence of an outer courtyard, not necessarily bordered by stone walls.

Behind the façade on the south came a huge courtyard, approximately 160 m (525 ft) square. The foundations of the eastern and southern sides survive as broad strips of gypsum concrete. That on the east is marked with a series of rectangles that are likely to have been stone bases to support red granite statues of which thousands of fragments have been found in the vicinity. The study of the pieces is still in progress.[14] They derive from over-life-sized figures of Akhenaten and women of his family, and are likely to have stood in front of tall limestone walls covered with carved and painted scenes. The walls continued across the southern end of the great court, as apparently did the statues, as far as the centre. Here, on the axis of the building, a stone platform projected forwards, its roof supported on columns. This was a reduced version of a grander scheme initially marked out on the gypsum, which was intended to make the platform four times as wide.

South of the dividing wall and the great court, the foundations mark out three main subdivisions, one on the central axis and one on either side (east and west). The central subdivision is likely to have been Akhenaten's principal hall of state. The foundation plan leaves many aspects ambiguous, and the reconstruction in **4.12** reflects one choice of architectural solution among several.

At the rear of the court was a square hall of columns, apparently subdivided to create two side aisles. On the central axis, at the back, I have interpreted the extra foundations as the basis for a long throne dais perhaps partially screened by walls extending outwards from the main side walls. (This is contrary to the excavators' interpretation. They put a rear doorway here, approached by a ramp.) In front of the columned hall came a courtyard of similar size, its various entrances approached by ramps that led upwards to the threshold of the doorway, then down again. The square foundations on either side of the main axis were not offering-tables, but may have supported free-standing granite stelae, of which two fragments have been found. The northern end was filled with a colonnade, three columns deep, which must, because it had to be reached by a ramp, have stood on a platform, provided with short side wings. The line of the axis, when taken across the main wall, then passes through the colonnaded platform that projects into the great court on the far side. This is surely the principal Window of Appearance, at one end of an axis at the other end of which was the throne. The great courtyard lined with colossal granite statues was a place of assembly for the crowds who gathered to witness

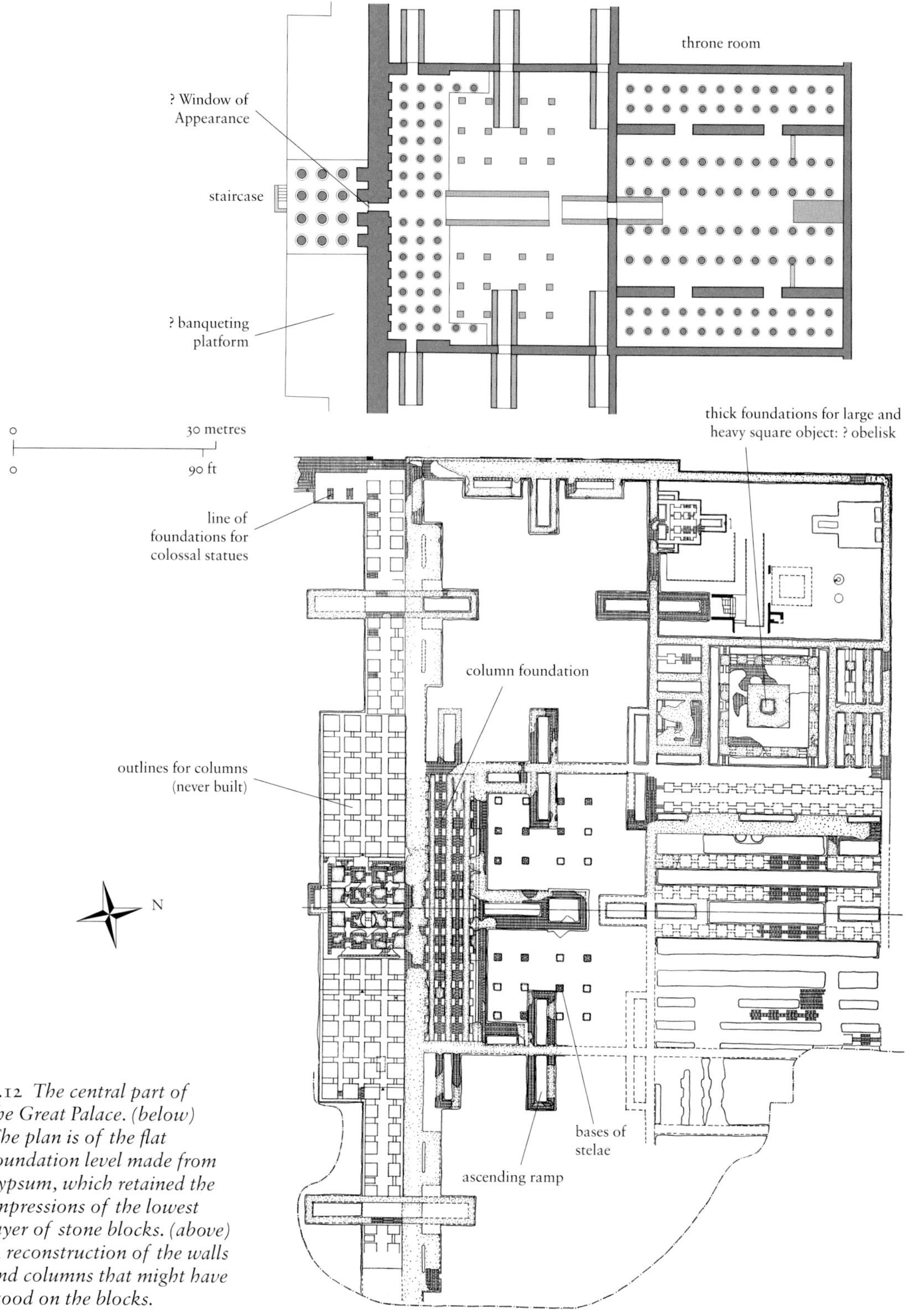

4.12 *The central part of the Great Palace. (below) The plan is of the flat foundation level made from gypsum, which retained the impressions of the lowest layer of stone blocks. (above) A reconstruction of the walls and columns that might have stood on the blocks.*

Akhenaten's moments of 'appearance'. The same basic arrangement, of a wide platform with two smaller platforms against the side walls, can be recognized at a raised mud-brick building centrally placed in the sun-temple enclosure at Kom el-Nana at the southern end of Amarna [**4.13**]. The similarity in layout suggests that this, too, may have acted as a Window of Appearance.

On either side of the hall of state in the Great Palace, foundations for stonework mark out paired courts and built features. The most conspicuous, on the east side of the throne room, is a broad square border of gypsum concrete that has been made to a greater thickness than normal. It had supported limestone blocks and surrounded a square hole, 2.5 m (8.2 ft) across. Could this have been for an obelisk?

The extravagant development of the architectural spaces in this complex was accompanied by exceptional care devoted to the finish. This is visible in the faience mouldings and tiles [**4.14**], the inlaid hieroglyphs carved from separate pieces of hard stone, the stelae and balustrades in travertine, the inlaid and gilded columns in a variety of plant forms. The building would have been ablaze with colour and shiny surfaces and the dull glitter of gold leaf. A constantly missing element that hinders our appreciation is the decorated stone walls, of which very few fragments were left behind after the ancient demolitions [**4.16**]. As will be explained later (see Chapter 8), for a while the whole city – Akhenaten's captive workforce – was put to work to manufacture the materials needed for this building. It might never have been completely finished, to judge by pieces of column that appear to show partially finished decoration.[15]

The stone halls of the Great Palace were separated from the Royal Road by a long range of buildings that, in their design and use of mud brick rather than stone, point to a more private zone of royal life, though still one imbued with formality. One part (the North Harem) seems to have been a self-contained

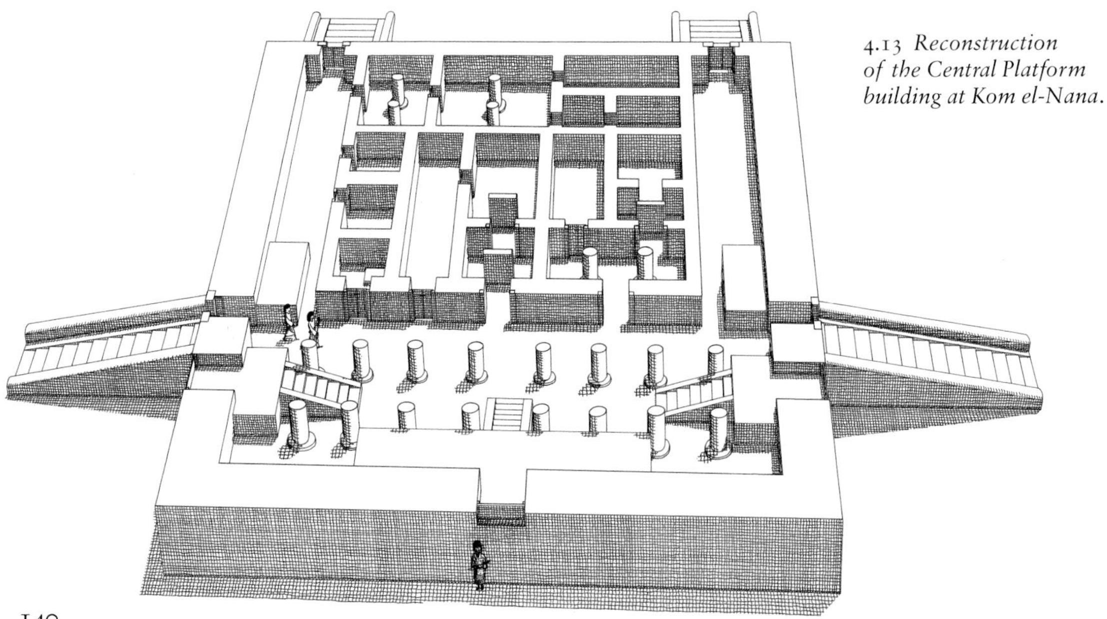

4.13 *Reconstruction of the Central Platform building at Kom el-Nana.*

4.14, 4.15 *Inlays from the Great Palace. (above) Stone blocks* a, b *and* d *were cut with recesses to hold rectangular inlays of coloured faience held in place with gypsum (cf. figures 8.11, 8.12). Block* c *is part of a stone frieze carved as a series of cobra heads wearing sun-discs. (below) A group of green faience tiles depicting papyrus stems that had covered the surface of columns.*

suite of apartments the core of which was a throne-room complex extensively decorated with painted gypsum pavements and wall paintings [**4.17–4.19, Pl. XVII**]. Although many of the walls were reduced to their foundations such that the locations of doorways have been lost, one can still recognize a progression of diminishing spaces ending in a tiny throne room, as at the North Palace. Rather than a Window of Appearance facing a court there was an enclosed garden that could be appreciated from a covered terrace.

4.16 *Four limestone wall blocks excavated from the Great Palace. Blocks* a *and* b *show corners of a building surrounded by a buttressed wall, with trees planted outside; block* c *comes from a scene of domestic activity, in this case including a line from which hang strips of meat curing; in* d *a building that contains a bed stands beside a park in which horned animals run free amidst vegetation.*

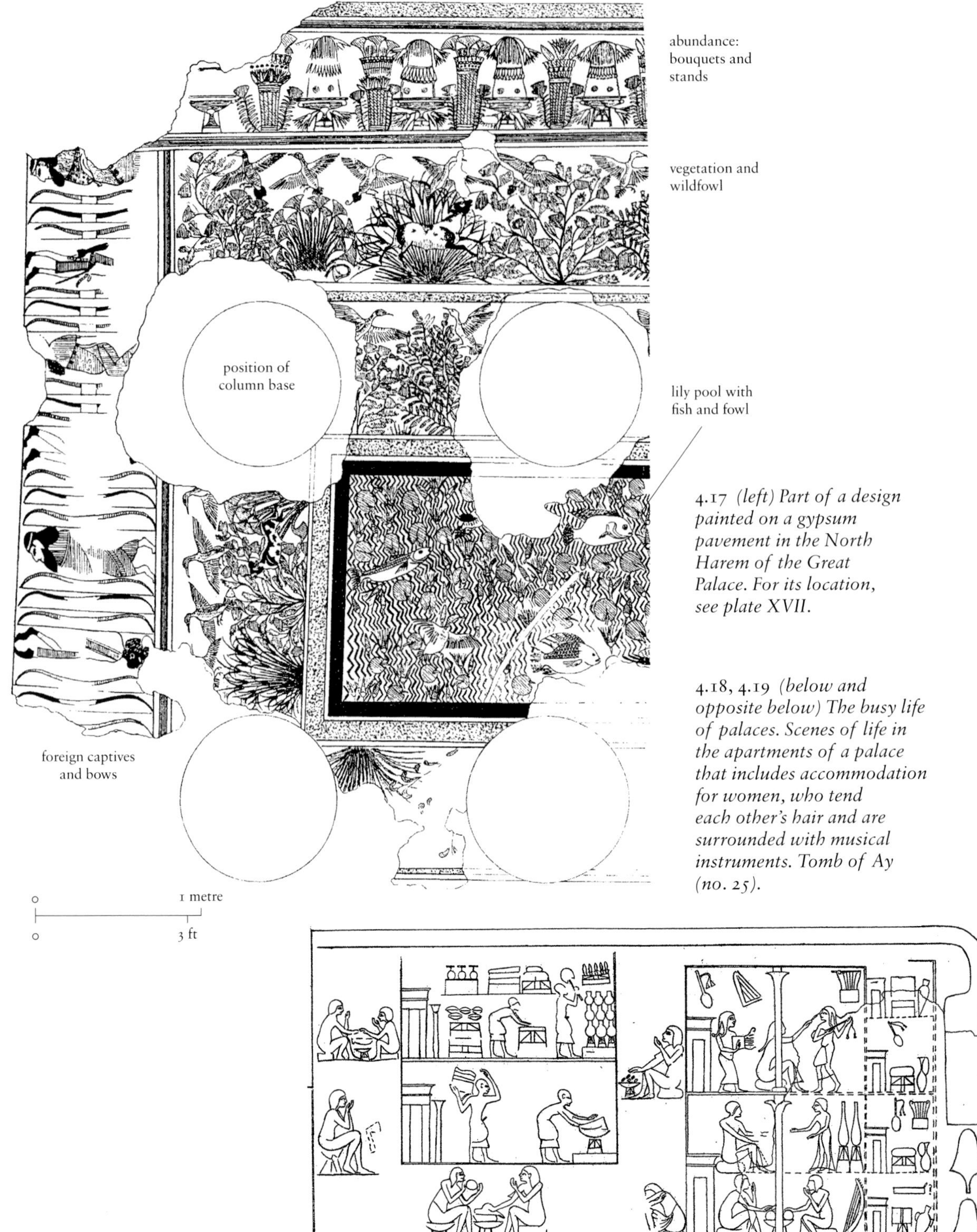

4.17 *(left) Part of a design painted on a gypsum pavement in the North Harem of the Great Palace. For its location, see plate XVII.*

4.18, 4.19 *(below and opposite below) The busy life of palaces. Scenes of life in the apartments of a palace that includes accommodation for women, who tend each other's hair and are surrounded with musical instruments. Tomb of Ay (no. 25).*

4.20 The king's bedroom. In the top picture (tomb of Meryre, no. 4) it appears in the top left corner of an abbreviated picture of the palace as a whole. In the bottom picture (tomb of Ahmose, no. 3) it is shown in more detail. The bed, with its mattress and headrest, lies beneath a sloping roof, presumably a representation of a wind funnel (compare figure 5.26). Note the Window of Appearance, closed with wooden shutters, in the middle of the picture.

Despite the huge spread of excavated buildings in the Central City, where and how members of the royal family lived the non-ceremonial parts of their lives still remains elusive. Where did Akhenaten normally sleep, for example? Tomb pictures show his bedroom [**4.20**], but one cannot locate it on the ground.

The Palace Occupants

Was the Great Palace a near-deserted monument or was it thronged with its own population? Some of the tomb pictures of palace life depict rooms occupied by women, who seemingly sit and chat, eat, play musical instruments and attend to one another's hair [**4.18, 4.19**]. Male guards or attendants sit, chat or snooze outside, while other male servants sweep the palace and tend to the food supply. It is to be expected, as well, that the palace was guarded all the time, even when the king was not present, to prevent access by people who might be a danger to the king or covet valuable items. The duties of the king's vizier, cited above, included a section on his responsibility for the security of the palace. The tomb scenes show, in attendance on the royal family, groups of men who belong to security units, some of them foreign. They carry weapons and sometimes have chariots.

The city as a whole was built around an assumption familiar to most readers: that individual families need a house of their own, which they thoroughly colonize. But not everyone lives in this way. Some choose, or find themselves living, a communal life, in army barracks, migrants' hostel, monastery or archaeological dig house. Personal space is reduced to one room or less, a space in a dormitory perhaps. For everything else, one shares common spaces and facilities. If we see Amarna palaces in this light, suddenly they offer accommodation to a significant number of people. What might be labelled storerooms might just as easily be personal rooms for one or even several individuals.

The Great Palace offers two possible places of accommodation, very different in their distances from the royal person. One is a series of small individual houses at the far northern end of the palace (as it is preserved), amounting to a small village, formally laid out (visible in 1.10). The other comprises rows of modest rooms on either side of the sunken garden in the North Harem [**Pl. XVII**], a location that must have brought intimate contact with the royal family. Adjacent to them a few small houses have also been incorporated into the scheme.

The single cubicles measure about 3 by 2 m (9.8 by 6.6 ft), a perfectly adequate space in which to sleep and keep a few boxes of clothes and other possessions if one is an attendant without family. Most of the day would be spent in communal living. As a point of comparison, the harem of the main palace of the Ottoman sultans in Istanbul consisted of some 300 rooms on half a dozen levels, almost all of them small; while the 'living quarters of the Black Eunuchs [were] arranged around an inner covered courtyard in three storeys with a tall fireplace at one end. There are ten or twelve little rooms on each floor, but even so [their inhabitants] must have been very crowded since there were several hundred of them; doubtless they served in watches and slept in relays'.[16]

Later in this chapter we will see that the same approach, when applied to the North Palace, easily turns it into a home for a substantial community of servants and attendants. Unfortunately, insufficient of the North Riverside Palace is preserved to support a comparable discussion.

4.21 *A royal banquet, seemingly in the open air, depicted in the tomb of Huya (no. 1). The musicians in the register at the bottom right appear to be foreigners from the Near East.*

Feasting and Banqueting

If we return to the palace functions listed at the start of this chapter and take the Central City as a whole as constituting the palace in the broad sense, we will find that many of the functions are covered: official and ceremonial (Great Palace and King's House), religious (the two Aten temples), defensive (the barracks and stable building on the eastern edge), administrative, service and residential. Those that are left unaccounted for are the social (banqueting), those involving a 'public' and the recreational. The last was, in part, catered for at other royal buildings, notably the North Palace and the 'sunshades' with their gardens and shrines. The 'public' elements belong to the Hellenistic world and seemingly had no close equivalents in ancient Egypt. But banqueting?

The written and pictorial sources from ancient Egypt are very sparing on the subject of royal banquets, but it is hard to believe that this was not a customary practice.[17] In the tomb of Huya (Queen Tiye's steward) at Amarna, the royal family is shown banqueting. Tiye and her own daughter (Baketaten) are present as guests [**4.21**]. Attending them are musicians, courtiers and servants. Food and drink are piled on tables and stands. The courtiers stand and observe, but they do not participate in the eating. The general reticence in sources could, however, reflect the long-standing rules of politeness that governed representations of kingship in Egypt.

European societies, faced with periods of cold, wet weather, have provided shelter for communal eating in the form of banqueting halls and refectories. The Mediterranean climate is (and was) kinder, however. During the Hellenistic period, the palace courtyard was considered to be the best setting for banqueting.[18] This might supply the answer for Amarna. The huge courtyard at the Great Palace, surrounded by colossal statues of the king and queen, looks like a very suitable place. A few New Kingdom scenes of feasting show the guests seated on the ground, with or without a mat. The dais at the southern end of the Great Palace courtyard, partly protected by a huge roofed area that also fronted the place where, I suggest, the Window of Appearance was located, separated the king and those honoured to be close to him from those who had been summoned to the feast, but took their places on the ground in the great courtyard. This would have been Akhenaten's high table.

A little after the Amarna period, King Horemheb (an ex-general of the army) issued a decree that corrected various abuses of power and affirmed certain procedures. Here he talks about the soldiery that formed his personal bodyguard. The first day of their ten-day shifts was to be regarded as a

> feast for them, each man being seated and receiving a share of every good thing, consisting of good bread, meat and cakes from the royal property ... [with the king] passing out honours to them from the Window of Appearance and calling each man by name.[19]

This combination of feasting and rewarding would fit well into the layout represented for us by the Great Palace.

And the source of the food? The last chapter introduced the subject of feasting and banqueting, and the destination of the food for whose display such generous provision was made in the two Aten temples, which lay across the road from the Great Palace. As far as it is preserved, the Great Palace itself shows nothing similar, not even the remains of ovens. As the plans show [**1.10, Pl. XXXV**], the central food depot lay across the road from the main courtyard of the Great Palace. Maybe on some occasions, food was spread out on the offering-tables in the temples; but a far more practical route would have been to take it directly from the depot, go across the road and through a gateway at street level that entered the main court of the Great Palace in the southeast corner.

The North Palace

Of all of the royal buildings at Amarna, the North Palace requires the least imagination to turn it into a habitation [**4.22, Pls X, XXXVIII**]. It is now an isolated building between the North Suburb and the North City, facing west towards the river and standing perpendicularly on a line a little back from the prolongation of the Royal Road. It was excavated in 1923 and 1924, and parts were re-examined in the 1990s. It occupies a walled rectangle, 148 by 115 m (485.6 by 377.3 ft) in extent, the built-up portions filling three sides, the long central space subdivided by brickwork that resembles a pylon. Many

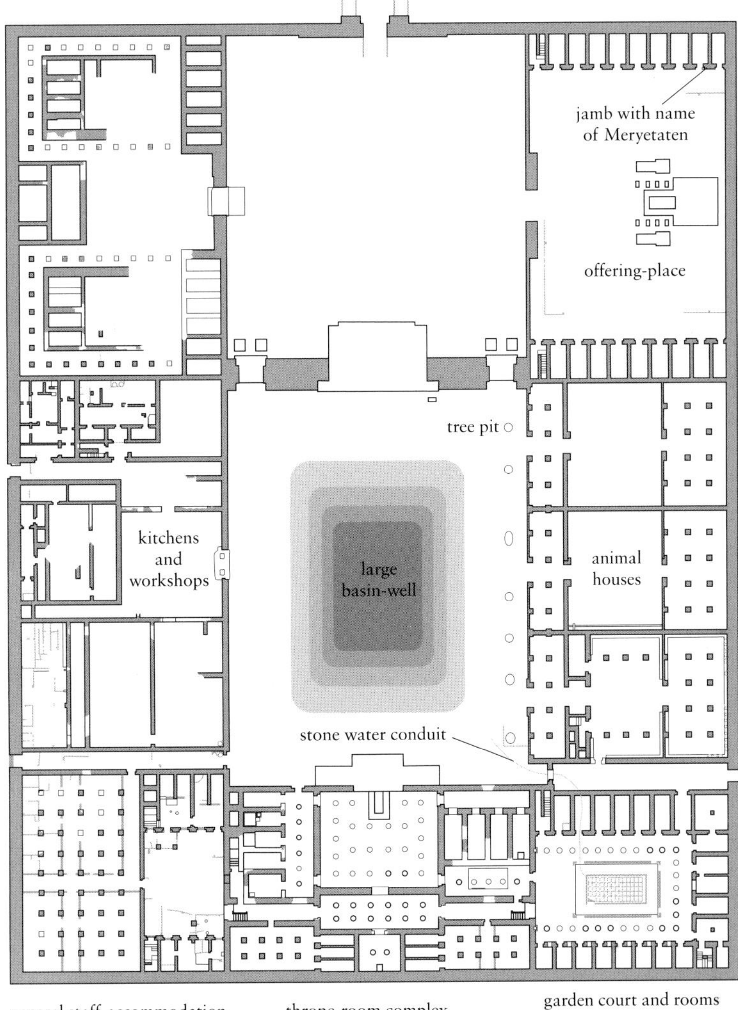

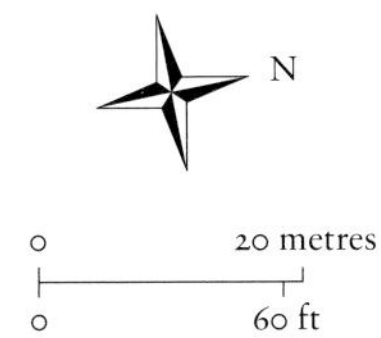

4.22 *Plan of the North Palace. For the central rear part, containing the throne room, see figure 4.10.*

inscriptions show that it belonged to Meryetaten, Akhenaten's eldest daughter who came to have a particularly prominent place at the Amarna court, seemingly responsible for running Akhenaten's household before becoming queen.[20] Its east–west alignment and axial symmetry have drawn the comment that it resembles a temple as much as a palace.

The heart of the building was at the rear, facing the court and the palace's water supply, a deep basin that was probably fitted with a chain of shaduf water-lifts that eventually fed water to a stone conduit. A neatly laid out suite of rooms enabled a formal style of life that moved between a small throne room at the back and a columned hall and stone-built balcony that faced the open air (and might have contained a Window of Appearance, as mentioned earlier). It lay adjacent to a private suite that included bedroom and bathroom on one side, and a set of rooms probably for close companions or personal servants on the other [4.10, 4.23]. Further to one side, towards the cooler north, was an enclosed garden surrounded by rooms that probably also housed personal servants [**Pl. XVIII**], perhaps in two tiers, the upper reached by staircases in the corners. And can we read a humorous comment on the captive yet pampered status of their occupants in the paintings of fowl feeding on grain (supplied by men) that were painted on the walls [**Pls XXXI–XXXIII**]? Taking these various parts together, we are looking at a place of communal living that could have housed, say, fifty persons at the least.

The corresponding southeast corner contained a few houses and a large roofed area that together were probably accommodation for staff who were more distant from the palace's owner, though even the interior of the roofed area had been painted with scenes from nature. Their realm continued along the south side of the palace, a place of kitchens and workshops where probably, as generally throughout the city, faience jewelry was made as a semi-domestic occupation. We might even have the name of someone who lived in this part of the building. The two papyrus letters written by the unguent preparer Ramose place him in the household of Princess Meryetaten.[21] The size especially of the kitchen area points to a substantial number of people living at the palace.

These various elements, which cover more than half of the roofed space of the North Palace, represent a 'working' residence that is fairly easy to comprehend. The remainder falls into that ambiguous category where practical needs encounter ritual and symbol. The northwest corner was given over to ritual centred on offering-tables and platforms reached by flights of steps [**4.24, 4.25**].

4.23 *The bathroom at the North Palace (whose last resident was probably Meryetaten as queen), when first excavated in 1924, looking towards the south.*

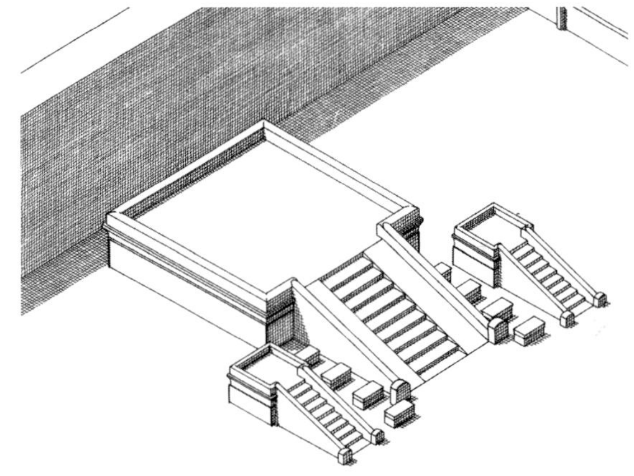

4.24, 4.25 *Perhaps an Aten temple in miniature, at the North Palace. A set of three stone platforms reached by stairs are represented by flat foundation beds of gypsum. Some of the original foundation blocks for two rows of offering-tables still stand. The picture looks to the southwest. (right) A reconstruction of the platforms, as if viewed to the northeast. In the model (Pl. XXXVIII), as an alternative interpretation, the main platform has been given a roof supported on columns and containing a throne dais for the royal owner.*

They face north, as did a similar construction at Maru-Aten (M II, the 'artificial island'; **2.16, Pl. XXXVII**), which seems unsuited to a cult of the rising sun. They could have supported statues of the royal family, but no fragments of broken statues have been found.

Filling the remainder of the north side of the palace was a building subdivided into three similar sections, though the easternmost contained more features, most strikingly rows of limestone feeding-troughs or mangers for animals, combined with tethering-stones, constructed against the walls [**4.26–4.28**]. The mangers in the innermost area were decorated with carvings of cattle, ibexes and antelopes. The numbers of animals provided for seem

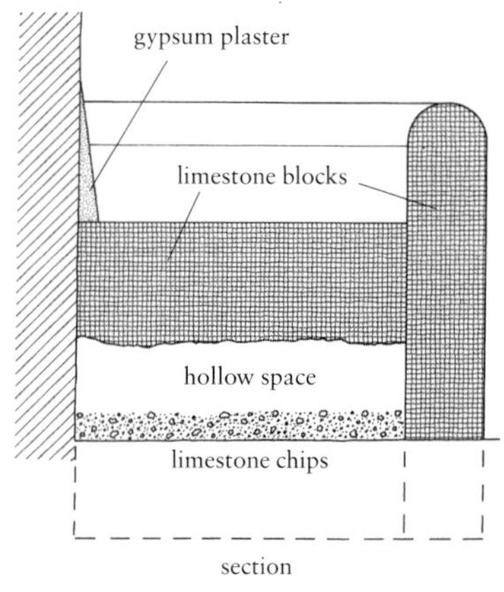

4.26, 4.27, 4.28 *View of the north wall of the court in the North Palace, which was provided with limestone feeding-troughs or mangers for cattle (as carved on the front of each manger), each pair separated by a tethering-stone. (right) Drawing of manger carved with pictures of ibexes feeding.*

excessive. In the rear portion there was space for forty-eight animals tethered along the four sides. The other two adjacent sections to the west lacked the mangers, but the middle one had a continuous brick trough against the east wall. A plausible explanation is that this court (and presumably its neighbour) were for birds (geese and other fowl), since painted scenes elsewhere in the palace depict them feeding [**Pls XXXI–XXXIII**].

We can take a straightforward approach to this layout and, noting the presence of kitchens on the opposite side of the palace and offering-tables in the northwest court, conclude that the prime purpose of the three animal houses was to maintain livestock for consumption. But is this credible, given their proximity to the royal quarters and the noise and smells they must have generated if used in this way to any extent? Moreover, there were signs that the walls had been decorated with paintings.

An alternative interpretation is that they were part of the fantasy atmosphere that the palace strove to create, of living within the realm of nature, partly that of the untamed papyrus marsh and partly that of domesticated species controlled by humans. The animals and birds could have been there to enhance the illusion and to provide a living tableau of the gifts of life that came from the Aten and the pleasurable spectacle of nature that had long held a place in the Egyptian imagination. Ibex-like animals appear running free in one of the scenes from the Great Palace [**4.16d**], for example. By this view, the numbers of animals might have been low. The builders, asked to provide a cattle stall covering a certain area, had fitted it out as if it were a farm building, but only a few token animals were actually installed. As a diverting spectacle it could probably be viewed from above, since a staircase in the southeast corner took one up to a gallery that ran along the front of the whole building.

As seen now, a mud-brick ruin, the North Palace is almost monochrome in appearance. Originally, however, a large part of it was adorned with coloured paintings, often though not exclusively devoted to natural life [**Pls XIX, XXXI–XXXIII**]. Traces of a marsh scene were even found on one of the external walls of the cattle court, facing the basin-well. For the Egyptians, lavishness in buildings included the addition of gold leaf. A pair of column bases in front of the bedroom-bathroom suite are pierced with small circular holes to support the ends of a wooden screen, the posts originally fixed in place with gypsum. Tiny traces of gold leaf in the gypsum point to the gilding of the woodwork.

If this is what a working palace looked like, one might have expected other examples to be preserved at Amarna, but this is not the case. Unfortunately, river erosion and later agriculture have deprived us of the greater part of what might have been the principal royal residence, the North Riverside Palace.

The North Riverside Palace

In Akhenaten's time, as you approached Amarna from the north by river, coming perhaps from the old capital at Memphis, you would first pass below the northernmost boundary stela standing out whitely in the limestone hillside, which, for a distance of about 1.5 km (0.9 miles), descended directly to the water's edge. As the cliffs receded, they gave way to a huge citadel of brick walls that ran to the waterfront. It is likely that it was here, in seclusion, that the king lived with his family and his personal army units. If your destination was a landing-stage at the Central City, just beyond the further end of the Great Palace, you would still have 3 km (1.9 miles) to travel.

Time has treated this huge building complex badly. A 270-m (886-ft) length of the double enclosing wall on the inland side runs just outside the present limit of the modern fields, but most of what it enclosed is likely to have been completely lost. The desert shelves down quite steeply towards the river and this must have necessitated constructing much of the building on terraces with deep foundations. In the late nineteenth century AD, the river ran closer to the present edge of the desert than it does now and is likely to have washed any surviving foundations away. The little that was left of the building, on the desert, was excavated in the early 1930s [**4.29, 5.7**].

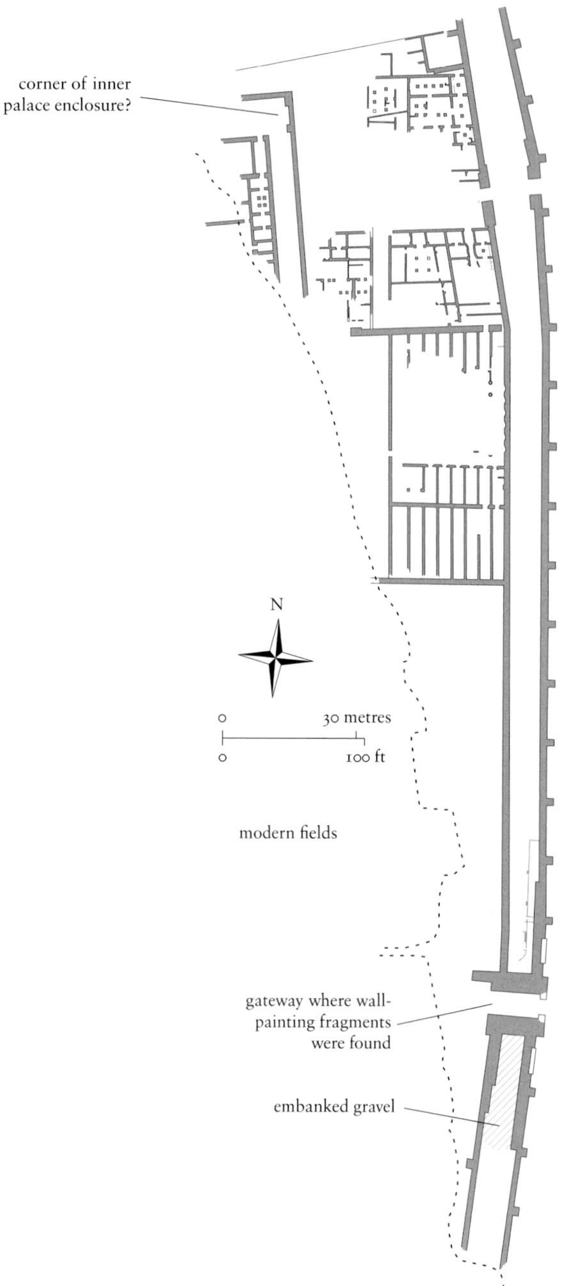

4.29 *Plan of the North Riverside Palace.*

The enclosing wall was 1.5 m (4.9 ft) thick and had possessed square towers or buttresses on the outside face. A tomb scene that might depict this building shows battlements along the top [5.5]. On the inside ran a space, 7 m (23 ft) wide, bounded by an inner wall. How far to the south this double wall originally continued has not been determined. If it ran as far as the limit of the adjacent housing of the North City, it would have had a total length of 350 m

(1,148 ft) and would have been the wall of a large citadel, perhaps of 5 ha (12.4 acres). A space of this size could have included gardens and even parkland. Near to where the wall vanishes beneath the fields stood a gateway, 5 m (16.4 ft) wide, originally with a stone doorframe at the front and stone-lined niches on either side. When excavated, the debris filling the gate produced many pieces of fallen plaster painted with a scene of the royal family in chariots [**Pl. XXXIV**]. Had it simply fallen from the inside of the gateway? This is the simple explanation, but the excavators imagined a painted room situated above the gateway, necessarily reached by stairs from the back, now lost.

The only part of the interior to have survived is at the northern end. The outer parts could easily have been for storage and for housing servants or soldiers, and had their own gateway. We will be forever tantalized by the survival of just the corner of an inner enclosure of thick walls, neatly laid out inside its own surrounding wall. Is it the corner of a palace, of *the* palace where Akhenaten spent most nights?

The Royal Road ran southwards from the North Riverside Palace, its course almost immediately vanishing beneath the modern fields [**2.1**]. On the desert opposite a point some 500 m (1,640 ft) south from where the line of the road meets the fields, a strange brick construction emerges, dug in 1925, and mistakenly thought to have been a granary. It appears rather to have been an elaborately constructed ramp, which took a roadway, 7 m (23 ft) wide, up a slope towards the line of the Royal Road. Constructed as a bridge, it implies the existence of a major building on the other side of the road.

The Royal Progress

We have no direct statement as to how the royal family divided their day, except for the requirement in the vizier's traditional routine that he be ready to greet and to brief the king every morning at a place that, at Amarna, was presumably the Great Palace. The rock tombs give prominence to scenes of royal land travel by means of a cavalcade of chariots, and imply that it was between formal buildings. The obvious route for them to have taken is the 2.5 km (1.5 miles) between the North Riverside Palace and Great Palace, the last stage along the line of the Royal Road where it enters the Central City. Several of the royal family's destinations were buildings that were themselves laid out for processions.

Depictions of the royal family stress the theme of their togetherness. Ruling Egypt was the family business. Yet, if we include the 'sunshade' garden-shrine enclosures for named women of Akhenaten's family as destinations, as well as the North Palace, the places that were 'theirs' were widely dispersed. Maru-Aten and the North Palace, both belonging to Meryetaten, were more than 7 km (4.3 miles) apart.

One is left wondering to what extent the royal family did live and move as a single unit, and if any one of them ever remained still for very long, or was always about to leave for somewhere else, for another elaborate station along a corridor of travel, forever the object of attention in a highly structured lifestyle.

5.1 *Length of ancient desert track behind the northern part of the city. View to the south.*

5.2 *A desert track close to the Workmen's Village descends a steep slope, before being lost on the eroded surface of the desert wadi floor. In the distance is a large modern irrigation scheme. View to the south.*

CHAPTER FIVE

CITY OF PEOPLE

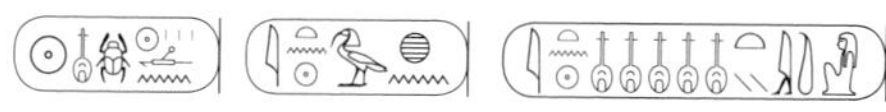

Nowhere in his surviving texts, including those of the boundary stelae, does Akhenaten use the word 'city'. Yet as a consequence of creating Akhetaten, several tens of thousands of people moved there to live out a significant part of their generally short lives in its houses. Whole neighbourhoods have been excavated, and give us the clearest and most extensive picture we are ever likely to have of what an ancient Egyptian city looked like (at least in the immediate aftermath of its construction). From a wealth of added archaeological detail we can also draw tantalizingly near to understanding how the city worked, though not near enough to be definitive. The attempt to understand Amarna also leads to considering what cities are, not just in appearance – buildings and streets – but as something intimate in the lives of their inhabitants, perhaps on the limits of perception.

Control Without Walls

Amarna the city had no boundary line, no surrounding wall nor even, as far as we can tell, a fence. The boundary that mattered was the one that defined, via the boundary stelae, the tract of land sacred to the Aten, Akhetaten. The built city (as we see it) was of no symbolic importance. Moreover, Egypt was a country that, at this time, felt no serious threat from within or without, and the old practice of surrounding towns with walls had seemingly been abandoned. Nonetheless, there may well have been constraint at Amarna on the free movement of people eastwards, out into the desert, and thus a tacit limit to how far people could continue to build houses on the eastern fringe of the city.

The desert behind the city is criss-crossed with trackways, made by sweeping into a pair of low parallel ridges the loose stones that form a natural cover to the sandy-gravel desert surface [5.1, 5.2].[1] Sometimes they run in fairly straight sections that can form arcs in a very shallow curve, or they can remain straight for long distances; or they can curve quite tightly when the landscape demands. They are mostly to be found on the low desert, but a few run up to the top of the cliffs, taking an uncompromising gradient as they do so, and there they join others that span the high desert. They were first recorded at the end of the nineteenth century AD, and from the way they often link, or at least respect, constructions of the Amarna period, we can be sure that they were created in Akhenaten's time.

Two sets of tracks had an obvious purpose [**Pl. XI**]. They ran generally from west to east and provided straight routes out from the city to individual rock tombs of the northern and southern groups. Close to the tombs, some of them fan out from feeder tracks. In three instances we can identify both the house and the tomb of the same person. The vizier Nakht (or Nakhtpaaten) and the general Ramose located their tombs (nos 12 and 11, respectively) in the southern group, and their houses were south of the Central City. The main residence of the high priest Panehsy was also south of the Central City, but his tomb (no. 6) lay in the northern group, close to that of his colleague, the high priest Meryre (no. 4), both tombs connected to the desert offering-place (which has the modern name Desert Altars).

These tracks to the tombs imply the existence of recognized points of departure within the city for people who were heading out towards the rock tombs and perhaps the lesser cemeteries that lay not far away. Funeral processions would have been part of this movement. They must have begun from individual houses where a death had occurred. Instead of making their way directly to the tomb, however, they first passed northwards or southwards through the city, making for the start of one of the desert tracks, at which point they turned to head eastwards.

Another set of tracks cut across the first and followed inconsistently concentric lines that skirted around the city on the low desert and on top of the plateau beyond. Individual tracks along various alignments divided the whole into unequal sectors, and the two kinds of tracks also joined one another. The system has not been completely preserved. Flash floods have washed out some stretches, the surface of the zone close to the edge of the ancient city has been eroded from long usage by tracks linking the modern villages, and a large swathe of the desert criss-crossed by tracks (as we know from old maps) is now under recent cultivation.

The Tomb of a Policeman

Tomb no. 9 at Amarna (in the southern group) belonged to Mahu, 'Chief of the Medjay of Akhetaten', Medjay being an old ethnic term for people of the eastern desert who were, so the Egyptians found, good at fighting and were, by this time, employed as desert police. The scenes carved on the walls depict Mahu performing his duties [5.3]. They show chariots, numerous running 'policemen' (sometimes armed with sticks), the supplying of a military-looking building and Mahu reporting to high officials (including the vizier) where he hands over three manacled prisoners (two of them bearded), with the words: 'The officials will hear [the case] of the people who join those of the desert'.[2] This is the clearest statement of the objective of the policing. It implies the presence in the desert of people who were outside the jurisdiction of Egypt, but did not represent the kind of threat that necessitated a city wall.

Trespassers in the desert were not the only people who ended up on the wrong side of the law and there were other reasons for putting oneself beyond

5.3 *The chief of police of Akhetaten, Mahu, goes about his tasks (tomb no. 9). In the lower register, he presents three manacled prisoners to the vizier and other senior officials; their crime: apparently that of trespassing in the desert.*

the bounds of normal life. Slaves formed an element in Egyptian society, and the state also conscripted ordinary people for building, quarrying, agricultural work and soldiering. We know from written sources of the period that some people in these categories absconded from their servitude and were hunted. Robbery was also well documented. We can imagine the background. A major new city – with palaces, wealth, workshops handling precious materials, and a population from among whom many will die and be buried, including royalty – rapidly takes shape in a previously uninhabited spot. It is bound to have attracted people who saw an opportunity for plunder. The most direct evidence we have for this is the extensive robbery of the cemeteries of the ordinary inhabitants, apparently carried out not very long after the burials had taken place.

The later New Kingdom has supplied us with abundant written records of the situation at western Thebes, where there were major temples on the edge of the desert, tombs in the desert hills and the royal tombs in the Valley of the Kings. All were the target of robberies. Mostly, it seems, the thieves were people living in a town that had grown up around the last of the major temples, that of Ramesses III at Medinet Habu. The main line of protection for the royal tombs was the same kind of police force of which Mahu at Amarna was in charge, the Medjay. The Theban written evidence also implies that the area of the royal tombs was considered to be sacred, and that the men who worked to create the tombs (who lived in the village of Deir el-Medina, see below) had a sense of self-identity that approximated to that of a guild.

The topography of Amarna favoured policing more than did that of Thebes. There were fewer places in which to hide. An expanse of mostly flat and open desert lay between the city and the tombs and could not easily be crossed

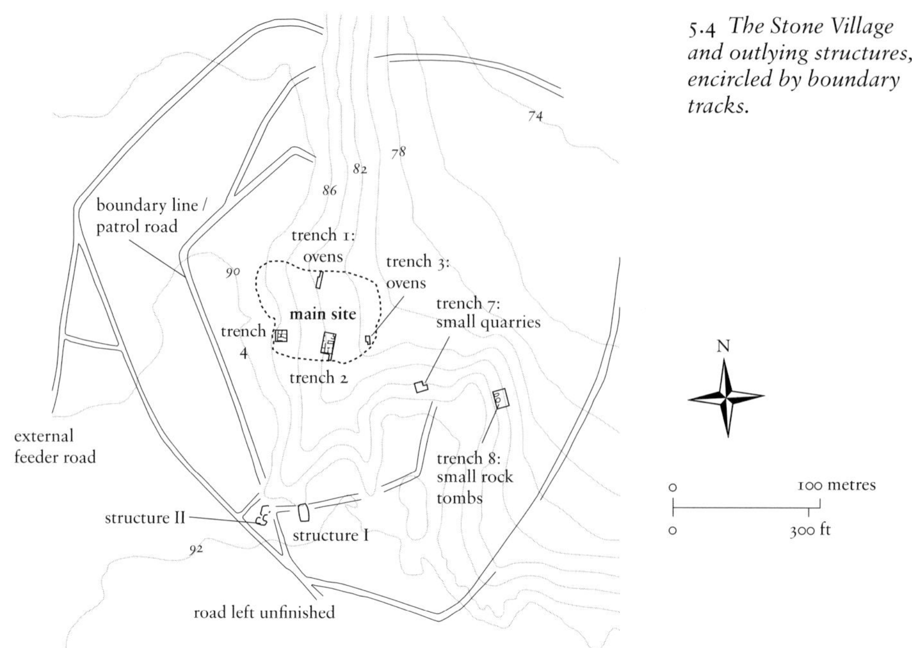

5.4 *The Stone Village and outlying structures, encircled by boundary tracks.*

unobserved, at least by day (and even in starlight the eye picks out quite distant movements). The one part that offered 'cover' was the low ridge that ran out from near the southern side of the entrance to the valley leading to the royal tombs. But this became the base for two 'official' communities, the Stone Village and Workmen's Village, on the north and south sides, respectively. The communities that lived in them were incorporated into the trackway system, making this the densest part of the routes and also the best preserved. Even a false start in laying out the system is still visible, where a track southwards had been started from the middle of the plateau, perhaps intended to join up with the concentric set around the Stone Village. It was placed too far to the west and was abandoned in favour of one that was 100 m (328 ft) to the east, and served as the feeder road to those around the Stone Village.

The Stone Village system is particularly well preserved and clear on account of the smallness and isolation of the site [5.4]. A single feeder road from the south entered a partially concentric double circuit around the village, with lines of connection between the two. At the larger Workmen's Village site, the system is similar but more complicated, with feeder roads to the north and northeast as well.

Roads or Boundaries?

At both sites, topography dictates natural paths of communication. Access to the Workmen's Village from the main city is most comfortably achieved by taking a path that curves around the base of the spur that protects the village on the west [**Pl. XI**]. A sparse trail of sherds from broken storage vessels follows this path from a point on the edge of the city where a well and workshops were located (building Q48.4) until, just before the Workmen's Village, it is checked by a barrier of stones laid across it, served by a small building at one end.[3] The ancient trackway system ignores this most obvious of routes, cutting across it. The same is implicit at the Stone Village. The track system is evidently independent of the needs of the occupants of the two settlements.

The Workmen's Village had a parallel at western Thebes, in the necropolis workers' village of Deir el-Medina. It lay isolated in its own valley, the employed men carrying out their tasks in the royal tombs reached by a winding pathway over the Theban hills. Theirs was a special calling, which gave them a sense of collective identity as if they were a guild. They were 'servants of the Place of Truth' (a respectful euphemism especially for places associated with the dead, including the royal tomb; the 'mountain of Akhetaten' was itself a 'Place of Truth'). Along with the village's separate location went boundaries, the crossing of which was a cause for observation by scribes who kept a record of events.

Dissatisfaction with the payment of rations provoked the workmen of Deir el-Medina to go 'outside', usually to stage protests at various of the mortuary temples on the low desert edge. To do this they had to pass one or more 'walls' (there were at least five of them that could be passed in succession). This is a conventional translation of a word (*ineb*, plural *inbu*) that can also be translated as 'redoubt',[4] or even 'fence' (when written with the determinative for wood). At these times they came under the scrutiny of a force of guards, none other than the Medjay, whose leader at Amarna, several generations earlier than these accounts, had been Mahu. The written records concerning Deir el-Medina reveal that the villagers sometimes had personal dealings with individual Medjay men, too.

The situation at Amarna was evidently similar. Some of the scenes of Mahu's duties place him and his men in schematically rendered settings that include what seem to be fences, arranged in parallel pairs, made of posts linked by rails or ropes [5.5]. Would the Egyptians have called them *inbu* ('walls', 'fences')? We cannot be sure; and it seems hardly feasible that the entire road network at Amarna was marked in this way, although some parts of it could have been.

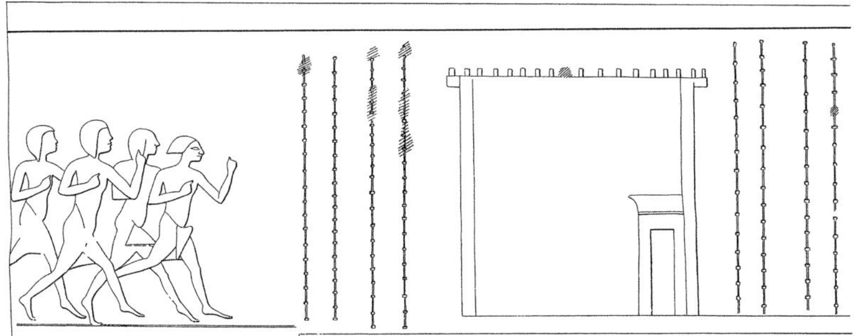

5.5 *Mahu's policemen and a representation of the roadways? They flank a fortified building that might be the North Riverside Palace. A scene in his tomb (no. 9).*

The point of this discussion is to suggest that the primary function of the tracks (other than those leading to the groups of tombs) was to act as boundaries, linear markers. This would, in turn, imply that the Theban necropolis, where Deir el-Medina was located, had its own network of boundaries. It need not have been a series of tracks like that at Amarna. It could have been an improvised mixture of stone walls, tracks, wooden posts and other markers. It would have been these – to a total of five – that the necropolis workers had to cross to reach the outside world. At Amarna, anyone heading from the Workmen's Village to the main city would also have had to cross five trackways. The scribal accounts of disputes at Deir el-Medina reveal that the workmen could breach the system with impunity if the motives seemed justifiable. When the scribes noted that men from the community had passed the five 'walls', no retribution necessarily followed, although in one instance the scribe, having sent the men out, threatened them with legal action after they had passed the first boundary.[5]

Mahu's scene of the manacled men shows that being out in the desert without permission was an arrestable offence that could be brought to the attention of the vizier. The short accompanying text quoted above ('The officials will hear [the case] of the people who join those of the desert') is open to slight modifications in translation, so another rendering is: 'O officials, judge [these] people who climbed the *gebel* [a useful Arabic term that combines the meanings "desert" and "mountain"].'[6] This makes their crime the simple one of crossing into the closed-off zone (with grave-robbing the most likely motive).

At Thebes, the closed-off zone contained the royal tombs. This would have been true at Amarna also. Akhenaten's boundary stelae had, however, designated the whole of the eastern desert mountain of Akhetaten as the special domain of the Aten. It was 'his'. A possible parallel case can be found at Abydos, 200 km (124 miles) upstream from Amarna, already cited in connection with the Great Aten Temple at Amarna. Here, too, was a sacred landscape, specifically called 'the holy land'. The natural topography is a large tract of flattish desert surrounded by an arc of cliffs cut by wadis. Over a long period of time, a town and a string of temples developed along the desert edge, but did not intrude much into the desert plain.

An important focus of attention was a tomb from the earliest period of Egyptian history (that of King Den of the 1st Dynasty), which was identified later on as the tomb of the god Osiris. It lay far back in the desert. A wide processional route ran from the temple of Osiris beside the alluvial plain across the desert out to the tomb of Osiris. Although it was left as an unimproved shallow depression in the desert surface, its perimeter was marked by large granite boundary stelae (one has survived). They bore an edict that specified death to anyone other than a priest who entered the demarcated tract of land or who made their tomb within it. It is a useful pointer to how seriously the sanctity of a piece of largely open desert could be taken.[7]

The eastern edge of Amarna was not marked with a boundary that has remained visible (if a trackway had run along the edge, it has long ago been lost to modern village traffic). Perhaps the sense, when stepping into the flat empty desert, that one is crossing a threshold was enough to deter most people from wandering off towards the cliffs, and put a natural break on eastwards expansion of housing. As for the two desert villages, more will be said about them later in this chapter.

The layout of the tracks is also a guide to how Akhenaten and those who worked for him perceived the landscape of Amarna. It is the antithesis of geometric appreciation, the product of a simple 'can-do' philosophy devoid of abstraction. It offers a good introduction to how the city itself took shape.

How the City Grew

Amarna was built by a king capable of thinking differently, possessed of the power of the absolute ruler at a time of peak prosperity, preparing himself to create a sacred place on a roughly flat extent of empty desert. Behind him lay centuries of building colonies, forts and work-camps that were, in some cases, planned on a rectilinear grid of streets contained within a perimeter wall provided with gates. Yet little of Amarna suggests that it followed a plan that went beyond general intentions; nor do the boundary stelae convey the idea that a city, as we would think of it, was about to be created.

Akhenaten's 'plan' seems to have involved a series of palaces and temples strung out on a line that ran roughly parallel to the riverbank [**2.1**]. Those in the centre (the Central City) formed roughly the sides of a rectangular space through which ran a broad highway (the Royal Road in modern nomenclature). To the north, the highway extended for 2.5 km (1.5 miles) to the North Riverside Palace, passing the North Palace and the Great Ramp on the way. To the south, the line pointed towards one of the 'sunshade' enclosures, Kom el-Nana (probably the sun-temple of Nefertiti). It looks, therefore, as though the city began with a single setting-out line. Once marked out on the desert, however, a good part of this line's usefulness quickly lapsed. The North Riverside Palace obeyed its alignment where it began on the south, but then swung northwestwards, the better to reflect the natural topography. To the south of the Central City, once it had fixed the front line of Kom el-Nana, it was ignored and lost beneath the housing areas as they developed according to their own local dynamic.

The great 'square' around which the state buildings of the Central City were arranged was not treated as a significant architectural space, and only one of the buildings (the King's House) faced it with a prominent entrance. Instead, as we have seen, the space was filled with an irregular complex of service buildings, which lost their parallel alignment to the Royal Road further back. It must have been obvious from the outset that Amarna would also become home for a substantial population, but this seems to have been an incidental consequence. No perimeter to the city was fixed nor was a grid of streets laid out ahead of the arriving hordes. Amarna appears to be the antithesis of geometric planning.

5.6 Aerial photograph of the southern part of the North Suburb, taken in 1935 by the Royal Egyptian Air Force, after the excavations of the EES, 1926–30.

5.7 (below) Aerial photograph of the North City, taken in 1932 by the Royal Egyptian Air Force. The wall of the North Riverside Palace and its gateway run just in front of the modern fields.

From the preserved traces, housing filled around half of the city. It fell into three separate zones. The largest extended from the southern limit of the Central City southwards for 2.5 km (1.5 miles), ending where the desert dipped, corresponding to land now cultivated behind the modern village of El-Amariya. The southernmost part (the South Suburb) seems to have been more lightly built up (and probably occupied for a shorter time) than the more northerly part (the Main City). On the north side of the Central City, the desert seems to have been left largely empty, apart from a scatter of houses close to the north enclosure wall of the Great Aten Temple. Then, after a distance of 0.5 km (0.3 miles), came the North Suburb, which broadly resembles the Main City though on a smaller scale [2.1]. Finally, after a further gap of 1.3 km (0.8 miles) (and ignoring for the moment the North Palace, which remained without associated housing), the North City covered a triangle of ground that rose up the lower slopes of the cliff as it swung towards the river bank [5.7].

For people in the Main City and the North and South Suburbs, it was clearly desirable to live not too far from the Nile. This must have been for access to travel and perhaps to riverside markets, as well as to a source of water that was more drinkable than the brackish water from the wells dug into the desert. Proximity to the riverbank evidently counted for more than closeness to the palaces and temples, an interesting comment in itself on the society of the time. The house of the vizier Nakht lay 1.7 km (1 mile) south of the Central City, far from Nakht's main point of contact with the king, but not far from the likely location of the riverbank.

The Alternative City

Amarna seems like the antithesis of city planning, a notable avoidance of what, to us, looks like a perfect opportunity to engineer a complete society. The city grew in two ways: by lateral expansion, spreading across the desert in a generally eastwards direction, and by the infilling of spaces left over from the initial stages of colonizing. The ground plans hint at innumerable stories of personal claims to plots of land, sometimes followed by adjustments in the face of the claims of neighbours, sometimes adversely affecting the boundaries of the larger houses. Most of those personal claims, however, are likely to have been made by people who arrived as (and remained) members of a small community: the clients, the dependants and the family relations of the officials who, in following their king, were the driving force behind the settlement of the desert. The pattern of colonization that they followed reflected an awareness not of a master plan for a city, but of a scale and shape of neighbourhoods that must have arisen from what was already familiar, an innate understanding of what worked in the existing communities from which they came. One obvious element was a common decision to maintain first one and then another wider means of access leading from the suburbs to the Central City, though neither their edges nor their general alignments were kept straight. On archaeological maps they have the modern names of East Street and West Street.

At the heart of the neighbourhoods lay the patron–client relationship outlined in Chapter 1. There, it was illustrated by the house of Panehsy and its dependent village [1.15]. This provides a template for analysing the city as a whole. It can only be a general analysis, with fuzzy boundaries and plenty of anomalies. The division into rich patrons and poor clients was not neat and absolute. The floor areas of Amarna houses, when plotted on a graph, follow a fairly even gradient of decreasing numbers of examples of ever larger houses, there being no obvious 'steps' along the gradient.[8] People were rich, poor and in between at all stages. The varied sources for the New Kingdom show that people did not passively accept their lot. Within the limits of their society, they strove to better themselves, edging ahead of their fellows and coming, in time, to build themselves a larger house.

Some heads of household, perhaps a great many, took or were given a title as a mark of status, such as Ramose, 'Unguent Preparer in the House of Meryetaten'. What status should we attach to this title? More specifically, what size of house should we put Ramose in (though he might have been an occupant of the North Palace, where Meryetaten came to live)? The example of the house U35.26 in the North Suburb illustrates the difficulty. A limestone basin found in the adjacent kitchen area was neatly inscribed with the words: 'The servant Menkheper'.[9] The excavators wondered if this was the name of the house owner, although the house is one of medium size, standing in its own enclosure, of the kind we think of as belonging to 'officials'. So could a 'servant' count as an official, or was Menkheper the servant of the house owner, whose name has been lost? The standing of a 'servant' was, to some extent, relative to who the master was, a god (the high priest Panehsy's title was 'Chief Servitor of the Aten'), king or abstract concept ('Servant of the Place of Truth' for whom the title was evidently a matter a pride).

Often the villages comprise groupings of houses that share walls, perhaps a sign that their owners belonged to a single closely knit community. Panehsy is a rare case where an obvious one-to-one relationship seems to exist between a rich-man's estate and a dependent village [1.15]. In other cases, the links between estate and village are less clear and the numbers of both do not coincide. We are not looking at an engineered society, but at one in which the strivings of thousands of individuals reflect tendencies, but not rigidly determined paths.

The following examples are attempts at applying the template – of larger estates generally lying close to dependent villages – to other parts of the city. The larger houses are identified by their catalogue numbers (and name of owner, where known). They stand in their own enclosed space, often provided with a well, a chapel for the royal cult and granaries (groups of circular constructions). Sometimes the dependent village stands beside its large house and separates it from its neighbour; sometimes several large houses form a continuous group and their dependent villages likewise form a contiguous neighbourhood.

- North City, house U25.11 [5.8]: one of the largest and most carefully laid out estates at Amarna stands opposite the monumental entrance to the North Riverside Palace. The owner is unknown. The particular interest here is that the village, of perhaps seventeen small houses, was incorporated into the planned interior of the estate, along the rear eastern side, with other larger houses filling wider spaces at the north and south ends, their owners presumably related or connected in some way to whoever it was who lived in U25.11.

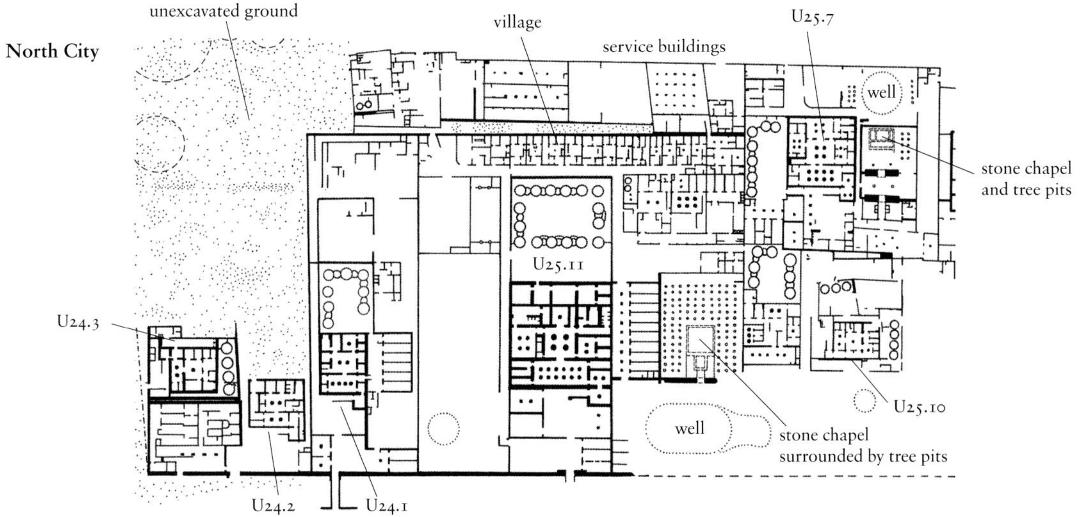

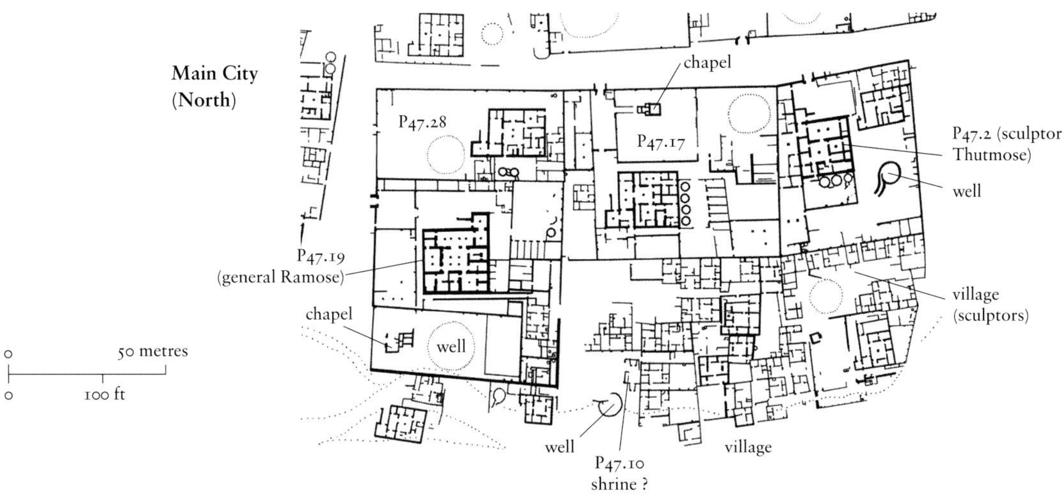

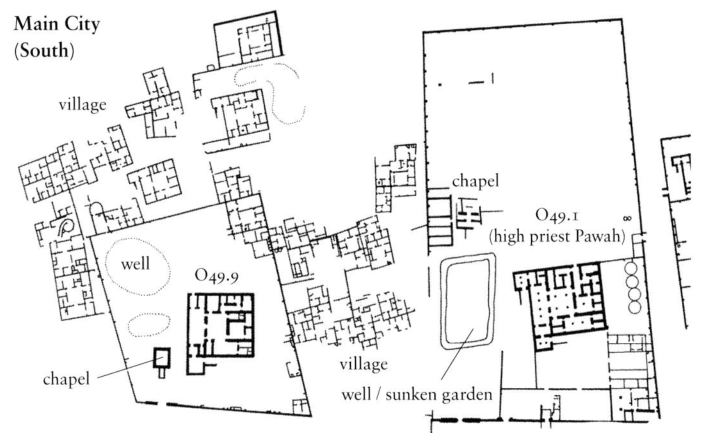

5.8, 5.9, 5.10 *Plans of three groups of houses that illustrate different relationships between the larger houses and dependent villages. Note the small building that looks like a shrine in the lower centre of the middle picture, 5.9.*

- Main City, square P47 [5.9]: four large houses have been built along two sides of a rectangular plot of ground: P47.2, P47.17, P47.28 and P47.19. The first belonged to a chief sculptor (Thutmose) and the last to an army officer (Ramose). The dependent small houses must represent at least two villages, one of them housing other sculptors, something that helps to affirm the close association between large house and dependent village.
- Main City, square O49, southeast sector [5.10]: two large houses (one of them of the high priest Pawah) must represent some of the last houses to be built in the area, for they lie on the fringes of the city. A small village lies adjacent to each.
- North Suburb, squares T36, U36 [5.11]: perhaps seven large houses lie along two sides of a square, creating a neighbourhood block. The development came late in the city's occupation. The villages, which amount to around six or seven clusters of joined houses, help to complete the other sides of the square. Had Amarna been longer occupied, in time the central space would presumably have been further built up.

Consent Rules

The people whose city we excavate and study built their houses by reference to what their neighbours or peers were doing. They had no predetermined plan to consult. The result is a classic example of self-organization or 'emergence', in which small-scale local decisions, made by a large number of people following a few simple rules of interaction, collectively and more or less spontaneously, create a complex kind of order. It is by this process that 'informal settlements' or 'squatter cities' come into being in the modern world. The big difference at Amarna was that the rich and powerful were part of the process as well. Amarna was not a shantytown of the disadvantaged.

For most people at Amarna, the basic rule was to situate your house close to those owned by people of shared standing and relationship, but beyond that, also to those more important than yourself, especially if you owed them deference. Conversely, you did not feel dismayed to live close to someone less important than yourself, if they had ties of subservience to you. This was a rule for aggregation and community-building that was valid from the bottom of the social scale upwards, until a cut-off point was reached. That cut-off point was not the king and his family, however. They followed life-rules of their own, and high officials seem to have placed little or no value on living close to them.

The cut-off point, where a different rule took over, lay with the high officials, men like Panehsy. Their rule was to select a space for their residence that was far enough away from their peers to give them a sense of personal territory, which would be rapidly colonized by those with ties of dependency upon

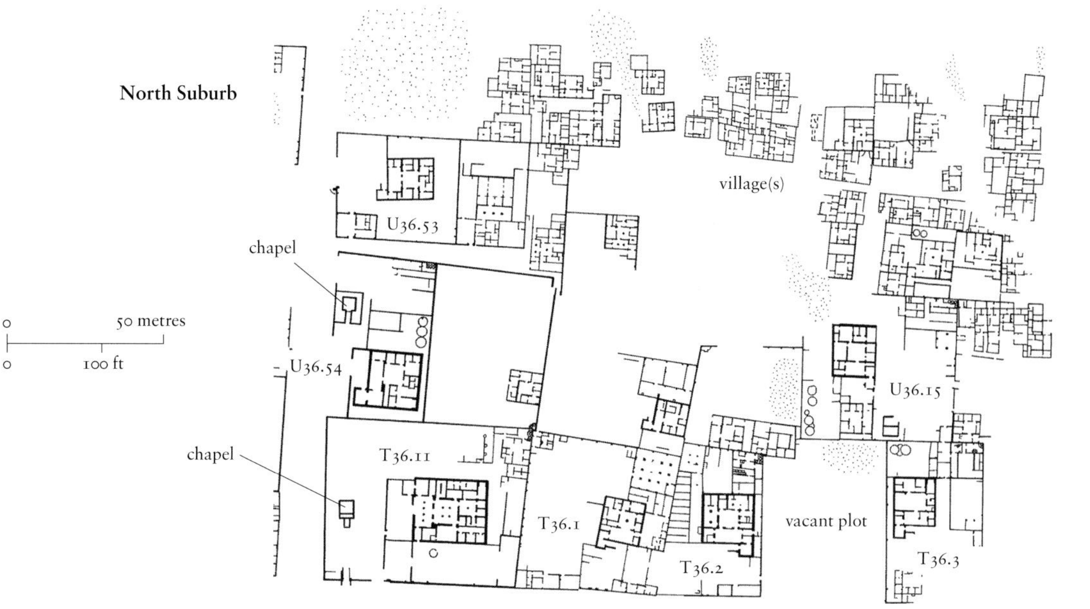

North Suburb

village(s)

U36.53

chapel

0 50 metres

0 100 ft

U36.54

U36.15

chapel

T36.11

T36.1

vacant plot

T36.2

T36.3

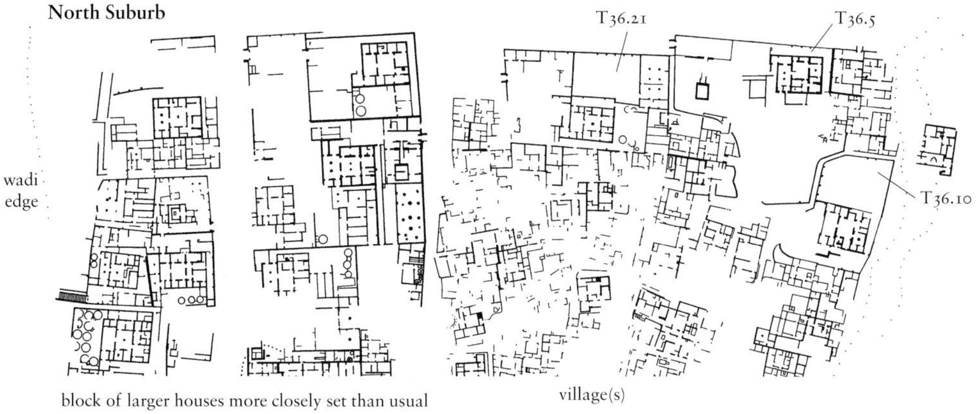

North Suburb

T36.21

T36.5

wadi edge

T36.10

block of larger houses more closely set than usual

village(s)

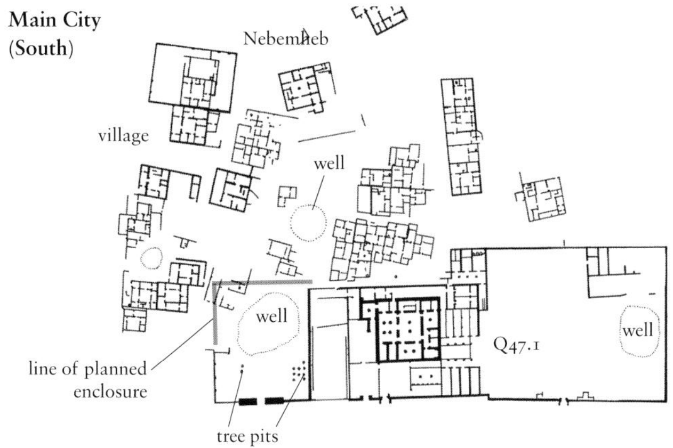

5.11, 5.12, 5.13 *Plans of three groups of houses that illustrate different relationships between the larger houses and dependent villages. In the example in the middle, 5.12, the tight packing of larger houses (on the left), for reasons unknown, has led to intense development pressure at village level, and the invasion of small houses into the grounds of the three larger houses, T36.21, T36.5, T36.10. Compare figure 8.13. (right) Another example, 5.13, of the breakdown of consent, this time in the Main City. The owner of Q47.1 lost part of his enclosure to the encroachments of poorer neighbours.*

them. They were the ones who maintained the necessary degree of dispersal, creating the spaces needed for the villages of the lesser folk. They buffered themselves by surrounding their houses with walled compounds, but otherwise accepted proximity to their dependants as the normal condition of life. Sometimes they seem to have had ties to others of similar standing, such that 'colleague groups' of large houses appeared, with a corresponding grouping of the dependent villages.

The result gave to the city a hint of blocks or islands of housing that never quite resolved itself into a proper grid. This kind of plan – the fuzzy grid – tends to appear in the modern world, in informal settlements that develop in places where government control is weak. This sounds at odds with how things were in ancient Egypt. We see pharaoh as all-powerful, but, in reality, he was so only in those areas over which he chose to exercise his power. The modern experience of political power, as something that can be applied across the board and can shape all parts of society, is not necessarily true for the more distant past. Societies have to learn, slowly, what power, beyond its most obvious manifestations, really is; how far it can reach. In the case of Amarna, designing a complete city fell outside the limits. Akhenaten's self-assembled city worked, in that it brought his officials and their support populations into reasonable proximity; and that was sufficient.

Rules of consent did not invariably prevail. Within the patterns of frozen growth that Amarna gives us, we can sometimes glimpse personal storylines that illustrate how, when restraint weakened, a free-for-all scramble for space developed. In one example, in the North Suburb [**5.12**], the story began when a few large houses (T36.10, T36.5 and T36.21) started to occupy two sides of a rectangle. The three owners evidently experienced a delay in the building work (a sign that they shared more in their lives than just neighbourliness), and a mass of village houses carved pieces out of their estates. In this part of the city, many of the larger houses were packed quite closely together (as shown in the left-hand part of the plan), perhaps creating greater pressure among dependants for space for village houses, with some owners of large houses unable to withstand invasive development around or within their estates.

In a second example [**5.13**], the owner of a large house (Q47.1) had wished for a long walled estate that included a separate walled garden with pylons fronting the street. A brick chapel was probably intended to be located on the far side of the well (or sunken garden). Before he could finish, however (did premature death intervene?), a good part of his plot had been invaded by small houses, and he lost control of the ground. This took place despite the location being on the eastern edge of the city. People evidently wanted to live in this part of Amarna, even though it was furthest from the river.

Being a senior official entitled you to great deference, and probably at all times polite and respectful speech and comportment from others. Nevertheless, it did not prevent those of lesser status from encroaching on your property when your attention was engaged elsewhere.

XV, XVI (below) Reconstruction made by F. G. Newton in 1922 of a painted 'date-palm' column from Maru-Aten (height c. 3.5 m, c. 11 ft 6 in.). The excavator C. L. Woolley commented: 'The column-capitals were in limestone, of the palm-leaf type, the surface of the leaves being cut into cloisons (as if to give the veining) which were filled with coloured paste'. (below left) Two pieces of original leaf tips from Maru-Aten, the left-hand one (obj. S-7124) plain, the right-hand one (obj. 22/346) with cloisons that were originally painted.

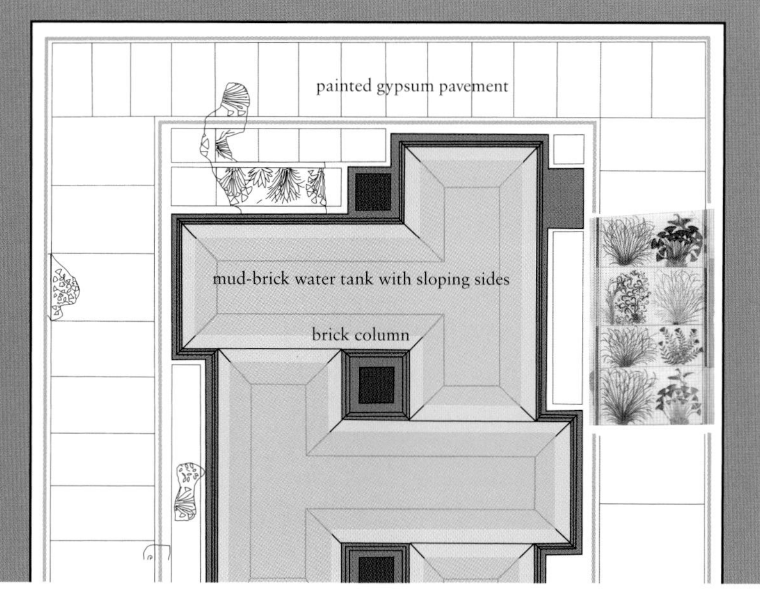

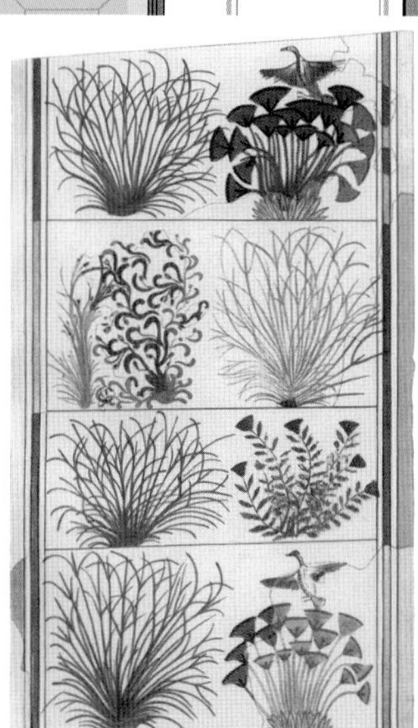

XII, XIII, XIV (top) In the northeast corner of Maru-Aten (building M I), a gypsum pavement painted with pictures of plants and waterfowl surrounded a series of interlocking T-shaped mud basins intended to be filled with water. The parapets of the basins rose 50 cm (19.7 in.) above the floors, and the basins were 1 m (39.4 in.) deep. Brick pillars must have supported a roof. (above left) Faience tile from the Great Palace with plant decoration. The daisies were made separately and fixed into their circular beds by means of gypsum. Width 11.4 cm (4.5 in.); thickness 1.3 cm (0.5 in.). (above right) F. G. Newton's watercolour copy of part of the pavement made in 1922 (width 1.8 m, 5 ft 11 in.).

XVII Isometric approximation of the North Harem of the Great Palace at the time of discovery. Elevations are derived from photographs of the 1930s. The southeastern part, dug only by Petrie, was never photographed and so heights of wall remains are estimates (shown by broken lines). The main themes of the painted gypsum floors of the throne-room complex are rendered in separate colours. See also Weatherhead, *Paintings*, 11, Fig. 11.

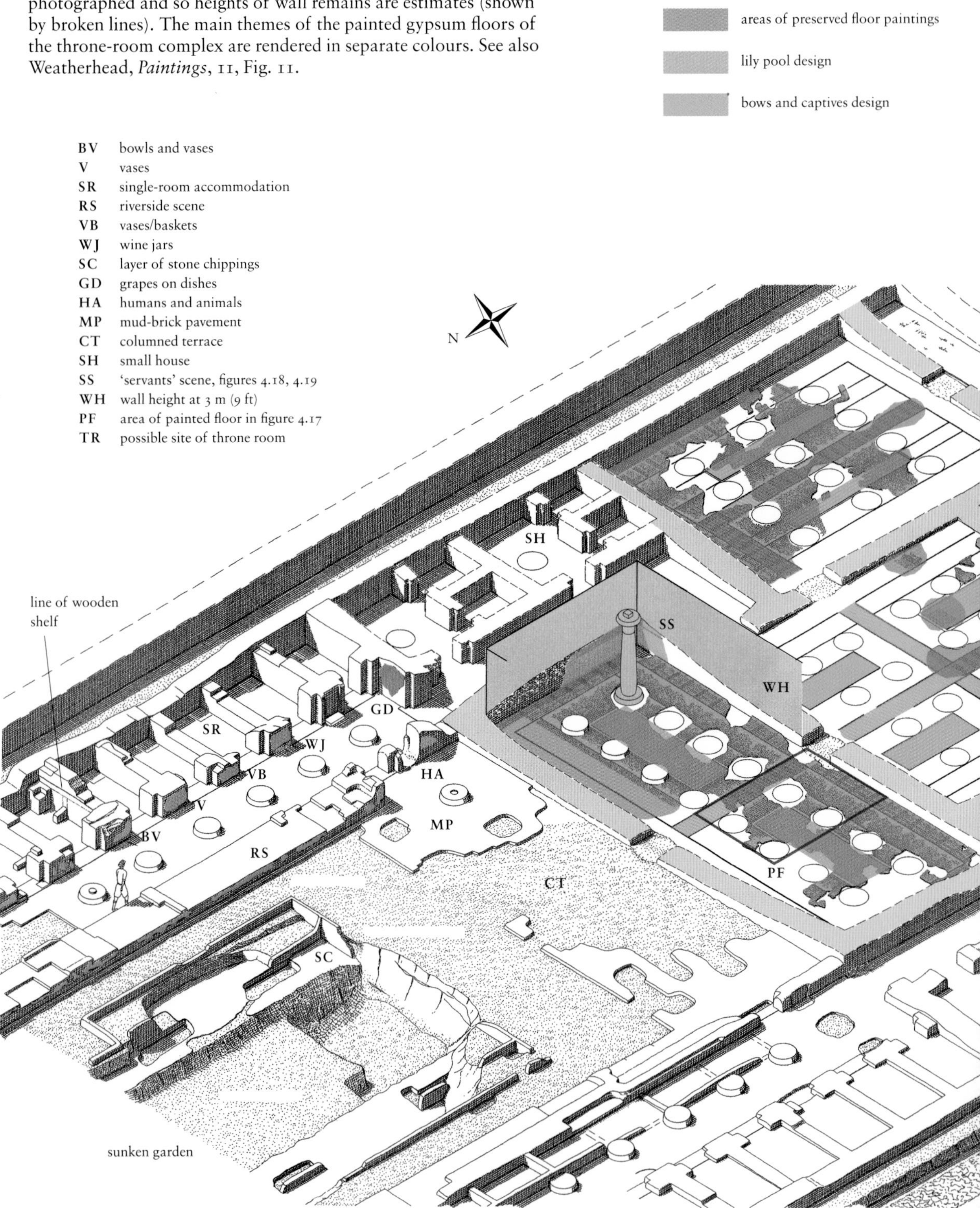

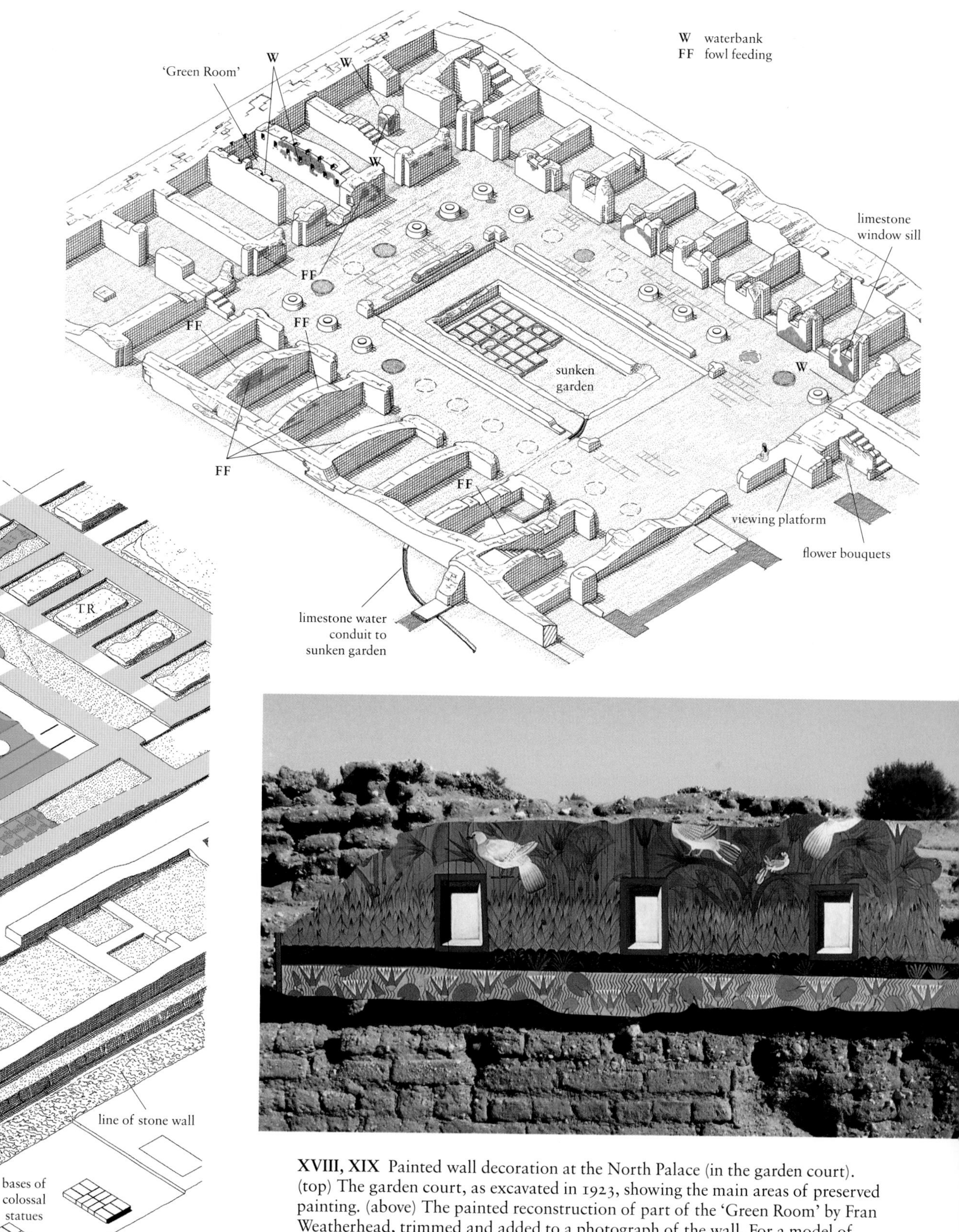

XVIII, XIX Painted wall decoration at the North Palace (in the garden court). (top) The garden court, as excavated in 1923, showing the main areas of preserved painting. (above) The painted reconstruction of part of the 'Green Room' by Fran Weatherhead, trimmed and added to a photograph of the wall. For a model of the building itself, see Pl. XXXVIII, and for some others of the paintings, Pls XXXI–XXXIII.

XX Reconstruction of the wall painting in the King's House, which included the 'Princesses Panel', now in the Ashmolean Museum, Oxford. The width of the painting is *c.* 1.63 m (5.3 ft).

XXI The 'Princesses Panel' wall painting in the King's House.

XXII, XXIII (top) Reconstructed façade of the sanctuaries at the rear of the Main Chapel at the Workmen's Village (compare figure 7.7). (above) The fragments from the winged sun-disc panel, restored by F. Weatherhead. The length of the panel is 1.77 m (5.8 ft). See *Main Chapel*, col. pl. 3.2.

XXIV (left) The busy life of palaces. Wall painting from the North Harem of the Great Palace. It shows servants preparing the building for the coming of people in chariots (presumably the king and his entourage). For its location, see Pl. XVII and, for a detail, figure 2.30.

XXV, XXVI (above) Reconstruction of the rear wall of the front reception room or transverse hall of Ranefer's house. The 'false door' on the right (detail at bottom) is based on how it must have appeared when first excavated in 1921. The reconstruction of the central double door is based, in part, upon fragments of the jambs from Ranefer's house, and on the design of the lintel from the house of Hatiay in the North Suburb (plate XXX).

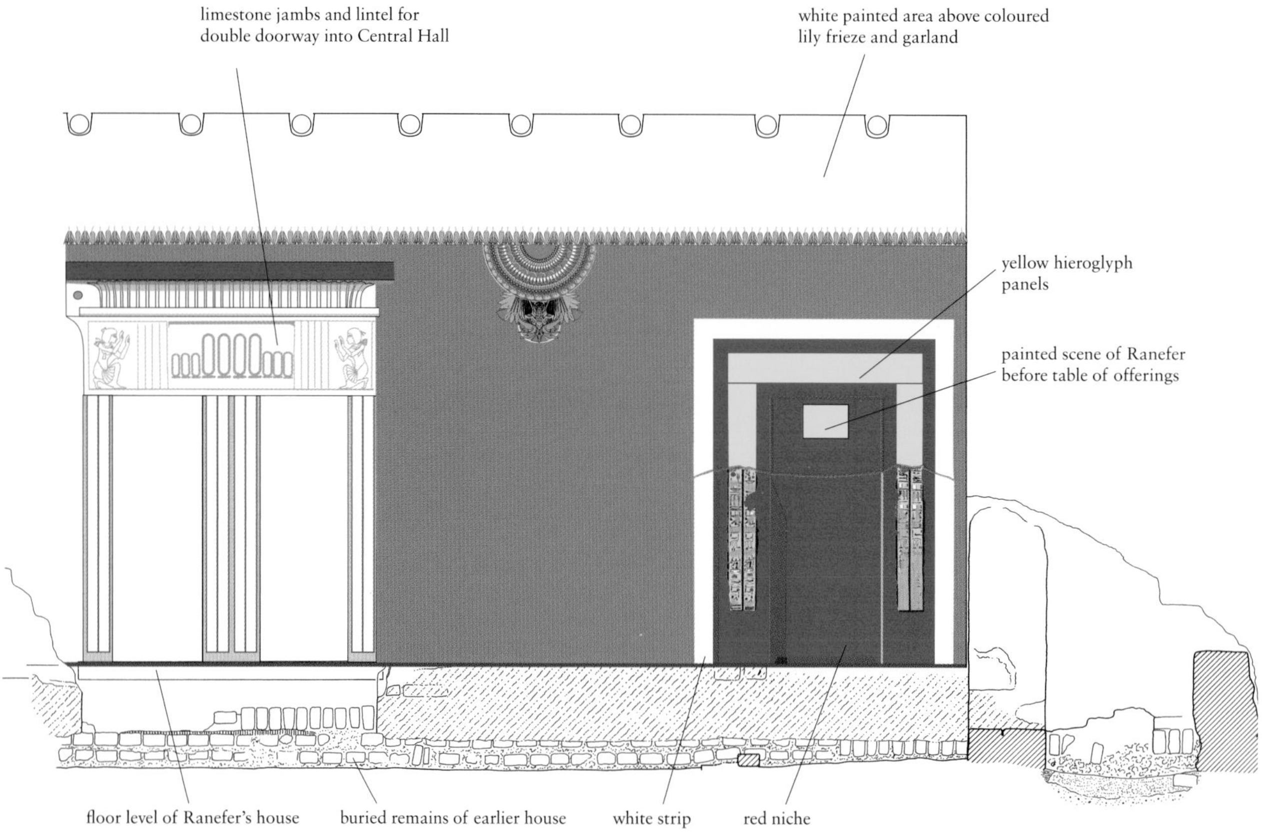

limestone jambs and lintel for double doorway into Central Hall

white painted area above coloured lily frieze and garland

yellow hieroglyph panels

painted scene of Ranefer before table of offerings

floor level of Ranefer's house

buried remains of earlier house

white strip

red niche

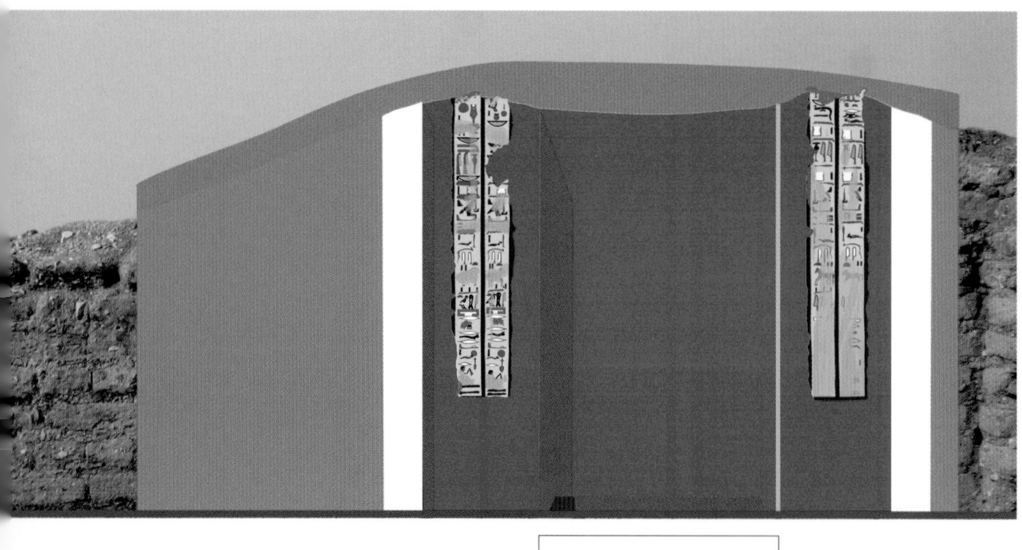

XXVII (below) The colour scheme for house interiors. The red door frame is based upon the one found in house M50.13; the red window upon those found in P46.11, and in T34.1; and the wall pattern on designs published in Frankfort, *Mural Paintings*, Pls. XVIII–XX. Some window-grilles were painted yellow, see Kemp and Stevens, *Busy Lives* I, 361–63.

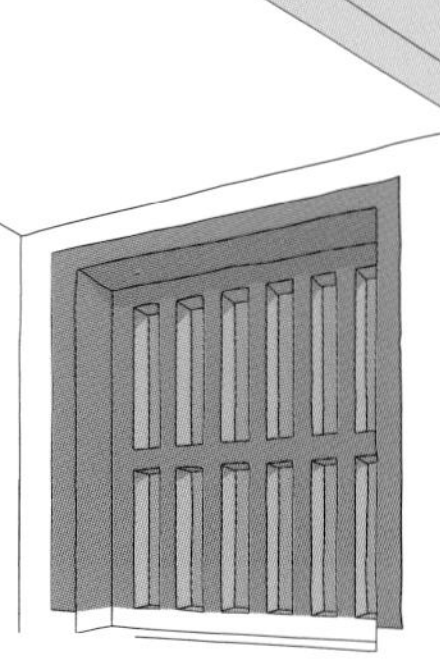

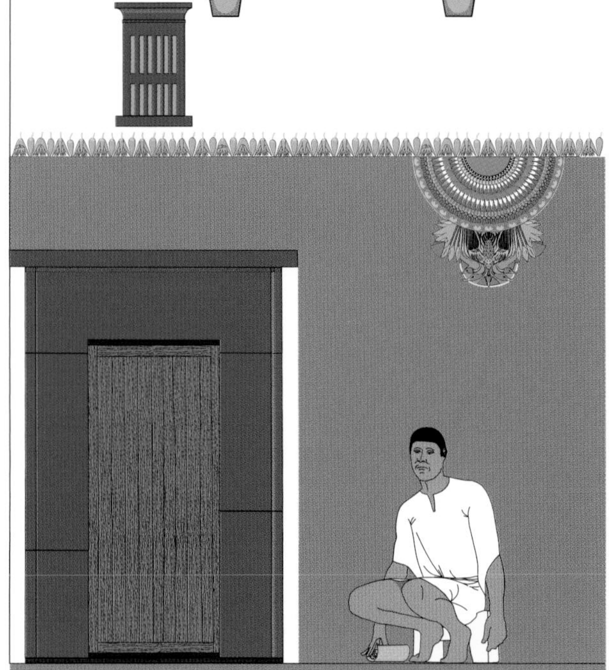

XXVIII, XXIX (above) Further choices for interior features. The source for the painted false window-grille (to the right), made from mud plaster, is Frankfort, *Mural Paintings*, Pl. XXI and the original facsimile in the EES archive. The ceiling pattern below from house V36.6, *COA* II, Pl. LVI.

XXX (below) The limestone lintel of the 'Overseer of Works, Hatiay', from his house in the North Suburb, T34.1. Now in the Egyptian Museum, Cairo. The holes in the top corners were probably for ropes securing the lintel to a wooden beam that ran into the brickwork, and stopped the top-heavy lintel from falling from its place. Mud plaster would have covered this part (see plates XXV).

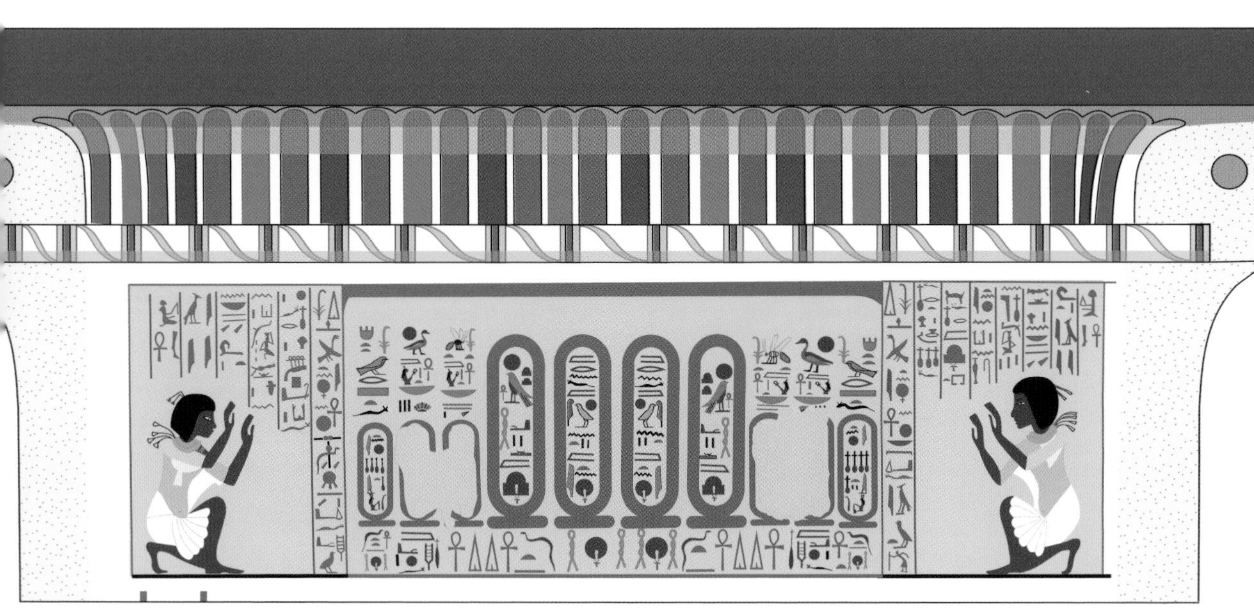

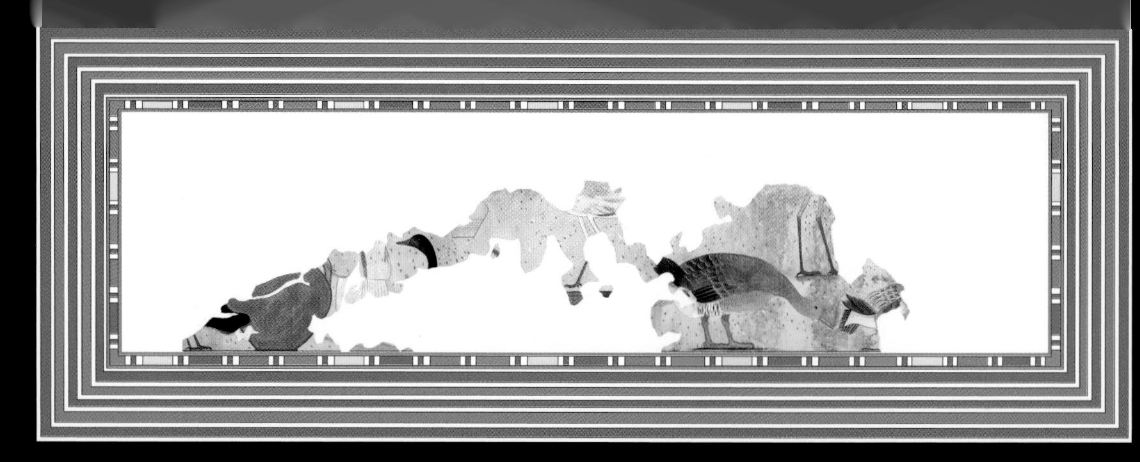

Room 7, south wall

Room 6, north wall

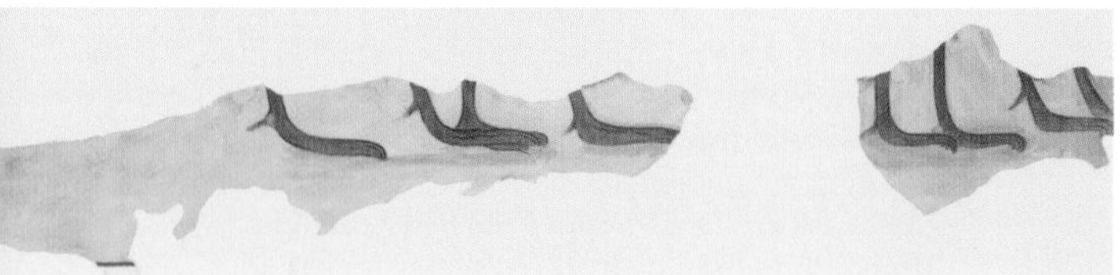

unspecified room

XXXI, XXXII, XXXIII (above and left) Wall paintings in the rooms of the garden court at the North Palace. The black surround is authentic. For their locations, see Pl. XVIII. The painted scenes are watercolour copies made by F. G. Newton at the time of excavation.

XXXIV (below) Fragments of painted wall plaster fallen from the walls of the main gateway, copied in watercolours by Hilda Pendlebury. They showed a king in his chariot, and part of the wall was painted to simulate wooden panelling. The cartouches refer to Nefertiti and to a successor king, Ankhkheperure beloved of Neferkheperure (perhaps Smenkhkare, Neferkheperure being Akhenaten).

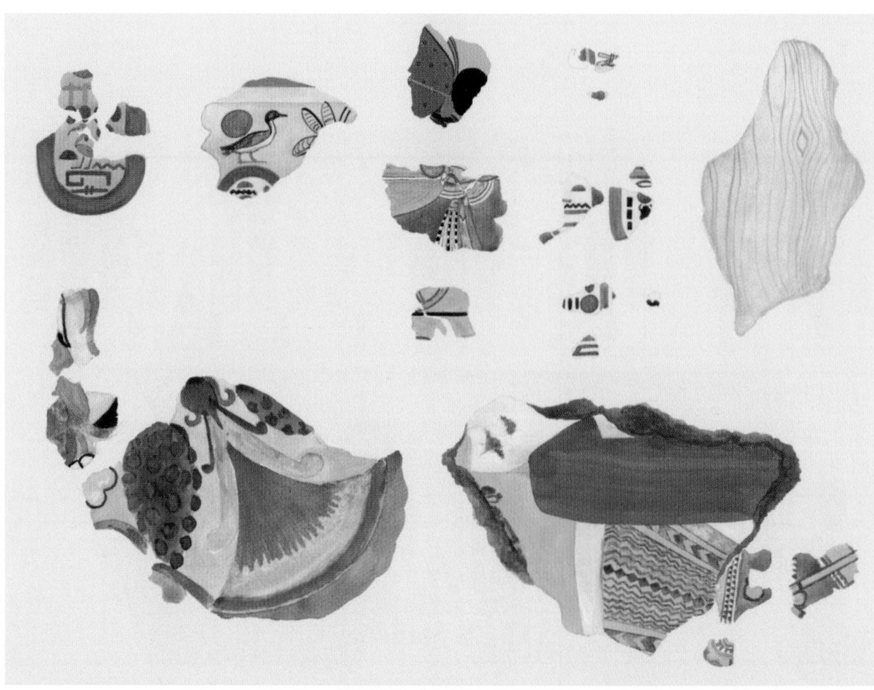

5.14 *Plan of a group of houses (part of Grid 12), excavated 2004–5, showing joins between sections of wall, and the two different brick types used. The information leads to reconstructing the order in which the houses were built.*

How it was Done

By taking a small area of housing and examining the way that individual walls abut one another, it is possible to work out roughly in what order they were built and so to follow in detail how the land was enclosed. The following example comes from an area of modest housing in the Main City with the modern designation Grid 12 [5.14–5.17].[10] The walls, having mostly lost their plaster surfaces, reveal how they were put together. They were often built in relatively short, separate lengths, either in a single line or turning at least one corner. Each length could represent the work of a builder (who might have

5.15 View of house N50.39 in Grid 12, towards the northeast.

5.16 (below) View of the Grid 12-group of houses immediately after excavation, towards the southwest.

been the house owner) in a single day. Bricks were made in small batches, in part from soil dug from the desert, and the batches varied somewhat in colour, ranging from orange-yellow to grey-brown. These distinctions also help to highlight individual wall lengths. Brick courses were not levelled other than by eye, but wall lines were normally kept straight, evidently by the use of a builder's line, a taught length of string. In this way the lines of some walls were maintained even when crossing from one independent section to another, implying co-operation and simultaneous work.

Walls were commonly the thickness of a single brick's width, thus around 16 or 17 cms (6.3 or 6.7 in.). The foundations were normally a single course laid in a shallow trench and therefore no wider than the wall it supported. When a new wall was built at right angles to an existing wall, it was abutted directly and not bonded into the existing wall. But to increase the surface area of mortar in contact with the older wall, a common practice was to begin the new wall with a short L-shaped turn that, in effect, doubled the thickness at this point of contact and presumably helped to stabilize it, at least while it was being built (just as one might find when gluing together cardboard models where some of the edges are provided with 'tabs'). Joins of this kind point to the order in which walls were built. This particular characteristic shows up even on plans made by some of the earlier archaeological expeditions at a small scale, where wall outlines have been solidly filled with black.

The excavation of Grid 12 also revealed that people used this piece of desert for a short time immediately before the houses were built. The city grew from west to east. Any open ground behind houses temporarily on the fringe of the city had its uses. It was a source of clay for making bricks, and so pits were dug out that then served as convenient places for dumping rubbish. At the eastern end of Grid 12, before it was built upon, a much larger pit had been dug that, even when filled up, left a depression in the local landscape. Although excavation has exposed an insufficient part for a positive identification, it is likely that this was a well. Eventually all the pits and their fills of earth and rubbish were buried beneath the floors of the next wave of houses to colonize the ground, the houses of our Grid 12.

None of the Grid 12 houses is of the same size or design. They do not look like the work of a single builder independent of the occupiers, (a 'speculator'

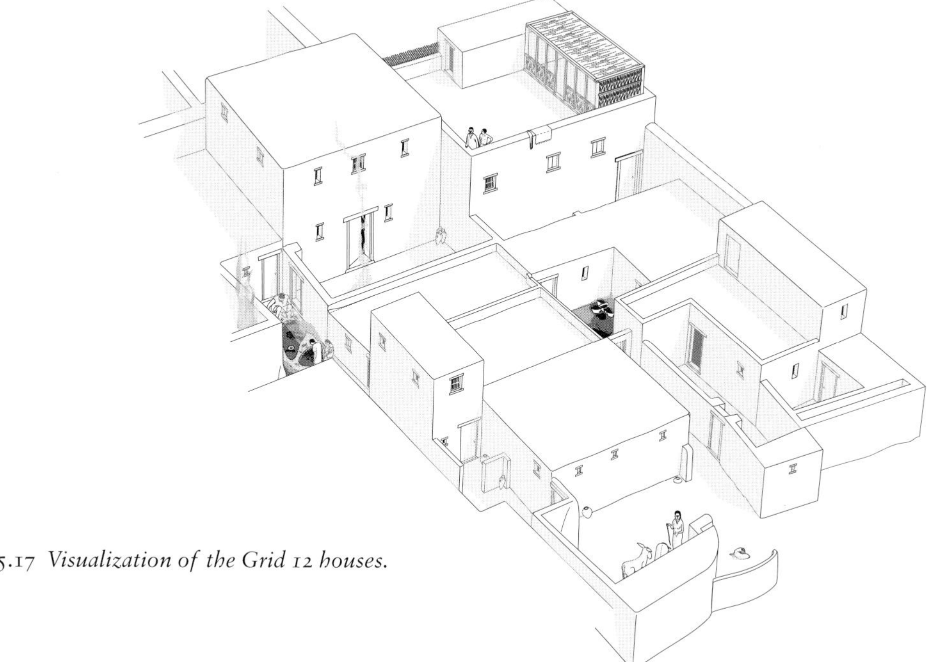

5.17 *Visualization of the Grid 12 houses.*

or contractor). Time and again, their idiosyncrasies point to decisions made on the spur of the moment by owners who were working simultaneously according to their own preferences, but also had to co-operate. The many asymmetries that are visible in the ways they were laid out represented variety of experience, the creation of surroundings unique to each family, which, on a tiny scale, became a home not quite like any other. The general impression is of an additive cellular process that maximizes the subdivision and occupation of a stretch of ground – and at the very same time minimizes the size of the individual stake through competition resolved through negotiation. It was a very efficient means of colonization.

Although houses show constant variety, that variety lay within fairly narrow limits. There was a standard Amarna house plan or template. How were those limits maintained? Part of the answer presumably lies in the largely unconscious sharing of cultural knowledge that happens because people normally experience the lives of neighbours or relatives who live at a slight distance and who are, in turn, points of contact for others, and so on, across whole tracts of inhabited land. Some people also sought to design their intended house or other building using a small-scale diagram. A few examples have survived of house (or house-like) plans drawn on sherds of pottery (with the likelihood of now-lost versions on papyrus, for which sherds tended to act as an improvised substitute; see **5.18**). No dimensions are written on them. One of the plans comes from the Central City. As we saw in the last chapter, this part of Amarna has supplied several natural rounded stones, which, inscribed with brief notations, served as markers to place on the ground to delimit building plots. A few have also come from the housing areas.[11] If stones, laid out on the ground (doubtless with much discussion), marked broad plot boundaries, then sketch plans without dimensions would have been helpful as the next stage.

5.18 *Two potsherds on which plans of buildings have been sketched (though not marked with cubit dimensions). Both were found in the Central City, at the bridge (one, perhaps both, as discarded debris in the fill of the ramps). The illustrations are taken from the excavators' record cards.*

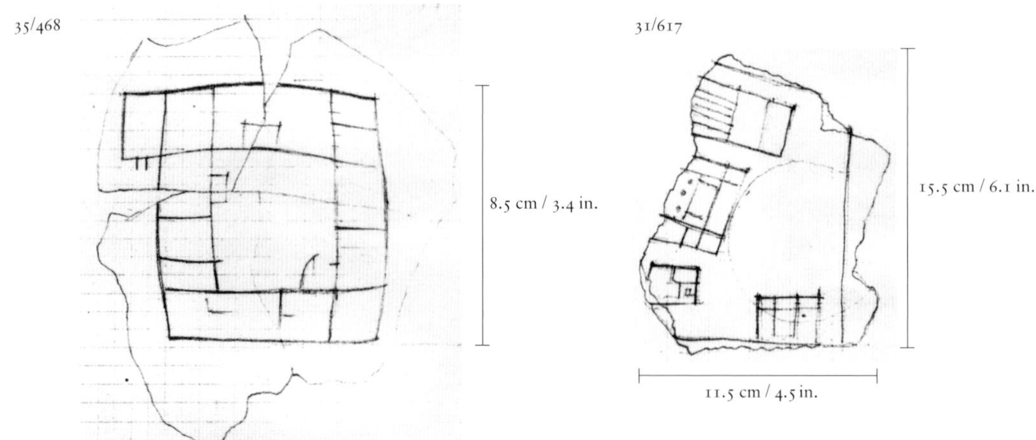

Continuing Development

The life of Amarna was short, perhaps no more than sixteen or seventeen years. In having no perimeter or predetermined design it could never be finished. It could grow, it could die, and in between it could modify itself. Growth came partly as infill of spaces that had been left in the individual neighbourhoods, and partly along the fringes of the city.

If the city had been occupied for a lot longer, the plan that we now see would have gradually changed. Mud-brick architecture does not encourage a sense of permanence. Because of the softness of the material it can be modified relatively easily, allowing houses to mirror the changing fortunes and tastes of individual families. An example is the house (N49.18) of a chariot officer named Ranefer.[12] This had been built over the foundations of a smaller house (N49.58) that was largely demolished, and probably over one or more adjacent plots as well [**5.19**]. We cannot tell if both houses had belonged to Ranefer, whose rising career had perhaps given him the means to expand his property, or only the second one, making him a wealthier newcomer who had purchased neighbouring plots to make way for his new and larger residence.

Since fragments of an inscribed door frame name not only Ranefer, but also King Ankhkheperure Nefernefruaten (Smenkhkare, the successor to Akhenaten), it is likely that Ranefer had only a short time in his new house before the exodus from the city began. Given more time, one by one the neighbouring houses would have changed, too, sometimes in innumerable small ways and sometimes through complete rebuilding, perhaps on different layouts. In this way, the city mounds of the ancient Near East – often given the Arabic name *tell*, 'mound' – came into being through hundreds of years of overbuilding. Ranefer's house represents the first step at Amarna in the formation of a *tell*, one that developed no further.

5.19 *An early sign of the transformation of Amarna (as first laid out) into a city mound in which layers of occupation are superimposed on one another. The chariot-officer Ranefer has built his new house (N49.18) over the remains of an earlier one (N49.58), raising the floor level with a layer of rubble. View, to the northwest, of Ranefer's central hall.*
1 = floor of the earlier house;
2 = floor of the later house.

The Amarna House

The Amarna house has become a textbook classic [5.20, 5.21]. Its character is most clearly illustrated by some of the larger examples, although these inevitably illustrate the lifestyle of a rich minority. This perspective is defensible because smaller houses, closer to the average, seem to represent similar though more modest aspirations.

The classic house, even if joined to other parts of its compound by walls or outbuildings, stood apart from surrounding constructions by reason of its height and the access path that directed attention towards it. Its height was determined by two factors. One was that it was built upon a solid base that raised the ground floor by around 40 to 50 cms (15.7 to 19.7 in.) above the surrounding ground level. This was advertised by an entrance stairway, which, by means of many very shallow steps, ascended to the main doorway set into a projecting vestibule. The other factor contributing to height was the existence of additional storeys. For a long time it was assumed that Amarna houses were of a single storey, except for the addition of an upper room over the front, its existence given away by the occasional finding of small column bases that did not fit the pattern of those from the ground floor and had evidently fallen from an upstairs room.

When first excavated, the walls of even the larger houses stand to no more than shoulder-height [5.22]. Everything above this level is reconstruction and thus based on imagination. A strong case can be made that much more of the ground floor of many houses than the single front room originally supposed was covered by a second storey, even a third. Thus some of the houses could have risen, tower-like, above their surroundings [5.23]. This is by no means a unanimous view, and it remains troubling to have uncertainty over something

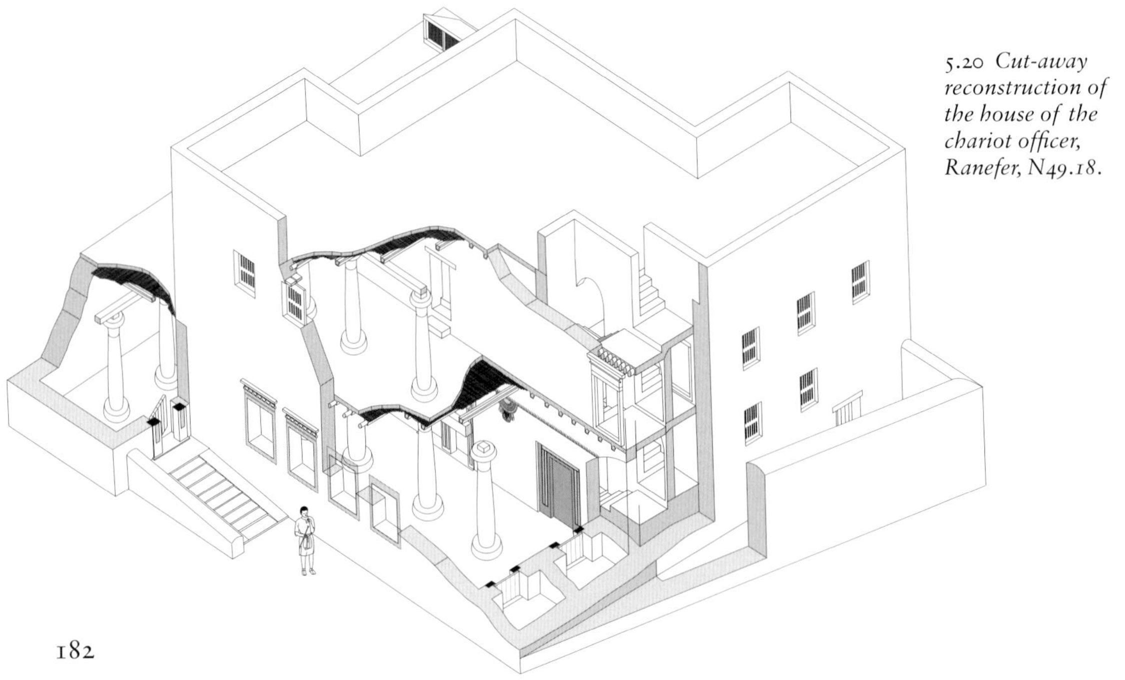

5.20 *Cut-away reconstruction of the house of the chariot officer, Ranefer, N49.18.*

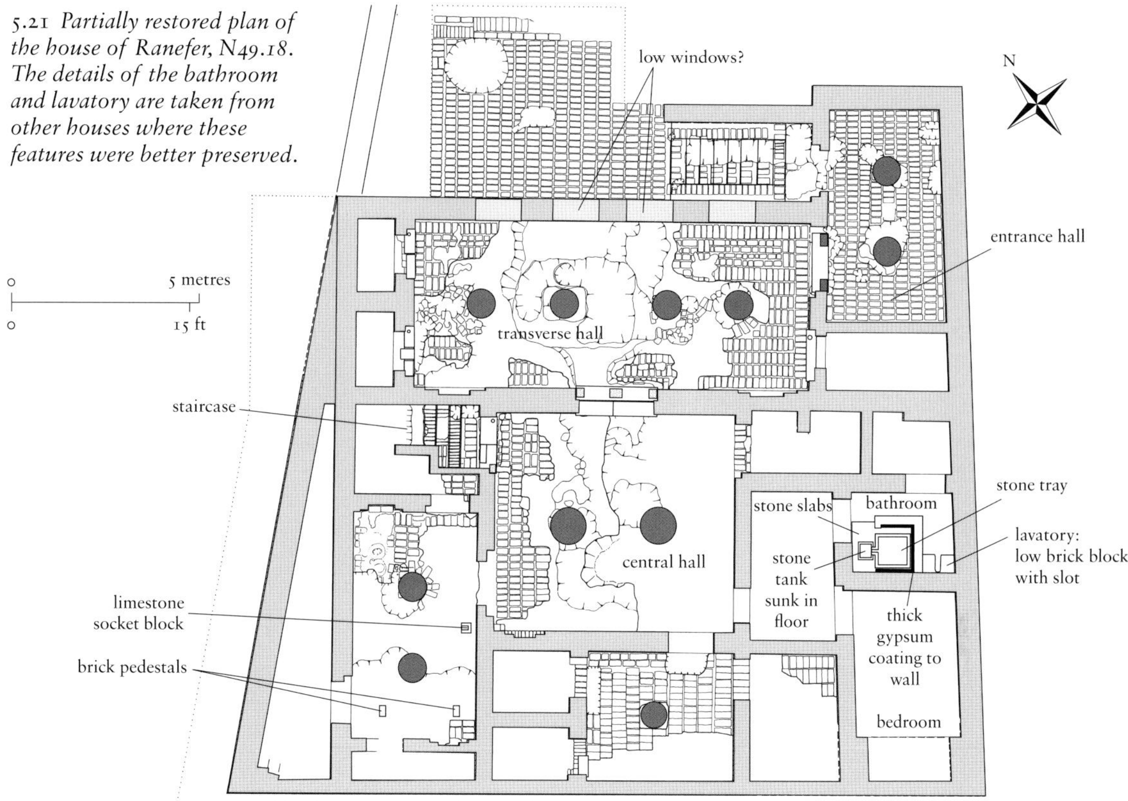

5.21 *Partially restored plan of the house of Ranefer, N49.18. The details of the bathroom and lavatory are taken from other houses where these features were better preserved.*

so fundamental.[13] Yet there is persuasive evidence (see below) that the small houses at the Workmen's Village also had an upper floor, implying that it was not a privilege of the rich [**5.24, 5.25**].

The typical ground-floor plan offered space for the reception of people from outside with space for private living behind. Towards the front came two columned rooms with signs of formality and display that showed off the owner's status. False doors (painted red, sometimes flanked with vertical yellow panels) were set into some of the walls, their positions symmetrically matching actual doors. The door that joined the outer and inner reception rooms could be of double width and was framed with heavy stone jambs and lintels that announced the name and titles of the house owner [**Pl. XXX**]. It was this doorway rather than the one at the house entrance that was, by its grandeur, intended to make its mark on the visitor. Thus the long wall of the outer reception hall was the real house façade, its other long wall serving as a protection against the elements [**Pls XXV, XXVI**].

The central columned room, and sometimes others of the inner rooms, possessed certain built-in fittings, though the digging-up of the floors of many of the houses in ancient and more recent times has deprived us of much evidence. As was the case with elements of the overall house plan, each household made individual choices in the exact placement and details of construction, which

5.22 House Q44.1 in the Main City, excavated in 1923. The name of its owner is not known. Some modern repairs have been done and the original column bases have been replaced, but the heights of the walls are almost as they were when first excavated. The fence follows the line of the enclosure wall that surrounded the house. The ruin in the mid-distance is the city house of the high priest Panehsy, R44.2 (shown in figures 1.15, 1.16).

5.23 Part of the Boston model of the city of Amarna, showing houses within the Main City.

achieved a common but not identical effect. When, on visiting another's house, you walked through the main internal door from the outer reception hall, you could not anticipate whether the low brick dais on which the owner would sit to receive you would be facing you or would be against the side wall. The owner might also have chosen to have a second dais against another wall. And the same was true for other fittings, for example the domestic altars, vertical painted niches and lustration slabs: they varied in design and placing, though they reflected a common style. Perhaps the most consistent element was the hearth, a pottery bowl for a fire set in a low brick surround – a measure against the chill of winter nights – which seems always to have been in the central room, a sign of how this room was at the heart of family life.

Beyond the reception rooms lay a separate suite that matches our expectations of how private needs should be served. Often in a corner and facing north was a room with an alcove at the back, to be identified as a bedroom (suited to the standard single bed of ancient Egypt). In one case (house V37.1)

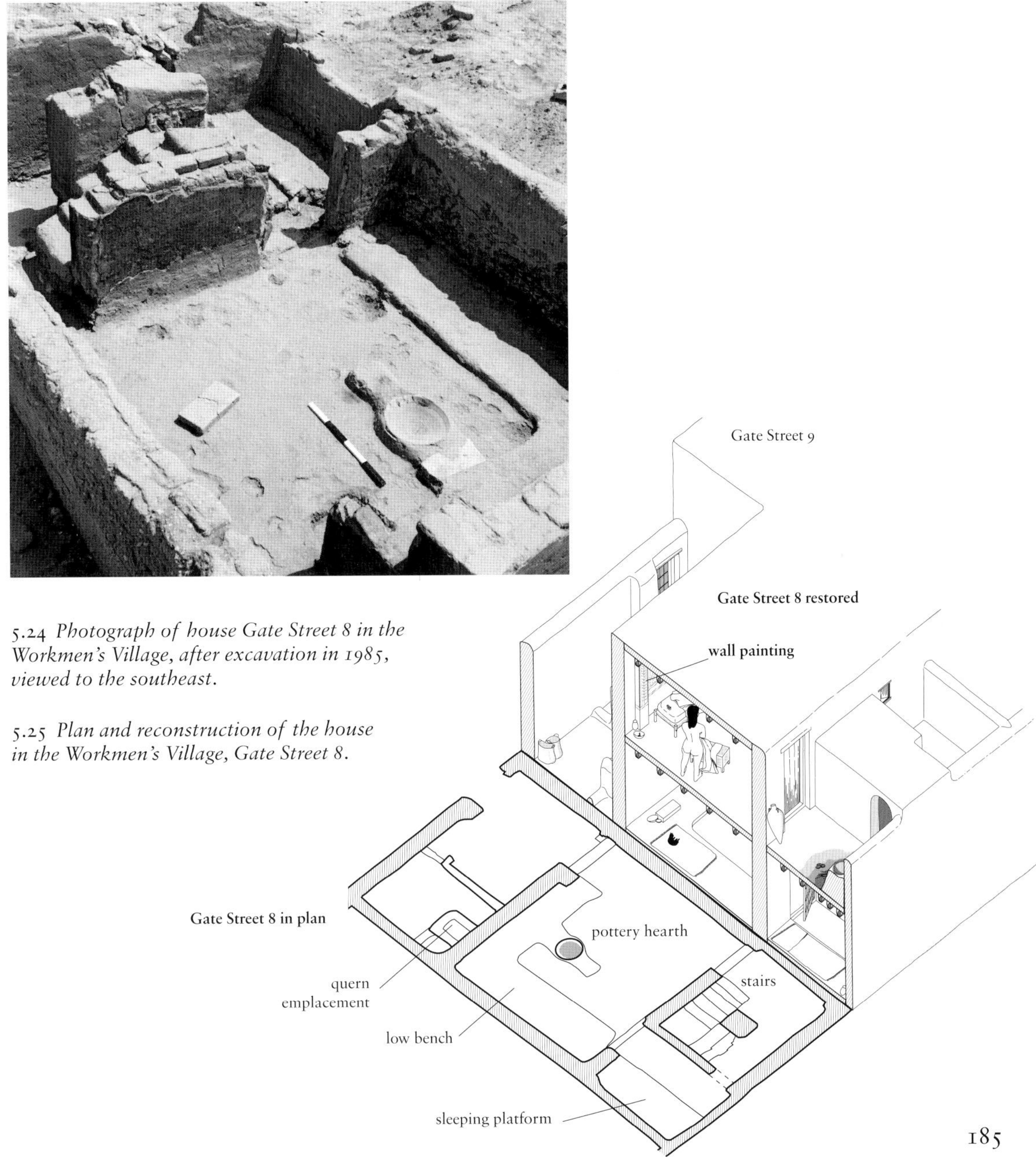

5.24 *Photograph of house Gate Street 8 in the Workmen's Village, after excavation in 1985, viewed to the southeast.*

5.25 *Plan and reconstruction of the house in the Workmen's Village, Gate Street 8.*

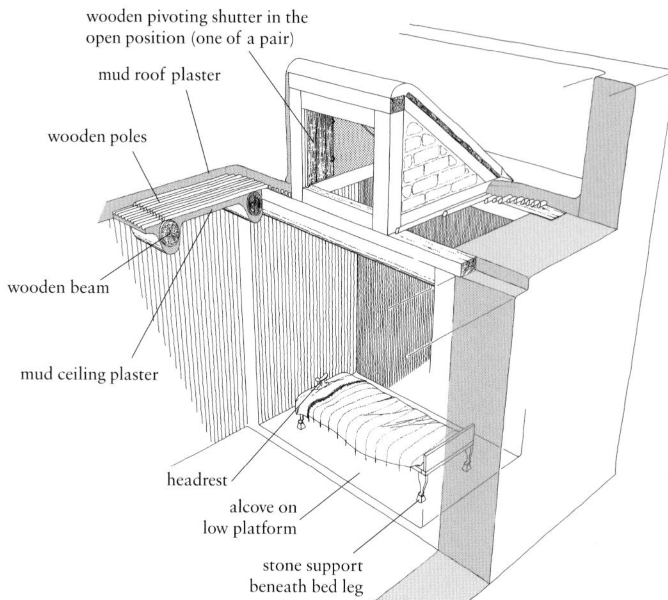

5.26 *Reconstruction of how a ventilator might have stood over a bedroom in one of the larger houses.*

5.27 *(opposite) Cattle shed with brick feeding-troughs or mangers and stone cobble floor, found at house Q44.1 in 1923, viewed to the southwest.*

the excavators found that: 'On the dais of the bedroom the four [limestone] cones which served for support for the legs of the bed were still in position', a valuable piece of confirmatory evidence [**6.6**].[14] It makes good sense to see the side thickenings of the alcove walls as serving to support a triangular wooden hood over a roof aperture that would funnel down the cool north breeze during summer [**5.26**]. Also to be found in the suite is what is self-evidently a bathroom, variously laid out with stone slabs, whitewashing and sometimes a crude external drain. A toilet might have been alongside (see Chapter 6). Some larger houses provided the owner with an inner columned room that could include a dais and small rooms fitted with supports for shelves.

What lay inside a house created the setting for lives whose components were a mix of the practical – writing or dictating letters and accounts, keeping warm in winter, gossiping and making things – and of thoughts and actions that were bound up with the Egyptians' conceptual world. By this I do not mean so much their interest in specific 'gods'; rather a view of what constituted a proper and harmonious existence, in which certain displays and forms of behaviour counted for much. Chapter 6 takes up this theme.

If the rear part of the house at ground-floor level offered sufficient privacy for the head of the household, what lay on the floors above, supposing we are right in adding floors to our reconstructions? In the nineteenth century AD, western painters and writers made their public familiar with Egypt under Ottoman rule. They were particularly intrigued by the harem (more properly written harîm) and what it stood for, the strict seclusion of women from society (as well as the idea of multiple wives and concubines). At the court of ancient Egypt it is possible to identify something that might be comparable, a 'secluded' institution for royal women that had its counterpart as a building, the palace at Medinet el-Ghurab being one example. There is, however, little or no evidence to suggest that it was imitated by people outside the royal family. Tomb paintings of the 18th Dynasty that show feasting put the guests in separate groups. Couples form one group; singles are separated into males and females. Nevertheless, they still seem to occupy adjacent spaces.

Many written sources for the period show women taking assertive roles in society, while 'love songs' written not long after the Amarna period imagine situations of unchaperoned openness between young women and men. The upstairs parts of Amarna houses offered greater seclusion, but we are not justified in thinking along the lines of a harem. The most useful tomb picture of life within a multi-storey house (the tomb of Djehutynefer at Thebes) places the male tomb owner in the prime position in all parts of the house, though being waited upon by a woman in the main part.[15] (Although one could argue that the male owner was likely to be the dominant figure everywhere.)

One constant element in the larger houses, and many that were smaller, is the exclusion of cooking and perhaps of food preparation generally. This was, for preference, done outside. It centred on one or more circular open-topped ovens set in the corner of a courtyard or a small separate building, often accompanied by emplacements for the various stages of preparing cereals for baking and brewing. For the richer households, the source of cereal grain for much of the year was a series of silos, tall tubular brick constructions with domed tops often set within their own enclosure (see **2.6**). In a few instances, they have been rebuilt as rows of parallel rectangular chambers, probably representing an increased capacity since it was within the latter kind of building that temples and other administrative bodies stored their grain.

Kitchens and silos are straightforward to identify. The house compounds at Amarna additionally contain other buildings, sometimes roofed on square brick pillars, for which we have very little evidence as to their purpose. In one case, the presence of well-preserved mangers beside a stone-cobbled floor points to cattle being housed and fed [**5.27**], presumably for a final fatten-

ing stage before slaughter, and we can suspect that other outhouses were for animals (some officials would have had chariot-horses to stable, for example). Excavation also produces evidence for widespread manufacturing, and this must have been accommodated somewhere (see Chapter 8). But for many of the parts of the house enclosures, even after a century of excavation and study, we have advanced little beyond guesswork.

Light and Colour

Imagine the collapse of an abandoned mud-brick Amarna house. Termites eat the roof timbers and whatever structural woodwork the owners left behind, such as door and window frames, perhaps even some wooden columns propping up the ceilings. Eventually the ceilings collapse. The walls might still stand for much longer. Sometimes the bricks fall piecemeal; sometimes a slab of wall will topple over and come to rest on the ground, its bricks still mortared together. Sand blows in. The rubble decomposes and the fine, light, dusty part of it blows away. The house eventually becomes a smooth low mound with a surface of sand and small pebbles. Archaeological excavation reveals what is left of the walls, but the process of digging them out naturally removes all that loose rubble and sand. The good archaeologist closely watches the rubble as it comes up, because it might contain, albeit jumbled up and fragmentary, key evidence for what originally covered or lay above the bare surviving stumps of the walls.

In 1921, the archaeologists Peet and Hayter came across a fallen slab of wall lying within the front hall of house N49.10 [**5.28, 5.29**].[16] One side of the slab had a finished surface, bearing patches of whitewash. They interpreted it as the side of a wide window in the centre of the outside wall of the house that had fallen inwards. It would have stood opposite the main doorway into the central room and so come close to making that inner doorway into the main entrance, and to giving the long front room something of the character of a veranda, or even a private version of the royal Window of Appearance. This would noticeably change the general character of the house and especially the amount of light reaching the interior. Many who have studied Amarna houses since have not accepted this interpretation, yet the evidence remains. Of course, some houses might have had openings of this kind and others not. In the end one has to keep an open mind, even on so basic a thing as this. I have incorporated similar window openings into the reconstruction of Ranefer's house [**5.20**], adding a painted cornice over each one.[17]

The finish to walls and the extent of painting is another subject where much depends upon chance and fragmentary finds. Given the quantities of gypsum that were brought to Amarna, the potential must have been there for painting the house walls white, inside and out. It would seem to be a very natural thing to do. The extent to which the people actually did this, however, is surprisingly hard to judge (even in the case of royal brick buildings). Mud-brick walls, both inside and out, were commonly coated with a mud plaster into which

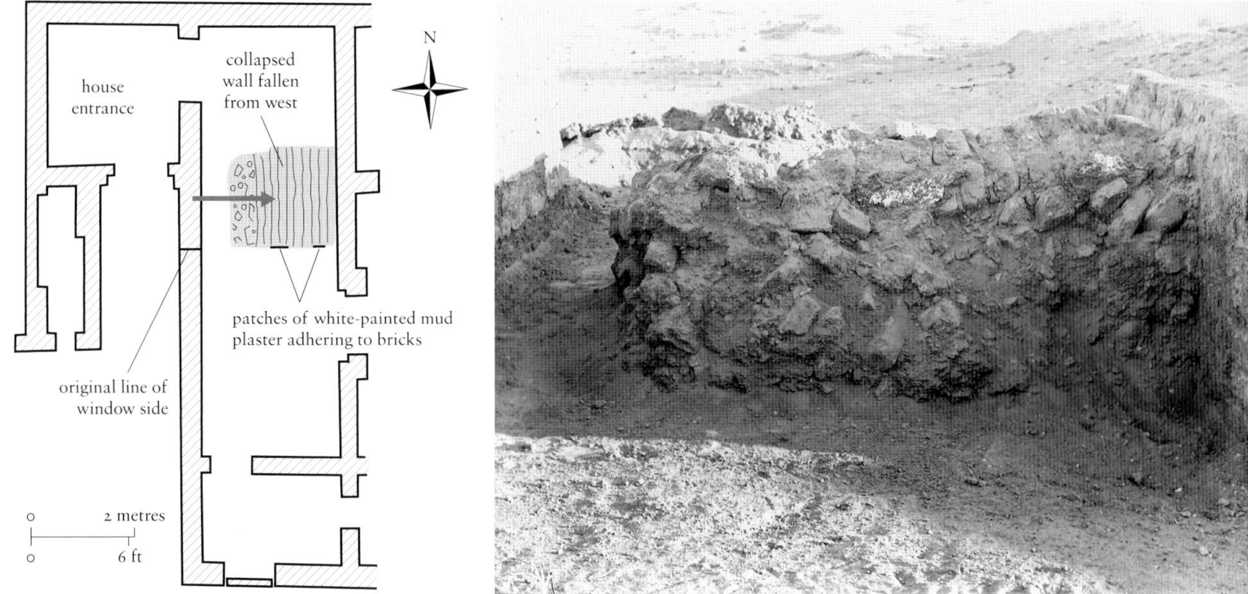

5.28, 5.29 *Evidence for large windows at the front, at house N49.10. (left) Reconstruction, built around the 1921 plan, of how the collapsed wall lay when first excavated. (right) 1921 photograph showing white plaster from the window sides on a collapsed stretch of wall.*

much plant material had been mixed. The same material could be used to coat the underside of ceilings and to spread on floors. The loss, over time, of the binding plant fibre leaves the plaster very friable and, for the most part, it has very largely vanished, leaving the bricks and mortar exposed in a way that the builders never intended.

Wall plaster preserves best at the very bottoms of walls and especially in corners. In certain buildings (chapels at the Workmen's Village, for example) a white coating over the mud plaster has survived well, suggesting widespread internal whitewashing of these buildings. This being the case, where plain mud plaster survives with no trace of whitewash we should probably conclude that the walls were never painted. This situation seems to have been quite common, even in the larger houses, pointing to an ancient acceptance of mud-coloured surfaces (which in the case of larger houses cannot be put down to a need for economy). The picture is reinforced where white has been used in limited and clearly defined places: a strip of about a hand's width beside doors, for example, or the outside of house V36.4 where a strip of whitewashed plaster about 1 m (39.4 in.) wide extended beside the entrance vestibule.[18]

What was evidently admired was contrast: patches of bright colour set off by the muted background mud colour. Red was a major contributor. In being the preferred colour for wood, it coated doors and even their stone surrounds [**Pl. XXVII**] and the surfaces of columns. (The clues are drips and smears of red paint on stone door thresholds and column bases). It was used on window grilles even when they were not made of wood [**Pls XXVIII, XXIX**], although yellow was an alternative. A bold effect on the red surfaces of some false door niches was created by a central vertical strip of yellow. Some niches were also places for small scenes of people, either the royal family or perhaps the owner of the house himself.

The principal use of colour was reserved, however, for the upper parts of walls, at least the walls of the entrance vestibule, the long front hall and the central room. The evidence comes only from fragments of decoration that survived a fall of maybe 2 m (6.6 ft) or more. The decorative motifs, mainly of leaves, flowers and wildfowl, seem generally to have been laid out on a broad frieze of white paint that joined with the general white surface of the ceiling [**Pls XXV–XXVII**]. This was supported on wooden beams and these, too, were encased in mud plaster and painted, either a uniform pinky-brown or simple block-and-line patterns in the intense colours of thickly applied mineral pigments: red, blue, yellow and green. In one house, the inter-beam spaces, instead of being white, were decorated with 'tartan' patterns crossed with a broad band filled with a line of rosettes [**Pls XXVIII, XXIX**]. The overall effect of whiteness and bright colour patches at and around the level of the ceiling is likely to have created the effect of subdued ceiling lighting.

At the top of the social scale, the large house of the vizier Nakht preserved more traces of decoration than was often the case elsewhere. Here the internal walls were actually whitewashed (with coloured friezes at the top), the ceiling of the long outer hall had been painted 'a brilliant blue' and its floor, of mud bricks, 'had originally been whitewashed, but at a later period had received a fresh coating of mud plaster and had been painted in bright colours, of which only traces of red and yellow remained'.[19] What stands out is that Nakht's decorative scheme still stopped short of figurative wall scenes of the kind found in palaces. The great divide in Egyptian society was not between rich and poor – Nakht's house, although more splendid, was still a version of the standard house – but between the royal family and everyone else.

The Outlying Villages

The discussion at the beginning of the chapter on the desert trackways introduced two isolated settlements situated on opposite sides of the low plateau that partially divides the Amarna plain, the Workmen's (or Eastern) Village and the Stone Village. They are of great importance as archaeological sites, in part because of the unusually good conditions of preservation. Moreover, their isolation has preserved the 'footprint' of the two communities; whatever they did that disturbed the ground has left some trace. The landscape in which they are set seems to convey the messages of concealment (to judge from their locations within side valleys that shut them off from view from the Main City) and confinement (evidenced by the pattern of trackways and marker lines on the desert surface, **Pl. XI**).

The Workmen's Village, in its isolation and general scale and layout, resembles the village at Thebes (Deir el-Medina), which, as we have seen, housed the workmen and craftsmen who cut and decorated the tombs in the Valley of the Kings at Thebes. One of the inhabitants of the Amarna village actually had the same title as was borne by the Deir el-Medina men, 'Servant of the Place [of Truth]', the last a circumlocution for the royal necropolis and its environs.[20] The fact that Deir el-Medina was subject to a scheme of enforced separation from the outside world, under a regime of local policing by a group called the Medjay (the same as the term used at Amarna, see above pp. 156–57), reflected the sanctity of the work done and the security fears that it engendered.

In the boundary stelae, Akhenaten promised to create tombs for himself, for Nefertiti and for their eldest daughter Meryetaten. By the time that Amarna was abandoned, Akhenaten's own burial place within the 'Royal Tomb' had been completed [**Pl. XLIII**], as had an annexe made for his daughter Meketaten (and possibly used by others of the royal family). Substantial progress had also been made on four more tombs of royal proportions: one reached by a side corridor leading off from the 'Royal Tomb' and three more in a separate valley. A start had been made on a fifth.[21] This implies significant increases in the labour force as the Amarna period progressed, with several royal tombs being created simultaneously.

What might have happened is that, to begin with, the Deir el-Medina community was transferred to Amarna and was set up in the desert to become the Workmen's Village. (To judge from the apparent absence at Deir el-Medina of faience rings bearing royal names, an Amarna period fashion, the place was abandoned during this period.) Subsequently, to accommodate an expanding workforce, the walled village was enlarged by one third by building an extra portion on the west side. Later still, as more royal tombs were begun, even more workers were recruited. Instead of installing them at the Workmen's Village, they were allowed to build their own small settlement, the one that we know as the Stone Village. Perhaps they came from a different background (were they desert miners or quarrymen?) and needed to be kept apart from the others. They certainly adapted differently to the local conditions than did the people at the Workmen's Village.

The inhabitants of the Workmen's Village lived within a fully enclosed settlement, surrounded by a plain brick wall, approximately 69 m (226.4 ft) square [**5.30, 5.31, Pl. XLII**]. A total of seventy-two houses of similar design were built along a series of parallel streets. A larger house in the southeast corner was presumably for the official in charge; the western portion of the village also contained one larger house. The village came to have a single narrow entrance (a separate entrance to the later addition was walled up). Just inside the gateway, a low rectangular pedestal could have been a shrine.

The houses were laid out as identical rectangles, subdivided into three sections from front to back, but were then built up in such a way as to suggest that each owner or family was responsible for their individual house [**5.23**].

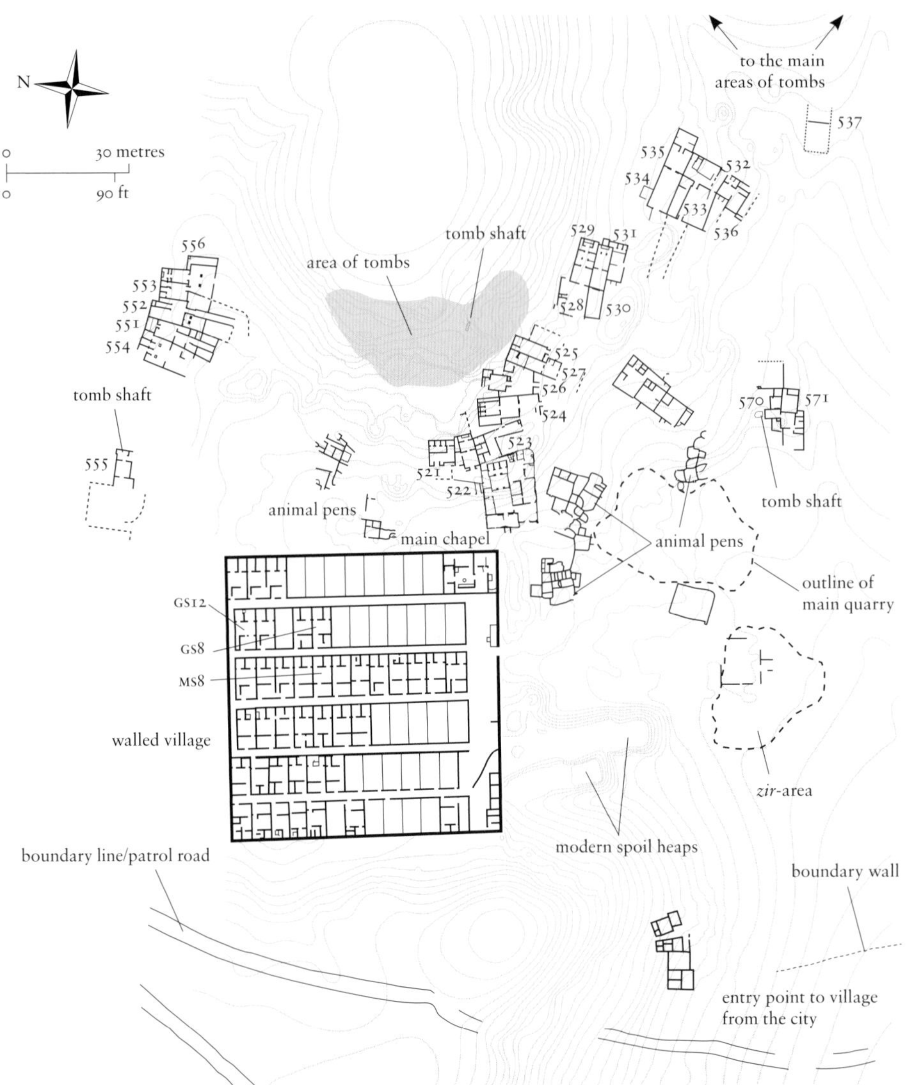

5.30 *Map of the Workmen's Village, showing its constituent parts. The numbered buildings are private chapels. The houses GS8 (Gate Street 8) and MS8 (Main Street 8) are the subjects of figures 5.24, 5.25, 6.2 and 6.3. GS12 (Gate Street 12) helps to locate the group of houses featured in figure 6.1.*

The central room resembled the central room of the standard Amarna house. Along its walls were built one or more low brick benches, and at its centre was a pottery hearth set in a low flat brick support. In terms of space in which to live, eat and sleep, this central room amounted to almost all there was at ground level, apart perhaps from a single small room leading off towards the rear. This was used in part for storage – in a few cases thin brick walls might have been for supporting shelves – but could also have offered a place of privacy. The remainder of the ground floor seems to have been given over to the kind of activities that, in the main city, people preferred to place further away from the domestic centre, either in outer rooms or in a courtyard. One of the spaces at the rear commonly contained the kitchen, while the front 'room' seems to have been a working-place, where there might be situated the equipment needed for milling grain and perhaps the large vertical linen looms in use at this time, and also a place where small food animals could be kept. We cannot even be sure if all these front rooms were roofed. On the other hand, perhaps because it was the most public part, one or more of the walls of this front area were thought suitable for simple painted panels that celebrated household spirits (see Chapter 7).

The lack of living-space in what seem to be poor and constricted dwellings was alleviated by the building of a second storey reached by the narrow staircase. Among the archaeological evidence pointing in this direction is a mass of painted wall plaster in one house (Main Street 9) that had fallen when the downstairs rooms were already part filled with debris, some of it from a fallen roof. It had come from 'a panel in which there was an inscription in black on a yellow ground and a polychrome design with a human figure', apparently bordered by a pilaster painted with a tall and narrow plant motif.[22] This is rare evidence for decoration in an upstairs room.

The walled village with its regimented houses that filled most of the available space is a good example of a settlement made by government order and represents a well-established tradition in ancient Egypt. The villagers themselves, however, had needs that could not be accommodated within this strict framework. They looked to the ground outside and seem to have been allowed to develop it as they wished, as long as they remained within the limits of the perimeter roads.[23]

5.31 *Aerial photograph of the Workmen's Village, viewed to the south, in 1993. The ancient trackways on the desert in the foreground are particularly clear.*

The village faced south, directly into the sun and the scorching sandstorms of the early summer. Beyond the narrow gateway lay the floor of a short valley into which large pits had been dug to extract the soft crumbly marl from which most of the bricks had been made. This same area, including the pits, became the principal dumping ground for the village rubbish. The valley ended on the west with a steep rounded headland that hid the main city from view. The main path from the city approached the village around the headland and led directly to a space floored with mud that supported numerous water jars (Arabic *zir*) set in piles of mortared boulders. Given the careful attempts at isolating the village, it can be interpreted as an interchange place where water was brought by carriers who were to be discouraged from approaching the village more closely.

The villagers' territory included the slopes of the eastern, opposite headland and the flat top of the eastern hill itself. On the top and, to a lesser extent, on the slopes, the villagers made their tombs. These have never been properly investigated. Their presence, however, explains why a row of painted brick chapels was built along the slopes. They served as places for family commemoration of ancestors in a setting that honoured traditional deities and mostly ignored the cult of the Aten. They will be discussed in Chapter 7. Although they form a 'ritual zone', emphasized by an approach pathway of tiny T-shaped basins cut into the ground, they overlapped with the rubbish area and also with a series of little brick complexes that were purpose-built for the raising of pigs [**8.21**]. These represent a substantial investment of effort, both in the building and in the rearing of an animal with a high requirement for water, which had to be brought from the city, 1.25 km (0.8 miles) away. The Workmen's Village makes a valuable contribution to the debate about where the boundary lay between state control and self-sufficiency, one of the subjects of Chapter 8.

The Stone Village is a smaller settlement and its surrounding 'territory' is also much less.[24] It seems not to have had an enclosure wall of greater thickness than is represented by the rear walls of the few buildings so far exposed [**5.4**, **5.32**]. These buildings probably offered accommodation, but space was also taken up by groups of ovens and heaps of ash. An important discovery has been of a small group of carefully cut chamber-tombs, which suggest the presence of a community that felt a sense of permanence. One interpretation of this village, already mentioned, is that it housed an expansion of the original community – one that came from a different background – which had to be kept separate and adapted differently and more modestly to the desert locale.

Missing Experiences

Amarna houses will have had many intangible attributes that elude direct recovery. Egyptian lives were shadowed by the existence of a parallel world of spirit forces that constantly threatened illness, misfortune and death. The house as the centre of personal life needed spiritual protection. Moreover, although we know little about the rituals of social life – we have no specific evidence for a

5.32 *View of the Stone Village, to the west, at the end of excavations in 2008.*

ceremony of marriage at any point in Egypian history, for example – it is to be expected that they existed and that in part they happened in the house. Within the house the senior figures were formally honoured (and in time became the similarly honoured ancestors) and the dead were probably laid out briefly (when, as was the norm, mummification was not intended) pending burial. Parts of the house are thus likely to have had associations that extended beyond the mundane, not necessarily to be invoked all the time, but perhaps on special occasions. These spiritual aspects will be discussed in Chapter 7.

Further beyond the limits of academic research is a whole range of lost experiences: the smokiness of house interiors in the winter, mingling with the smell of incense and, at different times in the year, of lily blossoms, in turn competing with the pungent smells of human waste. The experience of night when the city was hardly ever fully dark, but lay faintly visible in shades of silver-grey from the light of stars in a clear sky, but never silent, for night was the time of barking dogs, sometimes those on the city fringes developing an unearthly dialogue with the jackals and hyenas of the desert. Firelight visible through cracks in house doors; the arousal of a young man on seeing a neighbour's daughter; the grief of constant bereavements. Although archaeology can only deal with the material debris of life, we should not forget that the places we study were once lived in by real people.

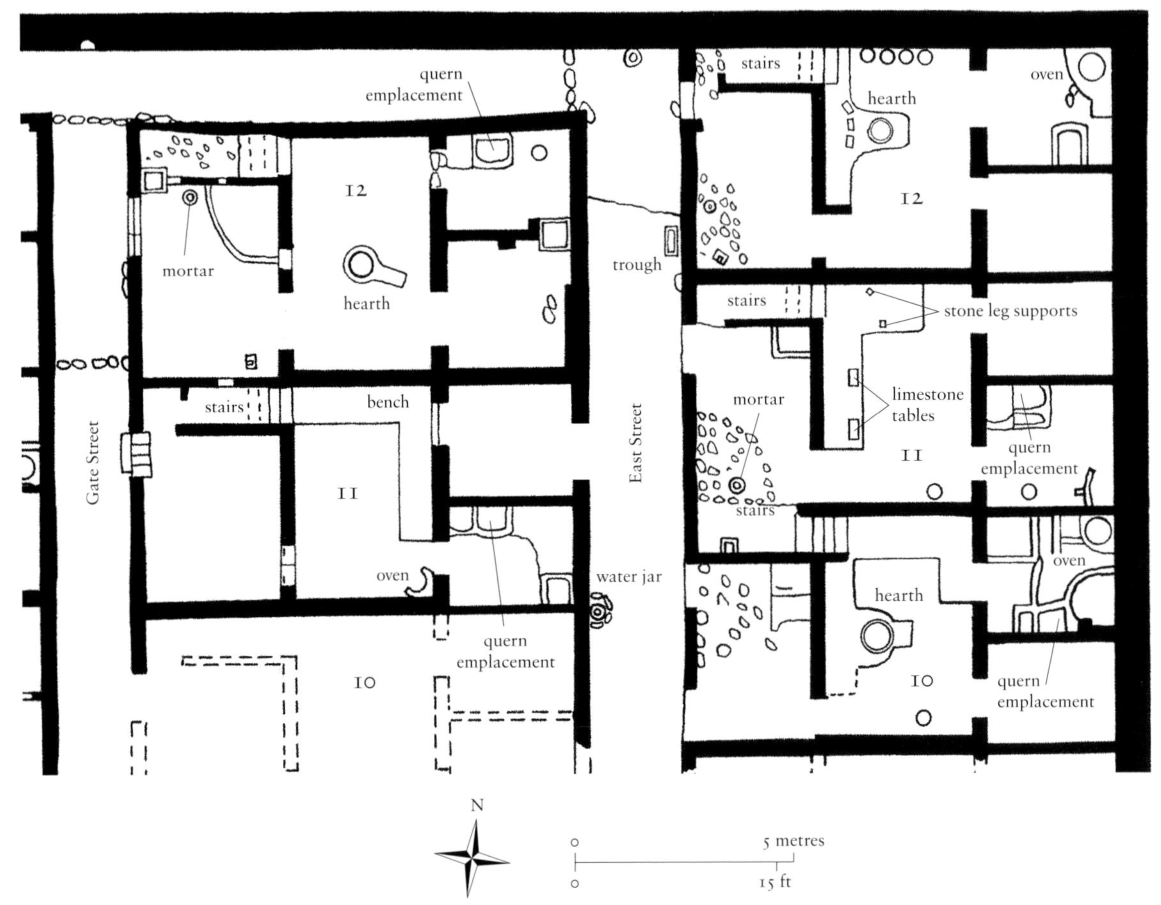

6.1 *Plan of the northeast corner of the Workmen's Village, one of the least disturbed parts of Amarna. For the location of the houses, see figure 5.30.*

CHAPTER SIX

THE QUALITY OF LIFE

Life from Objects

Amarna the city speaks to us mainly through the ground plans of its excavated buildings. Even though the houses are ruined and sometimes no more than foundations, we can, when working with ground plans, be fairly sure that we have a relatively complete outline of what was once present. Some information will be missing, especially if the buildings rose to more than one storey, but ground plans do supply a kind of basic currency of description. They offer a snapshot of life that requires relatively little commentary. Houses were also provided with 'fittings', minor elements constructed from mud brick or made of stone, and these, if they survive, can help us to understand how the different parts of houses were used [**6.1**].

With portable objects that were left inside and around the buildings, however, the picture is different. The evidence has widely differing characteristics and generally requires far more study to extract meaning. As a result, much more has been written about the architecture than the objects. Some of the difficulties are intrinsic to the material itself. Whole categories were simply too precious to their owners to throw away or leave behind, and some materials, even if abandoned, had poorer chances of long-term preservation. The excavated record of artifacts is therefore far more fragmentary, and heavily biased towards certain kinds of things. For example, because pottery was cheap, disposable and resistant to decay it has survived in huge quantities, sufficient to make us believe that, from studying large samples, we can derive conclusions about matters of trade and domestic economy that are fairly reliable.

Bronze, however, was valuable even as pieces of scrap. People did not throw bronze items away. Excavation at Amarna has produced sufficient bronze articles to show the range of things that were made in this material (e.g. **3.19–3.21**), but it will never be possible to know if one kind was more common than another, or if certain utensils were more likely to occur in kitchens or bakeries or temples than others. In the case of wood, papyrus and textiles, the basic material is itself subject to destruction through environmental factors, especially the eating habits of colonies of white ants or termites that live along the desert margins in Egypt. Thus at the Workmen's Village, far enough into the desert to be less affected, wood was the commonest material of the spindle whorls used in the making of yarn for textiles. In the main city, however, most of the spindle whorls found are of stone, but this is only because termites must have eaten nearly all of the wooden ones and, in the process, have probably destroyed the bulk of examples.

Archaeological practice has also had an effect. Excavators in the first decades of the twentieth century, funded by private donors or museums, tended to be very selective in what they kept and recorded, and even more selective in what they found space for in their publications. Whole categories of objects – especially various kinds of stone tools and pieces of industrial waste – were largely ignored. The parsimony of their attention paid them dividends. They were able to cover large tracts of ground fairly quickly and so increase their chances of major discoveries. That will not do any more. By following acceptable modern practice and adopting the simple combination of passing all the dirt through a sieve and of keeping everything that was manufactured (apart from bricks), the number of finds seems to have increased by at least one hundredfold over the rate of recovery of the earlier days, with a consequent major change in the pace and character of the archaeological work as a whole. If one counts potsherds as 'finds' the total has to be multiplied several times more, and beyond 'finds' lie other categories of potentially useful material, such as plant remains (including charcoal fragments), animal bones, organic jar residues, the waste products of manufacturing and the remnants of insects. They all have a tale to tell, a contribution to make to a fuller picture of life at Amarna.

Modern archaeology exchanges the broad view for the intensely detailed, and at the same time expects more to be done with the material found than dismissing it with brief and incomplete listings. At Amarna, any attempt at serious analysis of what has been found has to accept that much of what earlier archaeologists recovered is still not properly documented, and that certain categories of material are still lying in their old spoil heaps. These are a stable part of the landscape, and modern archaeology will gradually address them (for an example, see **4.5**).

The various categories of archaeological material open up innumerable pathways for study. One possibility is to track how they are distributed across the site with a view to explaining why they are evenly spread or not; another, related possibility is to seek the geographic origin of a class of material and thus its source, an aspect of trade and other forms of supply. The close examination of objects, of tools and of waste products serves the history of technology, how things were made.

The most elusive aspect of objects, however, is how they contributed to the texture of ancient life. From the time of waking in the morning until sleeping at night the occupants of our Amarna houses constantly brushed, physically and metaphorically, against all these material things. How objects were experienced could be their most important aspect, yet it lies outside the field of scientific enquiry, being available only through imaginative insight and the dangerous lens of empathy: the varied weights of pots and the touch of their often rough surfaces; the slight tastes they must have imparted to the liquids they held; the feel of linen of different qualities on the skin and the unthinking habits that came with wearing it with dignity, loosely draped and fastened by knots. And the judgments! On visiting a house that was not your own, what would you pick out as significant, which might mark that person as richer or poorer, or well connected to the court, or lacking in taste and perhaps indicative of humble or even foreign origins?

These are physical sensations and social cares, and much of this chapter is devoted to the range of things that will have shaped the outward experience of living at Amarna, albeit elements common to ancient Egyptians of all periods and elsewhere. But as explored in the next chapter, in Egyptian eyes the house and the neighbourhood and the world beyond will have had spiritual resonance as well, in which material objects had their place.

Living the Low Life

No matter what the plan of a building, furnishings profoundly influence how people see and use it. In our own homes, the arrangement of tables and chairs, fireplaces and television sets and the placement and design of rugs give a room its character. Furnishings are, however, a category of evidence often missing from archaeological sites. The ground plans of Amarna houses tell only a part of the story of how space was sub-divided.

The portion of an Amarna house most amenable to study from this point of view is the central hall. Two common features create an internal orientation from the sides of the room facing towards a central focus. That focus was commonly the hearth made from a broad pottery bowl sunk into a low mud surround [**6.2**, **6.3**]. In many of the smaller houses (including those in the Workmen's Village) a low bench, the height of a single brick, ran along one or two of the walls, and people sat or squatted on this, facing towards the room centre. In the larger houses, the bench was single, either on the wall facing the main entrance or on one at right angles. These are, of course, built-in fixtures. The placings of mats, wooden tables, stools and chests, pots in stands, even cushions, all of which we know existed, are, by and large, lost to us.

Here we also encounter a dividing line in the history of personal behaviour, a difference in height in the horizon of reach. When inside a building, I am most comfortable with a set of surfaces that are between about 70 and 180 cm (27.6 and 70.9 in.) above floor level, the latter being items on shelves, including those towards the top of a large refrigerator and coats on hangers in a wardrobe. Things that are below about 70 cm (27.6 in.) require stooping and reaching down, bringing slight discomfort because I am not so used to it. In an Amarna house, the horizon of reach was lower [**6.4**], from close to floor level up to around 50 cm (19.7 in.) (wooden tables, the height of wooden storage chests), because people were at ease when squatting and kneeling. A valuable pointer to the range of reaching-height is given by the domestic altars, places where you displayed, probably only from time to time, items charged with special meaning [**7.16**]. They were often close to the floor.

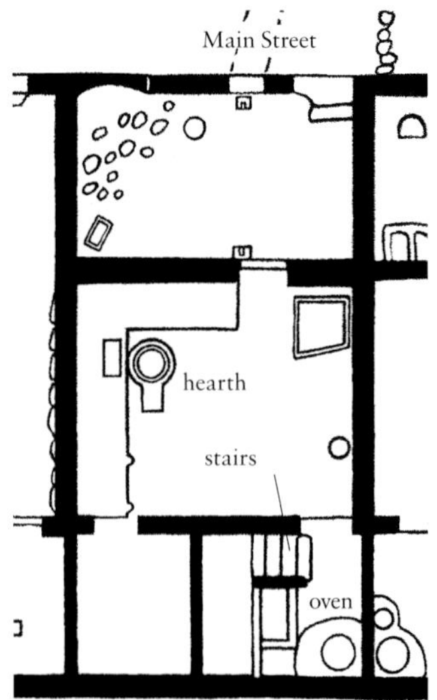

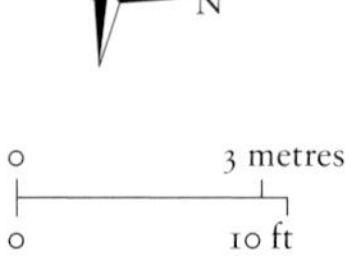

6.2, 6.3 (left) Plan of one of the houses at the Workmen's Village, Main Street, house 8. Compare figure 5.30. (right) View of the central living-room of the same house at the time of excavation in 1922, with a workman posing as one of the original occupants.

6.4 (below) At home in Amarna, mostly close to the ground. A series of ancient pictures showing Amarna people. From left to right: palace women tending their hair (tomb of Ay, no. 25); man warming his hands over a charcoal hearth (tomb of Mahu, no. 9); girl taking a snack in the palace (tomb of Ay, no. 25); two men, seated on wooden chairs, being waited upon by two women (design on a small stela from the city house of Panehsy, R44.2); female musicians in the palace (tomb of Ay, no. 25).

How people rest their bodies (when not actually sleeping) is an important cultural marker. The way that Egyptians wanted to be remembered – husbands and wives as well as kings – was, if not standing or striding, sitting on a chair that was roughly calf height. Two statuettes from Amarna depict men seated (in one case on a wooden chair with a back) holding the stem of a lily flower to their chest [**7.17**]. Fragments of chairs have sometimes been found. Nonetheless, squatting on the floor was not necessarily a less dignified alternative. Senior officials still had statues of themselves made in the posture of the squatting scribe [**7.6**], and this is how the gods of the Otherworld assembled when judging the dead, seated on a mat that was itself a symbol of authority in this context.

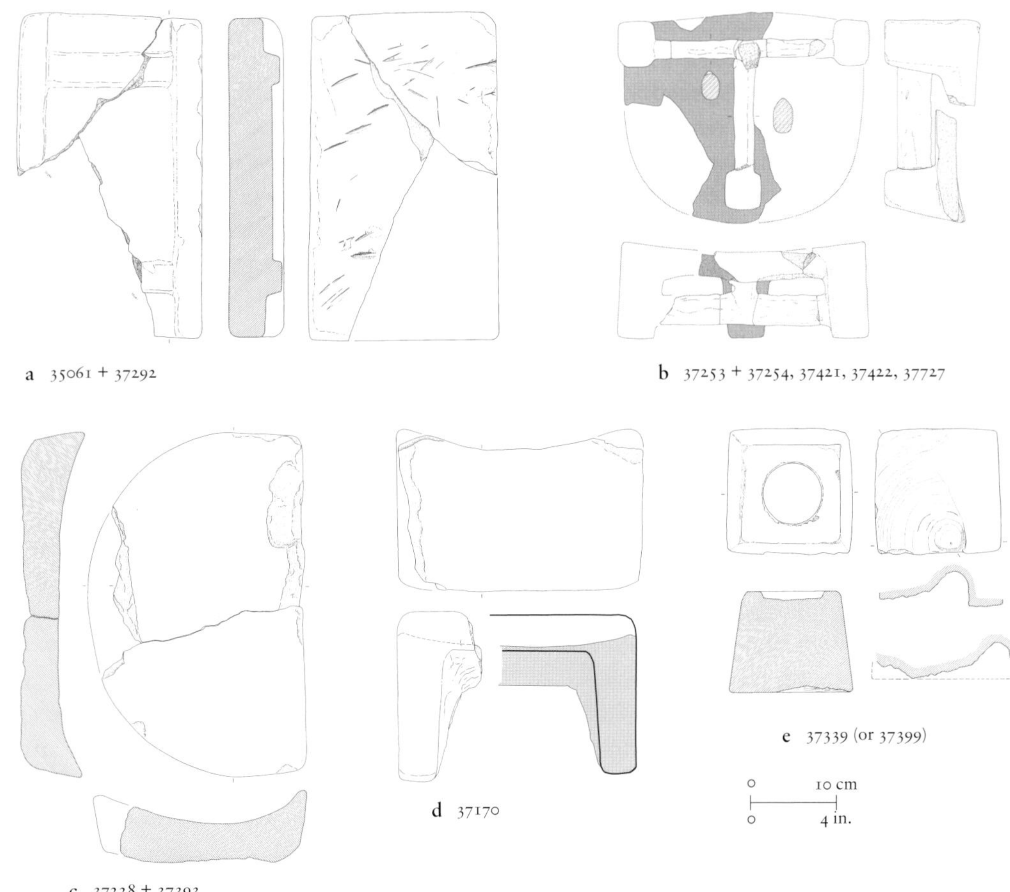

6.5 *Limestone furniture recovered from the excavation of the small houses of Grid 12.* **a** *Table scored with cut marks;* **b** *seat with carved support bars modelled on wooden furniture, the plan view being the underside;* **c** *concave seat to be placed directly on the floor;* **d** *seat slightly raised on two narrow supports;* **e** *block with sloping sides and circular recess on the top surface, originally intended to support the wooden leg of a bed or chair, and later (when turned upside down) used as the pivot block for a wooden door.*

Between normal chair height and the ground, any intermediate level also gave an acceptable height. One painted ivory leg of a chair was 19 cm (7.5 in.) high, for example; and a preserved lattice stool reached 30.5 cm (12 in.) in height.[1] In a painting from the King's House [**Pl. XX**], Nefertiti relaxes on a thick, richly decorated cushion spread out on the floor (her husband on a seat seemingly placed on the cushion). The lower height created scope for a range of stools made from limestone, carved with a concave seating surface, fragments of which are common at Amarna (though under-reported by the older excavations; **6.5**). One example copied a wooden design, in having an underlying framework of separated struts carved in the stone. The height of some chairs, however, was increased by standing them on little stone supports (see below).

Ancient pictures often show people eating while occupying a full-height chair. They reach for the food set out at elbow-height on a wooden table with thin latticework legs. When squatting on the ground, however, people might have chosen an option that archaeology also reveals: flat rectangular slabs of limestone carved with supporting bars on the underside [**6.5**; another is present in **6.3**]. They, too, are common finds. Mostly the top surface is smooth, but a few examples show diagonal scorings from blades, perhaps because the tables had a use in preparing food as well, although they could also have served as work-benches for the making of things.

The central room in many houses was provided with a low brick bench, rising by only the thickness of a brick (no more than 10 cm, 3.9 in.) above the floor. This was the height of the small throne dais at the rear of the North Palace [**4.10**]. One location, for a version wide enough to take two wooden chairs side by side on the bench, was in the middle of a wall in the central hall, sometimes placed to face the main entrance. The natural interpretation is to see the householder and his wife sitting rather stiffly on chairs to receive their guests (as so often shown in tomb paintings and on memorial stones), implying that the longer, narrower 'reception' hall in the larger houses was really there to give the sense of making a procession into the heart of the house.

In smaller houses, more of the wall space of the central room was taken up with low brick benches, which sometimes turned a corner between two walls [**6.2, 6.3**]. They were equally suited to wakeful squatting while eating and talking, and to sleeping at night. There is an archaeology of sleeping. Huya counted a made-up wooden bed as a desirable item for his tomb equipment [**7.23**]. Some of the pictures of the royal palace likewise include a carefully delineated royal bed complete with soft bedding, head-rest and short portable steps [**4.20**]. It is generally accepted that the beds of the elite, including the king, stood in an alcove on a low dais at the back of a fairly long 'bedroom' that also offered ample space for keeping, for example, chests of personal possessions [**5.26, 6.6**]. Most large houses had only one such alcove on the ground floor, and they occur sparingly in royal buildings.

By a very old custom, perhaps to guard against termite infestation, the four bed legs rested on stone supports shaped like steep-sided pyramids with flat or recessed tops [**6.6**]. Actual beds are rare discoveries. One, of simple design, was found upturned in the narrow street outside one of the Workmen's Village houses (Main Street 3, **6.7**). It measured 153 by 61 cm (60.2 by 24 in.), was 23 cm (9 in.) high and the frame was filled with a mesh made from tough grass. The length is short even for Amarna adults, whose heights (measured from their bones) were, on average, 164 cm (5 ft 4 in.) for men, and 154 cm (5 ft) for women. It should be noted that the standard Workmen's Village house did not have a bed alcove in a specially constructed 'bedroom'.

The distinctive stone leg supports, which would have helped to protect against termite infestation (though this was very much a desert problem), are a fairly common find at Amarna, including among the smaller houses in

6.6 (above) Bed alcove with four limestone supports in place, in house V37.1, viewed to the southeast. Compare figure 5.26.

6.7 (right) Wooden bed found upside down at the Workmen's Village, in the narrow street outside the house, Main Street 3.

the Main City and at the Workmen's Village. It might seem, therefore, that although special bed alcoves belonged only in larger houses, the wooden beds themselves were more widespread. Not all leg supports were for beds, however. In two Workmen's Village houses (East Street 11, **6.1**, and Long Wall Street 7) stone leg supports were found neatly placed on the brick benches in the middle room. In the latter instance, the set of four was set out in a square of 60 cm (23.6 in.), which would fit the dimensions of a wooden chair better than those of a bed.

When depicted, the king's bed, like Huya's, is shown covered with a rounded shape that has to be the bedding, which could have been a mattress or just a thick pile of blankets. Egyptians raised flocks of sheep, and therefore had access to wool. Preserved woollen textiles are, however, very rare, and it remains uncertain to what extent the Egyptians took advantage of the thermal properties of wool during the cool of winter. They did have an alternative. This was to add weight to linen sheets by threading lengths of linen yarn closely spaced across the surface, to create the effect familiar nowadays in bath towels (though the 'pile' was longer). We know from a fully prepared bed found in a Theban tomb (Kha) that lengths of linen prepared in this way served as blankets. Many such fragments (as well as a small amount of woollen textile) occur in the textile collection from excavations at the Workmen's Village.[2]

Because beds were made of wood, and wood does not preserve well, we have no idea how many individuals owned one. It might have been a social marker. Lying down on a mat-covered floor or low bench, closely wrapped in one of the large rectangles of heavy linen cloth that the Egyptians made as a matter of course, could have been the nightly experience of many people, as it is among poorer people in Egypt today.

Another determinant of personal behaviour and the use of domestic space was toilet practice. In common with ancient Egypt generally, Amarna had no drains or sewers, and it was a topic that Egyptian art and writing avoided, apart from spells in religious texts aimed at the avoidance of contact with excrement. The larger houses made some provision, at least for the family head. A private suite of rooms at the back of the house included a specially designed bedroom, bathroom and toilet [**5.21**]. The design of the bedroom was illustrated in **5.26**. In the bathroom, the floor was often covered with a large stone tray provided with a shallow raised rim and a spout [**6.8**].

In the absence of evidence for bathing tubs (even shallow ones), we have to picture water being poured over the bather, draining from the spout into a small stone tank (which had to be emptied by hand) or into a pottery vessel sunk into

6.8 *(below left) The bathroom and adjacent latrine, as found in house O48.1.*

6.9 *(below right) Bathroom in house Q45.45, from northwest.*

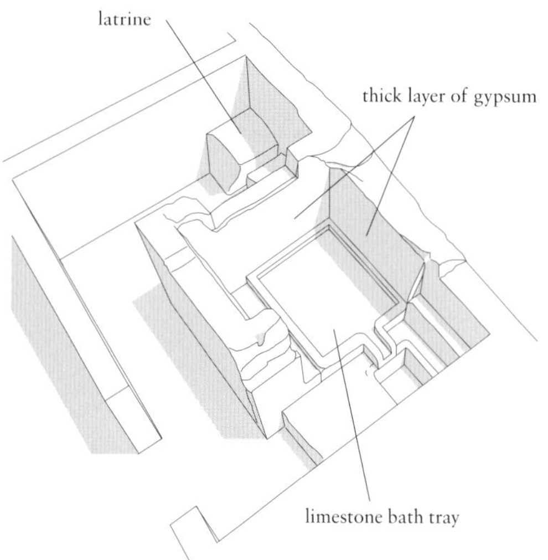

6.10 (right) Bath slab with adjacent brick latrine in house Q45.1, looking north.

6.11 (below) Limestone slab, presumed to be a latrine seat. On the underside are the remains of gypsum plaster used to embed it firmly onto a pair of supporting mud-brick walls. From house T35.22, obj. 30/182. Dimensions: 55 by 45 cm (21.6 by 17.7 in.).

the ground. To protect the surrounding walls from the effects of splashing, they were covered with a sloping layer of plaster coated with gypsum. In one house (Q45.45), the top surface of the side wall of the bathroom contained three rounded hollows or small basins [**6.9**]. Were they to hold scented oils for the skin? In the case of a stone version found in house T36.11, the excavators remarked upon 'traces of grease' still present within the receptacles. They continued: 'whether ointment or oil was poured into the cups, or whether the cups merely served to steady vessels which were put on the block, we cannot decide. The grease in the cups was not very extensive or deeply sunk in, so that the last assumption is perhaps the most probable.'[3]

Beside some of these bathing places is an unmistakable toilet on which one sat at a height of 20 to 30 cm (7.9 to 11.8 in.) above the floor, over a space that must have contained a removable vessel, for there is never a trace of a latrine pit underneath [**6.10**]. The size of the space would allow for a bowl with a diameter of no more than 25 cm (9.8 in.). Concern for cleanliness dictated that human waste must be removed altogether and not 'stored' in an underground pit. From another house (T35.22, not a particularly large one) was recovered a limestone seat, the concave surface of which was pierced with a central hole and wide slot to the front [**6.11**]. It was, at the time of discovery (and ever since), identified as a lavatory seat, and presumably spanned a similar little construction. Although they were simple, built toilets have not been common finds. A few examples have survived from other sites, however, of what are clearly toilet frames made from wood, with pierced seat and for use with a portable vessel. If they were a common household item at Amarna we would not know, because so little wood has survived.

It is natural to think of poorer people squatting to relieve themselves on areas of wasteland, and this must have been the custom for those who left their houses during the day to work outside. It was a less feasible option for the walled Workmen's Village, for example, especially if you lived at the further end of one of the streets. It might have been particularly unacceptable at night to head for the outside ground, especially given Egyptian fears of malevolent night-time spirits almost besieging people's houses. It is a near-inescapable conclusion that a bowl, of metal or of pottery and perhaps used beneath a wooden seat, was the standard temporary receptacle for human waste.

Imagining how people adapted to their houses begins with the assumption of good health, such that, for example, beds were for night-time sleeping. Yet the same houses and furniture also served the same people in sickness, injury and old age, and must have led to common rearrangements of routine and how things were placed in rooms.

The Smell of the Air

One benefit of the hot rays of the sun, especially when they touch the desert, is that they rapidly dry out moisture, including the moisture content of organic waste. In an index of unpleasant smells, ancient Amarna, which must have remained pretty dry for much of its brief existence, probably registered a fairly low score.

Where archaeological excavation uncovers floors of mud or mud bricks inside buildings they are generally clean and firm, without obvious accumulations of rubbish, although a build-up of earthy layers that is sometimes observable beneath a floor surface is a likely sign that the floor has been remade, perhaps more than once. As mentioned above, human waste did not accumulate in latrine pits, either inside houses or in their courtyards. In open spaces, including here and there along the main streets, deposits remain that are rich in broken pottery, small stones and pieces of charcoal, and they look like the remnants of rubbish heaps. Often, however, houses are so closely packed as to leave little space free for the dumping of rubbish, and some places where one might expect it, especially along the eastern edge of the city, show no signs at all. People were not in the habit of walking regularly from their houses out to the edge of the city and emptying baskets of rubbish. Perhaps it was forbidden.

The North Palace must have been the source of substantial waste, from the animals (including cattle) kept in special pens on the north side, and from an area on the south set aside for cooking and the making of faience jewelry. Yet the desert outside is clean, without adjacent buildings of any kind or signs of dumped rubbish. The only realistic explanation is that rubbish, including the dung from the cattle quarters, was carried away. The main residential areas of the city are not as clean as this, but still the limited amounts of rubbish imply either an organized system of disposal or a requirement for households to undertake this, in either case in the direction towards the river bank, leaving the surrounding desert untouched. One indicator of volume of waste is the amount of animal bone present. It gives the impression of being nowhere near as abundant as is to be expected. Since marks of gnawing by dogs or rodents are rare, animal scavenging is not likely to be the answer.[4]

If there was a policy of waste disposal, it was not universally followed. The most obvious exception is the Central City [**Pl. XXXV**]. The bakeries saw the accumulation of huge amounts of discarded pottery bread moulds within the buildings and over the desert behind, while to the south, two large dumps developed on the city edge, comprising a mix of pottery (excluding bread moulds, but including many imported Mycenaean vessels) and industrial waste from demolished kilns that must have stood elsewhere. A second exception is the Workmen's Village (which lay out of sight of the city). The practice there was to carry domestic waste outside the walled village and to dump it over ground to the east and south, and especially into abandoned pits and quarries, which had been used to supply desert clay for bricks.

Among familiar smells such as those considered briefly at the end of the last chapter, one would have been of wood smoke from ovens, open fires and occasional kilns for pottery and glass. Another would have been from incense: aromatic resin that, in the Amarna period, was imported in large quantities from the eastern Mediterranean, derived from the tree *Pistacia atlantica* (the incense now called mastic).[5] It was the normal accompaniment to the presentation of food-offerings in the temples. Potsherds coated with incense resin – either pieces of broken transport containers (amphorae) or sherds used to hold a patch of the substance – are also a common find in houses large and small. The Grid 12 group of small houses yielded fifty-nine resin sherds, for example. Incense, the substance 'with which the gods are placated', perhaps brought to the home a feeling of contentment and of enhanced separation from the outside world. At the Workmen's Village, where textile preservation was better than in the main city, many twisted wicks of linen have been found, some of them smeared with incense. They presumably took up oil and burnt in simple lamps, sputtering, fizzing and giving off their own smell.[6]

Material Signs of Success

Egypt in the New Kingdom was organized towards the large-scale production of goods: household, military and ritual. Amarna as a whole acted as a giant factory. What happened to this vast output of busy hands; what was its destination? The centre of consumption was the court. It must have become a repository of fine objects, both on display and in storage, within magazines. It is likely that the bulk of the items found in Tutankhamun's tomb were the result of a rapid trawl at the time of his death through palace magazines (no longer at Amarna) stuffed with fine objects many of which, inevitably, bore his name.

The over-production to which the country was geared could not be contained and inevitably spilled out into society at large, especially within a leading royal city like Amarna. The class of officials was responsible for control of the workshops, to the extent that they were integrated into the large households. Officials expected and received a flow of fine things directly from the palace as a reward for their services [1.13]. The larger Amarna houses are also likely to have become destinations for a portion of the goods manufactured on the premises.

In the small shrine at the rear of the tomb of the 'Chief Steward of Queen Tiye, Huya' (no. 1) are carved the outlines of the property that Huya wished or imagined would accompany his burial [7.22]. It includes a variety of storage chests or boxes (probably of wood) and vessels (including two Canopic jars to contain his embalmed organs), a chariot complete with bow case slung along the side, a wooden bed with its bedding, two chairs with cushions on each of which rests a staff from which hangs a pair of sandals, two or more upholstered footstools and a pair of tall shrines, the bases of which constructed like sledges.

Most of the objects we can recognize as markers of a successful life, the upholstered chairs and stools and the bed bringing comfort, the chariot denoting prestige, the chests there to contain items of value to be packed away, including folded linen. The shrines should have contained sacred images (Tutankhamun's tomb provides examples), which at Amarna might have been statues of the king, of Huya himself or even of household gods (for example, Bes, see 7.12). As mentioned in Chapter 2, the faience models of bunches of grapes often found in the city [2.15] probably decorated small wooden shrines with partially open sides (and thus somewhat different from those shown in Huya's tomb), which would have been attractive objects within the house.

Surviving pieces of wooden furnishings have been very rare and seem mostly to have belonged to boxes. Examples are part of a cylindrical wooden box with an incised design of an antelope and a tree picked out in white;[7] geometrically decorated panels of ivory that once covered a box with a curving lid;[8] the lid from a circular box delicately carved with calves running in vegetation [6.12]. They show a variety of design and a manufacturing skill that hint at a richness and sophistication in domestic furnishings easily underestimated from the small number of surviving examples. On some wooden objects, the decoration took the form of inlays in glass and carnelian, each piece in the shape of a hieroglyph or an element in a feather pattern.

Another glimpse of the things that people held to be precious is given by the tomb scene of the king rewarding the god's father Ay [1.13]. The king tosses down gifts for Ay to catch and then heap on the ground, and to pass to servants for carrying away. Much of it is jewelry in the form of broad collars, necklaces and armlets (presumably of gold), drinking-vessels and signet rings, also perhaps of gold, and a pair of (leather) gloves that Ay puts on. 'Look at that stool and that bag!' calls out a retainer as he hands them to a companion, introducing examples of less spectacular gifts. 'They [Ay and Tey his wife] have

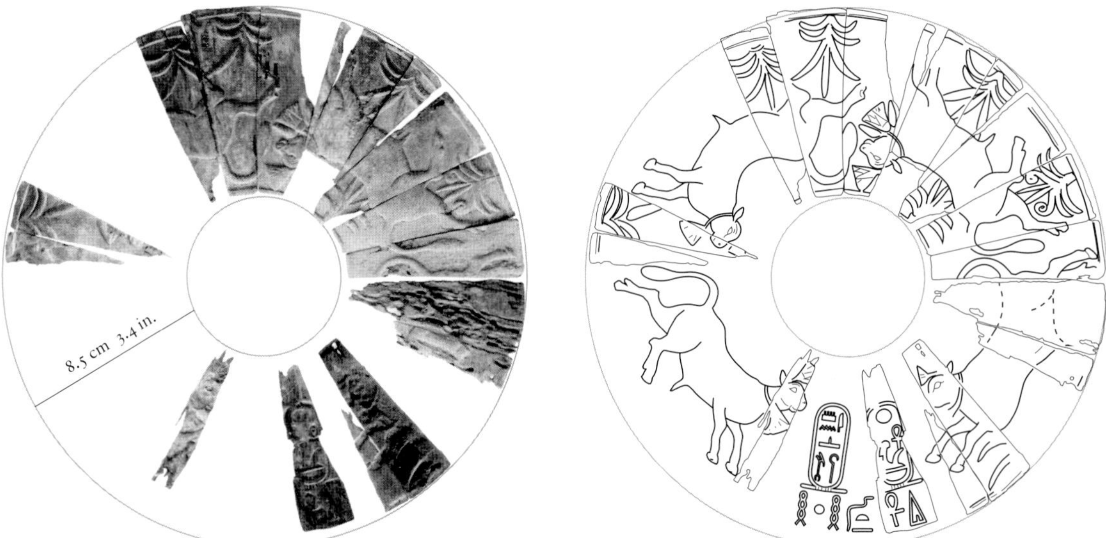

6.12 *Lid from a wooden box found at Amarna (obj. 33/256), made from separate strips placed side by side and carved in low relief. There are traces of gold leaf over gypsum. It depicts young bulls, garlanded with lilies, running among vegetation. The decoration also included the cartouches of Amenhotep III. The hole in the centre is for a separately made knob.*

become people of gold' states another.[9] The similar reward scene in the tomb of the cup-bearer Parennefer (no. 7) adds a crowd of his retainers carrying off bulkier commodities in amphorae, sacks and heaped baskets, suggesting that the king's rewards were not confined to ostentatious gifts.[10]

Though rarely found, an important part of daily life were articles of metal. The most widespread would have been made of a copper alloy approximating to bronze, although the most valuable would have been of gold (which could also be alloyed with copper). 'In my brother's country, gold is as common as dust' wrote envious foreign kings to pharaoh at this time.[11] Slightly later records show that a given unit of gold had at least 200 times the value of its bronze equivalent[12] and, as the furnishings in Tutankhamun's tomb show, its glitter could be spread further by covering wooden objects with gold leaf laid over a thin coat of gypsum.

Individual items illustrate the versatility of metal [**6.13**]: knife blades, long tongs, axes and adzes, chisels, needles, arms and pans from pairs of scales, weights used in weighing, mirrors, bowls and drinking-cups, razors, a tool for branding a design on cattle hide, tweezers, rivets, spoons and (made of lead) a decorated right-angled tube with strainer from which one drank beer [**6.14**]. A tomb picture of treasures held in a store includes vessels decorated with stand-up images of animals arranged around the rim. Temple cult was served by metal vessels [**3.19–3.21**]. Metal objects, whole or in fragments, their value determined by their weight, were a common form of currency.

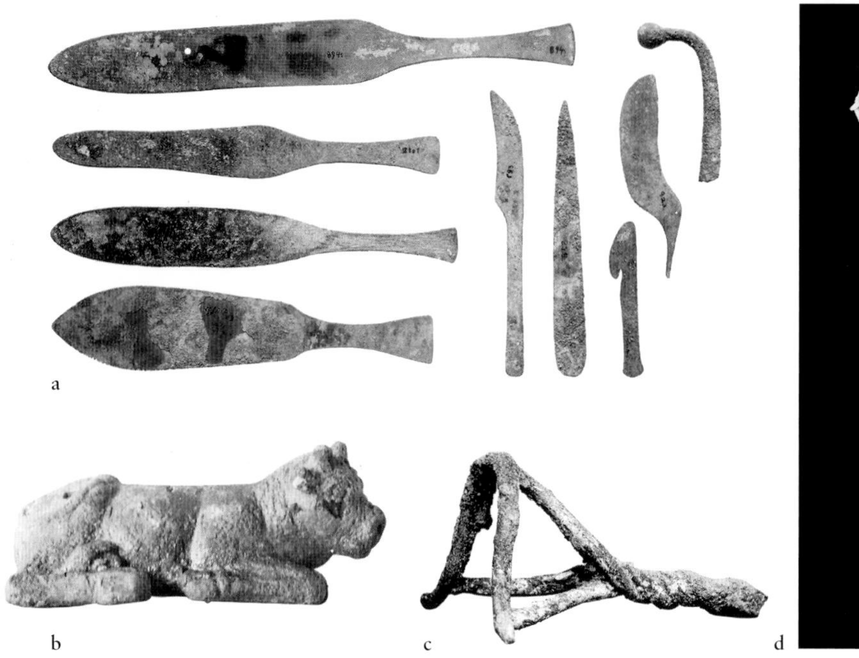

Most families probably owned some metal objects, particularly bowls for cooking, that were more suitable than their equivalents made from pottery, but examples are rare and not particularly large.[13] When the royal family is shown drinking, they use beakers or wide bowls with feet and a sharply angled profile, the same shape seen among the rewards given to Ay at the Window of Appearance [1.13]. Examples of this shape are fairly common in stone, but it is to be expected that the best ones were of precious metal.

A sign of status was the signet ring. These were made of metal (bronze, gold or electrum – which was a naturally occurring alloy of gold and silver) and

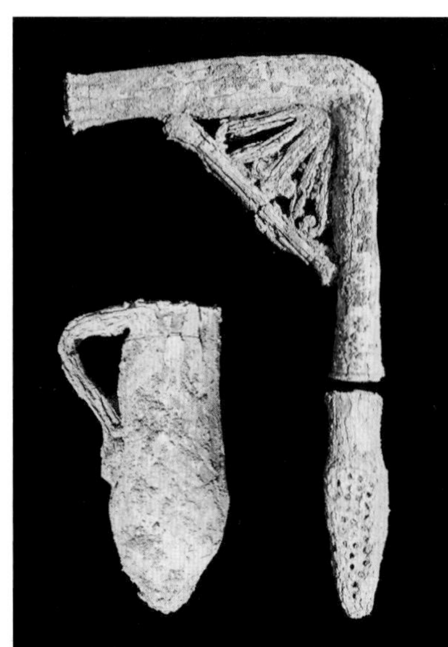

6.13 *(above) Metal objects from Amarna.* **a** *A selection of flat blades from the 1923/24 excavations in the Main City.* **b** *Obj. 33/280, bronze weight in the shape of a bull, length 5.8 cm (2.3 in.), marked '1* deben*', and weighing 92.9 g (3.3 oz).* **c** *Obj. 26/321, cattle-branding 'iron', length 8.2 cm (3.2 in.), from house V37.5.* **d** *Obj. 29/118, bronze plate with traces of gold leaf, made as a* menat-*counterpoise to a heavy necklace. It features images of the goddess Hathor. Height 19.5 cm (7.7 in.). The beads were found beside it, but are not necessarily restrung in the correct order.*

6.14 *(left) A drinking kit made from lead. It comprises three pieces: (left) 21/476, a tall vessel with handle; (below right) 21/477, a filter; (above right) 21/478, a right-angled length of tube (length of each limb of the tube, 10.6 cm, 4.1 in.). The last two were presumably fitted with tubes of a different material (wood?), one of them shaped to fit more easily between the lips.*

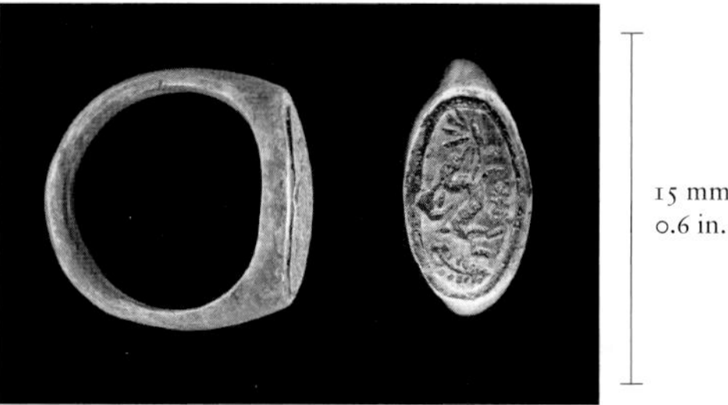

6.15, 6.16 *(above) Three examples of mud sealings bearing designs. Objs 21420 (a seated figure of Akhenaten wearing a feathered* atef*-crown, from Kom el-Nana), 9977 (a design that used the name of the Aten, from Kom el-Nana), and 4251 (with a clear writing of Amun-Ra, from the Workmen's Village). (right) The example of a ring (obj. 39447) is small in size, was made from a gold alloy, and was found in the grave of a child at the South Tombs Cemetery. The design shows an animal, perhaps a gazelle, amidst vegetation. All four objects are at approximately the same scale.*

sharply engraved with a design that could be impressed into mud sealings on the string that bound a papyrus document or was wound between the knobs of a box and its lid [**6.15**]. A few have been found,[14] one (of gold alloy and suitably small in size) in the grave of a child. Their designs are frequently encountered pressed into mud sealings. They might allude to the royal family, but they do not name the owner himself. Innumerable mud seals must have been broken from their string, as letters were received and boxes opened. Pieces of discarded seal impression are not uncommon among the finds from the excavation of houses, but only very rarely in groups, and none of those particularly large. Clusters can include several examples from the same ring[15] or impressions from several rings or seals.[16] Only limited numbers seem to have come from the offices in the Central City where there ought to be thousands.[17] The reason might be simple. The mud that was used for sealing had been prepared for the purpose, consisting of fine particles and able to dry hard and not crack. It would have been sensible to throw old sealings into a receptacle of water so that the mud could be re-used.

In addition to a signet ring, other accessories helped to convey the rank of a senior official. Again we know of these primarily from the tomb scenes: a long staff was one, another was the scribe's kit of ink palette and brush-pen. The god's father Ay holds in one and the same hand an ostrich-feather fan, a shepherd's crook and an axe; fan-bearer Ahmose carries slung over his shoulder the ostrich-feather fan to which an axe is tied. One finely made object (found in a private house) that could have signified status in a particular craft is a slate measuring-rod incised with multiple divisions of the cubit.[18]

Storing Possessions

In the developed world, richer people's assets are in part notional, statements of promised value – money and share certificates – and people (sometimes mistakenly) take for granted that these will always be honoured as a means of exchange for goods and services. In ancient Egypt, however, the concept of notional assets was barely developed. Assets were mostly things – bronze and gold, grain, cattle and textiles, and slaves, too – that had a tangible existence and could also be used in transactions for other things. The cautious or affluent person kept in the house a store of items that could be used as a means of exchange (forms of currency), as well as providing a sense of security against reversals of fortune. A married woman would also maintain an interest in the items of property that her husband had given her as her future security. In the absence of banks, where did people keep such things?

For some commodities, the answer was a special building: stalls for cattle, round silos or long vaulted chambers for grain [**2.6**, **5.27**]. Smaller things needed smaller receptacles and greater watchfulness. Egyptian houses held nothing that could be properly locked. As far as we can tell, many of the things of value were kept in the wooden chests and boxes described earlier, which stood on the floor. In one of the scenes of reward at the Window of Appearance (the tomb of Parennefer) we actually see servants packing the smaller gifts from the king into a wooden box. In his tomb scene [**7.23**], Huya displays at least three chests, made from a wooden frame with infilled wooden panels and a separately made lid that could be, for security, tied down to the body of the chest by means of string wound around a pair of knobs, the knot sealed with a lump of mud into which a personal seal was pressed, as described above. Other tomb scenes show sacks and baskets in common use, and baskets have occasionally been found [**6.17**].[19] Sacks or bags were not necessarily cheaper substitutes for chests. Ay's artist, in his reward scene, considered a bag to be among Ay's prize gifts from the king, a valuation reflected by the fact that Tutankhamun originally used one for the storage of valuable objects 'when he was a boy'.[20]

The means of storage that has left the most abundant remains was the pottery jar, which came in a variety of shapes, sizes and wares.[21] We might suspect a degree of correspondence between type of vessel and what it was used for, but, if that were so, the boundaries seem not to have been strictly maintained. Scribes wrote ink labels on the shoulders of some vessels (mostly the two-handled slender amphorae, **6.18**) and these generally state the contents and other information, revealing a wide diversity of materials that could be put into them, but such labelling was far from being a universal practice. Many jars, including amphorae, remained uninscribed and so whatever information one gleans from the labels may not be representative of the full picture. It was often important to close the vessel mouth, the standard practice involving first a bung (perhaps of grass) or lid and then a cap of mud or, less commonly, gypsum plaster, its lower edge pressed around the shoulder and its top neatly moulded. A seal stamped on the mud while it was soft left the impression of a design that

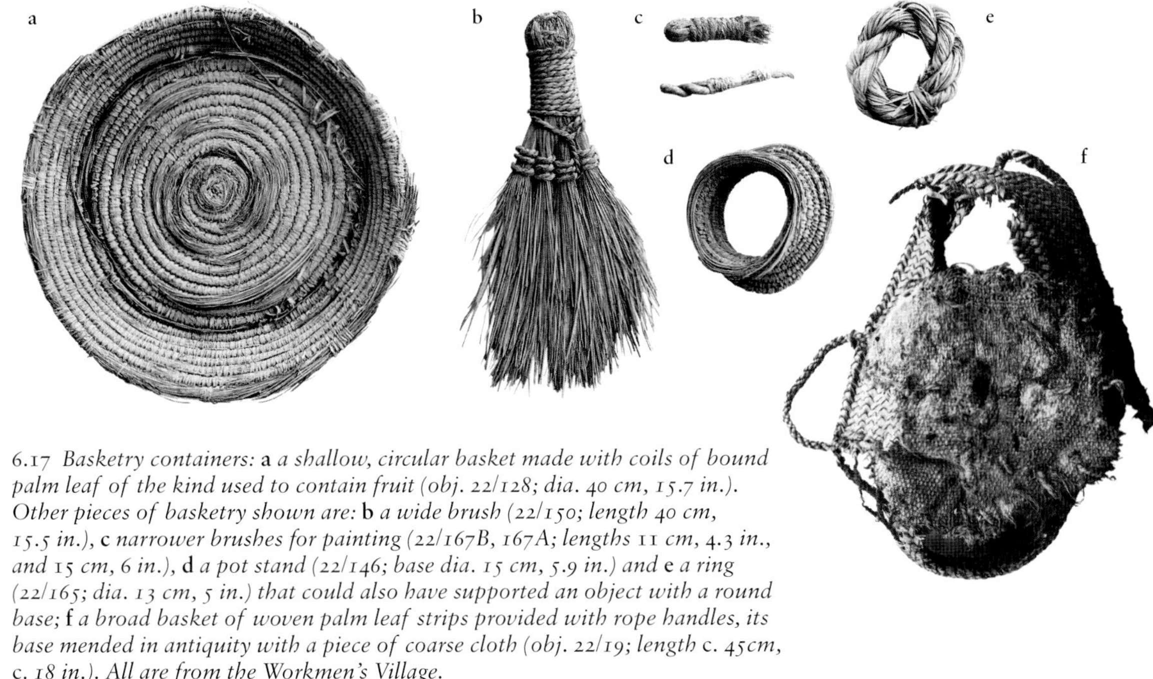

6.17 *Basketry containers:* **a** *a shallow, circular basket made with coils of bound palm leaf of the kind used to contain fruit (obj. 22/128; dia. 40 cm, 15.7 in.). Other pieces of basketry shown are:* **b** *a wide brush (22/150; length 40 cm, 15.5 in.),* **c** *narrower brushes for painting (22/167B, 167A; lengths 11 cm, 4.3 in., and 15 cm, 6 in.),* **d** *a pot stand (22/146; base dia. 15 cm, 5.9 in.) and* **e** *a ring (22/165; dia. 13 cm, 5 in.) that could also have supported an object with a round base;* **f** *a broad basket of woven palm leaf strips provided with rope handles, its base mended in antiquity with a piece of coarse cloth (obj. 22/19; length* c. *45cm,* c. *18 in.). All are from the Workmen's Village.*

might again contain information on what was inside and where it had come from. Opening a vessel of honey or fat needed care to prevent the friable mud of the broken seal from dropping in.

Pots, especially amphorae, could be re-used, at least for the carrying of water, and their broken-off bases were useful as makeshift containers. The storage of water, however, was better done in larger and wider jars made from porous Nile-silt fabric that allowed the water to percolate to the outside and, through its evaporation, to cool the jar as a whole. Outside the Workmen's Village, an area was set aside for what looks like a communal water supply held in these vessels (which approximate to vessels in modern Egypt that are called *zir*s, hence the *zir*-area of the map, **5.30**).

In common use was a big-bellied, wide-mouthed jar with short thick rim that was about as much as a person could readily carry empty. Some of them bear ink labels, and these labels are more or less exclusively for meat (which would have made them very heavy; **3.26**). It was also, however, a favoured jar for burying up to its neck in the floor to act as a form of secure storage, part of the attraction presumably being a mouth wide enough to receive a hand easily.

6.18 *Pottery amphora (obj. 6843, from the Workmen's Village), on the shoulder of which is written, in ink hieratic characters, the word* baq-*oil. Height: 65 cm (25.4 in.).*

The standard amphora shape had been borrowed by the Egyptians from the area of Palestine and Syria. Amphorae continued to be imported, but the Egyptians also manufactured them on a large scale, always from desert marl clay, which fires better than Nile silt to produce a hard and relatively non-porous fabric that can be burnished before firing to seal the surface even further. Equipped with vertical handles for carrying and a thick pointed base that could withstand the shock of being set down heavily, they were the standard means of conveying and storing a wide variety of commodities. Contents identifications come from ink labels on the shoulders of amphorae and impressions of hieroglyphic seals in mud jar-stoppers. They include wine, beer, incense, honey, fat, ducks, oil, dates, grapes, and various plant derivatives of uncertain identity.

Amphorae display variations in their shape and fabric that can, through analysis, point to their origin. Thus the clay in the thick distinctive walls of amphorae that are almost like drain-pipes in shape has been identified as coming from the western oases, implying knowledge of a desert route that, presumably by pack donkeys, brought wine to the Nile valley almost 400 km (248 miles) distant.[22] Sharp-shouldered amphorae from Syria similarly conveyed to Egypt the aromatic resin (incense) that was used in temples, shrines and houses. To judge from its ubiquitous presence in the soil and stuck to the insides of jars, it must have been imported in large quantities and been available to the whole population.[23]

Most Egyptian pottery of the period, although sometimes elegant in shape and with certain forms bearing bright blue decorative patterns [**Pl. XL**], was relatively coarse and heavy, made to be put to use and not valued. Alongside the Canaanite amphorae, which have the same characteristics, the Egyptians also imported vessels from the Mycenaean world and from Cyprus, though it is hard to be sure if they came directly or via middlemen based in eastern Mediterranean ports. Pieces of these imported vessels stand out from a background of Egyptian sherds by virtue of their fine clays and richer colouring, mostly reddish-brown, beige and black. They were not the preserve of the rich. They have been found in mixed housing neighbourhoods [**6.19–6.21**] and the Workmen's Village, as well as in the 'palace' rubbish heaps of the Central City. Mostly they are enclosed, flask-like vessels that were probably used for carrying oils or unguents, in the case of the little Cypriote bottles, perhaps a dissolved form of opium.[24]

A particularly secure form of storage was burial in the ground, often beneath the floor of a house. Burial took three forms. One was a brick-lined pit or cellar that could be in a courtyard or beneath the floor of a room [**6.22, 6.23**]. The pits sometimes seem inconveniently placed: in the living-room, for example. They could have contained various substances, including grain, especially when neatly subdivided by a central wall. They could be roofed with a brick vault, a slab of stone or with wood.[25] Another form of burial was within a pottery storage jar sunk up to its neck, as just mentioned. Deliberately buried pots are often found, though almost invariably they are empty. An exception was one

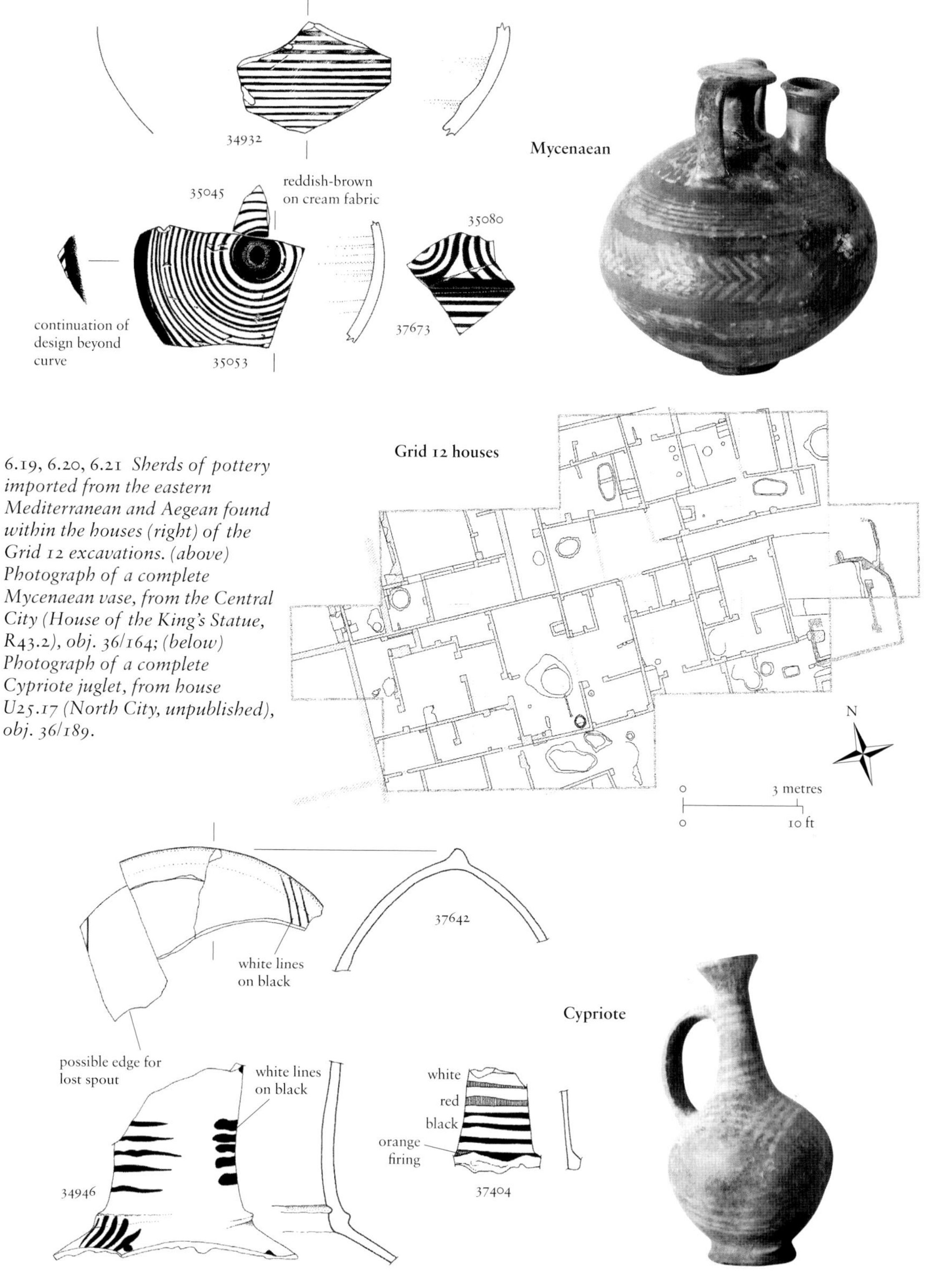

6.19, 6.20, 6.21 *Sherds of pottery imported from the eastern Mediterranean and Aegean found within the houses (right) of the Grid 12 excavations. (above) Photograph of a complete Mycenaean vase, from the Central City (House of the King's Statue, R43.2), obj. 36/164; (below) Photograph of a complete Cypriote juglet, from house U25.17 (North City, unpublished), obj. 36/189.*

buried in a small room (or possibly a court) in the North Suburb [**6.24**]. It contained twenty-three bars of gold and a quantity of silver fragments and roughly made rings, as well as a silver figurine of a Hittite god. The gold bars had been made simply by pouring melted-down gold into grooves scooped by a finger in sand. The total weight of the gold was 3375.36 g, equivalent in ancient terms to

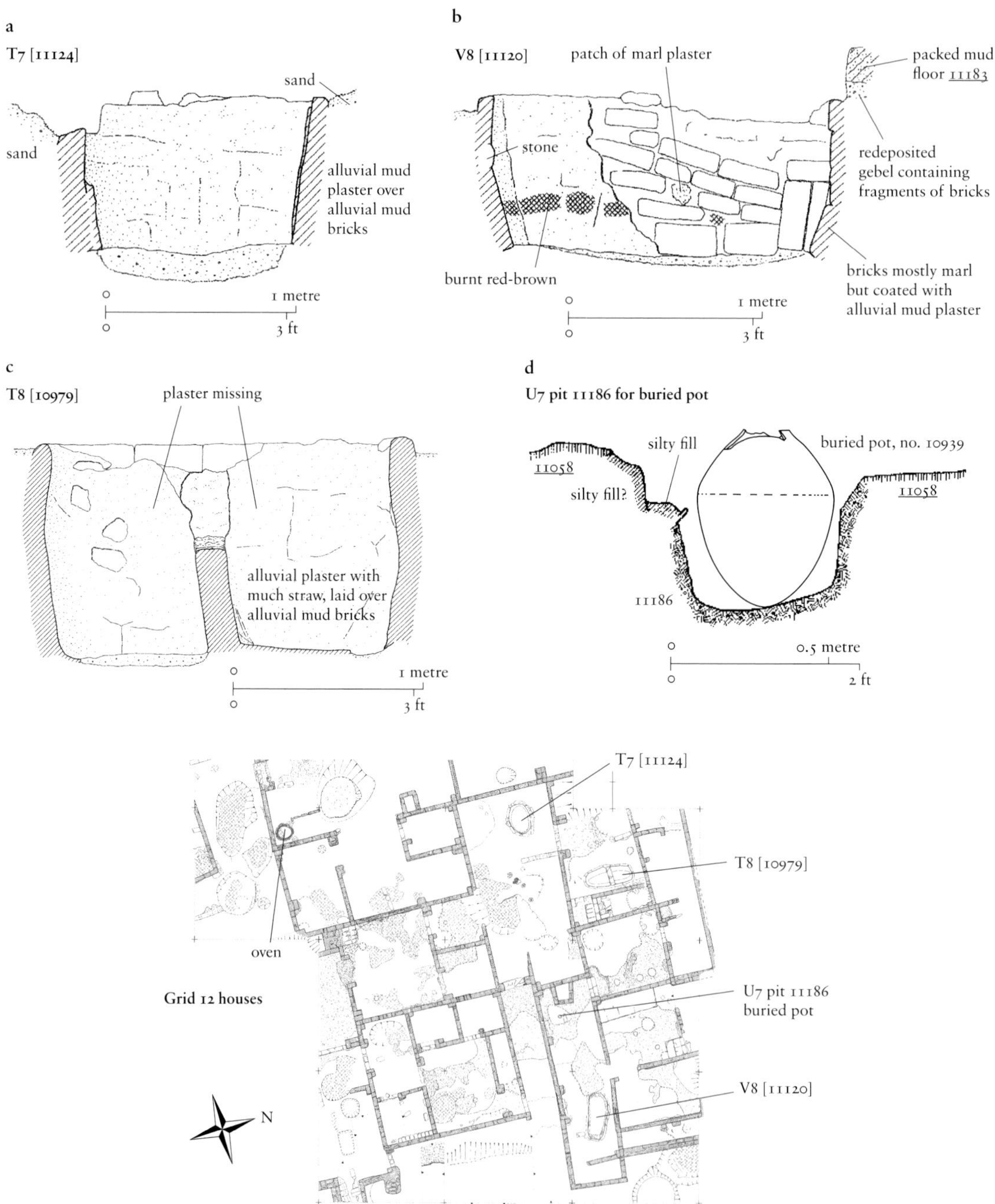

37 *deben* (a unit of weight for metals). The total weight of the silver came to at least 1085.85 g, or 12 *deben*. This represents a fair amount of wealth, though not a staggering sum. Some idea of its purchasing power can be obtained from the ratios of gold to silver (5:3 later becoming 2:1), and of silver to copper or bronze (1:100). The silver could have been used to buy, say, ten or twelve head of cattle. The archaeologist who made the Amarna discovery assumed that it was part of a thief's loot, yet we cannot be sure that the only remarkable thing about the find is simply that someone had failed to recover it. It might have been relatively common to bury valuable goods for safekeeping, with no necessary association of dishonesty. There is an uncanny parallel in a letter from a slightly later period (and unconnected with Amarna) in which the writer gives instructions as to where, in the pigsty beside the house, a mass of bronzework has been buried and, alongside it, a pottery jar containing a hoard of gold and silver items.[26]

6.22, 6.23 (opposite) A group of brick-lined storage pits or cellars found within houses in Grid 12. T8 [10979] is divided into two compartments.

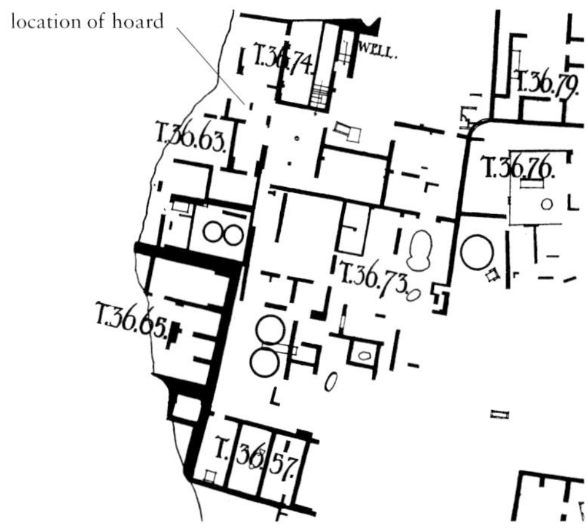

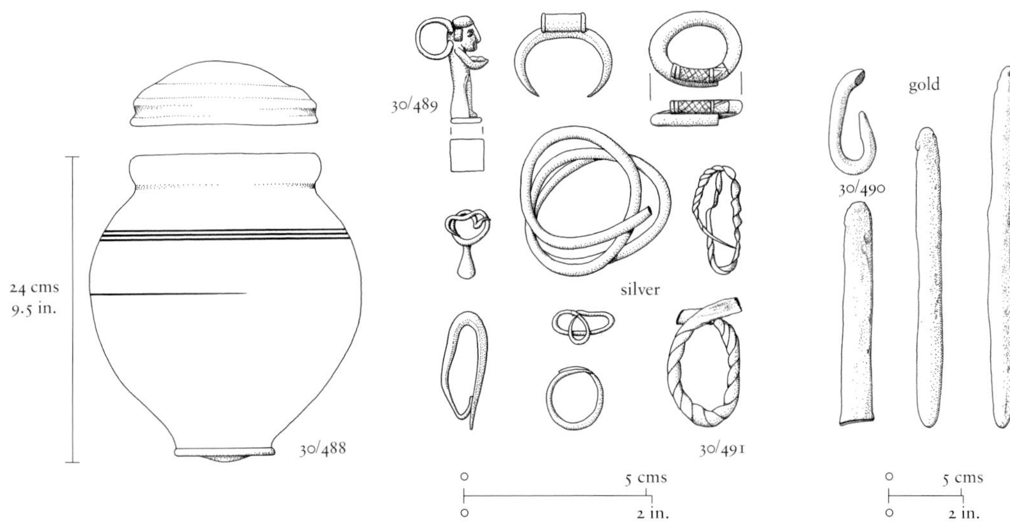

6.24, 6.25 Part of a hoard of gold and silver buried in a pottery jar in the North Suburb. The silver is made up partly of finished items (including the Hittite figurine, obj. 30/489) and partly of coils and irregular pieces, some cut from vessels; the gold in crude bars. A portion of the excavator's plan shows the approximate position.

A third form of burial was in a small and shallow hole cut into the floor of a room or courtyard, at least in the smaller houses. In house N49.20 a group of objects was found 'at the south edge of the room, under a double plaster floor', comprising two glass bottles, a glass bottle in the shape of a fish [**Pl. XLVIII**] and three vessels made apparently of lead (one of them a strainer, another a drinking-tube, **6.14**).[27] Beneath the floor of the inner sitting-room in house T34.1 were found 'fragments of copper and silver', three bronze adze heads, a bronze 'fleshing-knife 18 cm [7 in.] long', a piece of gold openwork jewelry, and a spoon with incised design made from travertine.[28] The danger for the occupants was that, over time, the locations of buried items would be forgotten, perhaps owing to a death. When, at the end of the Amarna period, the time came to leave the house for the last time, there must often have lurked in people's minds the feeling that things buried beneath the floor had been forgotten.

The floors, even when of mud brick, were soft and easily dug over. It would not have taken a great deal of time and effort to do this as a final check before walking out for the last time. Careful modern excavation of houses at Amarna has revealed extensive and thorough removal of floors, sometimes neatly up to the base of the walls, done while the walls were still standing to some height. If it was not the occupants themselves who did this, it was scavengers shortly afterwards, hoping to find those little treasures that had been forgotten; but it seems more logical to pin the responsibility upon the anxiously departing homeowners themselves.

People stored the things that kept their lives going, but also accumulated 'capital'. Traditionally, an important choice arose from time to time as to what to do with it. People could bequeath their property to their heirs. But they could also, out of respect, donate objects for someone's burial equipment and thus see it go out of circulation. The burial equipment depicted on the wall of Huya's tomb is an illustration of this ancient practice. He is, however, likely to have been a rich man. One of the cemeteries of ordinary citizens at Amarna (the South Tombs Cemetery, see below) gives a very different picture: of few grave goods or none, even when the graves are found to be undisturbed. People were evidently turning away from the age-old custom of surrendering valuable goods to the ground (they knew that robbers would quickly be searching for them), instead preferring to keep them in circulation among the living.

Eating In

Ancient Egyptian meals and mealtimes (like ancient Egyptian conversation) are hard to envisage beyond banal and universal generalities. But kitchens, at least, leave behind easily identifiable sets of remains. Moreover, we can, from the study of animal bones and plant remains, compile a list of foodstuffs for Amarna, which can in turn be supplemented by written and pictorial sources.

The Egyptian diet was heavily weighted towards cereals, consumed as bread and beer. The cereals came in two varieties: barley and a form of wheat called emmer. Unlike modern wheats, emmer is not free-threshing. The tough inedible husks enclose the edible grain so tightly as to require extra human force to split them off. This was done by pounding the grain in a limestone mortar set into the ground. Both barley and the separated emmer grains were then ground by hand in a backwards-and-forwards motion on a quern consisting of a lower stone (granite or quartzite), set in a box-like emplacement made from mud bricks, and a smaller rubbing stone, often made of basalt, grasped by both hands [**6.26**, **6.28**]. Mortars, lower quern-stones and sometimes the brick emplacements are straightforward to recognize when uncovered by excavation. The processing of cereals also left waste matter (husks and suchlike) that accumulated in open spaces and formed deposits found repeatedly during excavations.[29]

The rhythmic pounding of mortars and the sliding of quern-stones rubbed together must have been some of the regular sounds that accompanied life at Amarna. Experimental replication of the process has shown that reasonably fine flour can be produced, suggesting that the coarse gritty texture of a few loaves preserved as funerary offerings at other sites might not have been typical of the bread that the Egyptians actually ate.[30]

Meat regularly came from cattle, sheep, goats and pigs [**6.27**], as well as from geese and ducks, and from fish, too. Pictures of houses from this period show strips of meat hung up to cure [**4.16c**], allowing it to be stored and transported in pottery jars. In archaeological samples from the main residential part of the city, pig is the most numerous mammal species, making up more than half of those that were killed, although the majority were young animals and therefore not large. By contrast, the bones of cattle were far less frequent, but, especially given the large size of the animals killed, probably represent the main meat component of the diet.[31] A surprising addition, found at the Workmen's Village and attested by butchery marks on bones, is the striped hyena, an animal that, in the past, scavenged close to human habitation in Egypt (and is less fierce

6.26 Botanist D. Samuel demonstrates how grinding was done, on a replica of an ancient quern emplacement.

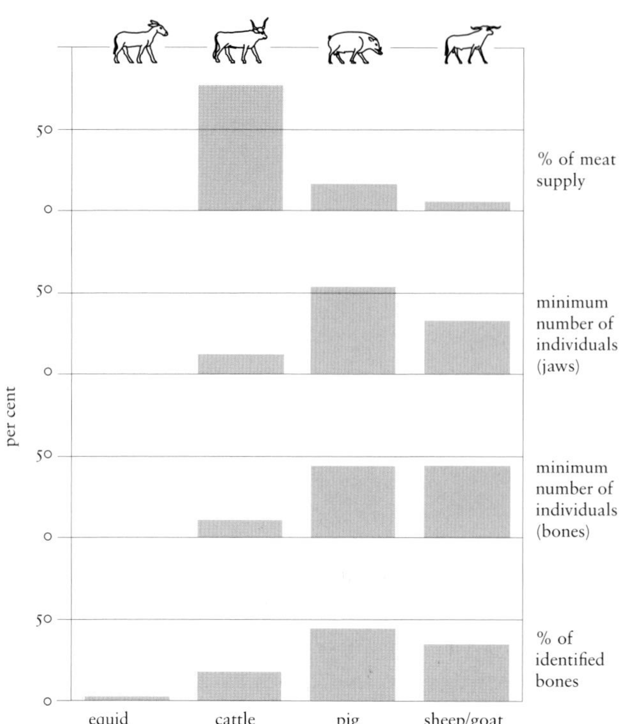

6.27 The common domestic mammals at Amarna, expressed in three ways: as percentages of meat supply (dominated by cattle); by the minimum number of individuals represented by jawbones and other bones; and by the percentage of identified bones (in which pigs and goats/sheep emerge as the most numerous animals killed).

than the spotted hyena of the African savannah).[32] Whether this was an animal enjoyed for its taste and possibly reared in captivity (as is attested from tomb pictures of earlier periods) or an opportunistic addition to the diet sought out by hungry people, we do not know.

Pictures of the royal family eating portray a very direct approach towards food. They hold cooked whole birds or long joints of meat on the bone in their hands and devour them [**4.21**]. Beside them, a supply of food, as whole loaves and whole joints, is stacked on a table, and not far away are rows of closed vessels evidently for drink. These, and the many pictures of private individuals seated in front of tables of 'offerings', and the lists of offerings themselves, give the impression that the main food items were prepared and consumed separately; that Egyptians did not have a style of cooking that blended foods and herbs and so produced 'dishes'. But could this be an artistic convention?

'Dishes' often involve boiling. Lentils have been recovered in excavation, and they would have required boiling – and heating water (though not actually boiling it) would have been a necessary stage in the making of beer. The Egyptians recognized and grew a variety of herbs. The names of many appear as ingredients in remedies for ills recorded in papyrus medical manuals, demonstrating a tradition of mixing ingredients. Then there are the extensive collections of plant remains recovered from excavations at Amarna that include coriander, black cumin, ajowan (a herb that smells and tastes like thyme), safflower and fenugreek, well suited to flavouring food.[33] But whether the

Egyptians used them in this way remains uncertain, and an attempt to write a modern Amarna cookery book would be largely a work of the imagination.

The principal source of heat was a plain open-topped cylindrical clay oven, provided with a small round hole near the base, but no internal shelves or floor to separate fire from contents [**6.28**]. These ovens seem suited to the baking of flat round loaves on the inside, and perhaps for roasting meat and for boiling liquids over the top. Traces of small open fires occur in and around buildings and these, too, could have been used for cooking.

The nature of what was eaten and the presence of querns, mortars and ovens are intimately tied up with the question of how food was supplied. The Central City complex, which incorporated the two Aten temples and the Great Palace, was designed to be a major source of food, including bread and joints of meat. The evidence from the housing areas, however, is that some of the cereals that were consumed arrived not already turned into bread, but as raw grains that needed processing by mortar and quern before being baked in an oven. At the Workmen's Village, many of the houses had their own full set of equipment, implying family autonomy in this area, understandable if the state were paying the heads of households an individual ration of emmer and barley from granaries that lay elsewhere. In the main city, however, where the larger houses possessed their own granaries, instances of mortars, querns and ovens are far fewer.[34] Does this point to a greater sharing or pooling of resources, or of the provision of certain services by designated individuals, remembering the picture of the urban village, exemplified by Panehsy, described in Chapter 1 (p. 34)? Did a portion of the prepared foods that passed through the Aten temples via the offering-tables find their way into the residential areas via an administered ration system (of the kind well attested from other periods)?

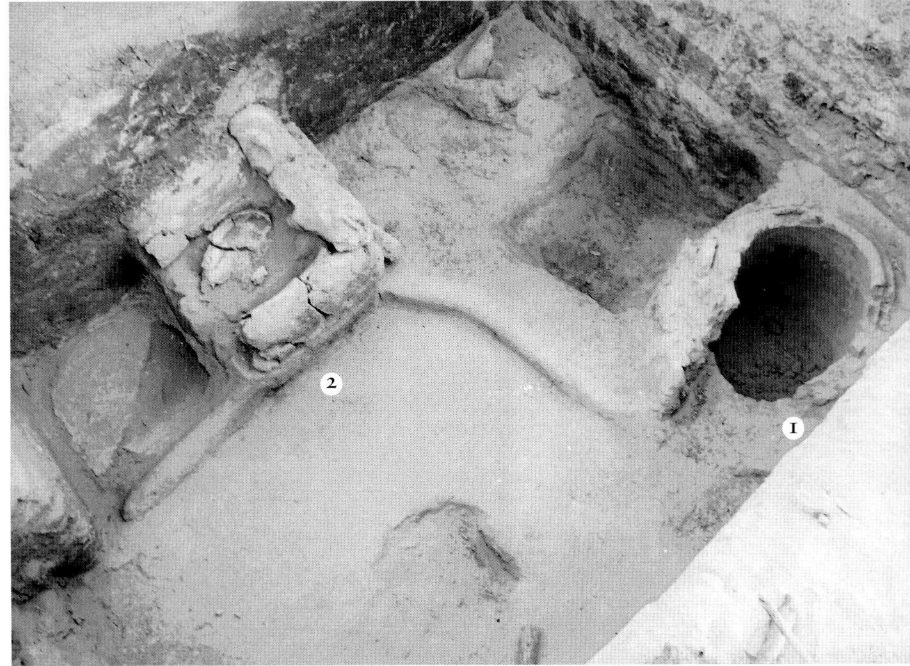

6.28 *Kitchen in Workmen's Village house Gate Street 11. 1 = quern emplacement; 2 = oven.*

Looking your Best

In some societies the elite develop extravagant dress, to the point of passing laws to prevent lesser people from trying to imitate them. Egypt seems not to have been like this. Even in the tomb scenes, which are likely to reflect an idealized view of the world, the rich simply wear more layers. Conversely, fragments of fine-quality textiles were not uncommon at the Workmen's Village.

The collection of 5,000 small textile fragments excavated at the Workmen's Village is a rare survival, brought about by unusually good conditions of preservation.[35] It offers a picture of dress that matches evidence from the tomb scenes and a few remarkably well-made statues of the royal family. Egyptians of both sexes had only a very limited range of tailored garments to choose from. Basically there were two [**6.29**]. One was a triangular loincloth definitely worn by men, though whether by women is uncertain. The other was a bag-like tunic made by sewing together the two halves of a rectangular length of cloth. A hole and slit for the head and neck were first cut in the centre, and two hemmed gaps served for the arms (although, since the tunics were wide, the arm-holes fell close to the elbow). Separately made sleeves could be sewn on to enclose the forearm. Some of Tutankhamun's tunics were elaborately decorated, but it is hard to judge how unusual this was. One accessory to the tunic was a linen sash that gathered it at the waist.

For the rest, Egyptians wound around their waists or draped over their shoulders rectangular lengths of linen of different dimensions and of different qualities [**6.30**]. Linen has the tendency to crumple and to resist a strong

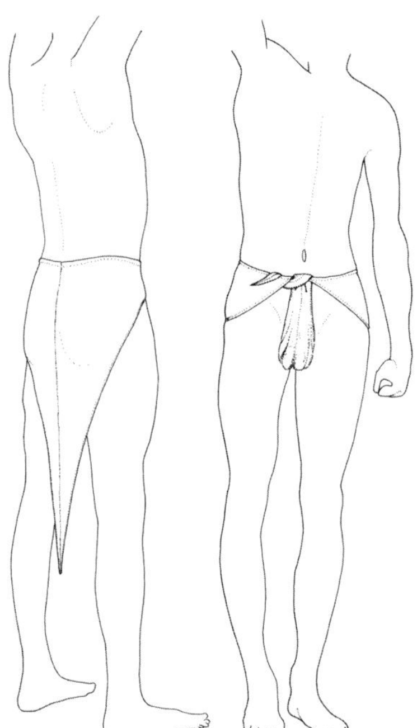

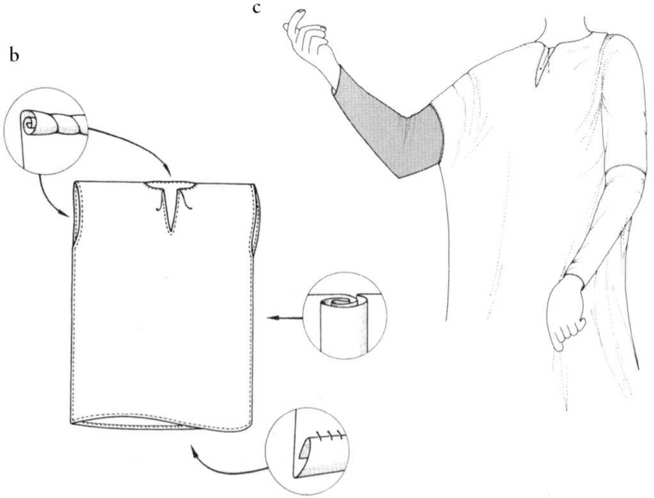

6.29 *Basic male clothing.* **a** *A simple triangle of linen provided with draw strings created a loincloth.* **b** *A rectangular tunic, much wider than the wearer's shoulders, created a loose, baggy garment, to which separately made sleeves (one of them shaded in* **c***) could be added, perhaps for winter warmth.*

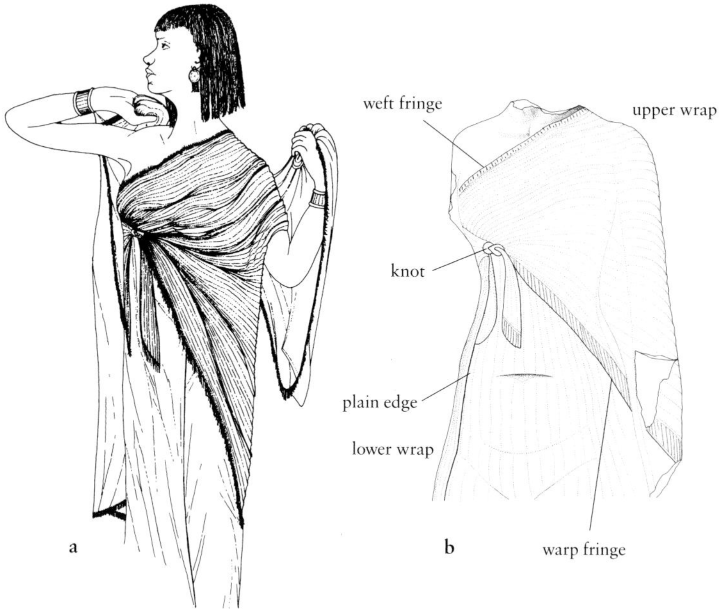

6.30 *Clothing styles.* **a** *The fashionable style of the times seems to have been based on untailored rectangles of fine linen, often provided with long fringes, that were worn in layers, fastened with knots and not pins.* **b** *A female member of the royal family shown dressed in two layers of fine linen, a lower, larger rectangle wrapped around the body and an upper, smaller rectangle, made with conspicuous fringes, worn as a knotted shawl (torso of a statue in the Musée du Louvre, Paris).* **c** *How an official might have looked, wearing a baggy rectangular sleeveless tunic, gathered at the waist with a wide, fringed sash.* **d** *How artists at Amarna portrayed the dress of an official, probably rendering the natural creases of the linen as if deliberately pleated (tomb of Huya, no. 1).* **e** *An older man dressed for warmth, having wrapped around himself a large, fringed rectangle of linen, covering his tunic.*

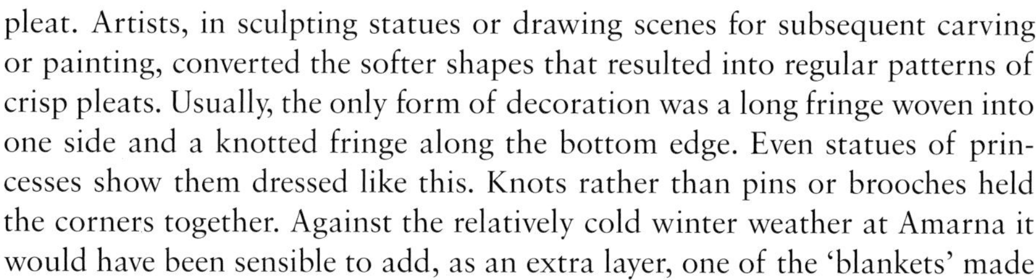

pleat. Artists, in sculpting statues or drawing scenes for subsequent carving or painting, converted the softer shapes that resulted into regular patterns of crisp pleats. Usually, the only form of decoration was a long fringe woven into one side and a knotted fringe along the bottom edge. Even statues of princesses show them dressed like this. Knots rather than pins or brooches held the corners together. Against the relatively cold winter weather at Amarna it would have been sensible to add, as an extra layer, one of the 'blankets' made with long pile, but we cannot be sure whether people did this. One has the impression from various sources that linen was abundant in ancient Egypt, and manufacturing it was a basic household industry. Stocks of linen, kept in wooden chests, were part of a family's wealth, a useful means of purchasing other things.

The draped whitish linen offered the maximum contrast for much of the jewelry of the time. The reward scenes show gold collars, but another ubiquitous industry at Amarna was the making of small beads and pendants in faience glazes of bright colour – predominantly yellow, blue, green, white and reddish-brown – that were threaded to make broad collars worn across the chest with a counterweight hanging behind the neck [**6.31**].[36] The small shapes imitated plant elements or depicted household gods (Bes and Taweret were popular, but never the Aten). The same range of colours, though primarily blue, was also used for the surface of a myriad small finger rings made from faience.[37] Facing outwards from the fingers was a flat plaque (the bezel) bearing a design drawn from a wide range of subjects. Two deserve comment. The most widely preferred was the eye of Horus (*wedjat*, see Chapter 7 and **7.9**), which represented wholeness and good health. The other was simply the first cartouche name of the king.[38] These were presumably made (in backyard workshops, see Chapter 8) on the accession of the king. The same colours (including white) could also be found at the ears, in the form of thick studs with a broad flat button-like end that was passed through a wide hole that had been made in the lobe (as seen on the reconstuction in **6.32**), or in the form of circles of glass or

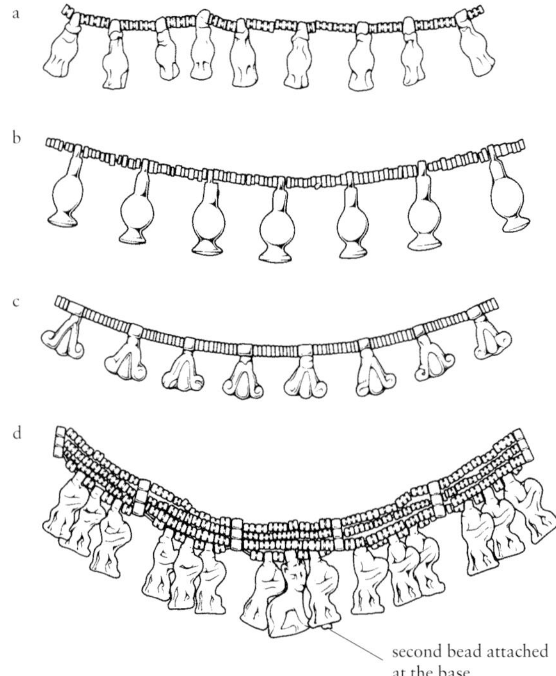

6.31 *Details of surviving necklace designs from Amarna. (a) obj. 30/272. Fifty-nine crudely moulded ?poppy seed-head pendants are attached with cylinder beads to the necklace string. Between the pendants are groups of segmented beads; (b) obj. 28/366. Sixteen blue ?poppy seed-head pendants, with red, yellow and dark-blue ring beads between; (c) obj. 26/142. A well made necklace of nineteen yellow Southern-plant pendants, with red, white and blue ring beads between; (d) obj. 28/328. Composed of four strings of yellow and red ring beads. The strings are held together by bead spacers. From the bottom string are suspended seven groups of three pendants in blue faience. These pendants depict the god Bes beating a tambourine, with the exception of the central pendant, which depicts a seated cat. One Bes pendant (arrowed) appears to have a second bead attached at the base.*

6.32 *Facial reconstruction of Individual 114 from the South Tombs Cemetery, a woman of between 40 and 50 at her death. She was between 161 and 162 cm tall (around 5 ft 3 in.). She had broken her left upper arm, but it had healed to a shorter length. She had suffered a blow to her head that had depressed her skull slightly and brought infection, but that had healed, too. She had been buried face downwards, and this had preserved her long hair plait.*

travertine, which, by means of a gap in the circle, could be pressed over the edge of the lobe. In the South Tombs Cemetery (for ordinary citizens), some people were buried with a single scarab or similar object (one group of three had a hippopotamus-shaped back, **Pl. XLI**), made of glazed steatite, which had been worn on a finger, held in place with thread. These objects look well worn and are carved with traditional symbols of power and protection. Some could have been heirlooooms.

For the further cladding of extremities, the god's father Ay received a pair of (probably leather) gloves from Akhenaten at a public ceremony of presentation, but we should regard these as rarities (Tutankhamun had a pair in his tomb). Several examples of leather sandals have been excavated.[39] They have been carefully made: two or more thicknesses for the sole are fixed with much stitching using a narrow thong, and an upright strap passes between the big and second toe to reach a circlet that held the sole to the ankle. Some examples have been found among the poorer houses, implying that they were not exclusive to the elite, something confirmed by the finding at the Workmen's Village of a wooden pattern of the kind one would use for cutting out the shape of a sole from a sheet of leather.[40] A sandal from the same site, the size of a child's foot, had red and green decoration around the edge.[41]

For both women and men, the desired appearance for the elite, as codified by art, was to go bare-headed. They could cover their natural hair with a wig, although we cannot judge how many people did this and in what circumstances.

Skulls from the excavation at the South Tombs Cemetery retain their original hair. In some cases, this had been plaited into many short braids, each one carefully whipped at the end to create a small knob. In other cases, the long hair of women was made into a single braid that hung down the back. Pictures of men and women of status (though not members of the royal family) often show a cone-shaped object placed on the crown of their head along with what are perhaps flowering lilies [**Pl. XLIV**]. The general assumption is that it was made of scented fat or wax. One woman was buried in the cemetery wearing what is probably the only known example on her head (its composition has not yet been determined).

Egyptian culture had long ago adopted the practice of emphasizing the eyes by rubbing a mineral powder (kohl) into the surrounding skin. Specimens of kohl recovered from the cemetery are of the grey metallic powder galena (lead sulphide). The Egyptians also produced or imported, and then used, a range of scented oils and unguents, known by individual names preserved in hieroglyphic texts. Such things were made to be rubbed into the skin. As noted above, it is tempting to see the cup-shaped depressions formed into a surface beside one of the Amarna bathrooms as receptacles to hold them [**6.9**].[42]

We have now formed a basis for the image of a successful, healthy Amarna citizen: a clean, perfumed, well-groomed body clad in carefully arranged layers of loose white linen, showing off gold and brightly coloured jewelry. Sometimes perhaps they touched or were close to other objects or articles that glowed with intense colours and intricate patterns, which have barely survived in the archaeological record [**Pl. XLV**].[43] Articles of this kind would have added to the contrasts between muted backgrounds and sudden colour areas – a juxtaposition that most Egyptians seem to have liked.

Impressions of a Good Life

The scenes in the rock tombs, and the tendency of modern reconstruction drawings or architectural models to idealize, give to Amarna a pleasing, positive character. It can seem almost like an early precursor to a modern garden city. An image of abundance and prosperity was consciously cultivated. Its symbols – food, drink, jewelry, incense and bouquets of flowers piled on light latticework tables and stands – appear in tomb scenes of palace interiors and in actual palace decoration. The same was true for the Aten, the hungriest of Egyptian gods. The signs of abundance filled the pictures of his temples. Among the many requests in the prayers of the rich officials in their tombs is to be well fed throughout eternity from the Aten's leftovers, a hope reinforced by pictures showing them sitting in front of a feast.

The desirability of foodstuffs in bulk, especially bread and beer, oxen and fowl, is characteristic of ancient Egypt generally. Akhenaten continued the tradition of showing himself as both generous consumer and provider. It would have carried greater weight than it does now. The Egyptian administrative system aimed to buffer the country against famine by maintaining full granaries. Temples, through food distributions, were a major instrument of implementing this policy. Moreover, Amarna was, in effect, an inland port receiving imports of commodities from elsewhere in Egypt and beyond: oil-based substances in distinctive pottery vessels from the Aegean and eastern Mediterranean, metal ingots (bronze or tin), incense from the region of Syria, wine from the Nile delta and the oases, craft products and also slaves from the courts of the Near East, tribute from Nubia. Yet, as a new city, Amarna also had to manage a major readjustment in its supplies, of foodstuffs as of everything else. Was this successful? Was Akhenaten able to live up to the promise contained in the pictures?

A Darker Side

Since 2006 a new source of evidence has become available for assessing what life was like at Amarna: the bones of the people themselves, excavated from a cemetery that lies in a desert valley behind the southern group of rock tombs [**7.26**]. As many as 3,000 people (possibly more) are likely to have been buried there. It offers a different, more sombre picture, of a state of health and well-being that is below what one might expect for the ancient past, especially for a population setting up home on a clean desert site at a time of high prosperity. At the time of writing, more than 200 individuals have been recovered and studied [**6.32**]. These are people who would have been alive at more or less the same time; many will have known one another or have been related. It is very rare in archaeology to have available for study a proper cross-section of a population from such a restricted period of time.[44]

Three characteristics of the group especially stand out: signs of inadequate nutrition in childhood, injuries to the skeleton and early death.

A common feature of the eye orbits of Amarna skulls is a minor distortion of bone growth (which the owners would have been unaware of) called *cribra orbitalia*. It marks prolonged nutritional deficiency up to the time of death. Acute illnesses in childhood have also left their record, in the form of banding in the teeth, which goes under the name of hypoplasia. A few cases of scurvy are known. Given this evidence, it is hardly surprising to find that, overall, the population was failing to achieve the normal stature for the period. On average, men and women were *c.* 164 cm (5 ft 4 in.) and *c.* 154 cm (5 ft) respectively, a few centimetres shorter than is expected of ancient Egyptians of other periods.

Injuries varied between those coming from blows and those, especially compression fractures of the spine, from bearing heavy loads. The latter affected young people as well as old. One older man's injuries, which included puncture wounds in the hip area received on two different occasions as if from arrows, identify him probably as a veteran soldier.[45] Five instances are known of a gruesome practice in which men had been stabbed through the shoulder, at an angle that pierced the muscle, but avoided penetrating the body cavity and endangering life (most easily achieved if the victim is spreadeagled on the ground with arms spread out). A form of punishment comes to mind.

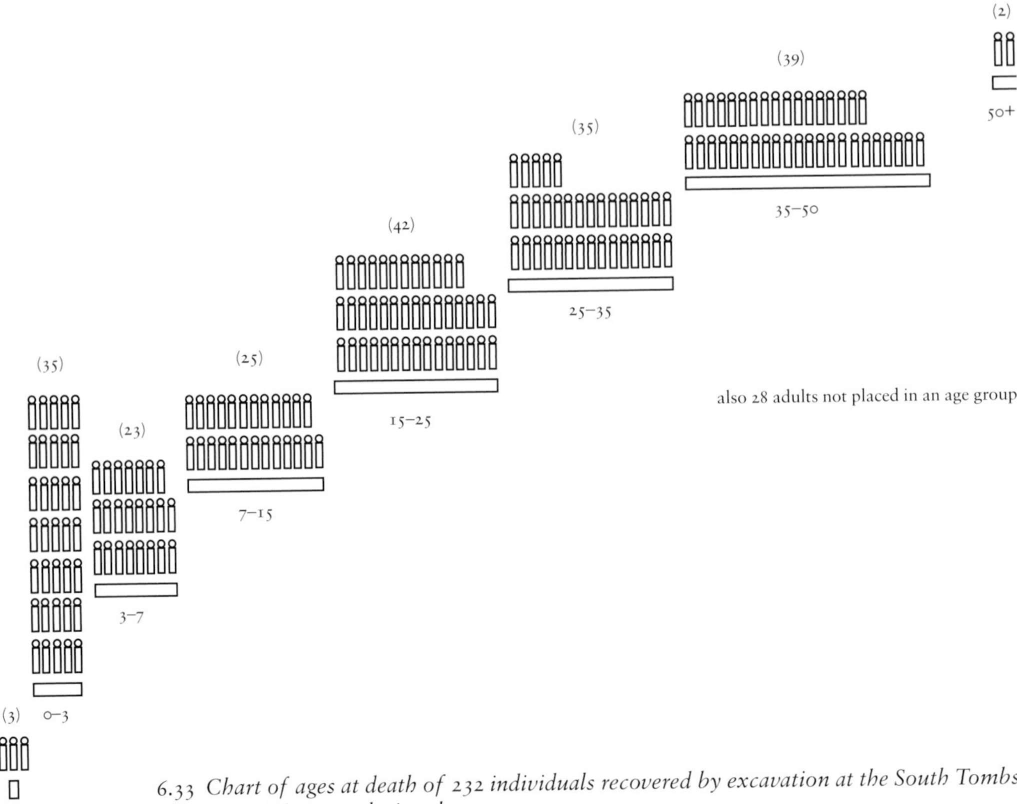

6.33 *Chart of ages at death of 232 individuals recovered by excavation at the South Tombs Cemetery at Amarna during the 2005–10 seasons.*

In a sample of 232 individuals whose ages have been ascertained, 70 per cent had died before reaching the age of 35 [**6.33**]. Many people thus had a much shorter lifespan in which to accumulate possessions and experience than is common today, and so many of the scribes, guards, women of the house and people engaged in manufacture will have been in their teens. The same, of course, was true for the royal family. They seem to have suffered a series of early deaths (including eventually that of Tutankhamun).

The abnormally high incidence of death among young people is consistent with patterns of death in populations known to have been victims of epidemics. So those individuals with hypoplasia might have survived one or more attacks of an epidemic, to which others succumbed. Hittite records from a generation later claim that, in Akhenaten's time, Egyptian prisoners of war spread an epidemic of some kind into Hittite society, something perhaps referred to obliquely in one of the Amarna Letters as brought on by the 'hand of Nergal', a Near Eastern god of pestilence.[46] The graves in the Amarna cemetery were dug into a bank of sand partially filling a narrow valley. They were often packed closely together, and they would have been difficult to open a second time to receive further burials. Where, in a significant number of instances, graves contained more than one individual, it is likely that they had died at the same time (bearing in mind the absence of evidence for mummification, as many of the skulls excavated retain brain tissue, and the consequent likelihood of very rapid burial after death).

Advances in analytical techniques, especially the growing confidence with which ancient DNA can be extracted and studied, make it likely that we are on the threshold of a much better understanding of the health of the time.[47] Tutankhamun, weak in health (malaria has been identified in his body) and dying young, looks like a representative of his people rather than a tragic product of an anomalous family.

How far should we allow the comparative bleakness of the cemetery evidence to influence our portrayal of the life of the times? Within certain bounds of reasonableness, people adjust to what is normal. What confronts them from birth to death is the baseline against which optimism and pessimism vie to become the dominant mood of the individual. Some lose out to despair, but overall, populations incline towards something more than fortitude, towards a degree of cheerfulness and optimism that can confound the expectations of people who have been brought up surrounded by the best of modern experiences. That said, those who moved to Amarna might have faced a drop in living standards severe enough to leave those who survived to the end of the Amarna period only too happy to move away when it became possible to do so.

7.1 *Carved limestone blocks from a shrine inside the house of the high priest Panehsy, reassembled in the Egyptian Museum, Cairo. Height 98 cm (38.6 in.), width 118 cm (46.5 in.).*

CHAPTER SEVEN

SPIRITUAL LIFE AT AMARNA

Religious reforming movements have sometimes come from below, from 'the people': Jesus of Nazareth, the village carpenter; the prophet Mohammed, the merchant from Medina. Their teachings spread through society as a result of enthusiastic adoption in household and neighbourhood, and became the religion of states only later. At that point we start to meet the familiar investment of large-scale resources by rulers in architecture and sometimes in warfare, as a way of glorifying simultaneously their religion and themselves. With Akhenaten we are looking at the reverse process. The one with the ideas was already an absolute ruler. With him lay the power and resources to bring the new ideas to the fore straight away and make them the approved religion of the state.

The approved religion of the state: two thousand years of intolerance and persecution have left an indelible impression of what that phrase implies. It is easy to expect that Akhenaten followed the same unsavoury route. But did he? Was he a bigot?

We can identify some of his aims: to purify the cult of the sun, leaving it without mythology; to establish a sacred home for the Aten; to instruct those around him in righteous conduct. We can take for granted a further aim: to perpetuate his dynasty. But Akhenaten did not live in a world that expected the relentless pursuit of consistency across a wide front. His reforming zeal might have been confined to particular, local targets of his choice.

Loyalty to the Regime

Fulsome adulation of the king was normal in ancient Egypt and was abundantly expressed at Amarna. He was its creator, and his images filled the stone buildings and dominated the decoration of the rock tombs of his officials. Collectively, however, these amounted to only a portion of the city and would not have been ordinarily visible to most people. The huge halls and statue-encircled courtyard of the Great Palace were hidden from the main thoroughfare by a mud-brick wall. In the streets of Amarna, so far as we know, there were no statues of Akhenaten to loom over passers-by.

Within their houses, officials combined commemoration of themselves with deference to the king and the Aten. The principal doorways, framed in stone, carried short prayers and showed the house owner kneeling in adoration before the cartouches of the Aten and the royal family [**Pl. XXX**]. A number of small stelae or plaques showing the royal family (including, in the city house of Panehsy, Amenhotep III and Queen Tiye) have been found in and around houses, though none in its original location. A wall niche is the most obvious place. A unique case is represented by the official house of the high priest Panehsy beside the Great Aten Temple. A shrine built of stone, carved and painted to appear like a small Amarna temple, stood in the central room of what was presumably his 'office' [7.1]. Sockets at the top of the sides of the doorway point to the original presence of a pair of narrow wooden doors closing the front. Inside, there is likely to have been a statue, most probably of the king.

Many of the larger houses possessed a small chapel that stood on its own in the surrounding enclosure, sometimes in a part laid out as a garden. Most were small brick chambers built on a low pedestal (one is at the rear of 7.2), but three of the larger examples were constructed of stone (although only the gypsum foundations survive). Two (U25.11 and .13) were part of the huge multiple-dwelling estate opposite the North Riverside Palace and must have belonged

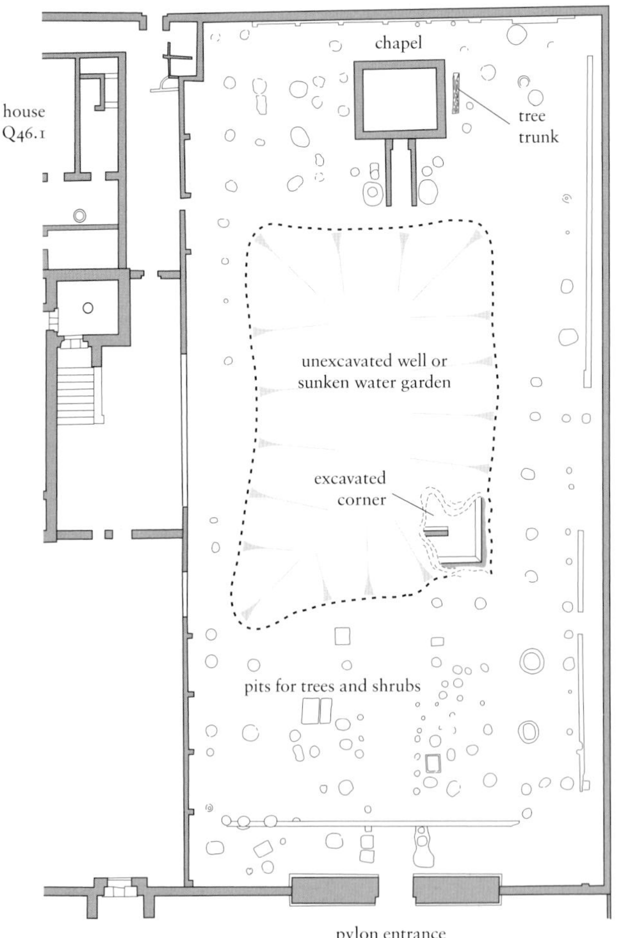

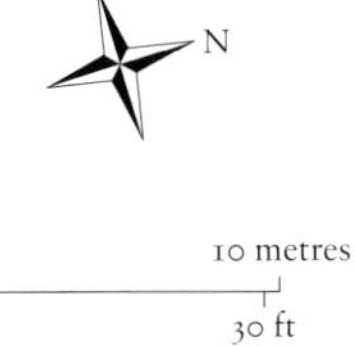

7.2 Garden, with central sunken area, shrine and tree pits, entered from the street between pylon towers and attached to the house of a high official (Q46.1). This could have been the setting for the funeral banquet prior to the burial of the deceased. Were some of the pits post-holes for a funerary tent?

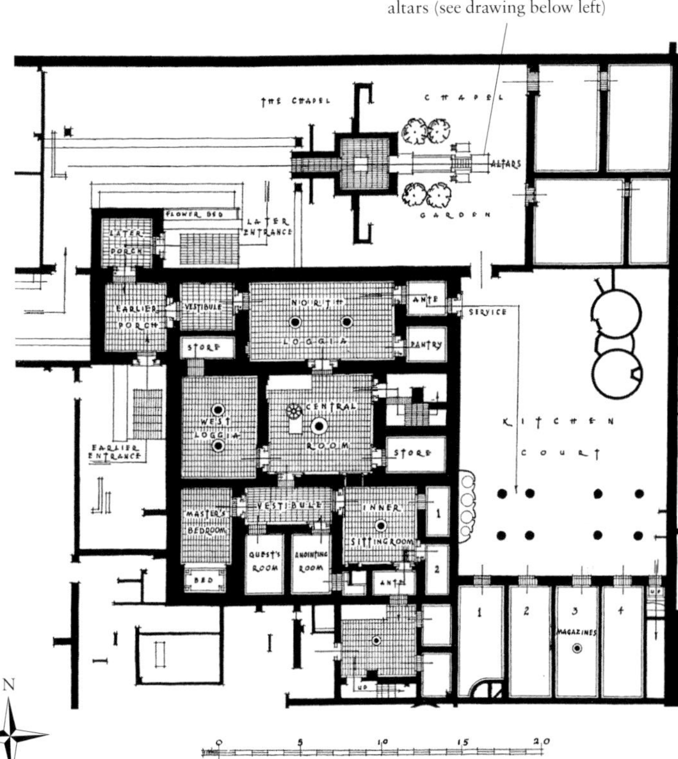

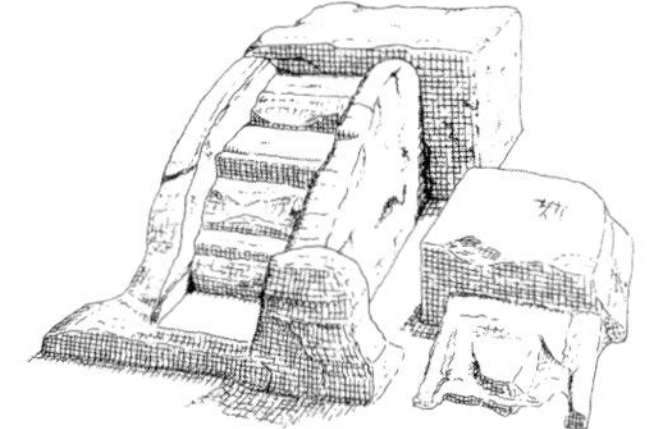

7.3, 7.4 Chapel and offering-place in the grounds of house T34.1 (of Hatiay). a partially reconstructed plan. The sketch of the two standing 'altars' is after the photograph. The left-hand 'altar' and the south half of the forecourt were not preserved. Stevens, Religion, *254, Fig. II.14.5 is another view.*

to people close to the royal family [**2.7, 5.8–5.10**]. They stood in groves of trees planted in straight lines and had pylons. The third example, belonging to the main city house of the high priest Panehsy (R44.2), had its own precinct containing ancillary brick buildings, and stood in a large space (probably a garden) fronted by a pylon opening to the street [**1.15**]. A few of the smaller brick chapels were likewise in a separately walled part of the enclosure with a pylon entrance to the street [**7.2**].

In a unique expression of private interest in the actual cult of the Aten, the chapel in the grounds of the North Suburb house T34.1 had two parts: at the front, a small court surrounding a single brick pedestal (for a stela or a small-scale version of the Benben-stone?); at the rear, a group of three tiny platforms reached by stairs, all facing towards the east [**7.3, 7.4**]. The owner of the house was not a priest, but an overseer of works, Hatiay.

Compared with the sizes and designs of the Workmen's Village chapels (see below), these garden shrines appear largely ornamental. At their best, when set in gardens, they recall in miniature the 'sunshade' temples (like that at Maru-Aten, **Pl. XXXVII**) and were likewise fitted with statues of the royal family and reliefs depicting them with the Aten. They represent a small-scale vision of an Arcadian landscape, of nature graced with sacred architecture. Perhaps it was sufficiently an act of loyalty to erect such places and maintain them in a token fashion without organizing a programme of cult. The garden shrines were little monuments to deference and also probably marks of status, advertising that the owner was a member of the king's establishment. Perhaps some people felt a sense of pride in identifying with a regime that was trying to change old ideas. Nonetheless, not all of the larger houses had one; it was not obligatory.[1]

Outside these pockets of loyalty, the material culture of the people who lived at Amarna paid little heed to the Aten. It is true that texts speak of Akhenaten as the only one who knows the Aten, and this can give the impression that he had set himself up as the sole mediator with the Aten, so that popular material expression was not necessary. Yet the owners of the rock tombs addressed prayers to the Aten, as well as to Akhenaten and Nefertiti, and – in a text quoted several times in this book – the unguent preparer Ramose speaks of the Aten as an intimate inner voice. The potential was there for an active interest in the Aten by people other than the king and queen. Nevertheless, while the cartouches of the Aten were occasional elements in jewelry, the distinctive sun-disc with rays was not adopted into the repertoire of popular designs. It did not appear on rings or as the subject of pendants. Only two or three examples have been found at Amarna of vernacular drawings of the image [1.2].[2] When set against the abundant use of traditional symbols at Amarna, the seeming failure of the Aten symbol to find a place in popular material culture is noteworthy.

One way in ancient Egypt of expressing piety or loyalty was to incorporate a god's name into personal names. A few examples that used the name Aten are known from Amarna, but they are rare (the general Paatenemheb, whose name means 'The Aten is in festival', owner of tomb no. 24, is one). None of the three senior priests we can identify (Meryre, Panehsy and Pawah, the last the owner of house O49.1) followed this practice, although the vizier Nakhtpaaten did (yet also abbreviating his name to Nakht). Thutmose, the sculptor in whose house the painted bust of Nefertiti was found, not only kept a name that honoured the god Thoth, he wrote the Thoth element in his name using an ibis-headed human figure, the kind of anthropomorphic divinity image that we are inclined to think Akhenaten abhorred [7.5]. Thoth in his alternative shape of a baboon is the inspiration for a statue of an unnamed scribe found in another probable

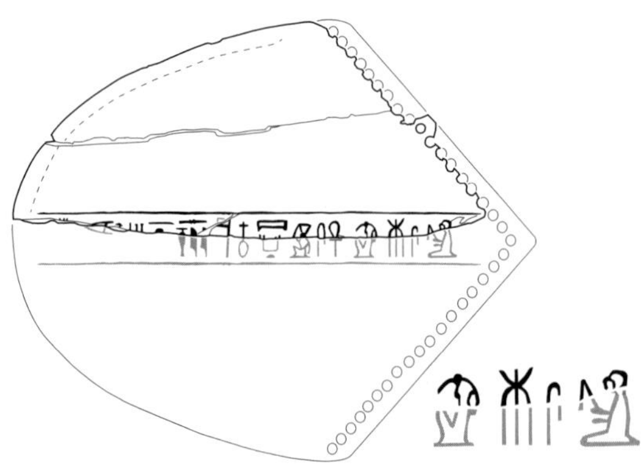

7.5 *Half of an ivory horse-blinker inscribed in hieroglyphs with the titles and name of the chief of works and sculptor Thutmose (Djehutymes) and found beside his house. He wrote his name (shown at an enlarged scale) using a traditional ibis-headed sign. Length 11 cm (4.3 in.).*

7.6 Statuette of a seated scribe beneath an image of the god Thoth, in his baboon manifestation, made from steatite. From house or sculptors' workshop O47.16a. Height: 10.8 cm (4.25 in.).

sculptor's workshop [7.6]. In neither case can we be certain that the pieces did not predate the Amarna period. Their significance lies in the fact that their owners did not suppress these symbols of the old gods and, in the case of Thutmose, the sculptor responsible for many statues of the royal family, in the fact that he did not change his name.

People do not, however, convert all their ideas into symbols. Material culture is not a full guide to inner life. We have previously met the man Ramose, of relatively low status (an unguent preparer in the House of Meryetaten), known from two personal letters that he wrote to relatives at Thebes.[3] In them, he refers to the Aten as a source of guidance in making personal decisions. Is this someone who has taken Akhenaten's moral teaching to heart and is equating the Aten with his own conscience? It will also be recalled, from Chapter 3, that there is scope for choosing whether to see the people of Amarna embracing the cult of the Aten in huge public gatherings at the temple that coincided with food distributions, or whether to accept a more exclusive view of the cult of the Aten, reserved for the royal family and a privileged group of attendants.

Divine Trespassers

The place Akhetaten, so the king declared, had not belonged to any god or goddess and was now to belong to the Aten. The implied exclusivity did not last for long. A quiet colonization by minor divinities took place once the city population began to move in, but whether Akhenaten or anyone else perceived the inconsistency and was troubled by it is impossible to tell. The Aten belonged to a separate plane of experience and so completely overshadowed everything else that perhaps people did not see it as competition.

Thoth was one of the colonizers. Examples of others come from one of the two desert communities, the Workmen's Village, which (along with the Stone Village) was made an exception to the policy of desert exclusion. On slopes beside the walled village, the inhabitants constructed small private chapels [5.30, 7.7]. They numbered around twenty-three, thus roughly one for every three houses (of which there were seventy-two). Like conventional temples, they had a single central axis along which several small courts or roofed spaces were arranged, entrances that hinted at the shape of pylons and tiny raised sanctuaries at the back. These were provided with brick benches suited to the support of small objects of veneration, one of which was a small limestone stela that commemorated the members of a family and depicted the goddess Isis and a god named Shed who offered protection against scorpions; prayers on the stela also embraced the Aten [7.8]. A painted wooden image of the sun's disc supported on cow's horns probably came from a statue of Hathor (perhaps in her cow form). The top of a wooden standard found in another chapel honoured a jackal-god, presumably Wepwawet, who was associated with the desert and cemeteries, and whose cult centre, at Asyut, lay about 70 km (43.5 miles) upstream [**Pl. XXXIX**]. The walls of the chapels had been painted with conventional scenes that avoided any hint of the Amarna art style [**Pls XXII, XXIII**, also **Pl. XLIV**]. One had been entered through a limestone doorway that contained a prayer to Amun-Ra.[4]

7.7 *View, to the east, of the Main Chapel at the Workmen's Village. At the rear is a line of three small chambers, a set of sanctuaries, each containing a shelf for the support of sacred objects (for a reconstruction of the front of the chambers, see plate XXII). The scale is 1 m (39.4 in.) long.*

7.8 *A family memorial, obj. 21/527. Limestone stela from the Workmen's Village, chapel 525. In the front panel stand the 'saviour'-god Shed and the goddess Isis, to both of whom a man named Ptahmay offers food and a prayer. On the sides are carved his family: left side, top, Ptahmay sits and is waited on by 'the lady of the house, Nubemshant (?)' accompanied by 'his son, Khaemmenu'; left side, bottom, standing in a line are 'his son, Khaemmenu', 'his daughter, Bakist', 'his daughter, Bakist', 'his daughter, Heket(?)'; right side, top: Ptahmay sits and is waited on by 'his sister, the lady of the house Thefy'; right side, bottom: 'his daughter, Heket (?)' and 'his daughter, Neferu' entertain with music and dancing. Height 44.4 cm (17.5 in.). See Stevens,* Religion, *143.*

A superficially attractive explanation is that at least some of the chapels had been built after Akhenaten's death, when the rejection of his style of rule had already begun. The chapels are, however, an integral part of the village layout, sometimes fitting closely between non-religious buildings. There is no definite sign that they are later insertions. Their decoration seems to show how far people felt able to choose their own spiritual path, in this case in a community that was deliberately isolated from the rest of the city.

The principal dilution of the Aten's exclusive occupation of Amarna came, however, from people's sympathies for protective deities that were expressed in ways that seem to have permeated personal and domestic life. Among the realities of ancient Egyptian life were the agents of an authoritative and bureaucratic administration that could bear down and make your life a misery, people in your own community who became your 'enemy' (Egyptian texts sometimes mention these), the accidents and illnesses that were never far away and, within generally small houses, the old age and often premature death that you witnessed from childhood onwards. It made sense to think that forces were at work that disturbed the possibility of a harmonious life.

One of the most widely owned – and presumably read – texts for the society from which Amarna's population was drawn was the Book of the Dead. Although it is primarily (though not wholly) concerned with existence after death, its unsettling world of gods and spirits was simultaneously separate from and identical to the conscious self of the individual reader. Eternity was a nervous voyaging through an imagined universe – an Otherworld – that the Egyptians seem to have recognized was actually within themselves. Its creatures, in having names and characteristics, had a degree of identity of their own that kept them separate. Yet, by the very fact that the individual reader knew their names, those creatures – and they included the greatest of the gods – were also potentially a part of that individual. The reader constantly slipped in and out of identity with gods who possessed positive characteristics, at one moment honouring them and at another assuming their powers in order to combat the forces of chaos.

> I am the daily sun. I am not grasped by my arms, I am not gripped by my hands. There are no men, gods, spirits, dead men, patricians, common people, sun-folk or robbers who shall harm me. I go forth hale, one whose name is unknown.[5]

The self-as-universe was the daily reality from which existence after death was a projection. This is brought home by collections of medical–magical texts (from periods earlier and later than Amarna) that had a place in the properly equipped household. Their viewpoint is the same as that of the Book of the Dead. In grappling with the forces that brought sickness, laid children mysteriously low or provoked scorpions to creep into the house and sting, the person who opened up the papyrus roll and found the appropriate spell drew power from knowing that he (they are written from a male standpoint), for that instant, was the controlling force in the universe. Addressing the power of a scorpion, the reader declares: 'If [you] bite: I am Osiris. If you take me along: I am Horus.'[6] From this point of view, every Amarna house had the capacity to be a theatre in a struggle between the householder and demonic enemies.

The logic of modern portrayals of Akhenaten as intolerant is that he is bound to have disapproved of magic and its demons, and even to have tried to prevent people from using it to sustain them in times of need and anxiety. That would indeed have been a serious blow, especially in the light of evidence that the country was suffering from a serious epidemic (see Chapter 6). The religion of solar light on its own did not explain the bad things of life and thus could not have offered remedies. Egyptian medicine was founded on pragmatic skill mixed with knowledge of the properties (or assumed properties) of substances, and with the confrontation of demonic powers in the way just described. Are we to assume that medical texts were edited at Amarna so as to exclude this last central element? One of the owners of a rock tomb, Penthu (tomb no. 5), was the 'Chief of Physicians' at court. What kind of remedies could he have offered Akhenaten that ignored the spiritual component of malady and thus the existence of a non-Atenist spirit world?

Friendly Forces

One of the commonest finds in the city is of pieces of faience finger rings and their decorated flat surfaces (bezels) . By far the most numerous of the designs is the *wedjat*-eye, or Eye of Horus, which was also worn in bead necklaces and on the finger [**7.9**]. It was a symbol of wholeness and hence of wellbeing, the fundamental meaning of the word *wedjat* itself. It was no ordinary eye. Although its basic shape was human, two decorative extensions imitated the markings beside the eye of a falcon. In this it represented one of the eyes of the god Horus (when in his falcon form), which was ripped out by his relative Seth in a fierce quarrel that stood for the archetypal conflict between legitimacy and disruption in the exercise of power, both political and supernatural. References to the myth permeated Egyptian thinking; versions of it recur in medical–magical texts. Although the symbol had other associations (with Ra, for example), it is reasonable to assume that, to the people of Amarna, its protective power lay in its evocation of the Horus–Seth conflict.

A symbol of attacking power that could be harnessed to a person's advantage when confronting hostile things was the cobra (or uraeus). The cobra was versatile in its imagined powers. A spell against nightmares that arise from evil spirits calls for the use of four cobras made from clay that are set in the corners of the bedroom.[7] In another spell, intended to provide protection against scorpions, Isis models serpents from earth.[8] Under the name Renenutet (the Greek form of the name is Ternuthis), the cobra offered protection to stores of grain (endangered by insect infestation). Numerous clay figurines of cobras, both fired and unfired, have been found at Amarna [**7.10**]. They take two forms. In one, the cobra stands on a flat base, sometimes with a tiny offering-stand attached to its front. In the other, it rears itself from the bottom of a shallow pottery bowl that has a wavy rim, suggestive of an intention to fill the bowl with water as a prelude to magical usage, divining being one possibility.[9]

The small brightly coloured glazed pendants from which collars and necklaces were made included a range of helper symbols [**6.31**]. One represented the god Bes, a bandy-legged dwarf figure who bore a lion's mane, protruded his tongue, banged on a circular percussion instrument and is often shown as if vigorously dancing. He evidently had the role of household protector and represented, through his image, release from the constrained behaviour that

7.9 *Two* wedjat-*eye finger rings made from greenish-blue faience. Obj. 34128, with a length of 1.86 cm (0.73 in.) across the face, comes from the house of Ranefer; obj. 34948, with a length of 1.73 cm (0.68 in.) across the face, comes from Grid 12.*

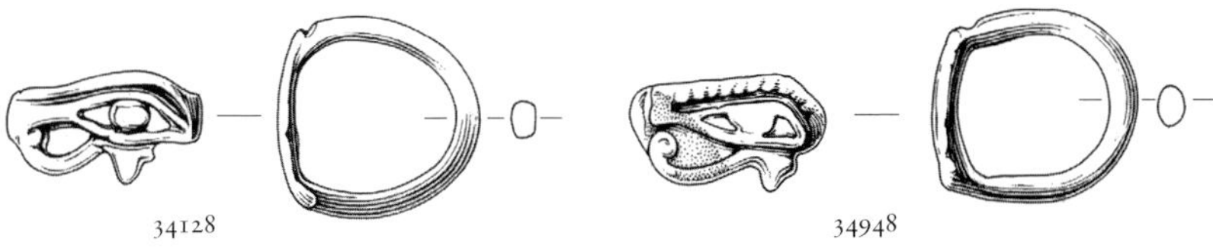

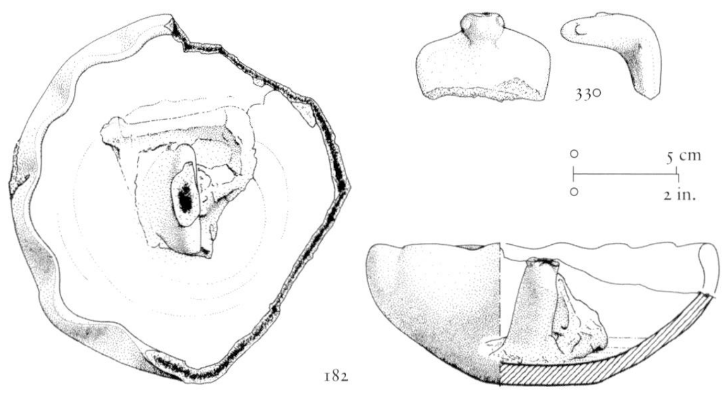

7.10 Pottery cobra bowl from the Workmen's Village, obj. 182, and the head from another bowl, obj. 330. The outline of this head has been added to the damaged figure in the bowl to complete the effect. Original bowl diameter c. 17.5 cm (6.9 in.).

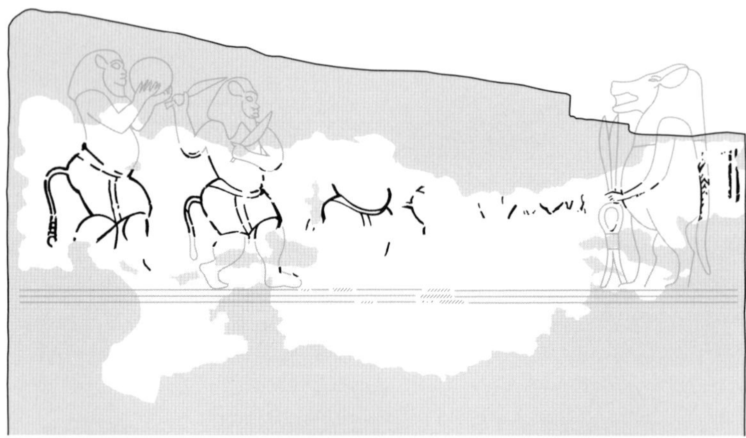

7.11 Painting of a procession of Bes figures in front of an image of the goddess Taweret. Workmen's Village, house Main Street 3, front room. The procession runs for the full length of the wall, c. 2.8 m (9.2 ft). The painted lines of the figures were white, on a mud-coloured background. Traces remained of three parallel lines along the bottom in a different colour, perhaps red or blue.

7.12 Statuette of the god Bes, obj. 29/283, made from steatite and standing on a base of travertine (not shown). Height 12 cm (4.7 in.). It looks as though it has been made for the insertion of a tongue and penis of a different material (red-painted ivory?). The holes on the back must belong to a means of support.

Egyptians aspired to and which, by and large, governed the portrayal of their gods. A procession of four or five Bes figures was painted across the full width of a wall in one of the Workmen's Village houses [7.11].[10] They dance their way towards a figure of the standing goddess Taweret (half crocodile, half hippopotamus), who faces them holding the hieroglyphic sign for 'protection'. The painting was an addition to the wall's original plaster and had transformed what was normally a workroom into a shrine. Might it have been added at the time of a marriage or impending birth? The bringing of children into the world is a subject that modern commentators assume was, in the past, so fraught with frustration and risk as to have warranted the invoking of divine aid in a particularly intense way. This was where the incongruous pair Bes and Taweret had their particular niche, as guardians of childbirth. Slightly larger statuettes or figurines of Bes in a variety of materials have been found in the housing areas at Amarna. One, finely carved in dark steatite on a travertine base, was large enough to have stood inside a small shrine [7.12].

Among the material found in the Amarna housing areas are figurines, most made of pottery, but a few in limestone, that depict women wearing heavy wigs, sometimes lying on a bed [7.13]. Pottery beds on their own, at a similar scale, also occur. They attract diverse explanations, often involving procreation or sexuality. We should not be too ready, however, to pick on a single explanation. One Egyptian text that demanded the use of a 'woman's statue [made] of clay', had, as its purpose, the alleviation of stomach upsets.[11]

7.13 *A collection of objects found together in N49.21, a medium-sized house in the Main City. They are shown at approximately the same scale.* a *Limestone stela, on which a woman and a boy stand before the protector-goddess Taweret, whose form was that of a standing hippopotamus with crocodile head. Height 15.2 cm (6 in.).* b *Pottery female figurine, wearing a heavy wig and a cone. Length 12.5 cm (4.9 in.).* c, d *Pottery model beds (with headrests), the lines painted dark red on a white slip. Length of 21/426 16.5 cm (6.5 in.). The objects are of compatible size, easy to pick up and hold, and to set out in a small space when needed. They all probably express the theme of regular and safe childbirth.*

7.14 *Face of the goddess Hathor moulded into the side of a large pottery bowl. Obj. 34149, from the Grid 12 housing area. Height 6 cm (2.4 in.).*

In their appearance, the figurines are reminiscent of images of the goddess Hathor. Her face was modelled on the outside of pottery bowls at Amarna [7.14; also **6.13d**] and it appears in an architectural drawing of a shrine originally on the wall of the Great Palace at Amarna, a clear sign of royal acceptance.[12] Artists found ways to hint at her association with the Amarna royal women, whose fleshy portrayals can also be interpreted as symbolic of fecundity.[13] More generally, she showed a kindly disposition to Egyptians who found themselves in desert outposts, in colonial towns and remote mines. She lent legitimacy to licence, in particular in the drinking of beer and in breaking free from the normal social constraints of Egyptian society. Women found a comfortable role in her cult.

Both the unnamed figurines and Hathor herself are perhaps ways of invoking a spirit of kindly femininity, who could soften the harshness of desert existence, alleviate pains, assuage fears and promise pleasure: the all-purpose comforter and a counterpart to Bes, the provoker of turbulence.

It is difficult to accept that this considerable body of material, which demonstrates a widespread retention of old beliefs [7.15], was an underground or clandestine sub-culture. The ties of dependency in the densely packed neighbourhoods, where privacy must have been slight anyway, would have ensured that the local patrons, the officials who owed so much to their king, would have known most of what was happening among their dependants. Moreover, the excavation of individual houses has occasionally yielded collections of objects that are sufficiently numerous to suggest that they are accumulations over time of the material remains of a single household. The house of a senior official, the overseer of works Hatiay (T34.1), had escaped depredation to the extent that the painted and inscribed lintel from the door to the central hall of his house had remained where it had fallen [**Pl. XXX**]. Among the objects found was an eclectic collection that represents 'religion' in several guises. It included:

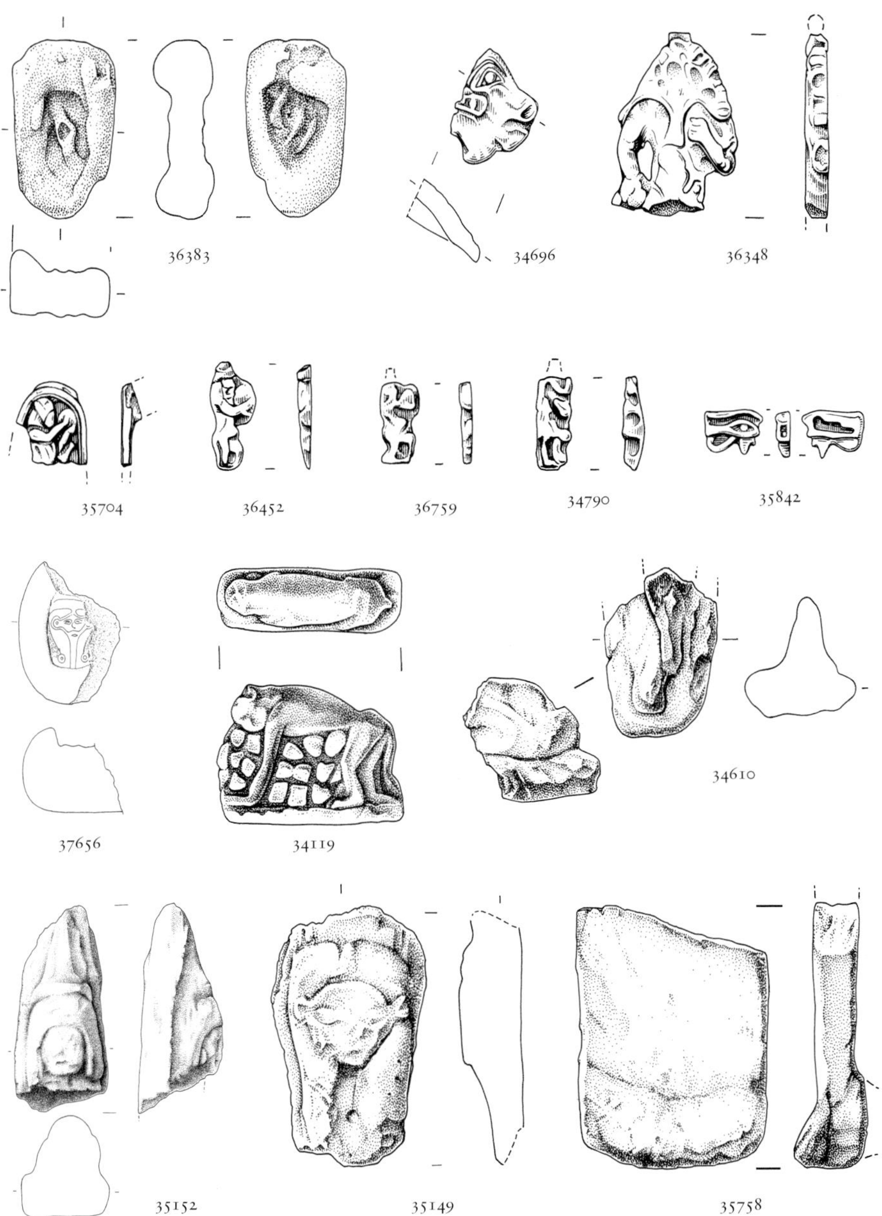

7.15 *A selection of objects and designs that express aspects of a world of supernatural forces, recovered from one small housing area, that of Grid 12. Obj. 36383, faience model of a human ear; obj. 34696, faience plaque in the form of the head of a bull; obj. 36348, faience pendant of Bes draped with an animal skin; objs 35704, 36452, 36759, Bes banging a drum or similar, designs on a faience finger ring and pendants; obj. 34790, faience pendant of Taweret; obj. 35842, the* wedjat*-design on a bead; obj. 37656, part of a pottery mould for making pendants bearing the face of Hathor; obj. 34119, limestone figurine of a monkey astride a pile of fruit; obj. 34610, base of a pottery cobra; obj. 35152, top of a pottery figurine of a woman with tall headdress; obj. 35149, face of Hathor from a pottery bowl; obj. 35758, part of a pottery model bed. See Kemp and Stevens,* Busy Lives II, *passim.*

- Round-topped limestone stela showing Thoth as an baboon.
- Fragment of a stela showing Aten worship (found near the garden shrine).
- Gold 'brooch' naming the Aten, found buried beneath the floor of one room.
- Variety of items of faience jewelry featuring images of power (including Bes and the *wedjat*-eye).
- Fragments of pottery vessels with the head of the goddess Hathor in relief.
- Pottery figurines, including those of women.
- Four faience cobra heads.[14]

A not dissimilar range was found in the city house of the high priest Panehsy (R44.2), a particularly valuable context in view of Panehsy's own role at Amarna and the relative isolation of his house:

- A stela depicting Amenhotep III and Queen Tiye.
- A stela showing two women serving food and drink to two seated men (ancestors?) [**6.4**, second from right].
- Other stelae now difficult to decipher (but probably showing human figures and offerings).
- Bovid-shaped vessel.
- Cobra bowl.
- *Wedjat*-eye finger rings.[15]

We have direct evidence for where some of this kind of material was made. Faience pendants and finger rings in the shapes of the familiar amulets, and glass *wedjat*-eye beads were made in small workshops scattered across the city, sometimes places where more 'official' articles were apparently also made. The workshop of the sculptor Thutmose (originator of the famous painted bust of Nefertiti) was one.

Another context, significant because, like the city house of Panehsy, it was isolated and thus less likely to contain material from other buildings, is the courtyard workshop Q48.4 [**8.3**]. It lay beside a large well that probably supplied the distant Workmen's Village with water and might thus have had an official status. It contained a pottery workshop. Among the debris were at least thirty fragments of female figurines (one of them not yet fired), an unfired figurine of a lion or sphinx and sixteen unfired sherds from wavy-rimmed cobra bowls. The female figurines were sufficiently alike to create the impression of having a common manufacturing origin, and also resembled figurines from the Workmen's Village.[16]

7.16 Mud-brick altar in the central room of house P46.24.

The rings and pendants were items to be worn, but this did not apply to the small stelae, figurines and statuettes. Within at least forty-one of the houses in the city, a small brick platform had been built, most often against one wall in the central room. Some of them preserve a raised edge and a tiny step or steps [**7.16**].[17] They range from around 25 to 90 cm (9.8 to 35.4 in.) in height, the lower ones belonging to that floor zone with which Egyptians were comfortable. Some of the houses in question were modest in size. A plausible explanation is that the platforms were 'altars' on which objects of veneration – the stelae and figurines – were set when occasion demanded, the larger ones perhaps in little decorated wooden shrines. When not in use, objects of this kind were presumably wrapped in cloth and stored in a wooden chest.

Egyptian towns and cities developed separate places of local sanctity, within housing areas. One example of a shrine to gods of a local community from elsewhere in Egypt can be identified at Amarna (building P48.4). Within it was found a stela honouring traditional gods, the Elephantine group of Khnum, Satis and Anukis.[18] Did it serve to counter the homesickness of a group of families drawn from this distant place? Another small brick building that looks like a shrine (P47.10) lay beside a well not far from the house of the sculptor Thutmose (it is marked on the plan, **5.9**).

There was, in addition, a source of quasi-spiritual authority that we are inclined to overlook: none other than the head of the household.

Ancestors-to-be

Amarna society revolved around its senior 'officials'. The division of authority was not absolute, since the official class itself had many grades. Most officials will have looked up to someone of greater standing and, at the same time, will have expected to command respect from people below them.

Modern accounts of ancient Egypt make regular reference to the 'deceased', people figured on offering-slabs or tomb walls or represented by statues, or the subject of journeys in the Otherworld. The only thing wrong with this is that individuals could also claim the key attributes of being 'deceased' while still alive. We should not see this as a morbid character trait, however. We simply lack, in English, a word that covers the condition in which a person is honoured in life in terms that are equally appropriate after death. People saw themselves, in a seemingly positive spirit, as ancestors-to-be. This was an aspect of the generous view that the Egyptians took as to where the property of 'being divine' was to be encountered, which was outlined in Chapter 1 (see pp. 25–26).

Men in senior positions at Amarna (and elsewhere) were honoured in their houses by texts that proclaimed their eternal virtues, by prayers addressed to their 'spirit' (*ka*) and by writing of their name with the accompaniment of the hieroglyphic sign of a swathed and enthroned man holding a flail, followed by the phrase 'true of voice' or 'justified', which referred to a successful outcome of judgment of one's life before the tribunal of Osiris [**Pl. XXX**] and was more normally associated with the deceased, who were to face trial more imminently, rather than the living. Small painted scenes on the wall showed these ancestors-to-be seated before the ubiquitous table of offerings. They were represented in their houses by statues [7.17]. In three houses (J49.1, M50.1, O49.9) brick constructions that filled the width of a small room are perhaps the remnants of

7.17 Limestone statuette of an unnamed man, obj. 29/331, seated on a chair and holding a lily (lotus). Height 18 cm (7 in.). Eyes and wig black, flesh parts red, chair red and black.

7.18 *Statue of the scribe Any, carved in the shrine at the back of his tomb chapel (no. 23) at Amarna. He sits on a chair placed on a platform reached by steps, waiting to receive food-offerings. He, and not the king or the Aten, is the object of veneration in this chapel.*

shrines,[19] closely resembling the shrine at the back of the tomb of Any [**7.18**]. Whether such a large statue of a head of household (living or dead), and presumably made of wood, was ever present, it is impossible to say. Tiny faience human busts, where the suspicion is that they represent heads of houses, living or dead, might be a miniaturized reflection of the same interest.[20]

The same phrases and offering-scenes were carved within the inner chambers of tombs, where the focus of the offering-cult was a statue of the man himself (and, in the case of the general, Ramose, owner of tomb no. 11, of his wife as well, the 'Lady of the House', Nebetint). Thus the spirit of the head of the family was commemorated in a way that blurred the transition from life to death. To be the head of a household (especially if also one of the king's officials) was to possess an aura of authority that placed one in the ranks of minor cult figures.

Had Amarna continued to be occupied, these honoured figures would eventually have died and their heirs would probably have left the house decorations in place, out of respect, until such time as fading memory had weakened the bond, and the time came for a descendant or new owner to see himself as of greater importance. A new cycle would then commence. The old decorated stonework would be ripped out for re-use, and new stonework inserted. An aspiring ancestor would replace the most recent real one. Given the generally short life spans, this unit of time might have had a duration of no more than about thirty years.

Another blurring of the boundary between life and death is seen in decorated tomb chapels of the immediately preceding and succeeding periods: a common scene depicted the tomb owner, often with his wife, presiding over a banquet. Relatives and friends, frequently named (the men and women segregated), sit either on chairs or on mats on the floor. They wear fine clothes, are waited on by servants and entertained by dancers and musicians. In a few tombs, the words of songs are written. They invoke thoughts of death, both positive and negative. We cannot tell if the individuals were alive or dead when the paintings were made. These family groups were intended to be timeless. In the Amarna rock tombs these scenes have been demoted in favour of scenes that featured the life of the royal family, but it seems reasonable to accept that the custom of celebratory family meals at which the spirits of recent ancestors were felt to be present was not itself abandoned.

Where were such meals held? The chapels of the rock tombs at Amarna (and other similar sites) seem too austere and show no signs of facilities for preparing meals. The painted mud-brick chapels at the Workmen's Village, which were provided with brick benches and where direct evidence for the presence of food has been found, fit the role perfectly. But they are unique at Amarna. What did the rest of the population do, those who lived in the main city? The only plausible answer is, they held such banquets within the houses themselves, perhaps beginning by honouring the couple who were the heads of the family in a way that recalled the offering ceremony, and making reference to those not long deceased. It could have been quite simple, but still a conscious mimicking of a familiar set of ritual gestures.

The permanent home for an ancestor of elevated status was a chapel cut into the face of the 'eastern mountain of Akhetaten, the place of Maat' [7.19].[21] A varied collection of officials chose locations for combined tombs and memorial chapels in the rocky slopes that face Amarna, in two groups: one in the north where the rock rises into a low cliff above a steep slope, and one in the south where the hills are low and broken by shallow desert wadis. Each of the two groups lay at the end of branches of the desert trackway system, perhaps laid out at a time when their points of departure were at the two ends of the city. Why a particular official chose the north or south group for the location of his tomb is not clear. The tomb of the high priest Panehsy is in the northern group, but his private residence in the main city was closer to the southern group and was on the line of a trackway that led to the southern group [**Pl. XI**].

The tomb chapels vary considerably [7.20 7.21]. The ideal was one or more rooms strung along a single axis, ending in a small shrine containing a statue of the tomb owner, the walls of all parts decorated with carved and painted scenes. A measure of ambition was the size of the internal rooms and, if they were at all wide, the number of columns supporting the roof. None of the tombs was finished. In many cases, as soon as it was practicable, the decoration of the area around the doorway and the first hall was started. The main theme was celebration of the life of the king and of the royal family, and of

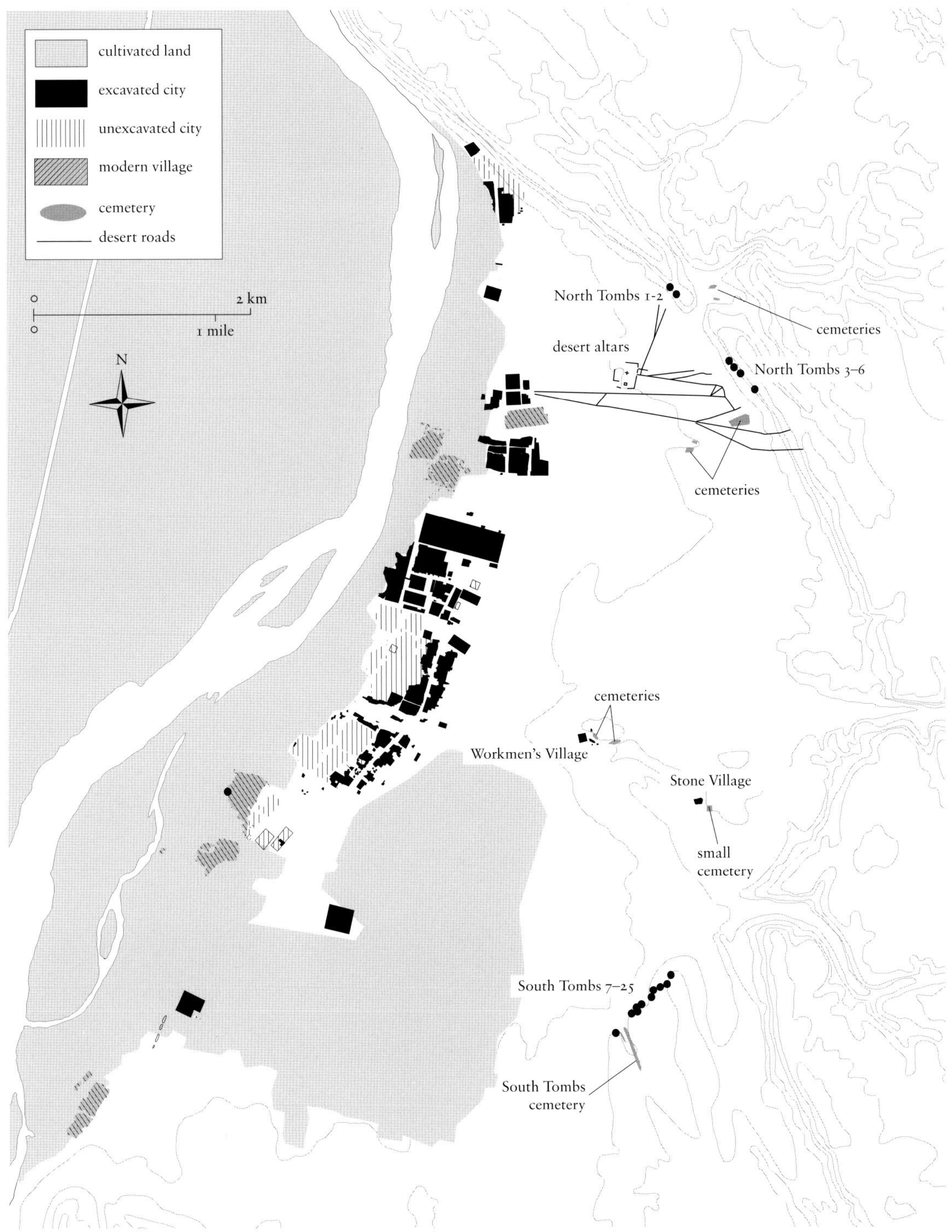

7.19 *Map of Amarna, showing the locations of tombs and cemeteries. The road system around the Desert Altars has been included.*

7.20 *(left) View of the interior of tomb no. 16 (anonymous).*

7.21 *(below) Section and plan of the tomb of Huya (no. 1), of the North Tombs group at Amarna. For some individual scenes, see figures 7.22, 7.23, 8.16, 8.17.*

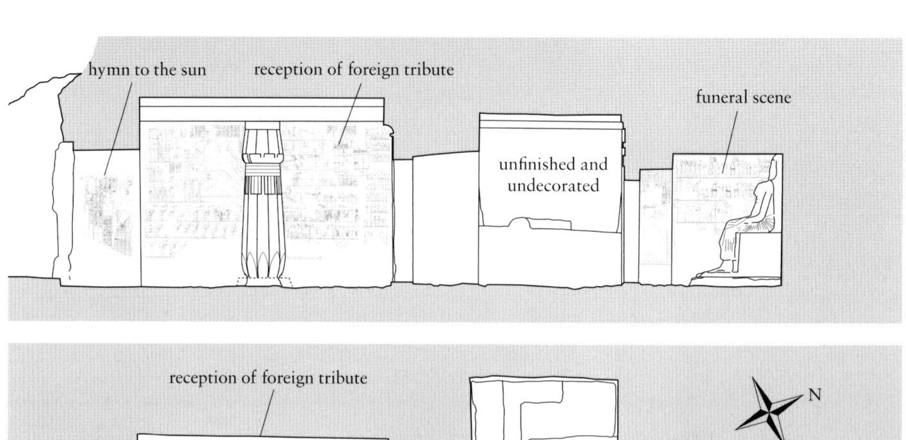

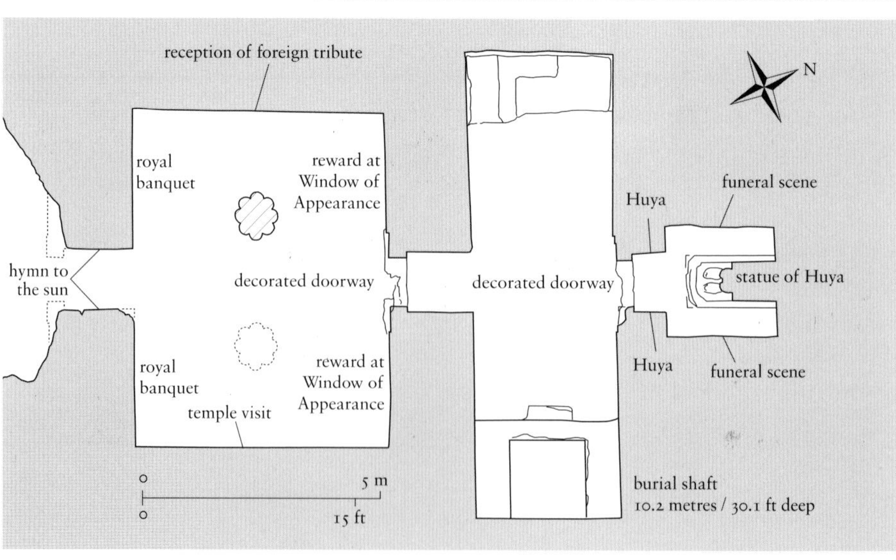

the owner's dependency on the king (whereas tombs of the preceding period celebrated the life of the tomb owner himself; a partial exception at Amarna is Mahu, the chief of police, of tomb no. 9, who included detailed scenes of his policing duties at Amarna as well as scenes of the royal family). This has contributed to the modern perception of Akhenaten intruding into what had been a largely private realm of ancestral commemoration, forcing on his people a more intensive cult of his person and of Nefertiti.

A second priority in these tombs was to develop the rear shrine to the point where it could become the next area for decoration, skipping unfinished rooms and doorways in between. This second priority partially counteracted the first. The rock tombs, although giving deference to Akhenaten in the outer parts, are actually shrines dedicated to the tomb owner, who sits enthroned awaiting the presentation of offerings by members of his family. The best preserved is that of the royal scribe, Any, where his life-sized image, seated on a chair, rests on a platform reached by a staircase [7.18]. On the side walls, rendered in paint, Any, accompanied by his wife, sits in front of a table of offerings tended by a man named Meryre (presumably a son or close relative).

Death and the Sense of Occasion

Among the higher ranks of officials, funerals were important events. The side walls of the shrine in the tomb of Huya depict what the funeral would look like [7.22]. Porters bring the grave goods and the food for the funeral banquet (including live oxen), mourners raise their hands over their faces and foreheads to express their grief. Behind a pile of food offerings stands the mummified body of Huya, adorned with a long narrow curving beard that, to any ancient Egyptian, would have identified him as already merged with the god of the Otherworld, Osiris. A short prayer expresses the hope that Huya will receive 'water from your pool, [probably fruit] from your trees'. It all looks very traditional, except for the conspicuous absence of overt depictions of, or references to, Osiris himself. Evidently Akhenaten disapproved, and his disapproval was taken seriously. Was this because, in Akhenaten's teaching, the judgment of one's conduct should not be postponed until after death?

In the same shrine, on either side of Huya's statue, are carved pictures of objects to be placed in the tomb (7.23; the author of the list looking ahead to a time of funeral that might have been years away). In addition to mundane items (a bed, chairs, a chariot) are Canopic jars and two shrines on sledge-runners of the kind intended to house sacred images or objects. Huya was evidently still aspiring to the traditional style of burial of kings and the elite, in which they went to the grave accompanied by expensive and sometimes bulky grave goods. If any major funerals did take place at Amarna, they would have been big and public events. The heavy coffin would have been dragged from the city to the tomb, and a line of bearers would have carried the funeral furnishings.

One tomb owner who probably died at Amarna (and before his tomb was finished) was the scribe and steward Any. Six men (among them a brother, his

7.22 *(above left) The funeral of an important official, the steward Huya, as depicted in the shrine of his tomb (no. 1).*

7.23 *(above right) Huya's burial equipment, as depicted in the shrine of his tomb (no. 1).*

charioteer and two servants) commemorated Any through small round-topped stelae cemented into niches in the sides of the short descending flight of steps leading down to the tomb entrance.[22] Some are conventional depictions of funerary offerings made to Any, but some seem to be memorials of a more personal relationship: his charioteer shows himself driving Any, for example. Another stela appears to record the gift of an ox for a funerary meal for which the king is thanked [**3.29**], something that fits the frequently repeated wish in other tombs to receive offerings in the Aten temple itself.

The presence of oxen, on the Any stela and in the Huya funeral scene, and the general sense that celebration of various kinds was best done to the accompaniment of food spread out, points to the funerals of important people having been an occasion for feasting. In some later New Kingdom tombs, some of them at Saqqara, funeral scenes use the setting of a garden with pool and shrine. Mourners are present, as are foodstuffs. New Kingdom desert cemeteries (including those at Amarna) have shown no signs of places of this kind. A few are to be found, however, in the city, in the form of gardens (with shrines and pool or well) attached to the larger houses [**7.2**]. Could it have been one of their functions, to serve from time to time as places of assembly for the mourners at the death of a rich person, perhaps involving the erection of a temporary tent to shade the coffin?[23]

The North Tombs (but not the South Tombs) seem to have possessed their own ceremonial area. Using modern nomenclature this is the Desert Altars, which lie 1 km (0.6 miles) in the desert due west of the North Tombs [**7.24**].[24]

They comprise: (1) a square platform reached by a long ramp on each of the four sides – a deep hole in the middle of the platform might point to the original existence of a standing stone; (2) a group of three platforms reached by ramps, two of them flanking the approach to the ramp of the larger one, which had been rebuilt in stone during the Amarna period; (3) a large rectangular platform, reached by ramps on all four sides – the complex pattern of its foundations suggests that several columned rooms stood on top, surrounded by an open colonnade.

The whole group stands on ground that has been cleared of stones, which have been heaped into a now faint ridge that surrounds the area on the north, south and east (but not the west). This perimeter is broken on the east by junctions with two of the desert trackways that also belong to the Amarna period (described in Chapter 5). The wider of the two led towards the rock tomb of the high priest Panehsy (no. 6). This connection, and the absence of a clear perimeter on the west, suggests that the altars as a group were intended to be approached from the east and so were an adjunct to the North Tombs and to their high officials, who included the high priest Meryre (owner of tomb no. 4), as well as Panehsy. It was perhaps their presence that justified the construction of this separate installation, which is a combination of architectural elements favoured in the Amarna period, here evidently assembled to create an outpost for the Aten cult in full view of the tombs of its two leading priests. If this involved the presentation and consumption of food-offerings, however, the

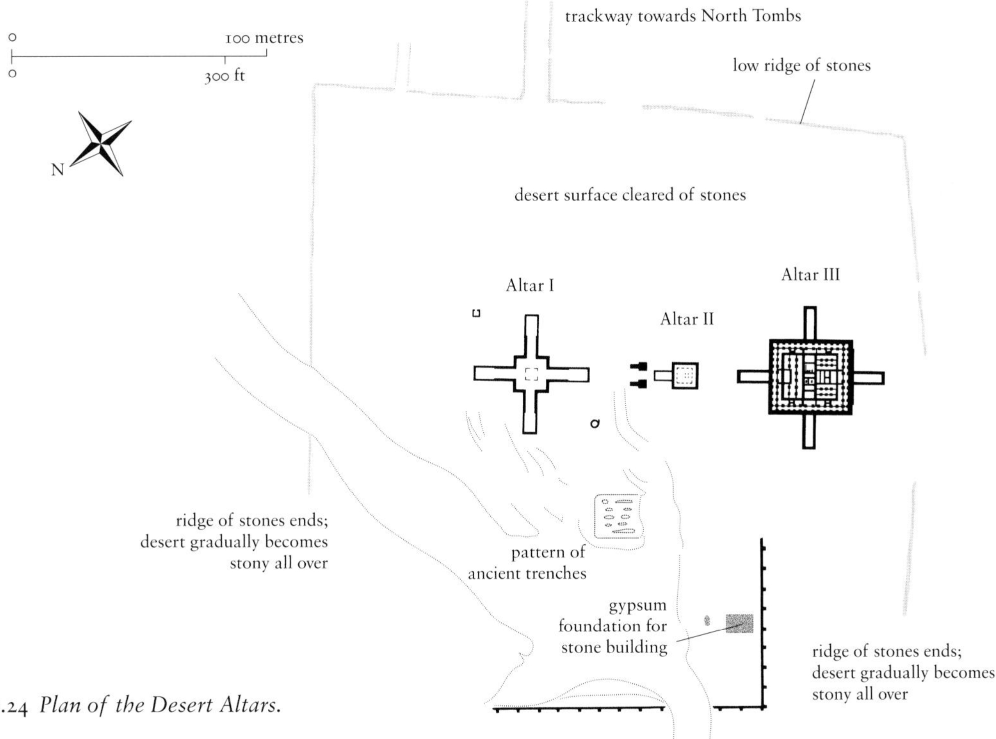

7.24 *Plan of the Desert Altars.*

food must have been brought out from the city (from the Great Aten Temple?), given the absence of ovens and related structures. The excavation of the site also produced remarkably little pottery or other kinds of material. Of course, if Meryre and Panehsy outlived the city, the altars might not have seen much use. Adjacent to the altars lay another example of an enclosure containing a small stone shrine, another 'sunshade'.

Existence after Death

The prospect – an ancient one – of the deceased existing as a spirit in the earthly world and able to receive food and drink is expressed in many of the Amarna rock tombs. Traditionally the aspect of the self that lived in the vicinity of the tomb was the 'soul' (*ba*). The decorated side panels of a model coffin buried in the city add details of how the deceased should be treated: they show the mummified body of a scribe Any (as well as his standing statue) receiving offerings, being mourned and having the 'Opening of the Mouth' ceremony performed over it, a ritual that opened up the body to receive the breath of life [**7.25**].[25]

In addition to this simple view of continuing spiritual existence after death, Egypt was home to a long tradition of creative speculation about a world that could be imagined, but was not visible in the normal sense. It was called the *Duat* (Underworld or Otherworld). To it the dead made their way. It had a landscape of waterways, mountains, caverns and mounds. It was home to innumerable beings, many of whom posed challenges of knowledge to the spirit of a

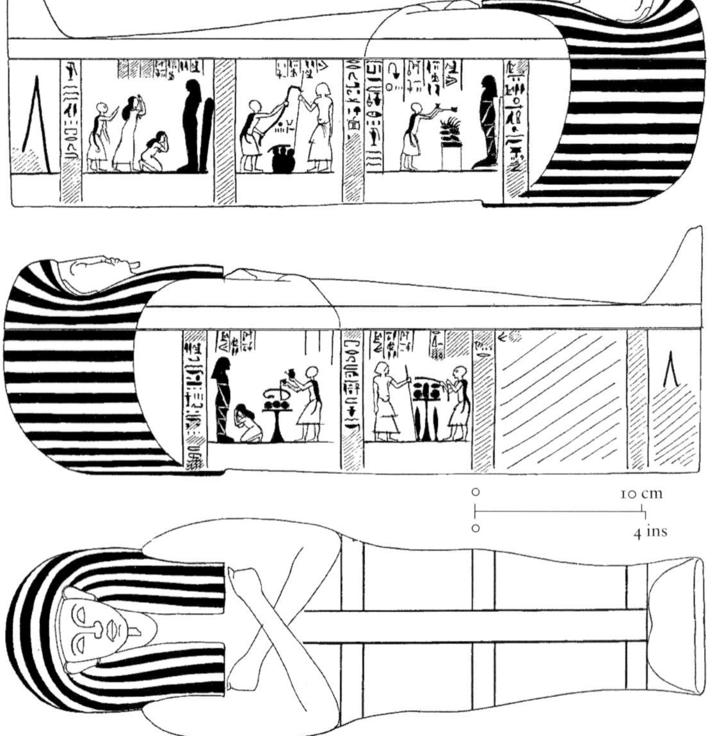

7.25 Wooden coffinette, reused for the burial of two pairs of ivory castanets. It was painted black with designs in yellow paint, and names the owner as 'the royal scribe, Any' (identical to the owner of tomb no. 23?). It could have been intended originally to contain organs removed during mummification (Tutankhamun's tomb offers a parallel) or it could have been a model prepared by a coffin-maker for his customers. Length 42 cm (16.5 in.). Obj. 31/591.

dead person wanting to journey to the presence of Osiris, ruler of the kingdom of the dead, who was encountered at the end of the journey. Through it also passed the long, repeated journey of the sun-god in his special boat, which constantly faced forces of disturbance and unrule that had to be subdued. Each morning the sun-god emerged into the visible world, serene and triumphant, an affirmation of the continuation of life and of a fundamentally orderly universe.

The Book of the Dead was a popular collection of texts aimed at equipping a person with sufficient knowledge to triumph in this Otherworld. Other 'books' (a Book of Caverns, for example) were composed that worked up various of its facets in more detail. Although composed on papyrus, the contents of these 'books' were copied on a larger scale inside the tombs of the kings of the New Kingdom in the Valley of the Kings at Thebes. These are the sources that preserve the core of ancient Egyptian serious, philosophical reflection. It is notable that the god Amun of Thebes, the great devotional focus of the New Kingdom, played virtually no part in this imagined world.

Akhenaten's own tomb at Amarna stands in contrast with what can be found in the Valley of the Kings. There are no depictions of the Otherworld, evidence that he had rejected mythical narrative as a way of exploring what could be thought about but not seen. Eternity for him was nothing more mysterious than the daily greeting of the Aten. Yet three of the men at the heart of Akhenaten's court anticipated at least a semblance of the familiar future existence. The high priest Meryre (who was presumably an authoritative voice in such matters) prays to the Aten: 'May he grant power on earth and glory in the Otherworld [*Duat*], and the *ba*'s coming out and refreshing itself in the tomb.' In a similar prayer, the god's father Ay is wished: 'May you stride through the gates of the Otherworld [*Duat*]. May you see Ra at dawn at his appearance in the eastern horizon; and may you see the Aten at his setting in the western horizon of heaven.' The standard-bearer Suty wishes similarly.[26] The mention of the 'gates of the Otherworld' points to the retention of one of the central aspects of the sun-god's journey, through gateways guarded by dangerous beings.

One of the chapters of the Book of the Dead, the sixth, encapsulated an ancient fear that the dead would be pursued by the threat of conscripted labour. To avoid this, the dead were provided with one or more figures – called *shabti* – that would substitute for him or her. The same chapter contains the activating spell that could also be copied on to the actual figures. Rather oddly, from our point of view, dead kings were not spared this danger and so had the figures in their tombs as well. Akhenaten was buried with many; one is known that was made for Nefertiti. A court lady named Py also had one, with a more extensive text that illustrates the amalgam between traditional beliefs and the new emphasis on the Aten. At the end comes the key traditional passage: 'O *shabti*: if you are detailed for work, if you are summoned, if you are assessed for work, "I will do it, here I am!" – so will you say.' It is preceded by a passage composed specially for the Atenist viewpoint: 'May you breathe the fragrant breezes of the north wind. May you go forth into the sky on the arm of the living Aten, your limbs protected, your heart content, without anything evil happening to your limbs, being whole, without decay. May you follow the Aten when he rises at dawn, until his setting from life occurs, with water for your heart, bread for your belly, clothing to cover your limbs.'[27] Such wishes occur on the door frames of rock tombs and on coffins from Amarna.

Akhenaten avoided creating a new spiritual landscape and narratives that could feed on people's imaginative powers. There were no new demons, even though people are naturally attracted to them. It is hard to escape the conclusion that the imagination of his people, even of his priests, remained with its stock of traditional imagery not far beneath the surface and occasionally finding overt expression.

Amarna's Citizen Cemetery

Our understanding of how the people of Amarna coped with death has been immeasurably improved by the discovery of several commoners' cemeteries, and excavations carried out at one of them, near the South Tombs (and hence called the South Tombs Cemetery) [7.26].[28] It occupies banks of sand along either side of a shallow wadi that runs back into the desert from a point near the tomb of the god's father Ay (no. 25), and might originally have spread continuously across the wadi floor. An estimate based upon burial density in the excavated areas is that the cemetery could contain as many as 3,000 graves or even more, some of them holding more than one body. Most had been robbed, evidently not long after the cemetery went out of use.

The graves were dug into the sand, mostly as narrow pits of varying depth, some of them very shallow [7.27]. Only one brick-lined pit has been identified. For the rest, rough stones were occasionally used to line the pit and, probably as a regular practice, stones were laid over the length of the grave, in part to mark its presence and in part to hinder animals from digging down [7.28]. Some graves also had markers of limestone or cement that could be mortared into the stones [7.29]. The markers show a preference for a pointed shape that could have the form of a pyramid or be a flat slab with up to three triangles on the top, seemingly invoking mountain peaks [7.30], which, in the context of Amarna, denote the place of sunrise [7.31]. Some had lightly carved scenes while others might have born inscriptions or scenes in paint, now lost to erosion. The best preserved is a round-topped stela cemented into a niche in a pointed slab [7.32]. It depicts a couple seated side by side, the man turning back to face the woman, his arm hanging down behind the back of the chair, his body slumped a little, emphasizing the roundness of his belly. Here are people from the city choosing to emulate the royal family's style of informality. The absence of Osiris, the god traditionally most associated with the dead, is notable.

The grave markers are broadly within the traditions of the New Kingdom, yet with sufficient variations to suggest the emergence of an outlook that was distinctive to this particular cemetery. The shapes suggest the place of sunrise, but ignore Akhenaten's way of depicting the Aten.

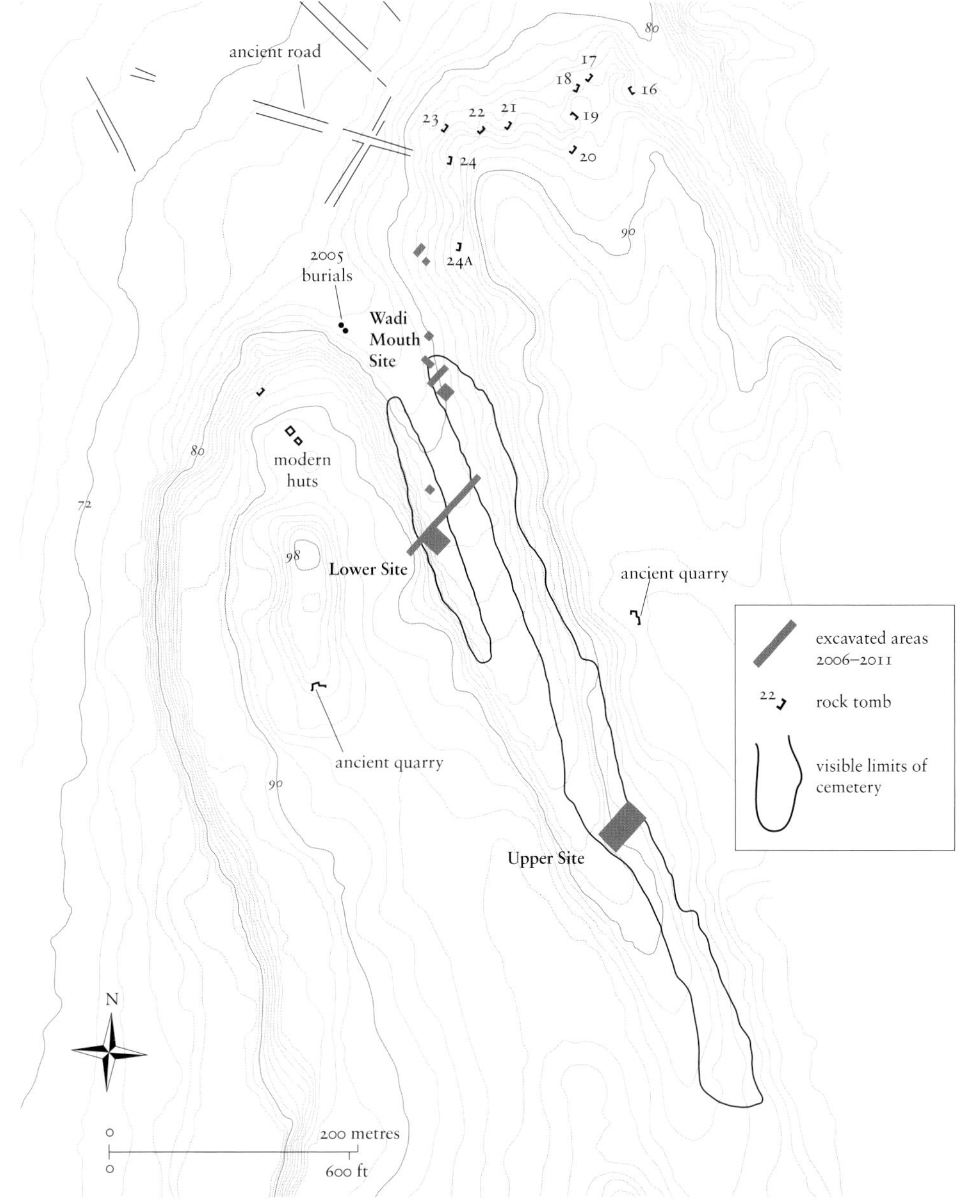

7.26 *Map of the South Tombs Cemetery, showing areas excavated 2006–11. In 2011 it was established that the cemetery extends at least halfway across the wadi floor. The numbered rock tombs are also shown.*

In many cultures, burial was an opportunity to lay the bodies of the deceased in a common direction (facing towards Mecca in the case of Muslim burials, for example). Despite the draw of sunrise on the eastern horizon at Amarna, the excavated burials show no common orientation. When the slope of the ground was appreciable, the bodies tended to lie in the position people naturally adopt when lying on a slope, head uppermost, torso and legs down the

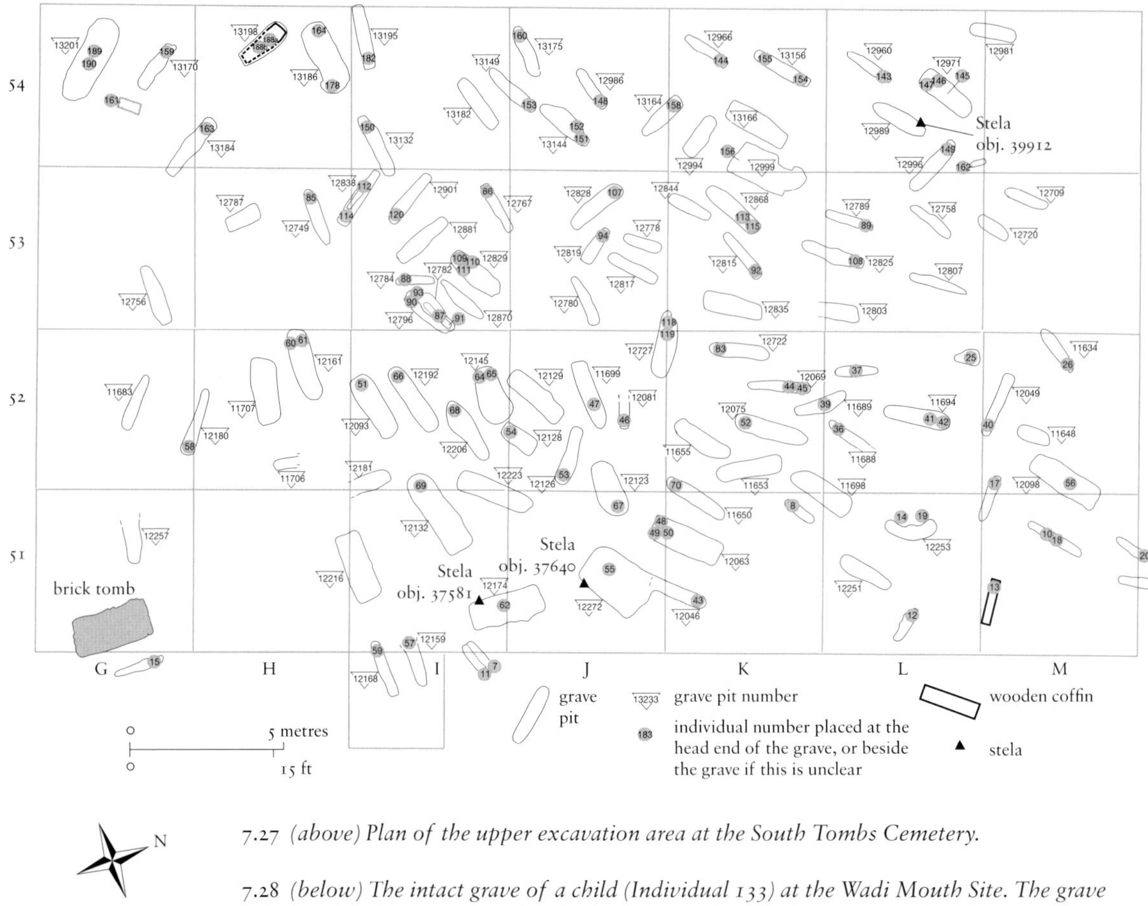

7.27 *(above) Plan of the upper excavation area at the South Tombs Cemetery.*

7.28 *(below) The intact grave of a child (Individual 133) at the Wadi Mouth Site. The grave (pit 13123) had been cut to a depth of only 80 cm (31.5 in.), then covered with a row of unworked stones.*

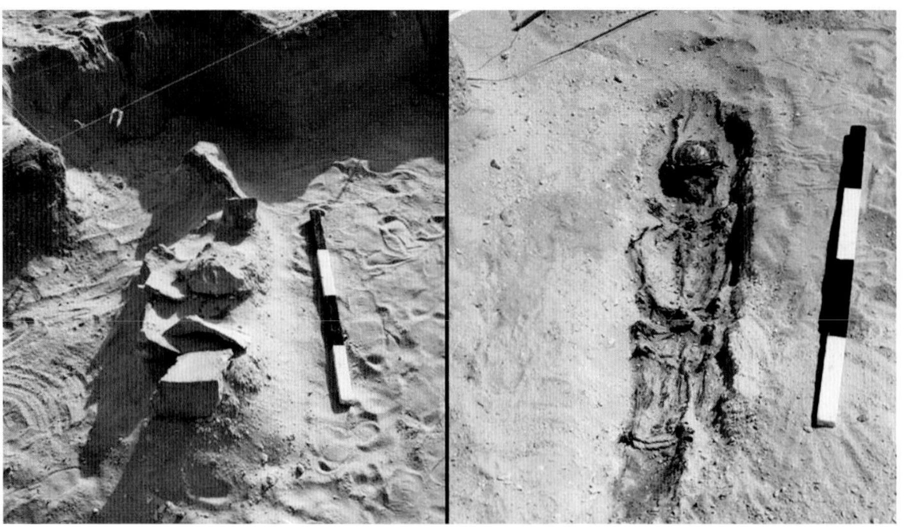

7.29 (left) Small stela (obj. 39448) cast in a mould from a gypsum and sand mix cement, with some of the plaster remaining that had attached it to a cairn of rounded stones. Height of stela 30.5 cm (12 in.).

7.30 (right) Stela (obj. 39446) carved with twin rounded peaks at the top, suggestive of the place of sunrise. Perhaps a separately made stela occupied the inner recess on the face of the stela, but this in turn seems to be within a doorway or chamber beneath the mountain. Max. height 32 cm (12.6 in.).

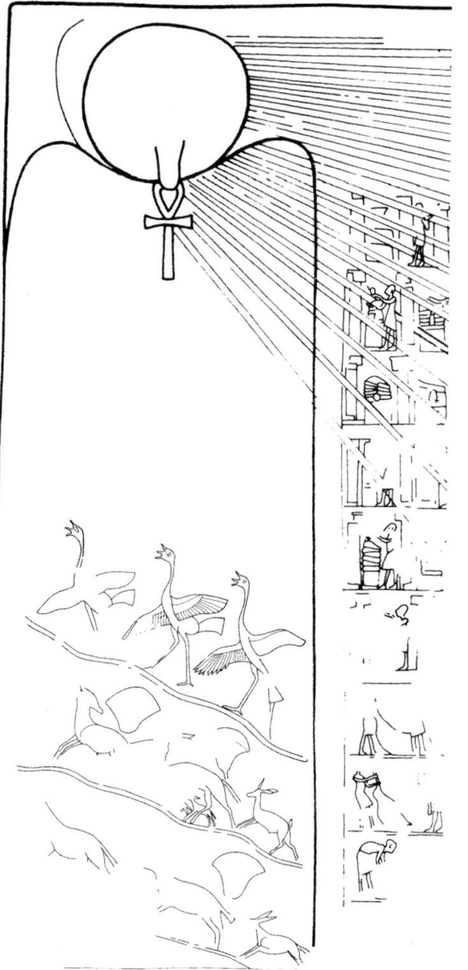

7.31 (left) Sunrise at Amarna, as depicted in the Royal Tomb at Amarna, chamber alpha in the Meketaten annexe.

7.32 (right) Grave marker (obj. 39938) from the South Tombs Cemetery. It is in two parts. A slab of coarse limestone with a triangular top has been cut to receive a round-topped stela of finer limestone. It shows a seated couple embracing, while being waited upon by a man. Height of inserted stela 25.5 cm (10 in.).

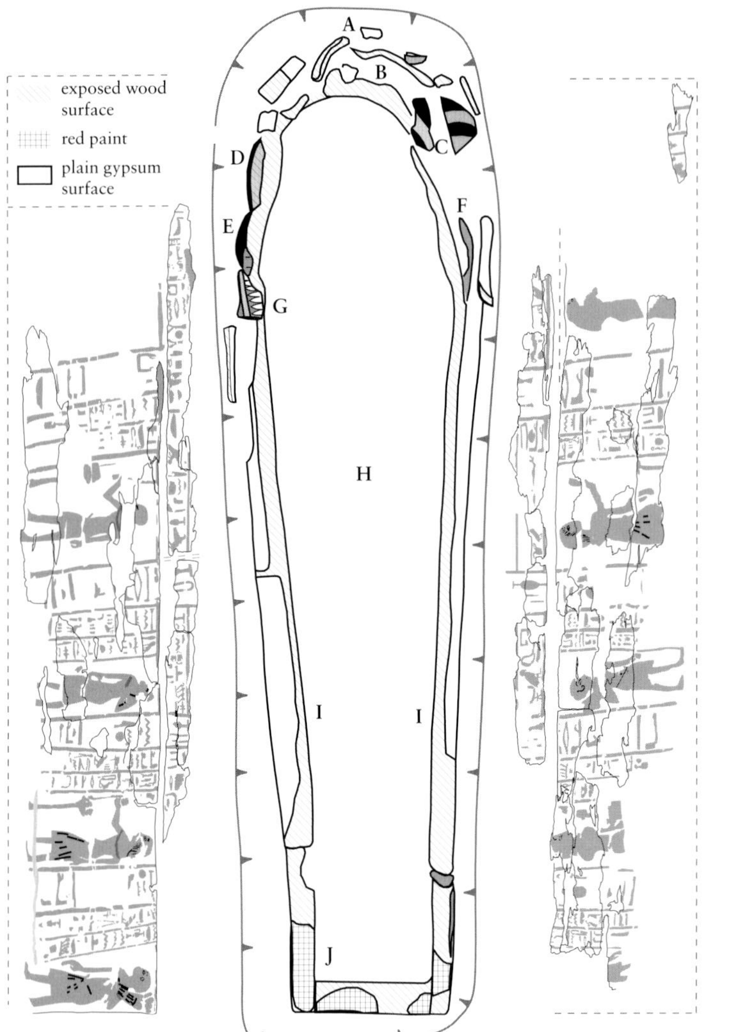

7.33 Coffin (13281), from square Y105 in the South Tombs Cemetery. One can pick out hieroglyphic phrases making wishes for the wellbeing of the deceased and, in wider vertical bands, the name of the deceased. This is given in at least two versions, Hesyenra and Hesyenaten, accompanied by the female version of the phrase 'true of voice'.

A at head, a mass of degraded wood and plaster, largely broken wig from the lid
B outer edge
C displaced wig strips
D *in situ* wig strips
E *in situ* side of collar
F indistinct traces of blue from the side of the collar
G displaced piece of collar from lid
H sand fill
I remnants of lower edge of lid
J top of coffin wall with patches of pink paint

line of the slope; whereas on flatter ground, the axis of the wadi itself tended to take over and burials lay at right-angles to the adjacent slope. The burials were often, however, closely packed and with varying orientations, suggestive of an attempt to maintain what was presumably a family grouping. There was no overriding preference dictated by the movement of the sun.

The bodies in the pits had, over time, been reduced to skeletons and, insofar as we can judge, had not been mummified. Each was wrapped in cloth and then rolled up inside a mat of rushes that was lashed tightly with ropes to create a rigid cylindrical 'coffin' that often fitted tightly within the grave pit. For some, however, a wooden coffin had been procured. Most were rectangular and had, over the centuries, been reduced to little more than brown powder. Four examples, however, were roughly in the shape of a human figure [7.33, 7.34],

7.34 Coffin (13262), from square Y105 in the South Tombs Cemetery. The hieroglyphs are reasonably clear, and some familiar groupings are present. In total, however, they do not form texts that can be translated by the familiar rules of the language, even with knowledge of the ritual texts.

A lid
B yellow and black wig stripes
C white gypsum on interior

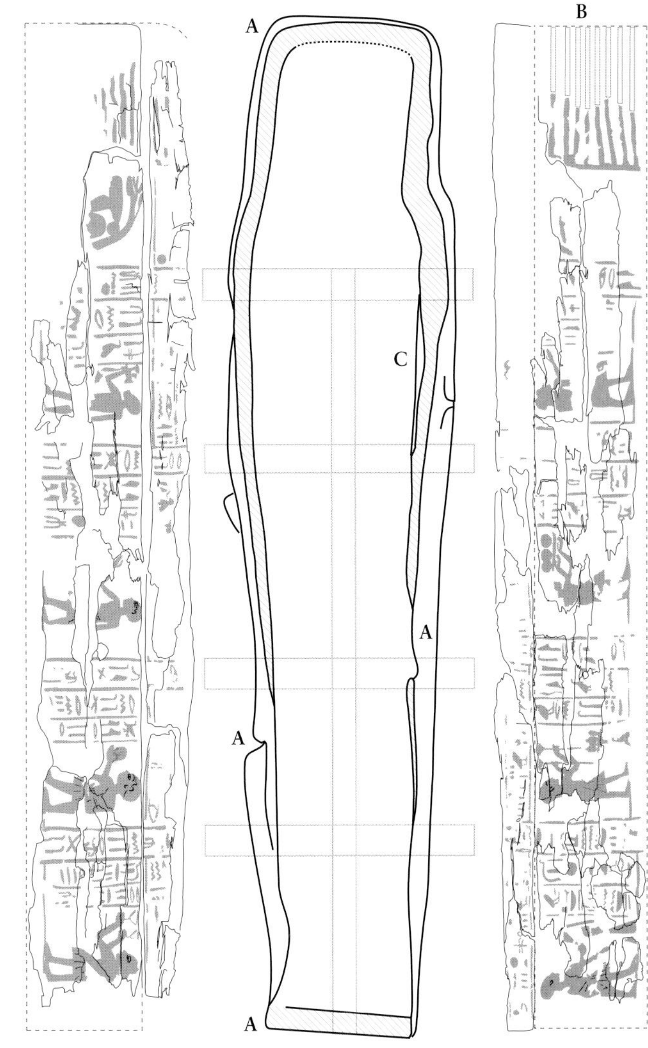

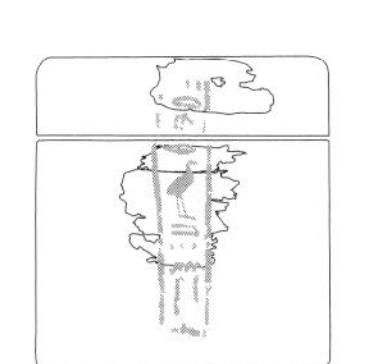

foot of coffin

one retaining a finely carved and painted wooden face. They had been coated with a layer of gypsum, then with black paint over which white decoration had been applied. In three cases, this depicted figures of men and women either mourning or making offerings, each one separated by one or more columns of hieroglyphic signs. These figures replace the traditional four gods (the Sons of Horus) who helped to safeguard the body. The name of the deceased is prominent and, for the rest, the texts are simple formulae that wish the deceased benefits in the future: food, cool water, the refreshing breezes of the north wind. On one of these three coffins, the Aten is mentioned as a provider of offerings. At the time of writing, the fourth coffin is still shrouded in conservation materials. In one part, briefly exposed as excavation progressed, the figure of a canine-headed god was clearly visible, either Anubis or Duamutef, one of the four Sons of Horus. This is a striking violation of the Amarna rule (as accepted in modern interpretations) that the old funerary deities should not be depicted. Some measure of personal choice in these matters evidently survived.

Two of the four coffins give the impression of being the products of 'village' craftsmen who worked to a standard coffin template, but had not trained as artists. The maker of coffin 13281 [7.33] must have had a set of correctly written standard funerary phrases from which to copy, and (with the help of the purchaser?) would insert properly written personal names. By contrast, the maker of coffin 13262 [7.34] must have worked from a 'copybook' far removed from correct originals, which produced a result that superficially looked right, but actually made no sense. The same applied to the personal names: the customer was presumably also unable to supply a correctly written version.

For the rich, buried in their rock tombs, the need to provide food-offerings was met, in part, by adding their names to the list of recipients of offerings in the House of the Aten. For the people of the South Tombs Cemetery, the appropriate gesture to this effect was to include a few pottery vessels in the grave pit. These did not normally include amphorae, but were a limited selection of locally produced small-to-medium storage jars and bowls. In a few cases, the remains of fruit (including grapes, dates, the small sour fruit of the Christ's thorn plant and probably juniper berries) survived, as well as cereal and cereal products.

The extensive ancient robbery of the cemetery does not wholly explain the small number of grave goods. Robbers were primarily seeking metal, and so would leave behind items that please us, such as finely made travertine vessels. Moreover, not all graves had been robbed, and they too often contain little or nothing. The people of Amarna, so it seems, preferred to keep their possessions in circulation among the living rather than to consign them to an uncertain fate in the ground. This remained the case for much of the population of Egypt (and of Egyptian Nubia) in the coming centuries. When objects were included, they tended to be small personal items of the 'charm' or 'amulet' variety, objects often made from glazed steatite, pierced to take a length of thread, carved with symbolic designs on the flat base and with varying shapes on the top: a scarab beetle, a simple dome or, in a case of a group of three, a reclining hippopotamus raising its head [**Pl. XLI**]. A bronze mirror is one of several objects for personal adornment. A small gold-alloy ring from a child's grave [**6.16**] illustrates, as do the painted coffins, that the people buried in the cemetery represent different levels of wealth and status.

We can see variation in the resources devoted to burials. Some people could afford a painted coffin or a carved grave marker, most could not. The variation is, however, small compared with the variation in the size of houses within the city. There, a gradient of continuing increase in house size linked the poor to the rich with every size in between. In their provision for death, however, most people seem to have resigned themselves to a minimal burial style, which left a wide gap between them and the elite in the rock tombs.

The material found so far makes no reference to Akhenaten, and the Aten at its rising is present only occasionally as a benign object of celebration. As in the city, Akhenaten's cult of the sun threw no protection over people. Although they mostly respected his wishes not to honour Osiris or to seek the protection of other funerary gods, they were buried with personal amulets that invoked the protector gods and goddesses of the household.

In Summary: Living in the 'Place of Truth'

We cannot doubt the overwhelming impact that Akhenaten had upon his society. At the heart of Akhetaten lay a huge establishment – a mixture of architecture and movements of commodities – dedicated to honouring the Aten and the unique role that Akhenaten played in creating the true form that piety should take. In their tombs, his officials and courtiers honoured the centrality of this in their lives. Because Akhenaten's drive for reform failed, however, there is a general modern view that, beyond obligations of loyalty, he won few hearts or minds with his ideas. To judge from the things they owned, the lives of the people of the city, from all ranks, incorporated thoughts and practices that belonged to older ideas of spiritual power. These filled a vacuum that Akhenaten's austere concept of the Aten had left, and they remained for people to clutch onto in moments of uncertainty.

To his courtiers, as expressed in their tombs, Akhenaten was also a teacher of righteousness. His choice of Akhetaten, a place of harsh desert sunlight, perhaps in itself signified a path of purification. Not only was the Aten the 'Prince of Truth [Maat]', the eastern mountain of Akhetaten was the 'Place of Truth'. If we take into consideration the evidence for funerary beliefs as well, especially the dropping of references to Osiris, we can perhaps reconstruct a part of his teaching: that an adherence to truth and righteous conduct was an absolute that should be followed daily for itself, rather than be something that lay ahead on a day of judgement after death and be then open to denial.

Akhenaten thus offered a path of deliverance from fanciful and complicated ideas about the hidden forces that were supposed to rule the universe. As long as the message was reinforced by his presence among them, it might have seemed attractive. The people of the South Tombs Cemetery seem to have felt sufficiently at ease to develop, in the variations on the stelae, individual ways of expressing the new pristine landscape of eternity.

We are accustomed to think of new religions finding their success in an expansion of followers. A way of life and belief is created that outlives its founder. Conversion is an essential. But Akhenaten's wish for a more righteous society does not seem to have been translated into a set of rules. Among his people, the climate of the times allowed the natural flexibility of the human mind to avoid a choice between one set of ideas and another. His main goals were to purify the cult of the sun and to create a new and special place for it. He achieved them, and nothing much was left for him to do, other than what all rulers do: to reign in such a way as to best ensure a continuation of the dynasty.

8.1 *Fragment of a relief on a* talatat-*block found at El-Ashmunein (Hermopolis), but probably originally from Amarna. It shows two houses beside a waterway (which could be the Nile), indicated by zigzag lines. At the far left, a group of women celebrates – perhaps watching a procession on the river. The inhabitants of the two houses carry out various daily tasks; some smaller rooms store food and drink and other household items. Note the bedroom in the top left room of the right-hand house, with bed and sandals. The equivalent space in the left-hand house is probably a kitchen containing an oven.*

CHAPTER EIGHT

WHAT KIND OF CITY?

There is a history to the city, as a worldwide creation of human societies that have reached a certain stage of development. It has a huge literature and divergent approaches. Sociologists and urban geographers pursue their studies from the unique vantage point of being able to observe and to question the inhabitants of the cities of the present-day. Archaeologists cannot do this, cannot distribute a questionnaire to Panehsy's people asking them to evaluate, by means of a numerical score, the quality and accessibility of the city's water supply, or to record social transactions with other neighbourhoods. For their cities, from the more distant past, they have to work with fragments of evidence that are of only marginal concern to their modern counterparts. An intellectual gulf separates the two groups.

In 1960, an American sociologist, Gideon Sjoberg, published a book, without illustrations, entitled *The Preindustrial City, Past and Present*.[1] His term 'preindustrial city' has passed into general terminology. Sjoberg was primarily addressing fellow sociologists who, so he felt, were inclined to imagine that cities could only ever be as they themselves experienced them in the modern, western world. Using the accounts of earlier travellers, and a certain amount of archaeological summary, he described a model of the city as it had widely existed before modern times. The cities of Seoul, Peking, Lhasa, Mecca, Cairo, Fez, Florence and Bokhara he found to be particularly useful as examples because they were well documented. The neatness and clarity of Sjoberg's summary sets up a model against which Amarna can be judged. Does Amarna fit the profile, or is it sufficiently different to suggest that it belongs in a separate category, the 'pre-preindustrial city' or even the 'urban village'?

The Preindustrial City

The next eight paragraphs are a précis of certain parts of Sjoberg's book. I have ignored several of his topics that cover themes, such as political structure, which go beyond the concerns of this book.

Amidst any number of local differences, the preindustrial city displays certain common features. It is normally surrounded by a wall, and thus entered by gates. Internal walls and gates seal off sections of the population from one another, increasing neighbourhood security and also the means of control by outside authorities. 'Within the walled precincts congestion is the order of the day',[2] because of the narrowness and crookedness of the streets and the constant traffic of humans and animals along them. Poor sanitation, inadequate removal of rubbish and easy contamination of the water supply encourage the rapid spread of epidemic disease.

At the heart of the city's life is the centre, where are located the most prominent governmental and religious buildings and usually the main market. They either crowd around an open square or stand along or at the end of a broad straight thoroughfare. The centre also attracts the luxurious dwellings of the elite. Consequently the 'disadvantaged members of the city fan out toward the periphery, with the very poorest and the outcastes living in the suburbs',[3] in conformity to a scale of values in which distance from the centre is a measure of status.

The city is also segregated in other ways: by ethnic groups and by occupation usually defined by the categories of goods made or sold. At the same time, buildings and pieces of land serve a variety of purposes so, for example, 'the residential units of artisans and merchants often serve simultaneously as their places of work'.[4] Most merchants, like the craftsmen, hold a lowly social position even though their activities are vital to the life of the city.

Sjoberg has much to say on the subject of marriage and family structure. In its ideal form, the 'feudal' city contains, among the elite, large extended family units, sharing extensive households, their members reaching to three or four generations and including cousins and their families, and some of the servants and their households as well. Among those of servant status might be artists or musicians living under the patronage of the head of the household.

Within the economic realm, the key unit is the guild, typically community-bound, that pervades manufacturing, trade and services. 'Within the city the various guilds are localized into specific quarters or along certain streets',[5] their main functions being to maintain a monopoly over a particular economic activity within a community and to regulate it and train apprentices for it. Manufacturing is a small-scale undertaking, confined usually to the homes of craftsmen or small shops in the market place. A few 'large' workshops have existed, but even these have rarely enclosed more than a few score of workers. Specialization in production occurs in product, not in process. The craftsman, instead of concentrating upon a particular step in the fashioning of an item, performs all or most of the steps from beginning to end and under one roof. At the end, he frequently markets the results of his handiwork at the site of manufacture, which may be his home or a special market.

Craftsmen may sell directly to the consumer or on a wholesale basis to retail merchants who may themselves belong to a guild. The large merchant may have his own brokers or agents, middlemen who serve a vital economic function and also enhance his status by removing him from direct negotiation with lower-class and outcaste persons. Most retail merchants function on a small scale, often from tiny shops or just a mat spread on the ground. They make little effort to gain customers through attractive display and, having inadequate storage facilities, keep only a small supply of goods on hand. Both sides exist from hand to mouth, customers tending to purchase minute quantities of food and other items on a daily basis.

Besides the merchants with fixed stations, itinerant vendors – peddlers – travel about the city hawking their wares. By visiting houses they eliminate some of the inconveniences of shopping for families of all classes and (since these societies generally restrict the outdoor movement of women) give the women an opportunity to examine goods and make purchases themselves.

In a chapter on 'religious structure', Sjoberg highlights religious sects, which seem to arise first in cities, and the prescriptive nature of the various religions, the way they lay down obligatory ways of behaving. Both reflect a world in which people distinguish between true and false belief, and therefore between believers and unbelievers. He also observes, across the societies that he studied, a fundamental cleavage in the religious beliefs and practices of the upper and lower classes. 'The folk religious rites of the lower class, whether in country or city, may bear little semblance to the more formal observances of the upper stratum. Local deities and a panoply of spirits, at times in astounding numbers, dot the religious scene for the lower classes, and these vary greatly from one locale to the next. We do not wish to minimize the impact of "folk beliefs", or the "little tradition," upon the elite.... Yet at the same time, the educated groups look with scorn upon the spirit- and demon-infested world of the common man.'[6]

In the measured prose of sociology, Sjoberg presents us with the academic version of the world that appears in countless adventure stories and historical romances set in an exotic 'east'. It is what Scheherazade might have seen from her window, Marco Polo have recounted as he entertained his friends and the Thief of Baghdad vanished into as he eluded his pursuers. It is where Indiana Jones might still go to buy his souvenirs (having first read Sjoberg's analysis of why people haggle).

Comparing Amarna

All cities are bound to have much in common. At the same time, they lie along a continuum of difference from one another. Turning those differences into historical stages – modern industrial, preindustrial and other categories – is to some extent a matter of convenience. How much of Amarna can we recognize in Sjoberg's description? His sources were primarily eyewitness descriptions of city life, allowing him to focus on the patterns of life rather than on the physical layouts of streets and buildings. One hardly notices the absence of illustrations. This immediately cuts Amarna off from many of the discussions. Marriage patterns, kinship ties and degrees of social mobility, for example, are not directly readable from the archaeological evidence.

At the beginning of Chapter 5, I commented on the absence of a city wall at Amarna and pointed out that this was in keeping with the spirit of the times. In earlier periods the Egyptians had, as a matter course, surrounded their towns with walls but had dispensed with them during the period of urban renewal that took place during the New Kingdom.[7] Large surrounding walls, sometimes given battlements, were reserved for major temples, as I pointed out in Chapter 3. Amarna followed an existing pattern that must have given to cities of the New Kingdom a different feel from those described by Sjoberg.

An equally telling difference concerns the way that people viewed the centre of the city. At first sight, Amarna conforms to the norm. Some of the most important governmental and religious buildings – the Aten temples and the Great Palace – were located in the Central City. But then the conformity breaks down. Amarna displays a strong reverse trend. The houses of the elite are dotted across the whole remaining area covered by the city, spreading all the way to its periphery. The elite clearly had a different scale of values. Fulsome praise of the king and gratitude for his generosity had its place. But the status that came from being prominent among one's local community evidently outweighed that of living close to the king. It is the lure of being a big fish in a small pond rather than the other way round. It fits literary and artistic portrayals of the ideal life of the official from the previous and ensuing periods, which revolve around material success and domestic pleasures at the family level and ignore attendance at court.[8] The intense Akhenaten-centred focus of the tomb scenes at Amarna did not represent how the city was arranged. Being big in one's village, even if that village was embedded in the city, was what mattered, the king being the instrument by which one obtained that status. It is an interesting bargain to have struck. It also has important ramifications in other facets of the city's life.

I have, in earlier chapters, touched on certain other aspects of Amarna that relate to the preindustrial city as described by Sjoberg. Religious structure is one. Amarna, of course, belongs to an earlier era in this respect. One could not describe Akhenaten's beliefs as a sect. As for differences in the beliefs and practices of the upper and lower classes, it is to be expected that the officials took a more nuanced view of Akhenaten's instructions than the rest of the population, but there does not seem to have been much there to encourage the pursuit of a higher level of abstraction. I have speculated earlier about the receptiveness of the common people to the changed spiritual climate, what ideas they might have developed in addition to the retention of an interest in traditional protector deities, but there is little enough to go on and the blurry nature of the subject might in itself be a pointer to how things were. Other aspects of Sjoberg's model, mainly connected with social status and economic activity, now require some further exploration.

Amarna's People

The larger houses advertised who lived inside, the name and titles of the owner written in coloured hieroglyphs on the jambs and lintels of doorways. Quite a few have survived, but they still represent only a tiny proportion of even the larger houses. Among them are the vizier Nakht, chief builder Maanakhtuef, chariotry officer Ranefer, chief of seers of the Aten Pawah, sculptor Thutmose, army general Ramose, first servitor of the Aten Panehsy and chief of works Hatiay. We cannot identify, however, the houses that belonged to most of the men to whom the rock tombs belonged, the high priest Meryre, for example (owner of tomb no. 4), or the god's father Ay (owner of no. 25); it is possible that their houses have not been excavated. One can see, nevertheless, that the leading houses in the city were distributed among administrators, priests and army men. One could not walk far in Amarna without passing close to the house of someone who was part of Akhenaten's court, and in their homes officials shared a lifestyle of comfort, affluence and local patriarchal authority (note the respective locations of the army general Ramose and sculptor Thutmose in **5.9**).

Within the rock tombs of the elite, the space allocated to the commemoration of the family was the shrine at the back [**7.21**]. In five cases some work had been done on the shrine even though the outer parts of the tomb were unfinished. All contained prominent statues of the owner; in the case of the general Ramose (no. 11) he sat beside a statue of his wife or sister, the 'Lady of the House, Nebetint'. On the shrine walls of three of the others (Huya, Any and Panehsy) are shown members of the family, mostly women. In the case of the high priest Panehsy (no. 6) they are 'his sister, the Lady of the House Iabka' and a boy and two girls, perhaps his son and daughters.[9] Lower down the social scale is a stela from a family chapel at the Workmen's Village that simultaneously honoured protector divinities – the god Shed and the goddess Isis – and members of the family of a man (without titles) Ptahmay [**7.8**]. They seem to be wife, sister, one son and maybe three daughters. Despite the tiny houses in which these families lived at the Workmen's Village, they are given a life of fashionable relaxation, with one daughter playing a large harp to which another daughter dances.

Apart from obvious imports, most numerous being sherds from Canaanite and Mycenaean pottery, the objects found at Amarna are overwhelmingly Egyptian. Many sources from the New Kingdom, however, document the presence of significant numbers of foreigners in Egypt, many of them people captured during Egypt's foreign campaigns, but others the result of the constant international interchange at this time of goods, information and people, including companions of foreign princesses who came to Egypt to become wives to the king. Men who are given the stereotyped features of foreigners regularly appear among the soldiers who form Akhenaten's bodyguard. The most intriguing evidence, however, is provided by a few cuneiform tablets that were not letters and were found in houses in the Main City. Tablet EA 368, a list of Egyptian words for everyday objects written for the benefit of an Akkadian speaker, was found in house O49.23; tablet EA 359 is a fragment of a Near Eastern epic (concerning King Sargon of Akkad) found in house O47.2. Were their owners Akkadian-speakers from the Near East temporarily resident at Amarna? Were they guests of Egyptian families or were they renting houses? Tablet EA 379 is a fragment of a sign list that might have been useful to someone

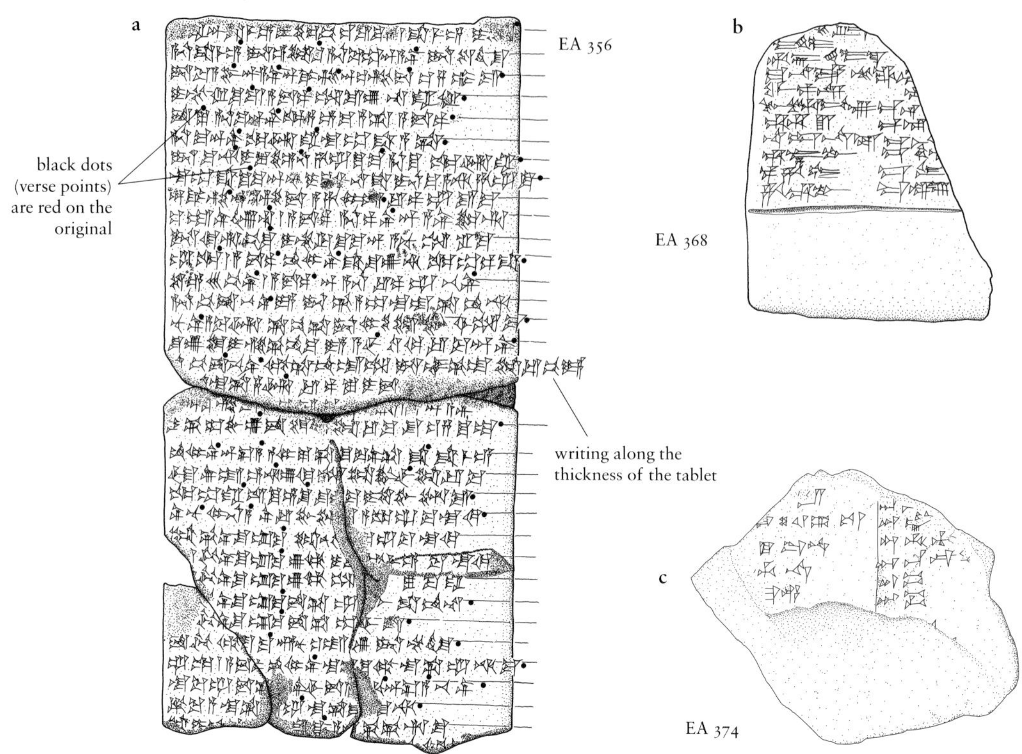

8.2 *Cuneiform tablets from Amarna.* **a** *EA 356, verso, contains a part of the myth of Adapa and the South Wind, the lines of cuneiform script are pointed with red dots in Egyptian style. Height 17.5 cm (6.8 in.).* **b** *EA 368, verso, a fragment of a vocabulary that transcribes ancient Egyptian words into the cuneiform script in the left column, and gives their meaning in Akkadian in the right. Height 6.5 cm (2.5 in.).* **c** *EA 374, recto, a fragment of a list of Near Eastern names of divinities. Height 5.2 cm (2 in.).*

(an Egyptian?) learning Akkadian. It was found in house N47.3. These three houses are too widely separated to imply the existence of a foreign 'quarter', but the owners of the tablets might have had a little cultural centre. Among the main group of the 'Amarna Letters', found in the Central City in the 'Office of correspondence of Pharaoh', were tablets that suggest that those who worked on the diplomatic correspondence nurtured wider cultural interests (EA 374 was a list of Near Eastern gods!) and came from several parts of the ancient Near East [**8.2**].[10] Amarna must have housed many people of foreign origin, but only written or pictorial evidence identifies them. If foreigners lived in particular parts of the city, even formed ethnic enclaves, the archaeological remains do not identify them.

One genre of ancient Egyptian literature encouraged 'scribes' to revel in a sense of superiority, contrasting, with contempt, the lives of others following different callings, from craftsmen to soldiers. The picture is one of a marked division in society, a classic instance of the us-versus-them view of life. Those who lived in the big houses (who might, in practice, actually be army officers or overseers of works) had obvious cause to feel superior. To judge, however, from the spread of artifacts that denote literacy – metal signet rings and their mud sealings – scribes are likely also to have occupied houses that were much smaller, indistinguishable from those of men who were not scribes. Two ostraca bearing extracts from one of the scribal compositions (called *Kemyt*) were found in a block of standard houses in the Great Palace. Described by the excavator as 'servants' quarters', a scribe is likely to have been one of the occupants.[11] Conversely, Ptahmay, whose stela was mentioned above and in the last chapter [**7.8**], gives himself no title (his name appears four times) yet the lifestyle depicted is what one would expect for the scribal 'class'.

It is reasonable to conclude that material culture barely distinguished, if it distinguished at all, scribe from non-scribe. Scribes might dream of urban villas for themselves or their teachers, but most must have lived in houses that resembled those occupied by the people they were taught to despise. A person can feel aloof while living a material life no different from those judged to be inferior. The scribal attitude was a cult of withdrawal, of inner separation. It is similarly not appropriate to apply the word 'slum' to areas of small houses when, in fact, it is likely that they were home to people who had specific callings and aspirations to better themselves that were, to an extent, realizable.

A telling instance of the spread of the 'good life' concerns music. Banquets in the palace and the celebration of the Aten in the temple were accompanied by musicians who both sang and played musical instruments [**4.21**]. Some of the female musicians lived in the palace alongside their instruments [**4.18, 4.19**]. Music was not an elite privilege, however. As just noted, Ptahmay of the Workmen's Village, who did not have a title, portrayed his life as enlivened by one of his daughters playing a harp [**7.8**]. One wonders who taught her and how the family acquired what was probably an expensive item. Did she play in one of the private chapels (where the stela was found) as well as in their house? Might she have already left home to live in one of the palaces? Was it only a dream, perhaps for the next world?

How Many People Lived There?

The total of excavated buildings with a separate modern catalogue number is around 1,150. Not all are actually houses, and some numbers cover more than one house. Several of the 200-m (656-ft) squares in the housing areas have been completely excavated. If we examine them, the number of houses in each is seen to vary considerably, a result of differing density, sometimes brought about by distance from or proximity to the outer edge of the city. The figures for a sample of six of them (the estimated numbers of houses are given in brackets, in some cases being slightly greater than the number of catalogued buildings) are: O49 (45), P47 (40), Q46 (62), T36 (88), U33 (15) and U36 (54), giving an average of 50.7 houses per 200-metre square.

How much of the total area of the city was given over to houses? In the Main City, housing did not extend all the way to the riverbank. It gave way to a line of large enclosures and storage buildings presumably connected with the fact that Amarna was a major inland port. If one takes this into consideration, housing (in both excavated and unexcavated areas) is likely to have covered at least fifty of the 200-m squares, to which a further ten might be added for areas both in the North Suburb and Main City/South Suburb that are now lost beneath fields (and might have seen a higher density than those further back). If one multiplies this figure of sixty grid-squares by the average of 50.7 the result is 3,040 for the number of houses at Amarna.

This becomes the basis for estimating the population, except that any multiplier can only lie within broad limits. What was the size of the average family and how many slaves were there? Written sources from the New Kingdom reveal that it was not necessary to be particularly wealthy to own slaves. Where did slaves live? They are, to us, an invisible population. They need not have been allocated any special building or architectural space, but could have slept in the house (perhaps in shelters on the roof), or in the outbuildings.

As a counter to this, we ought to factor in the low survival-rate of older people. If we choose a multiplier of ten persons per household (including slaves), then the population of Amarna comes out at around 30,000. The margins of possible error are large enough to set this figure within the bracket of 20,000 to 50,000.[12]

In fitting lives to the houses and to the objects discovered in them, we need to have some idea of how those lives were patterned. Nothing in the sources tells us for how long each day an official worked in his office or attended the king's court. The instructions for viziers of other reigns imply that attendance for a morning briefing was an obligation, at least for the most senior officials. When they were present in the Central City, so presumably were their juniors. Their juniors might well have been members of their extended households. Did they run behind their master's chariot along with the bodyguard (remembering the steward Huya's contingents[13])? Amarna's pattern of housing and the corresponding pattern of living imply a broad dividing of the population each day, with some of the men leaving for the Central City, either to work or to spend time in what can loosely be termed attendance. The remaining males – craftsmen, servants, the sick and the elderly – and the women and children perhaps generally did not move far from their neighbourhoods. At the Workmen's Village and Stone Village, it is likely that the male heads of each household left each day to work in the distant royal necropolis although, unlike at the Valley of the Kings, there were no huts on site where the workmen could stay. They must have journeyed back to their villages each night. The security measures that were in place imply that the lives of their women and children were wholly spent inside the villages and the immediately surrounding desert zone.

The king would not always have been in the city. He allowed for the possibility, in dictating the text of the first set of boundary stelae, that he and Nefertiti

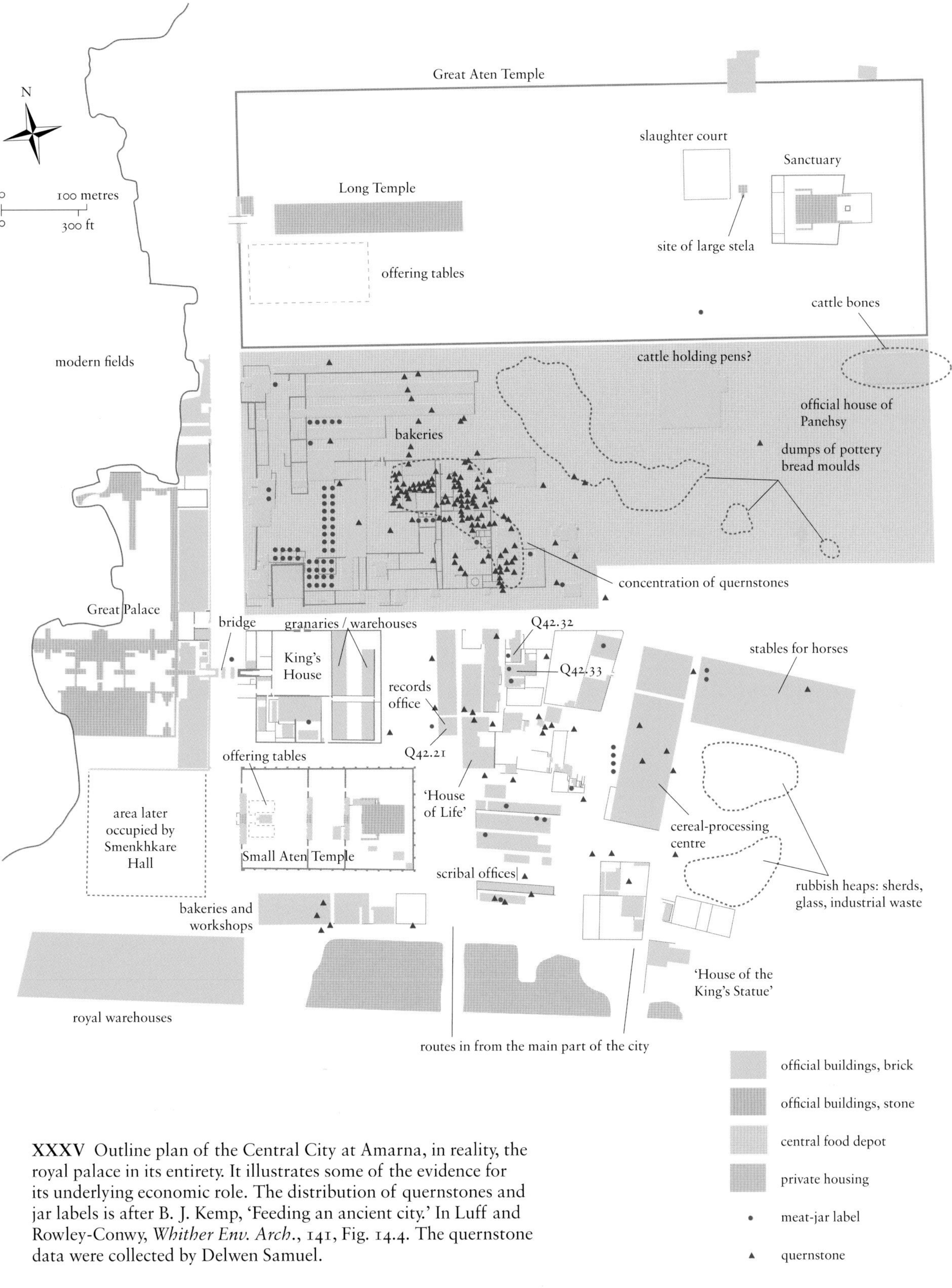

XXXV Outline plan of the Central City at Amarna, in reality, the royal palace in its entirety. It illustrates some of the evidence for its underlying economic role. The distribution of quernstones and jar labels is after B. J. Kemp, 'Feeding an ancient city.' In Luff and Rowley-Conwy, *Whither Env. Arch.*, 141, Fig. 14.4. The quernstone data were collected by Delwen Samuel.

XXXVI (left) Model of the main part of the 'House of the Aten', namely, the Long Temple at the front of the enclosure. The flagpoles have been added to the outer, mud-brick pylon. The tomb pictures (see figures 3.9, 3.10) imply that they stood in front of the second pylon, but this would place them behind the colonnades (see figure 3.11). Outside the temple is the field of 920 mud-brick offering tables.

XXXVII (opposite below) Model of the Maru-Aten sun-temple, based on the plan of excavations made in 1922 (see figure 2.16), as if looking towards the southwest.

XXXVIII (below) Model of the North Palace, viewed as if to the northwest. In the far corner (the offering-place of figure 4.22) a roof supported on columns has been placed over the platform (compare figures 4.24, 4.25). A Window of Appearance has been made part of the columned architecture set into the thick walls that separate the outer and inner courts (compare figure 4.10). Reconstructions often involve choices of more than one possibility.

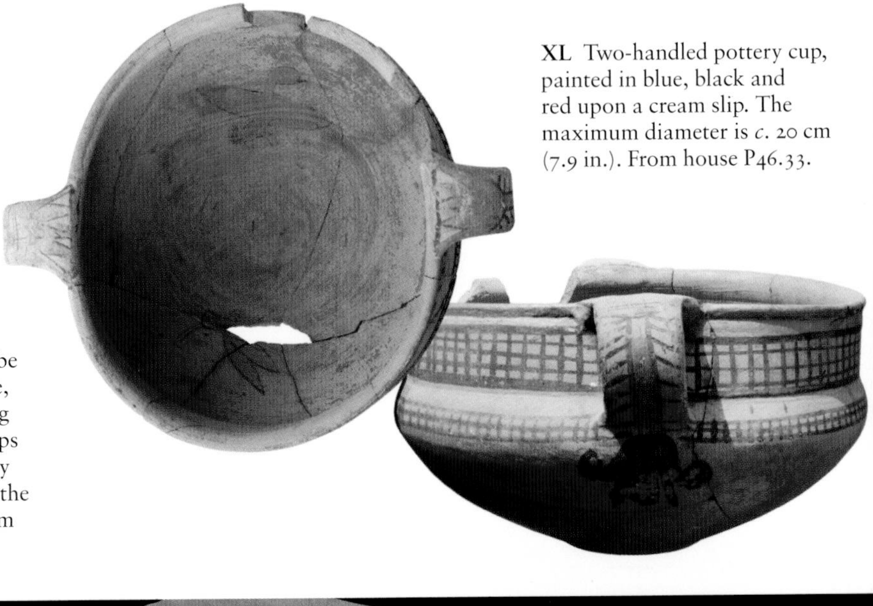

XL Two-handled pottery cup, painted in blue, black and red upon a cream slip. The maximum diameter is *c.* 20 cm (7.9 in.). From house P46.33.

XXXIX (above) Two sides of a painted wooden plaque, made to be mounted on top of a wooden pole, obj. 5239. It depicts a man adoring a standard of a canine god, perhaps Wepwawet. Found in the sanctuary at the rear of the Main Chapel at the Workmen's Village. Height 11.3 cm (4.5 in.).

XLI (opposite above) Three scaraboid beads with hippopotamus backs, made from glazed steatite, all from the South Tombs Cemetery, square H54 (13199), debris from the base of a wooden coffin that had contained an adult (Individual 188A, a woman aged 40–45) and a child (Individual 188B). The base designs show (left to right) Bes, a seated goddess and Taweret. Objs 39933a, b, c.

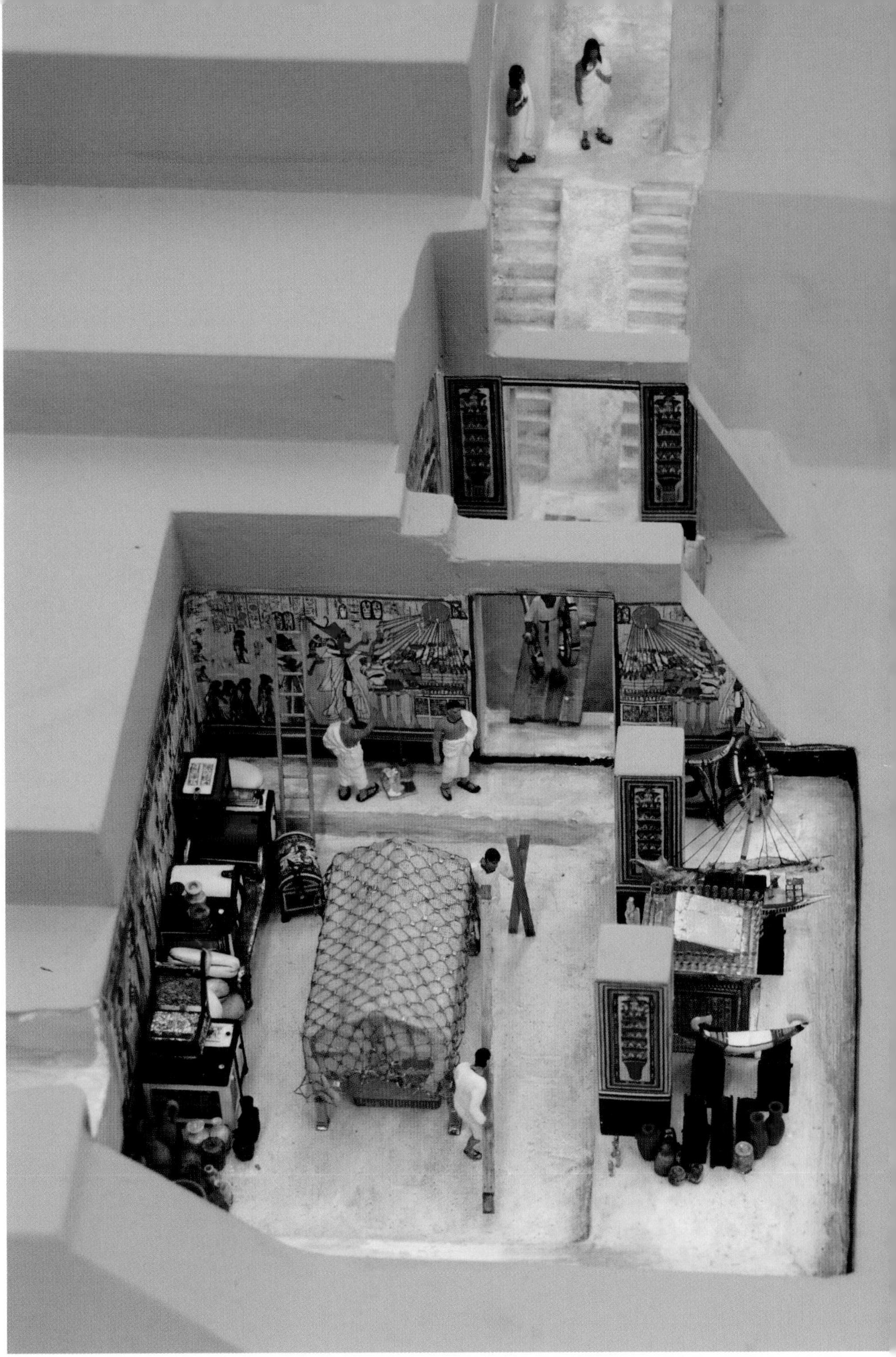

XLII (opposite below) Model of the Workmen's Village. The corner of the walled village is at the left edge. Beside the corner stands the Main Chapel, with other chapels ranged behind. In front are three groups of pens for the raising of pigs. Compare figure 5.30.

XLIII (above) Part of a model of the Royal Tomb, equipped as it might have been for Akhenaten's burial. The painted scenes on the wall repeat the familiar subjects of worship of the Aten. There are no scenes that depict the journey of the sun-god through the hours of the night, facing constant dangers before emerging, reborn, at dawn.

XLIV (above) A couple dressed for a special occasion. They wear wigs, a scented cone, necklaces of plant-shaped pendants, and they carry bouquets of flowers. Restored by F. Weatherhead from fragments found in the Main Chapel at the Workmen's Village.

XLV (above) Two decorated leather fragments from building R43.2 (House of the King's Statue), now in the British Museum, EA 74101. One shows a flying heraldic falcon, the other a feather pattern.

XLVI (left) Fragment of a faience tile showing two bullocks browsing among marsh plants. Possibly from Amarna (and very similar to others definitely found there). Height 10.8 cm (4.2 in.).

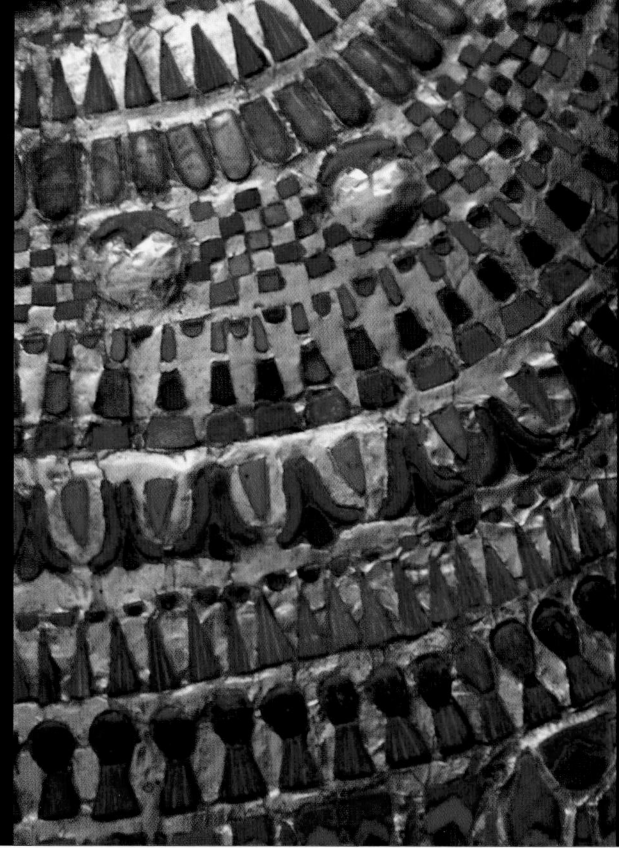

XLVII (above) Two parts of the coffin from Valley of the Kings tomb 55, originally for one of the royal women of Akhenaten's court and thus probably made at Amarna. The decorative patterns consist of myriad small inlays of glass and (in the case of the red pieces in the left-hand photograph) of carnelian. Gold leaf covers the spaces between the inlays.

XLVIII Glass vessel in the shape of a fish, obj. 21/475. Found with other objects buried beneath the floor of a room beside or belonging to house N49.20. Length 14.5 cm (5.5 in.).

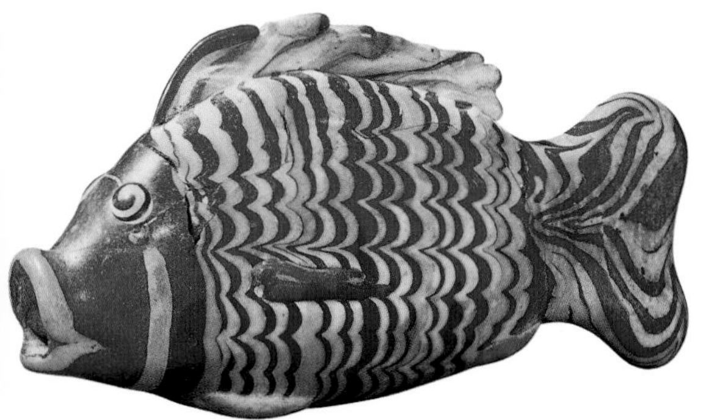

XLIX (above) Pieces of coloured glass inlay from Grid 12. All pieces are at the same scale, obj. 36158 being 2.8 cm (1 in.) long. Obj. 35992 is at an early stage of manufacture: a poured glass bar has been roughly chipped to shape, but not yet ground and polished. With obj. 35982, one side (on the right) has been polished. Obj. 35648 is a partially finished chevron, not yet polished. The thickness of obj. 36158 might be a sign that it still remains to be ground thinner. Obj. 35905 is finished and could be the hieroglyph 'mouth' that wrote the letter *r*. Obj. 36504 looks still unfinished, although inlay pieces were not made with great precision.

L Faience inlays from Grid 12, made as architectural inlays. (top) The red-brown pair, obj. 34847 (length 2 cm, 0.8 in.) and obj. 34956 (width 2 cm, 0.8 in.) were made in a shallow mould lined with cloth. (above) Those that are green-blue were roughly cut from larger sheets; (obj. 35600, left, width 1.2 cm, 0.5 in.); on the reverse of obj. 34346, (right, length 0.8 cm, 0.3 in.), the cut for the removal of a rough edge is visible.

LI Obj. 8761, fired clay mould (2.47 cm, 0.96 in.) and, obj. 8762, the blue faience ring bezel made from it (1.98 cm (0.77 in.). The design gives Tutankhamun's first royal name, Nubkheperure, followed by the words 'chosen of Amun-Ra'. From factory building Q48.4.

LII Experimental melting of metal (brass filings) in a replica of an ancient crucible, using goatskin bellows to raise the temperature of the charcoal (see also figure 8.10). A pyrometer and thermocouple inserted into the charcoal monitor the temperature. The work of Mark Eccleston. Note the simplicity and ephemeral nature of the 'kiln'.

LIII (above) Sherd from a bellows nozzle, or tuyère, obj. 37100, (60 mm, 2.4 in. wide); (below) Two sherds from crucibles, obj. 37104 (34 mm, 1.4 in. wide) and obj. 37807 (60 mm, 2.4 in. wide). All are from Grid 12.

and Meryetaten might suffer death while not at Amarna, which makes sense if they spent time in other residences. When they went to Memphis, they would have worked with a separate, northern vizier and his own staff of officials, implying that the Amarna vizier stayed at home to look after southern affairs. Outside the Amarna period, the rhythm of life through the year was in part made up of numerous traditional festivals, with a working period of ten days in which one or two days were a holiday. The Aten had its festivals, too, as we saw in Chapter 3. And perhaps, like the royal family, the leading families also left Amarna from time to time, to attend to houses and estates elsewhere. Military men will have spent time abroad.

Not All 'Houses' were Houses

To say that housing appears to have occupied around half of the total area of the city is to make a generalized contrast with areas dominated by royal buildings and large storage and administrative complexes. When examined more closely, however, even the 'housing' areas contained buildings that do not look like houses and in total must cover a significant portion of the 'residential' ground. Many of these occur within the private estates around the larger houses and, as commented upon earlier, must in part have stored cereals and cattle or accommodated small-scale manufacture. Other non-residential buildings stood on their own, or at least outside private estates. Three examples will serve to characterize them.

First is the group Q48.4, located just beyond the edge of the city, so presumably a late creation and potentially the first step in creating a new neighbourhood, although sufficient time elapsed for the complex itself to be largely rebuilt [8.3]. Only a small part has been excavated, to reveal a series of small workshops occupying a corner of a rectangular brick enclosure. The enclosure wall had been carefully built, strengthened with regularly spaced external buttresses. The people who took it over then created rooms and spaces according to their immediate needs, without reference to a master plan. Kilns were built and later replaced, leaving circular holes in the desert floor and deposits of ash and charcoal. Numerous pieces of pottery vessels, broken before they were fired, together with the stone wheel-bearing from a potter's wheel show that pottery was one of the industries pursued. Other industrial waste points to the making of faience jewelry and small glass items, and evidence is also present for spinning and the weaving of textiles, though perhaps belonging to the later phase of building [cf. 8.15]. A small unfinished statue (a surface find) perhaps adds sculpting to the list.

Secondly comes the group P47.1–3 [5.9], which included the house of the sculptor Thutmose (famous for the painted bust of Nefertiti). Sculptors' debris was found not only around the house itself, but also in a series of small buildings (some looking rather like small dwellings) arranged informally around the sides of a court attached to the side of Thutmose's estate wall and comprising his 'village'. Some of the finds also point to the making of faience jewelry.

8.3 *Plan of the lower level of the excavated part of building Q48.4, a factory. Certain categories of industrial waste point to the manufacture of pottery and small faience and glass objects.*

8.4 *(opposite) An area towards the southern end of the main residential area of Amarna. A large enclosure faces one of the main streets, its entrance flanked by brick pylon towers. It contains granaries, storerooms and two wells. Close by, on the north side, are two large circular brick enclosures, the northernmost containing two deep brick-lined storage pits in the middle.*

In these two cases, the archaeology defines their purposes. For some non-residential buildings, however, no explanation is forthcoming from the evidence we have. They include a group of buildings towards the south end of the city, comprising a large enclosed polygonal space and, close by, two large circular

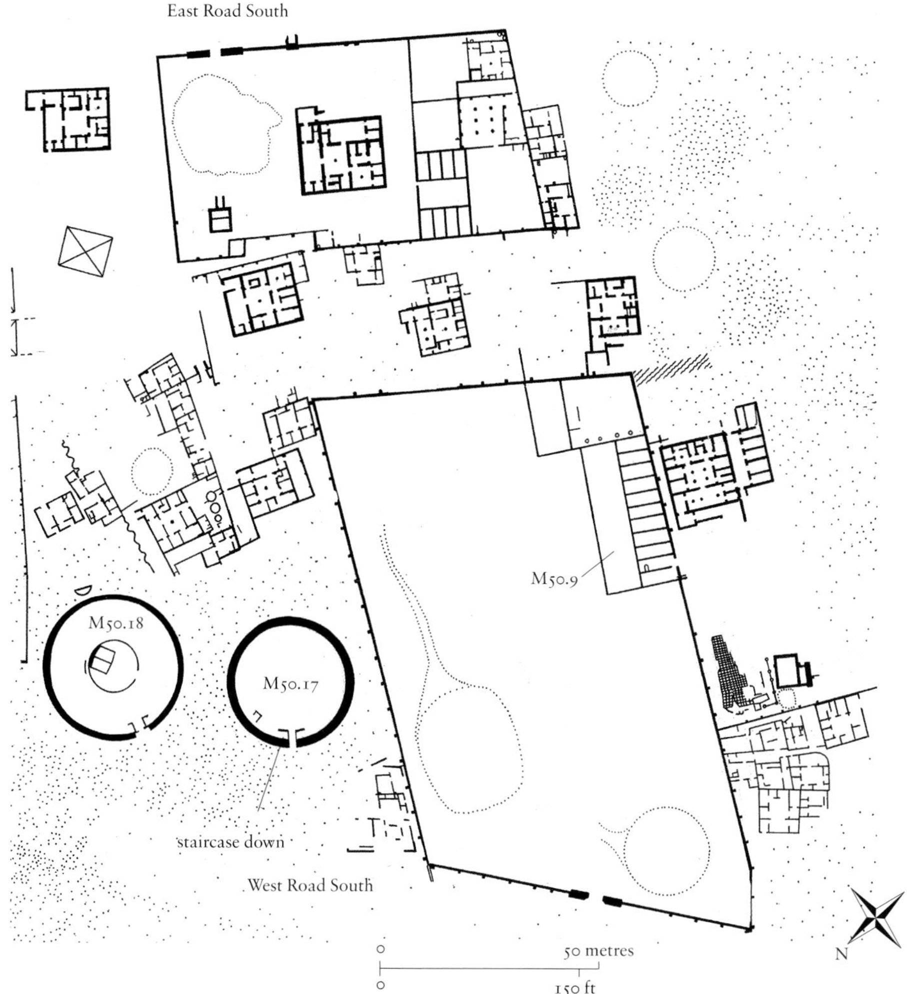

enclosures that were not wells [8.4]. They imply, in turn, the existence of institutions within the city that we cannot identify; and thus suggest that the picture I give of how the city worked, even though I think it valid at a general level, necessarily lacks other elements that would introduce a greater level of complexity.

A 'Vast but Loosely Structured Factory Serving the State'

My descriptions of the housing neighbourhoods rest largely on their ground plans. To recover those plans archaeologists have removed quantities of sand and rubble that have contained objects and waste material of various kinds. Within this material lie important clues to the economy of Amarna, a subject of key importance in defining the nature of cities.

When it was appropriate, the Egyptians in the New Kingdom could create something resembling a factory, specialized and with multiple units of production. This has been demonstrated by the discovery, at the slightly later royal city of Per-Ramesses in the eastern Delta, of a major bronze foundry in the vicinity of a chariotry barracks. The bakeries beside the Great Aten Temple are, in their way, an example from Amarna, and a glass-working factory of modest scale is mentioned below. For metals, however, there is no equivalent at Amarna, although bronze was widely used. There would have been a constant need for new items and for repairs to old. A small number of limestone moulds have been found, suited to the casting of the incised shapes in metal (which could have been gold or silver or even possibly lead) [**8.5, 8.7**]. The shapes are all, bar one, small items of jewelry (earrings, pendants, possibly appliqués to be sewn on to pieces of cloth, etc., the exception having the shape of a bent nail with head, no. 33/333). All except three (one of them the piece 33/333) come from the housing areas, the exceptions coming from some of the brick governmental buildings in the Central City; three of them come from the Workmen's Village. Casting was only one method of creating bronze objects. The other was to fashion them from bronze sheet that had been hammered out from ingots. This was probably the way that the bulk of bronze vessels was made. Shapes were also cut from sheets of gold foil that had been pressed into a mould [**8.8, 8.9**], the shapes perhaps to be sewn as pieces of appliqué onto pieces of cloth (a large example covered the shrines in the tomb of Tutankhamun).

Among the debris found in the city are broken pieces of coarse, thick pottery bowls that have been heated on the inside to the point when the surface starts to bloat into a black foamy mass in which metal particles are embedded (which

8.5, 8.6, 8.7 *Limestone metal-casting moulds for small objects: earrings, Bes pendants, a strip of lilies that were presumably cut individually and perhaps used as appliqués, rectangular or oval plaques with designs and long narrow support strips. (left) obj. 30/20; 10.8 by 8.9 cm (4.3 by 3.5 in.). The design at the bottom is described as: 'amulet having in relief the vulture and snake'; the third design from the bottom is described (on the object card) as 'a scarab'. (right) obj. 36/150; 12 by 9 cm (4.7 by 3.5 in.). The design near the right edge is an ink sketch. (centre) obj. 31/65 is probably an earring, said to be made of lead(?), cast from such a mould; 4 cm (1.6 in.) high. The moulds are of one piece, provided with drainage channels.*

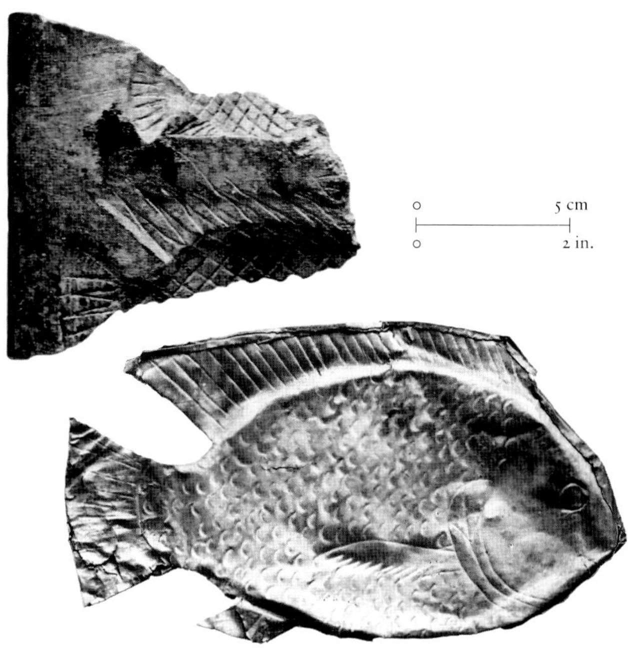

8.8, 8.9 *(above) obj. 36/184, another kind of limestone mould, for fish ornaments, to be made not by casting, but by pressing and cutting a sheet of gold foil. Length 11 cm (4.3 in.). (below) obj. 34/177, a fish ornament made of gold foil, pressed in a mould and trimmed. Length 17 cm (6.7 in.).*

turn green over time) and occasional pieces of charcoal. They are from crucibles, within which the temperature must have been raised by bellows forcing air into the glowing interior mass via thick pottery tubes, fragments of which have also been found. Sand grains cemented together by splashes from the operation also took on a green hue. This varied debris, not found in particular concentrations or associated with obvious workshops, is of a kind that earlier generations of archaeologists at Amarna must have discarded. It forms a distinctive component – though not a numerically large one – of the material from the excavation of the area of smallish houses in the main city (Grid 12) described in Chapter 5 (pp. 177–80).[14] These belong to a much larger area of similar houses dug in the first part of the last century and from which nothing equivalent was recorded. Yet pieces of crucible with a dark fused surface can occasionally be found on the ground in the city, adding to the impression that this material forms a regular though not a large part of the blanket of sandy debris that covers the entire city ruin.

The bright green colour of corroded bronze makes it easy to spot even when the pieces are small, but the corrosion hinders identification. Small and delicately made items of bronze, sometimes broken, often become unrecognizable. Even so, among the fragments of corroded bronze from Grid 12 are several that seem to be pieces of metal sheet that have been cut and folded to be even smaller, down to the size of a fingernail. The evidence fits into a picture if we imagine a very small-scale industry of remaking bronze sheet out of pieces of bronze scrap. The absence of heat installations is only partly explained by the ancient destruction of most of the floors in these houses. The installation may have been no more than the crucible itself, propped up on bricks [8.10]. A few near-contemporary tomb scenes at Thebes, however, add the disconcerting fact that the Egyptians, by this time, had small portable furnaces, raised to waist height so that the smith could work from a stool. Once carried off, they would probably leave behind no identifiable trace of their presence.[15]

The Grid 12 debris, sieved as it was excavated from the first day to the last, contained a constant mixture of fragments of different materials, easily dismissed on first viewing as too broken or formless to have value, yet on closer inspection having a contribution to make. Next to potsherds, the commonest object was a fragment of flat thin faience slab, shiny and turquoise-coloured on one side and rough on the other, the edges frequently irregular. They are pieces of inlay, in simple shapes, made to be inserted into similarly shaped recesses in a larger object of a different material and held in place with gypsum plaster. The Great Palace in the Central City possessed columns and other architectural embellishments made of stone and inlaid in this way [8.11, 8.12].

The method of making the inlays was akin to cooking. A thin layer of powdered quartz, held together with a moist adhesive, was spread on a flat surface to make something that looked like a large biscuit. Over the top was spread first a thinner and finer white paste to give a smooth surface and purer colour, and then the glaze mix. The whole was then heated, perhaps in a small oven. Once fired and cooled, the 'biscuit' was turned over. Using a sharp instrument, the rough underside was scored with closely set v-profile lines. When the 'biscuit' was snapped along these lines, its irregular outer edges were discarded and a heap of small rectangular or triangular inlays was left. It is a simple but somewhat crude way of making inlays, and used only for those of turquoise colour. Other similar inlays, fewer in number, were made in a red-brown glaze using a different method, in shallow moulds covered in cloth.

8.10 *A replica ancient crucible used to melt brass filings. Part of an experimental metal kiln at Amarna, by Mark Eccleston (see Pl. LII).*

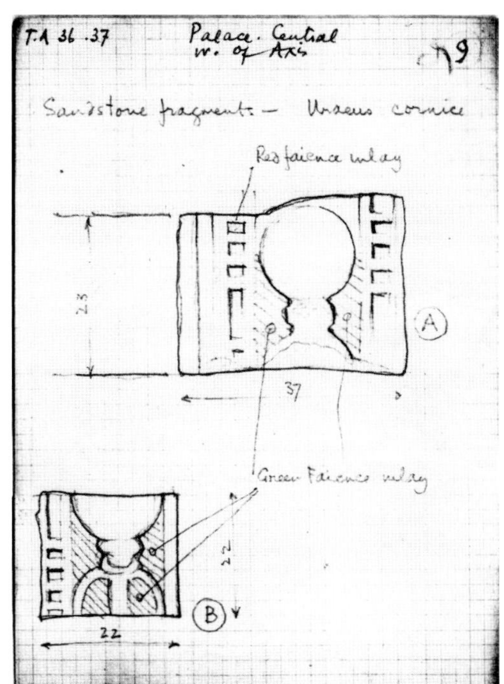

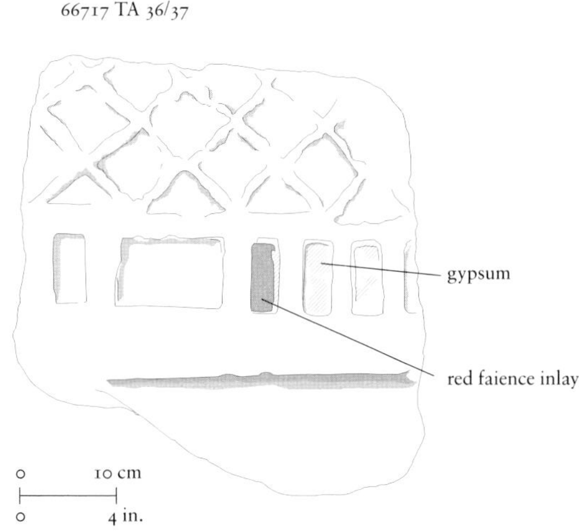

8.11, 8.12 *(left) Field record (made in 1936) of two stone blocks from the Great Palace that are part of a frieze of carved cobras or uraei (compare figures 4.14, 4.15). They were decorated with inlaid green and red faience tiles (compare plate L). (right) Obj. 36/no no. Limestone block from the Great Palace, which retains an inexactly fitting piece of red faience inlay and the gypsum in which it was set (see also figure 4.14a). Width 22 cm (8.5 in.).*

If these pieces were intended for architectural inlay, they must have been collected in sacks and taken to the Great Palace (for example) and there set into the stone architecture. But the inlays are not constant in size. They needed to be fitted one at a time into the most suitable spaces, gypsum cement helping to fill the gaps that would often have been left at the sides. It was an inexact industry that produced, nonetheless, an overall blaze of colour. In being individually set within narrow frames carved in the underlying stone, however, they were not quite like mosaics.

Amarna was home to a glass-working industry. On the preserved western edge of the city, close to the limit of the modern fields beside the river bank, part of a workshop of modest scale has been found equipped with kilns (more substantial than those for faience mentioned above) for the making of circular glass ingots, about 12 cm (4.7 in.) in diameter, from the raw-material mix of quartz powder, alkali (ashes from suitable plants) and colouring agent (cobalt for deep blue, for example).[16] From the ingots, when reheated with further colouring agents, long thin canes of glass were drawn out: light and dark blue, green, yellow, brown, red-brown, black and white. They were used to insert coloured wavy patterns in small glass vessels and pieces of jewelry. The brittle, short broken lengths of glass cane have been found almost everywhere at Amarna, including at Grid 12.[17] There they are joined by other remnants of the making of small items from coloured glass, including small inlays (either for stonework or wooden objects, such as coffins). These reveal a cautious technology that relied upon much secondary hand-work. The small shapes, instead of being cast, were cut and polished as if gem stones. The same applied to small beads and pendants made from glass. One gets a picture of people, perhaps children, spending long parts of each day rubbing small pieces of glass against an abrasive, a task that required little attention.

What survives for the archaeologist to find are mostly waste products. We can only speculate about the size and nature of the finished objects themselves. Several items from royal tombs of the period (including Tutankhamun's and the royal reburial, perhaps of Akhenaten or his successor Smenkhkare, at Thebes in tomb 55) are of wood covered with gold leaf, and inlaid with small pieces of coloured glass and hard stone. The king's coffin in tomb 55 at Thebes was originally created for a woman of his family and so was probably made at Amarna [**Pl. XLVII**]. It is inlaid with just the kind of small and somewhat inexactly cut pieces of coloured glass that were being made in the housing areas, where pieces of gold leaf are also not infrequently found. There is no intrinsic reason why expensive things of this kind could not have been made in these small domestic workshops, under the control of the local patron-official.

An almost indestructible remnant of jewelry manufacture is the small flattish fired-clay moulds for rings, beads and pendants that were made from faience [**Pl. LI**].[18] An original object was carefully pressed into a ball of prepared mud, to leave its impression, and the mould was fired. It was then filled with a glazing paste to produce a new example of the object. After drying, it was removed and separately fired. Faience-jewelry moulds are sufficiently distinctive and attractive to have been collected and recorded by the earlier archaeologists. They occur in large numbers across the site, sometimes in clusters suggestive of workshops, though these turn out to be particularly among smaller houses [**8.13**], including those of Grid 12.[19] Again no special firing installations can be recognized; they were probably made in the standard small cylindrical kilns used at other times for baking bread.

The myriad kilns, cooking fires and hearths of the city required a steady supply of fuel. As pointed out in Chapter 2, the uniformity of firewood at Amarna, documented from the identification of charcoal samples, implies a system of supply probably managed by the state.[20]

The Grid 12 debris also produced a bewildering variety of rough stone hand tools, for hammering, rubbing and polishing surfaces – but the surfaces of what kinds of things? They are still poorly understood. The only unfinished articles to be recognized are heavy querns of quartzite that have been roughed out, but not given their final surface. It means we can add stone-working to the list of crafts of these busy people.[21]

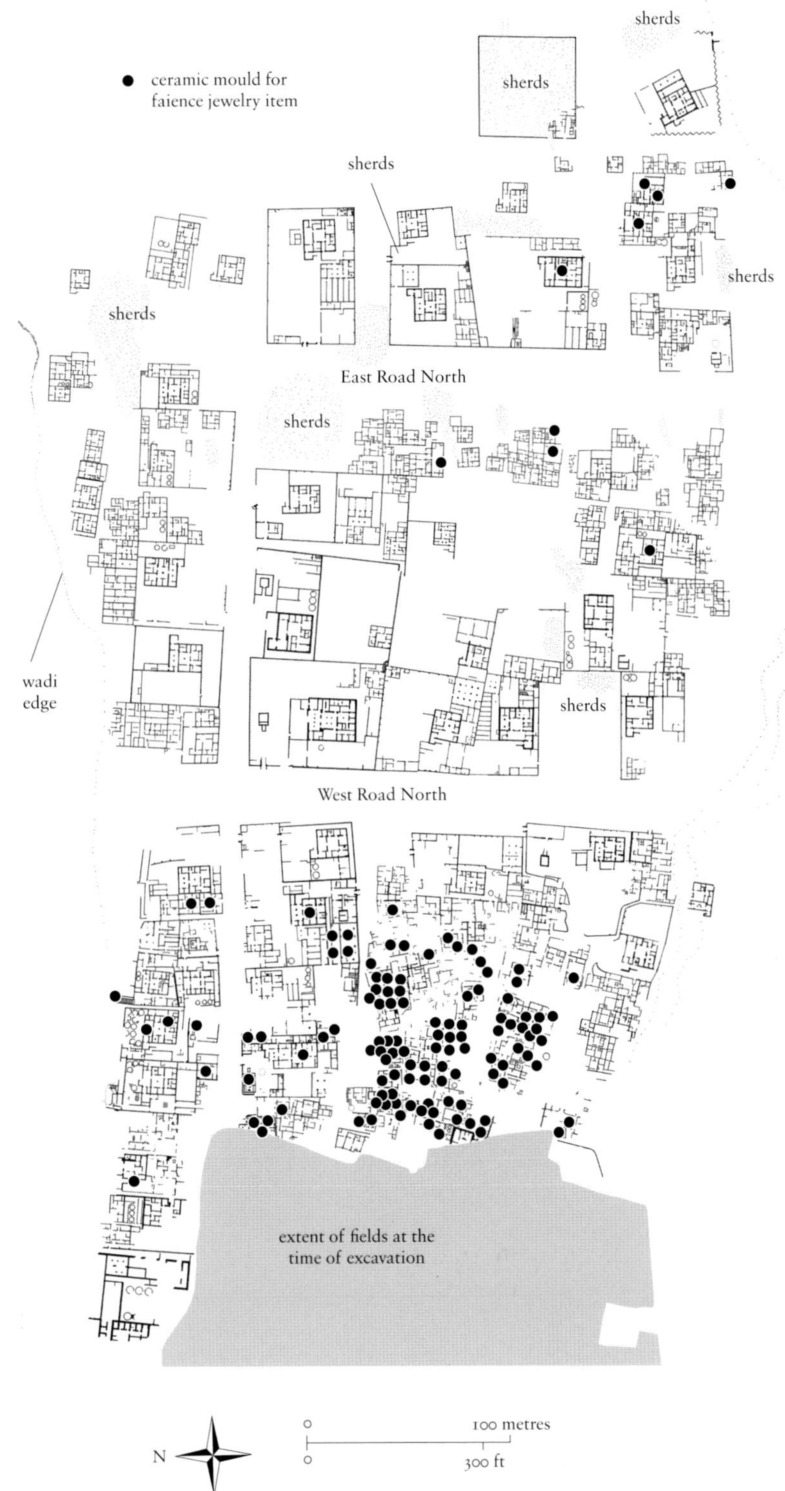

8.13 *Distribution map of small ceramic moulds for producing faience jewelry items, as found in the southern part of the North Suburb. A degree of caution is needed in interpreting the map. The houses east of West Road North produced generally less archaeological debris, including sherds, than those to the west. To judge also from the extensive open spaces, this eastern zone was still in the process of development when Amarna was abandoned. The open spaces would subsequently have been filled with just the kind of smaller houses that served as workshops. The map is based upon the excavation field records rather than the publication,* COA II.

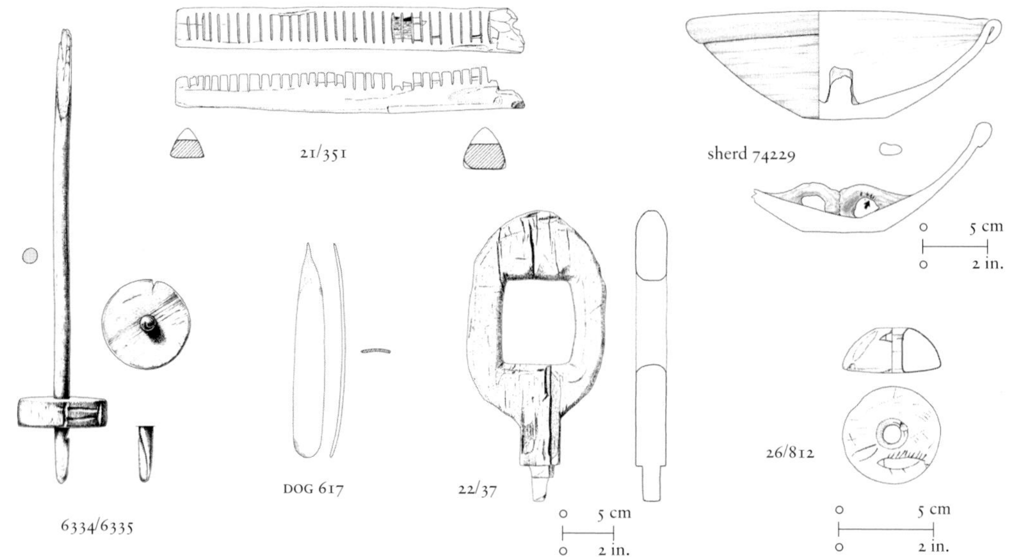

8.14 *Objects used in the making of textiles. Obj. 6334/6335, wooden spindle whorl mounted on its spindle; obj. 26/812, limestone spindle whorl with incised decoration; sherd 74229, pottery bowl used for plying two or more yarns together. On the section drawing, the arrow points to grooves worn into the underside of the pottery loops; obj. 21/351, wooden warp-spacer from a loom; obj. 22/37, probably another loom part, a wooden heddle support; DOG 617 (1913/14 season), a bone spacer or pin beater perhaps used for fine control of the warps during weaving (an alternative explanation is that they were used in leather working).*

Textile production is another industry that leaves telltale signs behind, from both the spinning and weaving stages [**8.14**].[22] Textiles in ancient Egypt were overwhelmingly made from linen, relegating wool to a marginal place. The first step in making yarns and threads was to splice thin bundles of twisted flax fibres together by rolling them between the hands over the thighs. The next step was to ply two of the assembled lengths together to lock in the twist. This was done by rotating them by means of a wooden spindle weighted by a disc (a 'whorl'), made from wood or limestone, that acted as a spinner. Flax needs moisture as it is worked, so the lengths were passed through a pottery bowl filled with water, which had pottery guiding loops. The looped bowls and the limestone whorls preserve well at Amarna; at the Workmen's Village where conditions of preservation are even better than in the main city, wooden whorls greatly outnumber those of stone.

By the New Kingdom some weaving at least was being done on fairly complicated vertical wooden looms. A few loom parts survived at the Workmen's Village. Less destructible items from weaving are more difficult to identify. Heavy limestone grooved blocks might have supported the bottom loom beam, and narrow bone points might have been used by weavers for fine adjustments of the taught warp threads. If one marks the find-places of these various cate-

8.15 *Distribution map of three types of object associated with textile production (though with the bone points the association is less certain). The higher concentrations of finds at the Workmen's Village, building Q48.4 and Grid 12 reflect more methodical collection of finds during excavation. In the case of spindles and whorls the better preservation of wood at the Workmen's Village also makes a difference (only one of the whorls was of stone).*

gories of spinning- and weaving-tools on a map of Amarna, a familiar pattern emerges [**8.15**]. Around the palaces and temples the marks are few, in contrast to the housing areas where they are liberally and fairly evenly scattered. A particular concentration appears at the Workmen's Village (perhaps because of the better preservation of wooden items).

According to texts of the New Kingdom, temples and palaces owned textile workers, who seem to have been slaves. By contrast, the Amarna map of textile evidence suggests that, even if palaces and temples at Amarna were involved in production, they were so only indirectly, with the actual spinning and weaving distributed wherever there were houses, even out to the Workmen's Village where, as we have seen, the evidence is particularly strong and abundant. It implies a massive delegation of responsibility from state to officials, who (as we know from other texts) were locked into supply agreements with the state, obliged to deliver a certain quota of pieces of finished cloth (while presumably keeping a share for themselves). What applied to textiles probably applied to other craft products. The whole picture is the opposite of the modern concept of zoning or of the medieval practice of locating related crafts in particular market areas (the Arabic *souk*). 'In a sense, the Amarna suburbs appear as a vast but loosely structured factory serving the state.'[23]

Manufacture and Status

New Kingdom Egypt did not offer opportunities for wealth and position to people on the basis of their own endeavours independent of the king. In the manufacture of textiles, a proportion of the skilled weavers were slaves, their skills not a means to secure significant advancement in life. Some men responsible for crafts, nonetheless, achieved prominence because they were able to provide the king with desired products. They were successful because they achieved a convergence between their creative skills, ability to organize and attentive service at court. The most explicit case concerns the 'Chief of the Sculptors for the big and important monuments of the king in the House of Aten in Akhetaten' Bak (who also called himself 'Chief of Works'), son of the similarly titled sculptor Men. He stated in a sculpted memorial at Aswan (site of the main granite quarry) that he was 'a disciple whom his Person [King Akhenaten] instructed'.[24] We do not know if he also lived and worked at Amarna, but the sculptor Thutmose (who likewise called himself 'Chief of Works', see 7.5), owner of the house and workshops at Amarna where the painted bust of Nefertiti was found [5.9], was presumably in the same position. Other successful providers of crafted products with large houses at Amarna were two men with similar titles 'Overseer of Works' and 'Overseer of Builders', Hatiay and Maanakhtuef respectively. There is no sign that Hatiay had a sculptor's workshops beside his house and so presumably he plied his skill in another sector (perhaps building).

Not all sculptors of note were leading officials. Among the king's rewards to the steward of Queen Tiye, Huya, was a set of craftsmen who included metal-workers, jewelry-makers, woodworkers and sculptors, one of them sufficiently important in Huya's eyes to be named ('the Chief Sculptor of Queen Tiye, Iuty'), but presumably not of the same independent standing as Thutmose [8.17]. In sculpting, there was evidently a flexibility of organization, although its manifestations were still mostly to be found within the housing areas.

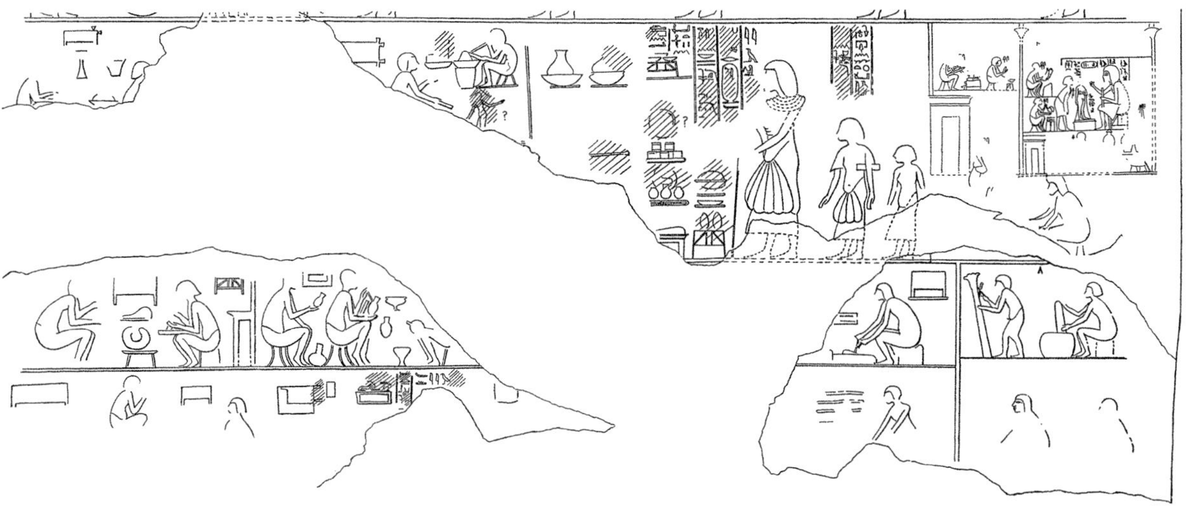

8.16, 8.17 Part of a tomb scene (from tomb no. 1) showing the steward Huya being rewarded at the Window of Appearance. Among his rewards is a set of workshops where furniture and jewelry are made, as well as statues. (right) The top-right part of the scene is shown at a larger scale. Men labelled as 'sculptors' are making a chair leg and other articles, including a head and a complete statue of Princess Baketaten, daughter of Queen Tiye. The chief sculptor in charge of that is named Iuty.

Thutmose maintained a degree of intimacy between himself and the products of his establishment. The painted bust of Nefertiti was found (by Ludwig Borchardt's workmen in 1912) in a small room leading directly from the front reception hall of his house, lying as if it had fallen from a shelf. Arranged on the floor of the same room was a large collection of heads and statuettes (some of them of the royal family), masks [**8.18**] and body portions, many made from gypsum plaster, but others in limestone and quartzite. Since the royal pieces would have been redundant even before the city was abandoned, the place where they were discovered might not have been their original location. Had they been a collection of models that Thutmose could show to potential cus-

8.18 *Plaster face from the house of the sculptor Thutmose, now in Berlin.*

8.19 *(below) Plan of houses O47.16a and .20, made by H. Waddington in 1932. Debris from sculptors' workshops was found scattered in both buildings though no individual find places were recorded.*

tomers or use as guides for his sculptors? Were the faces that were casts from moulds the faces of real people that were going to act as objects of domestic veneration because they represented a recently deceased ancestor?

Sculpting was not necessarily done, however, in establishments that were architecturally distinct from neighbouring buildings. An important group of material, similar in range to that from Thutmose's house, was found scattered in rooms and spaces that clustered around two houses of medium size (O47.16A and .20) [**8.19, 8.20**].[25] Debris from sculptors has also been found in the Central City, not associated with distinctive buildings at all. The variety of status and location contained within the evidence for sculptors illustrates once again the fluidity of social and professional boundaries in Amarna's society.

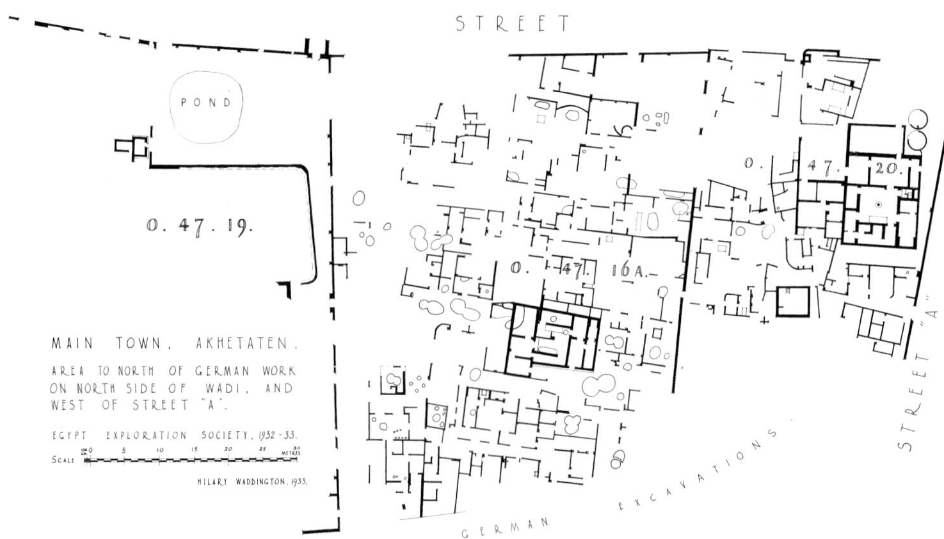

8.20 *Pieces from sculptors' workshop O47.16a. (above left) obj. 32/94, red quartzite inlay of a face of Akhenaten or Nefertiti, probably not finished. Height 12 cm (4.7 in.). (above right) obj. 32/90, gypsum plaster face of Nefertiti. Height 33 cm (12.9 in.). (below) obj. 32/205, brown quartzite head of a royal woman often thought to be Nefertiti and intended to be part of a composite statue. Height 35.5 cm (14 in.). Note the guide lines on the face. (Also from the same workshops, the statuette shown in figure 7.14.)*

Sjoberg's preindustrial city nurtured guilds. Evidence for guilds in Egypt in the New Kingdom is hard to come by. They seem to run counter to the nature of the urban village unit that is the foundation of Amarna. The people of the Theban necropolis workmen's village of Deir el-Medina, well documented in texts, behaved sometimes as if they were all members of a single guild, but this may have been a consequence of their separation from local society. In their own separation, the Amarna communities of the Workmen's Village and Stone Village were in a matching situation, but, in the absence of written records, we can only surmise that this created the same feeling of solidarity against the outside world that is visible sometimes at Deir el-Medina. Otherwise at Amarna, different crafts intermingled. Sculptor's workshops seem weakly concentrated in the middle part of the Main City, but they, too, shared spaces with other crafts. The intermingling and the varying involvement of officials seem the antithesis of the conditions in which guilds form.

For Whom were All these Busy People Working?

The evidence for manufacture – tools and waste material alike – spreads through the housing areas seemingly not distinguishing the houses of rich and poor. The little evidence we have from texts backs up the idea that the dependent life of much of the population, clients of their patron-officials, embraced their craft products. People made things initially for their masters, and secondarily for themselves. Many of the Amarna officials had mini-warehouses in their grounds, and these could have served as collecting-points for things manufactured in the dependent houses.

What happened next is illustrated in several tombs at Thebes of the immediately preceding period. Manufactured goods were given to the king on special occasions, including that of the New Year.[26] The amounts could be impressive. A scene in the Theban tomb of Qenamun depicts fifteen statues and a harvest of military equipment, which included 680 shields, 360 scimitars, two war chariots and fifty-eight horse blankets.[27] Where all this material came from is stated, if at all, in characteristically vague terms. In Qenamun's tomb it is said to be 'all kinds of artifacts of the craftsmanship of [Lower Egypt]'; in another (Theban tomb 73) the formula is: 'the best productions of the workshop and great places of His Majesty'.[28]

As for the final destination of these goods, we can surmise that the chariots and weapons were valuable supplements to the military resources that kings of the New Kingdom needed to maintain their military ambitions. For the statues and religious equipment, however, an annotation beside one of the donated statues in the tomb of Qenamun, to the effect that it was intended for the temple of Amun at Karnak, helps to confirm what we might otherwise suspect, that the king would subsequently present at least some, and perhaps most, of his gifts to a temple (although his own tomb would be a suitable home for a few of the pieces; for example, some fine wooden statuettes in Tutankhamun's funerary equipment had been donated by two of the king's officials[29]). This practice also helps us to understand the significance of Akhenaten's public comment to his chamberlain Tutu, quoted in Chapter 1: 'Pharaoh ordains that all the officials and chief men of the entire land be obliged to give him [i.e. Tutu] silver, gold, [cattle,] clothing and bronze vessels – they being imposed upon you like taxes' – this became an annual event.[30]

Amarna, with its ubiquitous evidence for manufacture, supplies the missing archaeological background to this practice of national donation of manufactured objects via the king's officials. It embraces Thutmose and the setting of his workshop. His clients would primarily have been fellow officials who had decided, for that particular year, to commission a fine statue as their annual gift to the king. An example would be the granodiorite statue of Akhenaten and Nefertiti seated side by side that was left unfinished (and subsequently smashed up) in his workshops.[31] Providing a flow of goods to the court was one of the city's main functions. The officials through whom it was mediated could be professionally involved, as an overseer of works, or, like Huya, a steward of the queen, but loyalty and local patrician authority were what mattered rather than technical interest in the manufacturing itself, although the sculptor Thutmose was one in whom the two aspects converged.

Goods of all kinds came back to officials through the king's rewards for loyalty. These men were not dependent upon this system, however, receiving income from farmlands and livestock they owned or rented outside Amarna. The most conspicuous signs are the private granaries (grain being a means of purchasing goods that one did not have) [2.6]. And just as the officials did not wholly depend upon the king, so it is unlikely that their dependants wholly lived off their patron's handouts. An informal economy, of exchanges through barter well documented elsewhere in the New Kingdom, must have satisfied individual wants: new sandals, an extra cooking-pot, a heavy mat needed for wrapping the body of someone newly and unexpectedly dead.[32]

No human system is ever fully homogeneous and complete. Exceptions and variations are a natural part. The economy of Amarna, though dominated by its officially orchestrated flow of goods, is likely to have had a place for people who were independent producers, even if only part-time. Examples of their products are the coffins and stelae from the South Tombs Cemetery [7.29, 7.30, 7.32–7.34]. In a different sector, the striking evidence from the Workmen's Village of a pig-rearing industry, represented on the ground by carefully laid out pig-pens [8.21, 8.22], points to a local initiative organized within the village. In addition to providing food for the village, pigs could also have been sold to the main city, where pig bones are also common. The incompleteness of the system will have extended to individuals and families who were outside the protective umbrellas of patrons, and thus had to obtain their own food. Some of them might have resorted to theft, from graves and from warehouses, and been hunted by Mahu and his police. These would be the people of a 'grey' economy (whose counterparts at western Thebes are well documented, 250 years later, in the so-called Tomb Robbery Papyri).

The blurring of boundaries in production and exchange meant that objects of fine quality entered the homes of relatively modest people, satisfying their aspirations to participate in the lifestyle of those further up the social scale. The most convincing demonstration comes from the Workmen's Village, a place isolated from rich patrons. With its incense, fine textiles and leather

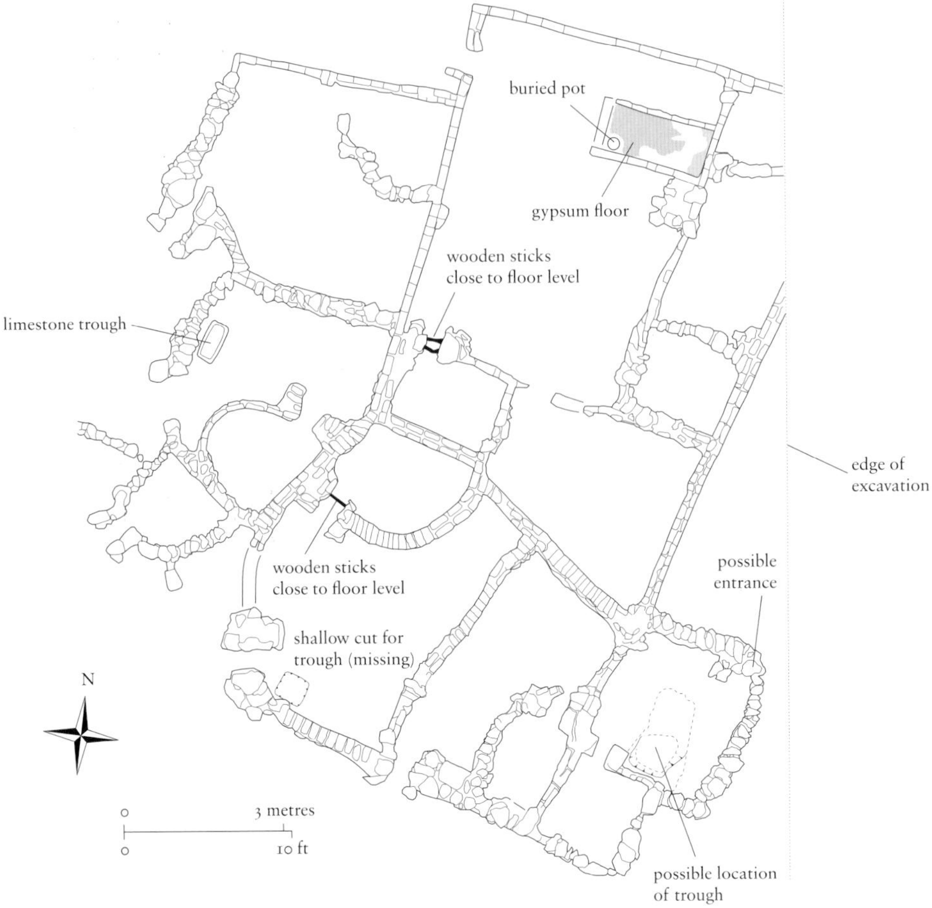

buried pot
gypsum floor
wooden sticks close to floor level
limestone trough
edge of excavation
possible entrance
wooden sticks close to floor level
shallow cut for trough (missing)
N
0 3 metres
0 10 ft
possible location of trough

8.21 (above) Plan of pig pens excavated at the Workmen's Village (see also Pl. XLII).

8.22 View, to the southeast, of one of the pig pens (building 400), with limestone trough beside one of the walls, at the Workmen's Village.

footwear, well-carved wooden objects, imported pottery, glass and faience jewelry and metalwork, it presents a selection of the material that is common across the main city. The archaeology of Amarna shows a generally egalitarian mix of fine and rough goods wherever one looks. It demonstrates the effectiveness of a system that, contrary to the way things were in Sjoberg's cities, offered no scope for the emergence of merchants who were not officials of the king.

The Urban Village

One way to view Amarna is to draw upon the concept of the distributed network, the 'small-world' phenomenon that seems to lie behind almost all kinds of complexity. It has been made popular through the idea that every person in the modern world is no more than six handshakes away from their national leader. When contact is frequent, flows of information or of goods will touch many more people if the lines pass through one or more centres or nodes (the person who shakes the hands of a lot of people, for example). This is how the World Wide Web works, in which a significant portion of the electronically exchanged information passes through points or nodes of further distribution: the forum, the chat-room, the site that is taken up by the big search engines. Likewise a grower of peas reaches many more consumers if the peas go to a packing and distribution depot owned by a supermarket company with many outlets than if he sells them directly to customers on a market stall (though he might have reasons of another kind for preferring the latter). Networks with nodes drastically compress the number of potential routes of contact that theoretically exist, and so make the world a smaller place.

The ubiquity of the small-world phenomenon is such that we can take it for granted that it existed in New Kingdom Egypt. Amarna's ground plan shouts out that it represents a small-world network. The map of Amarna is a diagram of connectedness, of interlocking proximity for the houses of the many, often clustered around a central node, which is the house of an official living at the heart of his little urban village and locked into the broader national web that centred on the office of the vizier. Although barriers of etiquette and palace design kept the king apart from his citizens, most of them were probably only two or three steps removed from Akhenaten: they had personal dealings with their patron, an official who met either Akhenaten in person or his vizier on a regular basis (as stipulated in the 'Duties of the Vizier' manual of the previous century, see Chapter 4).

This was a dense world of personal contact, a human hive. The physical scale was modest. Houses created bounded private spaces – cells – but the interlocking character of many groups of them ensured that, in coming and going, the routes of the inhabitants crossed one another and, for some, this involved people from the next 'village', the boundaries of which were not physically marked. Servants and slaves, whose own 'spaces' we cannot detect, must have constantly crossed boundaries – passing through gates to bring water or to dispose of baskets of rubbish, for example – acting as a kind of transmission fluid for information between the big and the small houses. Goods, too, flowed through the nodes, through the officials with their personal warehouses.

Part of the locking mechanism was registration. We have seen how, early in his reign at Karnak (as recorded on some of his temple blocks), Akhenaten raised extra taxes, one set of beneficiaries being 6,800 persons in some way attached to the 'House of the Aten' at Thebes.[33] The Karnak temple blocks also depicted (though without providing personal names) a register of officials in one way or another connected with the Aten temples: mayors of towns, the head of the treasury of the House of the Aten at Thebes, a couple of chief beekeepers and so on.[34] For the purpose of distributing rations and rewards, and for maintaining some supervision over people who often held responsible positions (and therefore opportunities to abuse the trust placed in them), the king's chief officials must have maintained registers of who held which position and how much each was entitled to from the ration handouts that were such a prominent feature of ancient Egyptian society. Although no court lists of this scope have survived from Amarna, the system could not have kept going without them, and such a practice (as documented in other periods, for example, Papyrus Boulaq 18 from the 13th-Dynasty court at Thebes) fits the overall way that Egyptian administration worked. The importance of central registration of people is that it made the court into *the* central node of the network. The location of its most significant component is likely to have been the vizier's office. As suggested in Chapter 5, this might have been the building we know as the King's House.

Private letter writing contributed to connectedness between more distant nodes. I have previously mentioned two papyrus letters that had been written by an unguent preparer in the household of Princess Meryetaten, named Ramose, and sent to their destination in Thebes (where they turned up, unopened, in a cemetery excavated in the 1920s).[35] Ramose complains about the failure or refusal of his brother and sister to write to him, but also asks that his greetings be given to four other named persons. He writes about certain contested matters that involve yet other people, including a daughter. The letters are a fragment of information intended to pass into an informal network. As with all New Kingdom letters, the address, written on the outside of the rolled-up papyrus, is simply the title and name of the intended recipient. The connectedness of Egyptian society ensured that the letters would most likely reach their destination (even if this recipient seems to have died before opening them).

Connectedness often seems a prominent characteristic of ancient Egypt. Sjoberg's preindustrial city is full of separations – walled-off city 'quarters', guilds that jealously look after their own, sects that view with suspicion everyone outside, an ocean of poor people living far from the centre-hugging mansions of the rich. This is not Amarna, nor by implication the society of New Kingdom Egypt. We are looking at a society that is still fairly close to village roots, which supports a superstructure of divine kingship and an empire run from mud-brick offices, but, at the end of each day, retreats into its small-scale localities.

CHAPTER NINE

AN END AND A BEGINNING

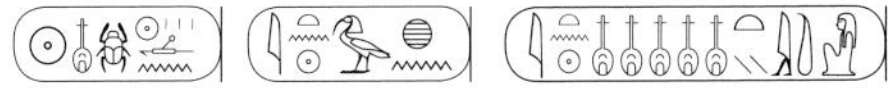

The End

Akhenaten died in the seventeenth year of his reign and was buried at Amarna (at least for a while). Endless speculation surrounds how power was then transferred to successors within the royal family. From the point of view of the city's occupation, the details scarcely matter. The inhabitants of Amarna celebrated two new reigns by making more of the cheap faience finger rings bearing royal names: an Ankhkheperure (whose second name was Smenkhkare) and a Nubkheperure (Tutankhaten who changed his name to Tutankhamun; **Pl. LI**). There is no sign that Tutankhaten/amun ruled from Amarna. Memphis and Thebes were his likely bases. Early in his reign he must have issued an order to withdraw what remained of the court and the administration from Amarna, closing offices, emptying storerooms. The officials went elsewhere and, inevitably, so did the bulk of the population. By normal Egyptian standards, the city was in an unattractive location, which, for the greater part, had no reason to be occupied other than as a result of Akhenaten's choice. The interval between Akhenaten's death and the abandonment was brief, perhaps only three or four years. This would mean a total of only sixteen or seventeen years for the entire life of the city (as it had not been founded immediately upon Akhenaten's succession).

One part that did survive lay at the southernmost end, close to the river (and now largely beneath the modern village of El-Hagg Qandil). Excavations early in the 20th century uncovered a quarter (misleadingly called the 'River Temple') that had continued to be lived in and rebuilt into at least the late Ramesside period (two centuries further on). It lay at the end of the road to the travertine (alabaster) quarries of Hatnub, and this perhaps explains its continued existence.[1]

It is a mistake to think that the rest of Amarna was wholly destroyed. The greater part of the city was of mud-brick and was left standing, open to scavenging for wood and anything else that was useful or of value. As far as we can tell, the paintings on the palace walls were not defaced. The stone buildings, however, were treated differently. Beginning in the time of Horemheb, the Amarna family's military successor, their systematic demolition commenced and was pursued so thoroughly that often nothing was left above the foundation level of gypsum concrete. The main purpose was re-use. Many hundreds of the blocks, mostly undamaged, have been found incorporated into later buildings at the site of El-Ashmunein (Hermopolis was its Greek name) across the river. They were mostly of the standard smallish size that characterizes Akhenaten's reign (the *talatat*-blocks), so demolition would not have been a particularly onerous task. It must have helped that the main stone buildings were close to the river, from where the blocks could be transported by boat to other destinations.

Later generations refused to accept Akhenaten's legitimacy as king, and referred to him as if he were a criminal. At Amarna itself, his names and that of Nefertiti were often removed from monuments, though frequently in a half-hearted way (e.g. **2.33, Pl. XXX**). The many fine statues of the royal family were broken into pieces. Amongst hundreds of fragments recovered, joins are so few as to suggest that much of what was broken was taken away to be re-used, the hard stones being the same as those used for querns as well as statues and statuettes.

By contrast, the names of the Aten in their cartouches were left alone. Moreover, the founding decrees for the sacred place Akhetaten – the boundary stelae – also escaped defacement, such that they still bear Akhenaten's names and still proclaim, in now weathered hieroglyphs, that the piece of desert they define continues to be the sacred home of the Aten. Stela A on the west bank is so close to a place where Egyptians of later periods were active (it is close to the main cemetery for El-Ashmunein/Hermopolis) as to make it likely that it was visited from time to time by curious scribes who would quickly have learned who Akhenaten was and what he stood for. He might not have been completely forgotten.

Akhenaten was defeated by biology in the first instance, by forces of reaction only secondarily. He did not produce a successor who could wield power effectively and who remained true to his ideas. Two or three generations of steadfast successors might well have seen Amarna and its style of rule cemented into place as the tradition that would shape Egypt's future. In the absence of a forceful successor, the military kings who followed, who benefited from this failure, made it seem as though Akhenaten's vision had no future. It suited them to destroy as much of it as they could and claim the authority of more ancient conventions. We should not see this outcome as inevitable.

The Seed of Atenism

Since his rediscovery in the nineteenth century, Akhenaten has intrigued people, at the very least because he was a rebel on a grand scale. Rebels are interesting. What to make of his vision, as viewed from a modern standpoint, is more complicated. Nowadays, we are unable to view what Akhenaten did free from the idea – which developed long afterwards – that promotion of a particular version of god or the giving of spiritual guidance has to have the familiar shape of a religion, perhaps one that we can call Atenism. So, following a variety of modern ideas, he has been recruited to monotheism, to cults of the forces of nature or to more mystic interpretations of what governs the universe, even to notions of Aryan superiority.[2] Although he was a teacher, I do not see that it was Akhenaten's intention to create a self-conscious community of followers or believers. No surviving text lays down rules to define what such a person should be, what kind of path they should follow other than to keep to a righteous life.

Let us imagine that Akhenaten's vision had succeeded and flourished in his country, finding acceptance in the Hellenistic world, competing successfully against Christianity and Islam to become a religion of solar energy that symbolizes the purity of truth and righteous conduct, with millions of adherents around the world. Amarna is its great centre, a place of pilgrimage. But almost nothing of its original archaeology survives. Over the centuries, the temples have been rebuilt, pious rulers eventually adding parts or whole buildings in an architectural style that has taken the ancient Egyptian style to a new plane of visual experience. To serve the administration of the cult and the needs of its pilgrims a large modern city has developed, with hotels and an on-site airport. The fragile mud-brick city vanished long ago. When a patch of very ancient walls is exposed in digging the foundations for the new residence of the spiritual leader of the worldwide Atenist faith, 'Ah', people say, 'so the legend of a real city built at the time of the great founder's move to Amarna was true after all.'

Perhaps in writing a 'what if?' story, it is the timing that I have got wrong. A sunny morning at the Small Aten Temple. A couple of small white-painted tourist buses, their wheels juddering on the rough dusty track, approach and stop outside the gateway in the barbed-wire fence. Not far away, the dark blue police truck halts and its khaki-clad officers emerge to stretch their legs. The buses have brought a group of foreign tourists. They walk through the mud-brick courts of the temple, to the sanctuary at the back. Some of them wear loose white robes. They have come to worship in the temple. Some groups bury crystals, others sit cross-legged and meditate. The only time I have tried to talk they were defensive and we did not get far. They must assume that I would mock, as most people probably do.

A modern Atenism has to be an invention. But so what? The validity of religious experience is not to be overturned by arguments from history. At the moment, we can note that a seed from Atenism is alive. Akhenaten's chosen and unlikely self-image of the beautifully sculpted freak has already gained in modern times compelling iconic status. Amarna's heyday might yet lie in the future. With religion, you never can tell.

Visiting Amarna

The parts of Amarna are so spread out that it is best to allow at least one full day for a visit. The site can be reached by rail and road. At the time of writing this note (February 2012) it was rumoured that river cruises through Middle Egypt might start again soon (dependent upon security assessments).

Access

Visitors usually base themselves in El-Minia, the provincial capital, 58 km (36 miles) north of Amarna, where several reasonable hotels are to be found. For access by road, whether from El-Minia or from further afield, there are several choices. An eastern desert highway (which can be reached from El-Minia by a bridge across the Nile) passes a turning to the west (signposted to Tell el-Amarna) that descends to Amarna near the South Tombs. If coming from the west bank, the river can be crossed by vehicle ferry, one at El-Till (from a turning eastwards south of Mallawi) and another further to the south, near Deir Mawas, which crosses to El-Hagg Qandil. South of Mallawi one can also access a second road-bridge across the Nile. Immediately at its eastern end an unmade agricultural road heads southwards and enters Amarna from the northern end, in front of the cliffs. Sharp right-angled turns make it unsuited to large buses.

However one arrives, it is necessary to go first to buy an admission ticket at the official ticket office on the road that leads from the village of El-Till to the North Tombs. Beyond the North Tombs the same road continues southwards and then eastwards to the Royal Tomb, passing Boundary Stela U on the way. A northern extension from in front of the North Tombs, in poor condition, leads to the North Palace, which is also on the line of the road coming into Amarna from the north. The Central City lies on the road (most of it with an asphalt surface) that links the two villages of El-Till and El-Hagg Qandil. A short distance to the north of El-Hagg Qandil another asphalt road leads eastwards to the South Tombs.

On Site

Amarna is under the guardianship of the Ministry of State for Antiquities and of the tourist and antiquities police. They require that visitors leave Amarna well before nightfall. Custodians are on duty at the tombs every day, and unlock them for visitors. A cafeteria with toilets is beside the ticket office. A Visitor Centre for Amarna has been built beside the ferry quay at El-Till, but, at the time of writing, was not yet open, pending the completion of the exhibits.

Chronology

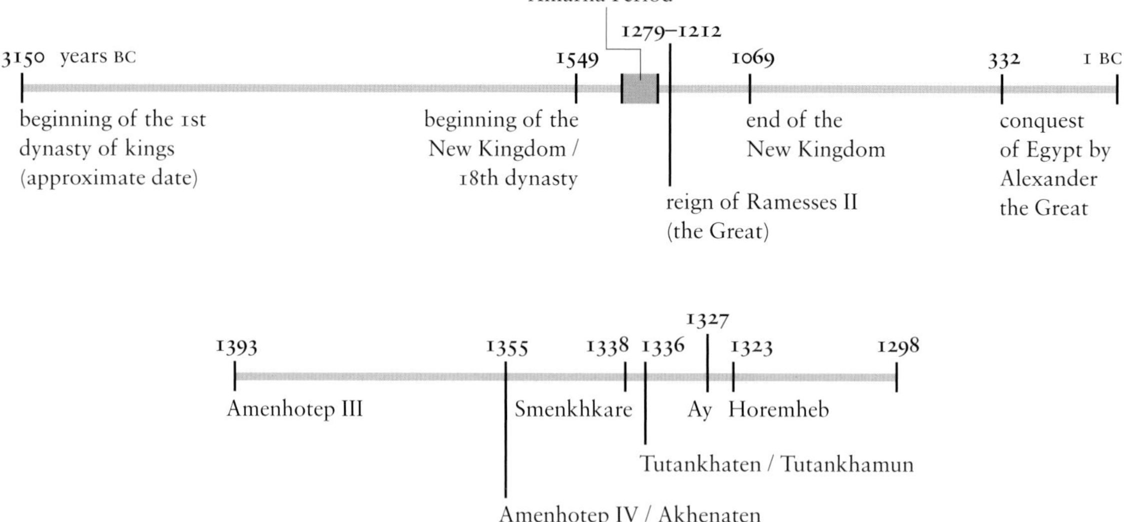

Abbreviations of works cited more than once in the notes or captions

The abbreviation EES refers to the Egypt Exploration Society, DOG to the Deutsche Orient-Gesellschaft.

Works abbreviated by title

AR – *Amarna Reports*, ed. B. J. Kemp. 6 vols. London, EES 1984–95.

AS – B. J. Kemp and S. Garfi, *A Survey of the Ancient City of El-'Amarna*. London, EES 1993.

CAJ – *Cambridge Archaeological Journal*.

COA – *The City of Akhenaten*. 3 vols. Vol. I, by T. E. Peet and C. L. Woolley; Vol. II by H. Frankfort and J. D. S. Pendlebury; Vol. III (in two parts), by J. D. S. Pendlebury. London EES 1923, 1933, 1951.

EA – *Egyptian Archaeology*.

JARCE – *Journal of the American Research Center in Egypt*.

JEA – *Journal of Egyptian Archaeology*.

Pharaohs – R. E. Freed, Y. J. Markowitz and S. H. D'Auria, eds, *Pharaohs of the Sun: Akhenaten, Nefertiti, Tutankhamen*. Boston, Museum of Fine Arts, and London, Thames & Hudson 1999.

RT – N. de G. Davies, *The Rock Tombs of El Amarna*. 6 vols. London, Egypt Exploration Fund 1903–8, reprinted as 3 vols, London, EES 2004.

TA – W. M. F. Petrie, *Tell El Amarna*. London, Methuen 1894.

Works abbreviated by author and title

Borchardt and Ricke, *Wohnhäuser* – L. Borchardt and H. Ricke, *Die Wohnhäuser in Tell el-Amarna*. Berlin, Mann 1980.

Borghouts, *Magical Texts* – J. F. Borghouts, *Ancient Egyptian Magical Texts*. Leiden, Brill 1978.

Frankfort, *Mural Paintings* – H. Frankfort, ed., *The Mural Paintings of El 'Amarneh*. London, EES 1929.

Izre'el, *Tablets* – S. Izre'el, *The Amarna Scholarly Tablets*. Groningen, Styx 1997.

Kemp, *Anatomy* 1. – B. J. Kemp, *Ancient Egypt: Anatomy of a Civilization*. London and New York, Routledge 1989.

Kemp, *Anatomy* 2. – B. J. Kemp, *Ancient Egypt: Anatomy of a Civilization*. 2nd ed. London and New York, Routledge 2006.

Kemp and Stevens, *Busy Lives* – B. Kemp and A. Stevens, *Busy Lives at Amarna: Excavations in the Main City (Grid 12 and the House of Ranefer, N49.18)*. 2 vols. London, EES 2010.

Kemp and Vogelsang-Eastwood, *Textiles* – B. J. Kemp and G. Vogelsang-Eastwood, *The Ancient Textile Industry at Amarna*. London, EES 2001.

Laboury, *Akhénaton* – D. Laboury, *Akhénaton*. Paris, Pygmalion 2010.

Lichtheim, *Literature* I – M. Lichtheim, *Ancient Egyptian Literature: A Book of Readings*, Vol. 1: *The Old and Middle Kingdoms*. Berkeley and London, University of California Press 1973.

Luff and Rowley-Conwy, *Whither Env. Arch.* – R. Luff and P. Rowley-Conwy, eds, *Whither Environmental Archaeology?* Oxford, Oxbow 1994.

Martin, *Royal Tomb* II – G. T. Martin, *The Royal Tomb at El-'Amarna* II. London, EES 1989.

Moran, *Amarna Letters* – W. L. Moran, *The Amarna Letters*. Baltimore and London, The Johns Hopkins University Press 1992.

Murnane, *Texts* – W. J. Murnane, *Texts from the Amarna Period in Egypt*. Atlanta, GA, Scholars Press 1995.

Sjoberg, *City* – G. Sjoberg, *The Preindustrial City, Past and Present*. Glencoe, IL, and New York, Free Press, and London, Collier-Macmillan 1960.

Stevens, *Religion* – A. Stevens, *Private Religion at Amarna: The Material Evidence*. Oxford, Archaeopress 2006.

Thompson and Hill, *Statuary* – K. Thompson and M. Hill, *Amarna Royal Statuary*. London, EES forthcoming.

Tietze, *Amarna* – C. Tietze, ed., *Amarna: Lebensräume, Lebensbilder, Weltbilder*. 2nd ed. Weimar, Arcus-Verlag 2010.

Timme, *Tell el-Amarna* – P. Timme, *Tell El-Amarna vor der Deutschen Ausgrabung im Jahre 1911*. Berlin and Leipzig, Hinrichs 1917.

Van den Boorn, *Duties* – G. P. F. Van den Boorn, *The Duties of the Vizier: Civil Administration in the Early New Kingdom*. London and New York, Kegan Paul International 1988.

Weatherhead, *Paintings* – F. Weatherhead, *Amarna Palace Paintings*. London, EES 2007.

Weatherhead and Kemp, *Main Chapel* – F. Weatherhead and B. J. Kemp, *The Main Chapel at the Amarna Workmen's Village and its Wall Paintings*. London, EES 2007.

Wente, *Letters* – E. Wente, *Letters from Ancient Egypt*. Atlanta, GA, Scholars Press 1990.

Notes

Introduction

[1] A. Stevens and M. Eccleston, 'Craft production and technology.' In T. Wilkinson, ed., *The Egyptian World*. London and New York, Routledge 2007, 146–59. The quotation is on p. 151.

[2] Herodotus, Book II.37; A. de Sélincourt, *Herodotus: The Histories*. Harmondsworth, etc., Penguin 1954, 143.

Chapter One: Building a Vision

[1] Murnane, *Texts*, 241.

[2] Murnane, *Texts*, 213.

[3] N. de G. Davies and A. H. Gardiner, *The Tomb of Amenemhet (no. 82)*. London, Egypt Exploration Fund 1915, 99–100.

[4] Murnane, *Texts*, 30–31.

[5] Murnane, *Texts*, 207–8.

[6] R. A. Caminos, *The New-Kingdom Temples of Buhen*. London, EES 1974, I, 18–19, though the removal of references to Amun-Ra at Buhen was not complete, see pp. 49, 56, for example; R. Krauss, 'Akhenaten: Monotheist? Polytheist?' *Bulletin of the Australian Centre for Egyptology* 11 (2000), 93–101; Murnane, *Texts*, 101–3.

[7] N. de G. Davies, *The Tomb of Rekh-mi-Rē' at Thebes*. New York, Metropolitan Museum of Art 1943, 81, Pl. XI.13.

[8] Murnane, *Texts*, 111–12.

[9] Murnane, *Texts*, 192.

[10] Murnane, *Texts*, 129, 142.

[11] Wente, *Letters*, 94–96.

[12] Z. Hawass et al., 'Ancestry and pathology in King Tutankhamun's family.' *Journal of the American Medical Association* 303, no. 7 (February 17, 2010), 638–47, make a case for identifying the body as Akhenaten's. The age of the body remains, however, an obstacle, for by conventional forensic criteria the body is that of a man too young to have been Akhenaten, see E. Strouhal, 'Biological age of the skeletonized mummy from Tomb KV55 at Thebes (Egypt).' *Anthropologie* (Brno) 48/2 (2010–11), 97–112; C. Duhig, 'The remains of pharaoh Akhenaten are not yet identified: comments on "Biological age of the skeletonised mummy from tomb KV55 at Thebes (Egypt)" by Eugen Strouhal.' Ibid., 113–15.

[13] Murnane, *Texts*, 73–86, provides translations of the boundary stelae.

[14] C. F. Nims, *Thebes of the Pharaohs: Pattern for Every City*. London, Elek Books 1965, 69.

[15] Murnane, *Texts*, 178.

[16] Murnane, *Texts*, 183.

[17] Murnane, *Texts*, 145.

[18] Murnane, *Texts*, 193.

[19] Murnane, *Texts*, 134.

[20] Murnane, *Texts*, 116.

[21] Murnane, *Texts*, 145.

[22] Murnane, *Texts*, 171; see also the sentiments expressed on pp. 172, 186 (the treasurer, Sutau).

Chapter Two: Akhenaten's Resources

[1] B. Kemp, 'Settlement and landscape in the Amarna area in the Late Roman period.' In J. Faiers, *Late Roman Pottery at Amarna and Related Studies*. London, EES 2005, 11–56, especially pp. 19–31.

[2] Kemp, 'Settlement and landscape', 30–31, Fig. 1.11.

[3] See also the suggestive profile through the modern storm-water ditch at El-Till, *AS*, 44–46, Figs 8, 9.

[4] For Amarna wells, see *AR* V, 1–14.

[5] *TA*, 10.

[6] *TA*, 10–11.

[7] *TA*, 15; Weatherhead, *Paintings*, 4–6.

[8] *TA*, 4; Timme, *Tell El-Amarna*, 52, Abb. 57 shows where the text was in the quarry. For the El-Bersheh quarries, see H. Willems and R. Demarée, 'A visitor's graffito in Dayr Abū Hinnis. Remarks on the source of limestone used in the construction of al-Amarna.' *Revue d'Égyptologie* 60 (2009), 222–26.

[9] Murnane, *Texts*, 29–30.

[10] *COA* III, 180–81.

[11] *COA* I, 113.

[12] Lichtheim, *Literature* I, 21.

[13] Kemp and Stevens, *Busy Lives* I, Chapter 6 (R. Gerisch); also R. Gerisch, *Holzkohleuntersuchungen an pharaonischem und byzantinischem Material aus Amarna und Umgebung*. Mainz am Rhein, von Zabern 2004.

[14] Wente, *Letters*, 104–6.

[15] Murnane, *Texts*, 29–30.

[16] *COA* I, 113.

[17] G. Owen and B. Kemp, 'Craftsmen's work patterns in unfinished tombs at Amarna.' *CAJ* 4 (1994), 121–26.

Chapter Three: The City of the Sun-god

[1] See especially *AR* VI, 203–15 (M. Mallinson); M. Mallinson, 'The sacred landscape', in *Pharaohs*, 72–79; M. Mallinson, 'Akhetaten: nothing comes from nowhere.' In S. Ikram and A. Dodson, eds, *Beyond the Horizon: Studies in Egyptian Art, Archaeology and History in Honour of Barry J. Kemp*. Cairo, Supreme

Council of Antiquities 2009, I, 223–40. A somewhat different symbolic interpretation is presented in D. O'Connor, 'City and palace in New Kingdom Egypt.' *Cahier de recherches de l'Institut de Papyrologie et d'Égyptologie de Lille* 11 (1989), 73–87.

2 L. Gabolde, <<"L'horizon d'Aton", exactement?>>, in I. Régen and F. Servajean, eds, *Verba manent: Recueil d'études dédiées à Dimitri Meeks par ses collègues et amis*. Montpellier, Université Paul Valéry (Montpellier III) 2009, 145–57.

3 R. Vergnieux and M. Gondran, *Aménophis IV et les pierres du soleil: Akhénaton retrouvè*. Paris, Arthaud 1997, 86, 102; Laboury, *Akhénaton*, 116–25.

4 Murnane, *Texts*, 30.

5 *RT* III, Pl. XXX.

6 Murnane, *Texts*, 158.

7 H. Frankfort, 'Preliminary report on the excavations at Tell el-'Amarnah, 1926–27.' *JEA* 13 (1927), 209–18, reference on p. 210.

8 The decorated faience tiles, not properly published, are: 32/16 (x10); 32/18 (not 17 as in *COA* III, 17); 32/23 (outside west entrance to temple); 32/30 (x11); 32/32 (x2; inside enclosure south of offering-tables); 32/41 (x2); 32/59 (front of the Long Temple); 36/103 (from the dump south of the temple), all listed *COA* III, 13, 17–20; at the Small Aten Temple: 31/338; 31/341; 31/466, 31/356 (single inlaid hieroglyph), listed *COA* III, 98–99.

9 Quoted in N. Reeves and J. H. Taylor, *Howard Carter before Tutankhamun*. London, British Museum 1992, 37.

10 *TA*, 18–19.

11 *COA* III, 13.

12 C. Aldred, 'The "New Year" gifts to the Pharaoh.' *JEA* 55 (1969), 73–81.

13 Murnane, *Texts*, 183; *COA* III, 188–89.

14 *COA* III, 18, obj. 33/30, Pl. LXI.5.

15 *COA* III, 12, obj. 33/16.

16 See note 36 for this chapter, below.

17 *COA* III, 10.

18 J. D. S. Pendlebury, 'Excavations at Tell El Amarna. Preliminary report for the season 1933–4.' *JEA* 20 (1934), 129–36, reference on p. 132; *COA* III, 11, 12. Other fragments, in the Metropolitan Museum of Art, New York, had been found earlier by Howard Carter, see C. Ransom Williams, 'Wall decorations of the Main Temple of the Sun at El Amarneh.' *Metropolitan Museum Studies* 2 (1930), 135–51.

19 H. Frankfort, 'Preliminary report on the excavations at Tell el-'Amarnah, 1926–27.' *JEA* 13 (1927), 209–18, reference on p. 212.

20 S. Ikram, *Choice Cuts: Meat Production in Ancient Egypt*. Leuven, Peeters and Departement Oosterse Studies 1995, 147–69.

21 *COA* III, 169–74, 218, Pl. XCII, nos 204–6 combined, all three from 'Magazines south of the Temple'.

22 *COA* III, Pl. XCI, no. 186, 218, from building R42.9.

23 *COA* III, 175, 218, Pls XCIV, XCV, nos 240, 256–67, from various locations, most of them the Great Palace.

24 B. J. Kemp, 'Food for an Egyptian city.' In Luff and Rowley-Conwy, *Whither Env. Arch*., 133–53.

25 *AR* IV, 119–21, area 12.

26 *TA*, 19.

27 *RT* I, Pls. XA, XIV; III, Pl. XXX.

28 Murnane *Texts*, 51–52.

29 Murnane *Texts*, 125.

30 Murnane, *Texts*, 151, 194, 120.

31 Murnane, *Texts*, 131, 160.

32 Murnane, *Texts*, 173; similarly 188 (Tutu).

33 Murnane, *Texts*, 141.

34 Murnane, *Texts*, 31.

35 Laboury, *Akhénaton*, 160, makes an assessment of a comparable scale for Akhenaten's main building at Karnak, as revealed by excavation.

36 The original report is in *COA* III, 140–41. A photograph of the first panel is Pl. LVI.2. Some discussion is in Kemp, *Anatomy* 1, 283–85; *AS*, 63; Stevens, *Religion*, 249–50. See also M. Hill, '"The Great Statue which the King Made" from building R43.2.' *Horizon* 9 (Spring 2011), 6–8.

37 J. Williamson, 'The "Sunshade" of Nefertiti.' *EA* 33 (2008), 5–7.

38 *AR* VI, 411–61.

Chapter Four: The Apartments of Pharaoh

1 K. Spence, 'The palaces of el-Amarna: towards an architectural analysis.' In R. Gundlach and J. H. Taylor, eds, *Egyptian Royal Residences: 4th Symposium on Egyptian Royal Ideology, London, 1–5 June 2004*. Königtum, Staat und Gesellschaft früher Hochkulturen 4.1. Wiesbaden, Harrassowitz 2008, 165–87; 'Court and palace in ancient Egypt: the Amarna period and later Eighteenth Dynasty.' In A. J. S. Spawforth, ed., *The Court and Court Society in Ancient Monarchies*. Cambridge, Cambridge University Press 2007, 267–328; C. Tietze, 'Das "Haus des Königs" in Amarna.' *Kölner Jahrbuch* 43 (2010), 779–96.

2 I. Nielsen, *Hellenistic Palaces: Tradition and Renewal*. Studies in Hellenistic Civilization 5. Aarhus, Aarhus University Press 1994.

3 *TA*, 24; *COA* III, 113, 162, Pl. LXXXIX.128, 129. For private examples, see Kemp and Stevens, *Busy Lives* II, 51–52.

4 *COA* III, 189.

5 *COA* III, 114, 150, Pl. LXXXIII.V.
6 Izre'el, *Tablets*; Kemp, *Anatomy* 2, 293–95.
7 *COA* III, 115; R. B. Parkinson, 'A papyrus from the House of Life at Akhetaten.' *EA* 38 (2011), 42–43.
8 *COA* III, 150–51.
9 Weatherhead, *Paintings*, Chapter 3.
10 Van den Boorn, *Duties*, 13.
11 Murnane, *Texts*, 149–50.
12 Van den Boorn, *Duties*, 55; T. G. H. James, *Pharaoh's People: Scenes from Life in Imperial Egypt*. London, Bodley Head 1984, 63.
13 The evidence for the Window of Appearance at Amarna is extensively reviewed in P. Vomberg, *Das Erscheinungsfenster innerhalb der amarnazeitlichen Palastarchitektur: Herkunft, Entwicklung, Fortleben*. Wiesbaden, Harrassowitz 2004; also in Tietze, *Amarna*, 87–89.
14 Thompson and Hill, *Statuary*.
15 *COA* III, 77, Pl. XXXVII.6.
16 H. Sumner-Boyd and J. Freely, *Strolling Through Istanbul: a Guide to the City*. 2nd ed. Istanbul, Redhouse Press 1973, 87–93. The quotation is on p. 88.
17 L. Green, 'Some thoughts on ritual banquets at the court of Akhenaten and in the ancient Near East.' In G. Knoppers and A. Hirsch, eds, *Egypt, Israel and the Ancient Mediterranean World: Festschrift Donald B. Redford*. Winona Lake (IL), Eisenbrauns 2004, 203–22.
18 S. Rocca, *Herod's Judaea: A Mediterranean State in the Classical World*. Texts and Studies in Ancient Judaism, 122. Tübingen, Mohr Siebeck 2008, 97–98.
19 Murnane, *Texts*, 239.
20 Her name occurs repeatedly in texts at the North Palace, in contrast to that of Nefertiti, which remains absent. In some instances, but not all, it has been carved over an earlier inscription. It has been claimed that this named, and so gave ownership to, Kiya, a secondary wife of Akhenaten. The evidence is ambiguous and perhaps not enough to justify conclusions that lead on to imagining an outbreak of harem politics at Amarna. See C. N. Reeves, 'New light on Kiya from texts in the British Museum.' *JEA* 74 (1988), 91–101.
21 See Chapter 1, note 11.

Chapter Five: City of People

1 Many of the roads were recorded by Borchardt's surveyor, Paul Timme, in his survey of Amarna: Timme, *Tell El-Amarna*. They were included in the GPS survey of Amarna carried out between 2000 and 2009 by Helen Fenwick. A short account of the roads is in *Horizon* 3 (February 2008), 8–9, and they are discussed in the article cited in note 24 of this chapter.
2 Murnane, *Texts*, 149.
3 *AR* IV, 124–26.
4 P. Vernus, *Affairs and Scandals in Ancient Egypt*. Ithaca and London, Cornell University Press, 2003, 57–58.
5 Vernus, *Affairs*, 61–62.
6 See also J. C. Darnell and C. Manassa, *Tutankhamun's Armies: Battle and Conquest during Ancient Egypt's Late Eighteenth Dynasty*. Hoboken, NJ, Wiley 2007, 195.
7 In general, D. O'Connor, *Abydos: Egypt's First Pharaohs and the Cult of Osiris*. London, Thames & Hudson 2009. For the text, A. Leahy, 'A protective measure at Abydos in the Thirteenth Dynasty.' *JEA* 75 (1989), 41–60.
8 Kemp, *Anatomy* 1, 300, Fig. 101; *Anatomy* 2, 312, Fig. 109; also P. Crocker, 'Status symbols in the architecture of El-'Amarna.' *JEA* 71 (1985), 52–65. Tietze, *Amarna*, 98–117 takes the analysis further and investigates subdivisions within the broad curve of house size.
9 *COA* II, 34, obj. 29/276, Pl. XXXII.3.
10 Kemp and Stevens, *Busy Lives* I, 473–78.
11 Kemp and Stevens, *Busy Lives* II, 51–52.
12 Kemp and Stevens, *Busy Lives* I, Chapter 2.
13 K. Spence, 'The three-dimensional form of the Amarna house.' *JEA* 90 (2004), 123–52 makes the case for extensive upper storeys. The many reconstructions in Tietze, *Amarna* assume that much more of the floor area was of a single storey only. The same is true for S. Lloyd, 'Model of a Tell el-'Amarnah house.' *JEA* 19 (1933), 1–7. H. Ricke, *Der Grundriß des Amarna-Wohnhauses*, Leipzig, Hinrichs 1932, is a sourcebook for plan analysis, as are the various excavation reports, especially Borchardt and Ricke, *Wohnhäuser* and *COA* I–III. Also useful for its fine detail is A. Koltsida, *Social Aspects of Ancient Egyptian Domestic Architecture*. Oxford, Archaeopress 2007.
14 *COA* II, 8, Pl. XVIII.2.
15 The Djehutynefer painting is illustrated, and plays an important part, in Spence's article cited in note 13.
16 *COA* I, 20, 39.
17 Taking my cue from the painted plaster found outside house J53.1, see Borchardt and Ricke, *Wohnhäuser*, 337, Taf. 25C, 29F.
18 *COA* II, 26–27.
19 *COA* I, 5–6.
20 *COA* I, 101, Fig. 15.
21 For the other tombs, see Aly el-Khouly and G. T. Martin, *Excavations in the Royal Necropolis at El-'Amarna 1984*. Cairo, Institut français d'Archéologie orientale 1987. Marc Gabolde has since investigated them again.
22 *COA* I, 59–60, 80, Pl. IX.2.

23 *COA* I, Chapter III; B. J. Kemp, 'The Amarna Workmen's Village in retrospect.' *JEA* 73 (1987), 21–50; Weatherhead and Kemp, *Main Chapel*, Chapter 5.

24 A. Stevens, 'The Amarna Stone Village survey and life on the urban periphery in New Kingdom Egypt.' *Journal of Field Archaeology* 36 (2011), 100–18.

Chapter Six: The Quality of Life

1 *COA* III, 125, obj. 33/272, Pl. LXXVIII.5; *Pharaohs*, 253, no. 168 (P. Der Manuelian).

2 Kemp and Vogelsang-Eastwood, *Textiles*, 34–55, 147–52, 218–21. For Kha's bed, see E. Schiaparelli, *La tomba intatta dell'architetto Cha nella necropoli di Tebe*. Turin, R. Museo di Antichità 1927, 121, Fig. 105.

3 *COA* II, 25, Pls. XIX.3, XX.3.

4 Kemp and Stevens, *Busy Lives* I, 499–503.

5 M. Serpico and R. White, 'The botanical identity and transport of incense during the Egyptian New Kingdom.' *Antiquity* 74 (2000), 884–97. Also *Busy Lives* II, 546–54.

6 The quotation is from the *Story of the Shipwrecked Sailor*, line 142, from the Middle Kingdom. Lichtheim, *Literature* I, 214. For the cloth wicks, see Kemp and Vogelsang-Eastwood, *Textiles*, 223, 226–30, 244–45.

7 *COA* II, 52, obj. 30/239, Pl. XLII.5.

8 *COA* II, 74, obj. 31/112, Pl. XLI.1; *COA* III, 247, Pl. CXI.1.

9 Murnane, *Texts*, 116.

10 *RT* VI, Pl. IV.

11 Moran, *Amarna Letters*, 39, 44, 48, etc.

12 The fundamental evidence for relative values of metals and of how the system of equivalences and exchange worked is to be found in J. Černý, 'Prices and wages in Egypt in the Ramesside Period.' *Journal of World History* I (1954), 903–21; J. J. Janssen, *Commodity Prices from the Ramessid Period: An Economic Study of the Village of Necropolis Workmen at Thebes*. Leiden, Brill 1975, 101–8, 510–38.

13 E.g. *COA* II, 42, obj. 29/396, dia. 34 cm (13.4 in.); *COA* III, 118, obj. 33/33, dia. 20 cm (7.9 in.); Kemp and Stevens, *Busy Lives* II, 344–45, Fig. 20.2, obj. 34961, dia. 16.5 cm (6.5 in.).

14 E.g. *COA* II, 72, obj. 31/78; 74, obj. 31/92; 75, objs 31/119, 31/173, all of them Pl. XLVI.1; *COA* III, 107 (objs 31/601, 32/216); 109, obj. 32/233; 118, obj. 33/160, Pl. LXXVII.2; 123, obj. 33/221, Pl. LXXVII.2; 125, obj. 33/245 (electrum), Pl. LXXVII.8.

15 *COA* II, 25, obj. 29/275, Pl. L.

16 *COA* II, 37, obj. 29/274, Pl. L.

17 *COA* III, 182, 219–23, Pl. C.

18 *COA* II, 70, obj. 31/250, Pl. XLVI.4.

19 *AR* V, Chapter 9 (W. Wendrich).

20 For Ay, see note 9, and for Tutankhamun's bag, Kemp and Vogelsang-Eastwood, *Textiles*, 448.

21 P. J. Rose, *The Eighteenth Dynasty Pottery Corpus from Amarna*. London, EES 2007.

22 P. J. Rose, '"Oasis ware" vessels from Amarna.' In R. Friedman, ed., *Egypt and Nubia: Gifts of the Desert*. London, British Museum 2002, 109–13, 128–31.

23 See note 5.

24 K. Koschel, 'Opium alkaloids in a Cypriote Base Ring I vessel (*bilbil*) of the Middle Bronze Age from Egypt.' *Ägypten und Levante/Egypt and the Levant* VI (1996), 158–66, building on an original suggestion by R. S. Merrillees, 'Opium trade in the Bronze Age Levant.' *Antiquity* 36 (1962), 287–92.

25 E.g. *COA* I, 21, house N49.11, where a lapis lazuli scarab mounted in gold was found beside the cellar; 32, house P46.13; *COA* II, 52–53, 73; Kemp and Stevens, *Busy Lives* I, 381–83.

26 Wente, *Letters*, 146, no. 196.

27 *COA* I, 24.

28 *COA* II, 66, objs 30/602, 30/605, 30/606, 30/609, 30/613.

29 *AR* II, Chapter 9 (J. Renfrew); Kemp and Stevens, *Busy Lives* I, Chapter 7 (C. Stevens and A. Clapham).

30 *AR* V, Chapter 12 (D. Samuel).

31 *AR* I, Chapter 11 (H. Hecker); P. Payne, 'Recovering animal bone at the house of the high priest Panehsy.' *JEA* 92 (2006), 45–52; P. Payne, 'Re-excavation at the Amarna house of Panehsy.' *EA* 30 (2007), 18–20; Kemp and Stevens, *Busy Lives* I, Chapter 8 (A. Legge).

32 A. Legge, 'Hyaenas at Amarna.' *Horizon* 6 (Autumn 2009), 8.

33 *AR* II, Chapter 9 (J. Renfrew); *AR* VI, Chapter 12 (D. Samuel); Kemp and Stevens, *Busy Lives* I, Chapter 7 (C. Stevens and A. Clapham).

34 D. Samuel, 'Bread making and social interactions at the Amarna Workmen's Village, Egypt.' *World Archaeology* 31 (1999), 121–44; Kemp and Stevens, *Busy Lives* I, 496–99.

35 Kemp and Vogelsang-Eastwood, *Textiles*.

36 *AR* VI, Chapters 2 and 11 (A. Boyce).

37 *AR* V, Chapter 8 (A. Boyce).

38 *AR* I, Chapter 9 (I. Shaw).

39 A. Veldmeijer, *Amarna's Leatherwork I. Preliminary Analysis and Catalogue*. Norg, DrukWare 2010, 24–26, and catalogues.

40 *COA* I, 69, obj. 22/179, Pl. XX.2.

41 *COA* I, 79, obj. 22/119, Pl. XX.2.

42 See note 3 of this chapter.

43 Illustrated by two fragments of decorated leather in the British Museum, from building R43.2 (House of the King's Statue), BM EA 74101 (see

our plate XLV). R. Parkinson and L. Schofield, 'Images of Mycenaeans: a recently acquired painted papyrus from El-Amarna.' In W. V. Davies and L. Schofield, eds, *Egypt, the Aegean and the Levant: Interconnections in the Second Millennium* BC. London, British Museum 1995, 125–26.

44 Reports by J. Rose and M. Zabecki are in *JEA* 92 (2006), 41–45; *JEA* 93 (2007), 53–59; *JEA* 94 (2008), 61–67; *JEA* 95 (2009), 32–34; *JEA* 96 (2010), 28–29; also *Horizon* 8 (Winter 2010), 5–9; *Horizon* 9 (Summer 2011), 5.

45 G. R. Dabbs and W. C. Schaffer, 'Akhenaten's Warrior? An assessment of traumatic injury at the South Tombs Cemetery.' *Paleopathology Newsletter* 142 (June 2008), 20–29.

46 J. B. Pritchard, ed., *Ancient Near Eastern Texts Relating to the Old Testament*, Princeton, Princeton University Press 1950, 1955, 1969, 394–96; Moran, *Amarna Letters*, 107–9, letter *EA* 35; also *ibid.* 21–23, *EA* 11. Also A. Kozloff, 'Bubonic plague in the reign of Amenhotep III?' *Kmt* 17, no. 3 (Fall 2006), 36–46, 83–84. It should not be taken for granted that the epidemic was of an identifiable modern kind.

47 See Chapter 1, note 12.

Chapter Seven: Spiritual Life at Amarna

1 S. Ikram, 'Domestic shrines and the cult of the royal family at el-Amarna.' *JEA* 75 (1989), 89–101; Stevens, *Religion*, esp. 133–38, 253–54.

2 Stevens, *Religion*, 136, Fig. 75, a stela where it is possible that there were figures beneath the Aten rays; and 154, Fig. II.6.2, the ostracon of Aten rays (our figure 1.2), and Fig. II.6.3.

3 See Chapter 1, note 11.

4 For this material, see *COA* I, 95–101; *AR* I, 27–30; Weatherhead and Kemp, *Main Chapel*; A. H. Bomann, *The Private Chapel in Ancient Egypt*. London and New York, Kegan Paul International 1991.

5 Book of the Dead, Spell 42. See R. O. Faulkner, *The Ancient Egyptian Book of the Dead*. London, British Museum Press, 1985, reissued 2010; B. Kemp, *How to Read the Egyptian Book of the Dead*. London, Granta Books 2007.

6 Borghouts, *Magical Texts*, 77, no. 106 (P Turin 1993 [17]).

7 R. K. Ritner, 'O. Gardiner 363: a spell against night terrors.' *JARCE* 27 (1990), 25–41.

8 Borghouts, *Magical Texts*, 51–55, no. 84; Stevens, *Religion*, 102.

9 K. Szpakowska, 'Playing with fire: initial observations on the religious uses of clay cobras from Amarna.' *JARCE* 90 (2003), 113–22; Stevens, *Religion*, 51, 100–3, 175–76, 292–93.

10 B. J. Kemp, 'Wall paintings from the Workmen's Village at El-'Amarna.' *JEA* 65 (1979), 47–53. For another similar painting, but done in colour, see B. Kemp, 'A wall painting of Bes figures from Amarna.' *EA* 34 (2009), 18–19.

11 Borghouts, *Magical Texts*, 32, no. 48 (P. Leiden I); Stevens, *Religion*, 93.

12 *COA* III, 69, Pl. LXX.8; Stevens, *Religion*, 288–89.

13 A. Stevens, 'The Amarna royal women as images of fertility: perspectives on a royal cult.' *Journal of Ancient Near Eastern Religions* 4 (2004), 107–27; Stevens, *Religion*, 287–91.

14 *COA* II, 65–66, 79–80; Stevens, *Religion*, 317–18.

15 Stevens, *Religion*, 146, 150–51, 306.

16 Stevens, *Religion*, 261.

17 Stevens, *Religion*, 219–34.

18 Borchardt and Ricke, *Wohnhäuser*, 222, Taf. 28; Stevens, *Religion*, 141, 252.

19 Stevens, *Religion*, 223–24, 231.

20 A. Stevens, in J. L. Keith, *Anthropoid Busts of Deir el-Medineh and Other Sites and Collections*. Cairo, Institut français d'archéologie orientale 2011, 18–21, 250–55; Stevens, *Religion*, 41–42, 128–29, 294.

21 Murnane, *Texts*, 187.

22 Murnane, *Texts*, 124–25.

23 Stevens, *Religion*, 294, 300–2, comments on the semi-public character of these gardens.

24 *COA* II, Chapter V, Pls. XXVI, XXVII; *AR* VI, 448–52.

25 *COA* III, 90, 92, 188, obj. 31/591, Pls LXXIV.9, CIV.

26 Murnane, *Texts*, 155 (Meryre), 120 (Ay), 185 (Suty), though in the last passage the word *Duat* is unnecessarily translated 'burial chamber'.

27 Murnane, *Texts*, 182.

28 Reports have appeared annually in *JEA* from 2006 onwards, and variously in *Horizon*, esp. 8 (Winter 2010). Also B. Kemp, 'The orientation of burials at Tell el-Amarna.' In Z. Hawass and J. Richards, eds, *The Archaeology and Art of Ancient Egypt: Essays in Honor of David B. O'Connor*. Cairo, Supreme Council of Antiquities Press 2007, II, 21–31; G. R. Dabbs, M. Zabecki and A. K. Stevens, 'Abandoned memories: a cemetery of forgotten souls?' In B. W. Porter and A. T. Boutin, eds, *Remembering and Commemorating the Dead: Recent Contributions in Bioarchaeology and Mortuary Analysis from the Ancient Near East*. Boulder, CO, University of Colorado Press (forthcoming).

Chapter 8. What Kind of City?

1 G. Sjoberg, *The Preindustrial City, Past and Present*. Glencoe, IL, and New York, Free Press, and London, Collier-Macmillan 1960. Strictly speaking, in

setting Sjoberg's account against Amarna, one is not comparing like with like. Sjoberg's account, because of the nature of his sources, was not based on archaeology. How would the distribution of manufacturing evidence look on archaeological plans of, say, Lhasa? Would it bear out the eye-witness descriptions or would there be an awkward disjunction, explainable only by saying that what people see and say is not necessarily the same as what they do? Statement and habit are not always identical. We will probably never know. But it highlights an inadequacy of descriptions of cities based on the accounts of observers: the hard material structure of cities, the plans of their buildings and the full spread of their artifacts are ignored or were not obtainable in the first place. Sjoberg's preindustrial city, in lacking an archaeological component, has a missing dimension. Moreover, how many ancient cities anywhere have yielded an excavated plan and an artifact record as large and representative as those from Amarna? Amarna is one in a very select category of places; it certainly has no peer in Egypt.

2 Sjoberg, *City*, 92.

3 Sjoberg, *City*, 97–98. He defines his use of the word 'outcastes' on pp. 133–37. He includes slaves, those that perform tasks that society considers defiling and minorities who might occupy a particular economic niche.

4 Sjoberg, *City*, 103.

5 Sjoberg, *City*, 189.

6 Sjoberg, *City*, 261.

7 B. Kemp, A. L. Gascoigne, N. Moeller and K. Spence, 'Egypt's invisible walls.' *CAJ* 14 (2004), 259–88 reviews the evidence for urban walling in Egypt from early to mediaeval times.

8 I. Shaw, 'Ideal homes in ancient Egypt: the archaeology of social aspiration.' *CAJ* 2 (1992), 147–66.

9 Murnane, *Texts*, 177. The term 'sister' was one of endearment that here could be referring to his wife.

10 See Chapter 4, note 6.

11 *COA* III, 162; Kemp and Stevens, *Busy Lives* I, 512–14.

12 Two discussions of population size are J. J. Janssen, 'El-Amarna as a residential city.' *Bibliotheca Orientalis* 40 (1983), 274–88; B. J. Kemp, 'The character of the South Suburb at Tell el-'Amarna.' *Mitteilungen der Deutschen Orient-Gesellschaft zu Berlin* 113 (1981), 81–97, both of them review articles of Borchardt and Ricke, *Wohnhäuser*.

13 Murnane, *Texts*, 134, and see Chapter 1, note 19.

14 Kemp and Stevens, *Busy Lives* II, Chapter 21 (M. Eccleston).

15 Depicted, for example, in a painting in the Theban tomb of Nebamun and Ipuky, N. de G. Davies, *The Tomb of Two Sculptors at Thebes*. New York, Metropolitan Museum of Art 1925, 62, Pl. XI.

16 P. T. Nicholson, *Brilliant Things for Akhenaten: The Production of Glass, Vitreous Materials and Pottery at Amarna Site O45.1*. London, EES 2007; P. T. Nicholson, C. M. Jackson and K. M. Trott, 'The Ulu Burun glass ingots, cylindrical vessels and Egyptian glass.' *JEA* 83 (1997), 143–53.

17 Kemp and Stevens, *Busy Lives* II, Chapter 26; A. J. Shortland, *Vitreous Materials at Amarna: the Production of Glass and Faience in 18th Dynasty Egypt*. Oxford, Archaeopress 2000.

18 *AR* V, Chapter 8 (A. Boyce); Kemp and Stevens, *Busy Lives* II, Chapter 25.

19 *AR* VI, Chapter 11 (A. Boyce); Kemp and Stevens, *Busy Lives* I, 481–85.

20 Kemp and Stevens, *Busy Lives* I, Chapter 6 (R. Gerisch).

21 Kemp and Stevens, *Busy Lives* II, Chapter 22.

22 Kemp and Vogelsang-Eastwood, *Textiles*.

23 See Introduction, note 1.

24 Murnane, *Texts*, 129. Presumably he is referring to the new style of statues of Akhenaten, many of which, erected in the Great Palace at Amarna, were carved in granite. But why was he at Aswan? Were the statues roughed out in the quarries and therefore required his presence to make sure that they had the correct proportions?

25 This important excavation, carried out by H. Waddington in 1932, has so far been described only briefly: J. D. S Pendlebury, 'Preliminary report of the excavations at Tell el-'Amarnah, 1932–1933.' *JEA* 19 (1933), 113–18, pp. 117–18. It forms part of a study of sculptor's workshops at Amarna being undertaken by K. Thompson, which will form part of Thompson and Hill, *Statuary*.

26 C. Aldred, 'The "New Year" gifts to the Pharaoh.' *JEA* 55 (1969), 73–81.

27 N. de G. Davies, *The Tomb of Ken-amūn at Thebes*. New York, Metropolitan Museum of Art 1930, 22–32, Pls. XI–XXIV; B. Cumming, *Egyptian Historical Records of the Later Eighteenth Dynasty*, fasc. II. Warminster, Aris and Phillips 1984, 101.

28 T. Säve-Söderbergh, *Four Eighteenth Dynasty Tombs*. Oxford, Griffith Institute 1957, 2, Pl. II.

29 A. R. Schulman, 'The Berlin "Trauerrelief" (No. 12411) and some officials of Tut'ankhamun and Ay.' *JARCE* 4 (1965), 55–68, especially pp. 61, 68.

30 Murnane, *Texts*, 193, and see Chapter 1, note 18.

31 K. Thompson, 'A shattered granodiorite dyad of Akhenaten and Nefertiti from Tell el-Amarna.'

JEA 92 (2006), 141–51.
[32] Kemp, *Anatomy* 2, Chapter 7.
[33] See Chapter 1, note 4.
[34] Murnane, *Texts*, 36–37.
[35] See Chapter 1, note 11; Chapter 4, note 21; Chapter 7, note 3.

Chapter Nine: An End and a Beginning
[1] *AR* VI, 446–48.
[2] D. Montserrat, *Akhenaten: History, Fantasy and Ancient Egypt*, London and New York, Routledge 2000, surveys the sometimes unexpected ways in which people have interpreted Akhenaten and Amarna.

Further Reading

For delving more deeply into the Amarna period, the starting point should be the collection of translations, W. J. Murnane, *Texts from the Amarna Period in Egypt* (Atlanta, GA, Scholars Press 1995). Mastering the texts will make you almost an expert. The most significant omissions are the short Hittite sources that relate to the end of the Amarna period which are translated in J. B. Pritchard, ed., *Ancient Near Eastern Texts Relating to the Old Testament* (Princeton, Princeton University Press 1950, 1955, 1969, pages 319, 394–96); the Amarna Letters, translated in W. L. Moran, *The Amarna Letters* (Baltimore and London, The Johns Hopkins University Press 1992); and the easily overlooked personal letters of the unguent preparer Ramose, to be found in E. Wente, *Letters from ancient Egypt* (Atlanta, GA, Scholars Press 1990, 94–96).

Amarna itself is well covered by source books. The two survey volumes, P. Timme, *Tell El-Amarna vor der Deutschen Ausgrabung im Jahre 1911* (Berlin and Leipzig, Hinrichs 1917) and B. J. Kemp and S. Garfi, *A Survey of the Ancient City of El-'Amarna* (London, EES 1993) together provide descriptions of the overall appearance of Amarna, the former including features that have now disappeared as well as a personal account of the place by an observant and enthusiastic German military officer. For the rock tombs of the officials, N. de G. Davies, *The Rock Tombs of El Amarna* (6 vols. London, Egypt Exploration Fund 1903–8), reprinted as 3 vols, 2004, remain incomparable. The Royal Tomb is covered in the two volumes of G. T. Martin, *The Royal Tomb at El-'Amarna* (London, EES 1974, 1989), and the boundary stelae in W. J. Murnane and C. C. Van Siclen III, *The Boundary Stelae of Akhenaten* (London and New York, Kegan Paul International 1993) as well as Murnane, *Texts*, 73–86. Pendlebury wrote his own account near the end of his work, J. D. S. Pendlebury, *Tell el-Amarna* (London, Lovat Dixon and Thompson 1935).

Excavation has produced a run of detailed volumes. In the order of excavation (though not of publication) they are:

W. M. F. Petrie, *Tell El Amarna*. London, Methuen 1894.
F. W. Von Bissing, *Der Fussboden aus dem Palaste des Königs Amenophis IV zu El Hawata: im Museum zu Kairo*. Munich, Bruckmann 1941.
L. Borchardt and H. Ricke, *Die Wohnhäuser in Tell el-Amarna*. Berlin, Mann 1980.
T. E. Peet and C. L. Woolley, *City of Akhenaten* I. London, EES 1923.
H. Frankfort, ed., *The Mural Paintings of El 'Amarneh*. London, EES 1929.
H. Frankfort and J. D. S. Pendlebury, *City of Akhenaten* II. London, EES 1933.
J. D. S. Pendlebury, *City of Akhenaten* III. London, EES 1951.
P. T. Nicholson, *Brilliant Things for Akhenaten: The Production of Glass, Vitreous Materials and Pottery at Amarna Site O45.1*. London, EES, and Oakville, CT, David Brown Book Co. 2007.
F. Weatherhead and B. J. Kemp, *The Main Chapel at the Amarna Workmen's Village and its Wall Paintings*. London, EES 2007.
B. Kemp and A. Stevens, *Busy Lives at Amarna: Excavations in the Main City (Grid 12 and the House of Ranefer, N49.18)*. 2 vols. London, EES 2010.

The six volumes of B. J. Kemp, ed., *Amarna Reports* (London, EES 1984–95) also contain much that derives from excavations begun in 1979. Preliminary reports for all seasons of the Egypt Exploration Society's work, as well as that of the Amarna Trust, are to be found in their *Journal of Egyptian Archaeology*, between 1921 and 1936, and from 1978 onwards. Similar reports by Ludwig Borchardt for his pre-1914 excavations are published in *Mitteilungen der Deutschen Orient-Gesellschaft zu Berlin* between 1911 and 1915. The Amarna Trust's newsletter, *Horizon*, has contained pictures and news of current work since 2006.

Certain categories of things found have also received specialist study leading to publication:

R. Gerisch, *Holzkohleuntersuchungen an pharaonischem und byzantinischem Material aus Amarna und Umgebung*. Mainz am Rhein, von Zabern 2004.

B. J. Kemp and G. Vogelsang-Eastwood, *The Ancient Textile Industry at Amarna*. London, EES 2001.

J. Kuckertz, *Gefässverschlüsse aus Tell el-Amarna. Sozioökonomische Aspekte einer Fundgattung des Neuen Reiches*. Saarbrücken, Saarbrücker Druckerei und Verlag 2003.

P. J. Rose, *The Eighteenth Dynasty Pottery Corpus from Amarna*. London, EES 2007.

J. Samson, *Amarna, City of Akhenaten and Nefertiti: Key Pieces from the Petrie Collection*. London, University College and Warminster, Aris and Phillips 1972.

A. J. Shortland, *Vitreous Materials at Amarna: The Production of Glass and Faience in 18th Dynasty Egypt*. Oxford, Archaeopress 2000.

A. Stevens, *Private Religion at Amarna: The Material Evidence*. Oxford, Archaeopress 2006.

A. Veldmeijer, *Amarna's Leatherwork I. Preliminary Analysis and Catalogue*. Norg, DrukWare 2010.

F. Weatherhead, *Amarna Palace Paintings*. London, EES 2007.

Details of the many *talatat*-blocks originally from Amarna that have been found re-used at El-Ashmunein (ancient Hermopolis) are to be found in G. Roeder, *Amarna-Reliefs aus Hermopolis* (Hildesheim, Pelizaeus-Museum 1969); R. Hanke, *Amarna-Reliefs aus Hermopolis: Neue Veröffentlichungen und Studien* (Hildesheim, Gerstenberg 1978); and J. D. Cooney, *Amarna Reliefs from Hermopolis in American Collections* (New York, The Brooklyn Museum 1965).

From time to time, exhibitions showcase aspects of Amarna and are commemorated by beautifully produced catalogues with perceptive essays. Prominent are

C. Aldred, *Akhenaten and Nefertiti*. Brooklyn, The Brooklyn Museum 1973.

D. Arnold, *The Royal Women of Amarna: Images of Beauty from Ancient Egypt*. New York, Metropolitan Museum of Art 1996.

R. E. Freed, Y. J. Markowitz and S. H. D'Auria, eds, *Pharaohs of the Sun; Akhenaten, Nefertiti, Tutankhamen*. Boston, Museum of Fine Arts 1999.

M. Jørgensen, *Egyptian Art from the Amarna Period*. Copenhagen, Ny Carlsberg Glyptotek 2005.

D. P. Silverman, J. W. Wegner and J. H. Wegner, *Akhenaten and Tutankhamun: Revolution and Restoration*. Philadelphia, University of Pennsylvania Museum of Archaeology and Anthropology 2006.

C. Tietze, ed., *Amarna: Lebensräume, Lebensbilder, Weltbilder*. 2nd ed. Weimar, Arcus-Verlag 2010.

Mary Chubb, *Nefertiti Lived Here* (London, Bles, and New York, Crowell 1954; reissued Libri 1998) is a happy account of what it was like to be a member of the Amarna expedition in the early 1930s directed by John Pendlebury. Charles Brasch was another member (though not overlapping with Chubb), but his account, *Charles Brasch in Egypt* (Wellington, NZ, Steele Roberts 2007), is less rose-tinted. Imogen Grundon, *Rash Adventurer: a Life of John Pendlebury* (London, Libri 2007) reveals much from behind the scenes of that EES expedition.

Given that this is a book about Amarna the city, I have not mentioned books that concentrate on Akhenaten and his ideas, of which there are many. Exceptionally, D. Laboury, *Akhénaton* (Paris, Pygmalion 2010) pays equal attention to Akhenaten the historical figure and to Amarna itself. M. Gabolde, *Akhenaton: Du mystère à la lumière* (Paris, Gallimard 2005) also stands out as the most elegant summary of the Amarna period.

Much information on Amarna and current research at the site will be found in the website www.amarnaproject.com where the newsletter *Horizon* can be downloaded (and at the site www.amarnatrust.com).

The last word should be with Dominic Montserrat, *Akhenaten: History, Fantasy and Ancient Egypt* (London and New York, Routledge 2000). His study is of how people have received Akhenaten and Amarna, interpreting them according to their own personal philosophies. I am sure I am now one of them.

Sources of Illustrations

Unless otherwise stated all photographs, maps and drawings are by the author. Where adapted, the source of the original is given below.

A key to abbreviations used may be found on p. 305 above.

0.2 Ägyptisches Museum und Papyrussammlung, Berlin, 21300 and 21351. **0.3** *Description de l'Égypte, Antiquités*, Planches IV, Paris 1817, Pl. 63.6. **1.2** After Stevens, *Religion*, 154, Figure II.6.2. **1.4** After *RT* IV, Pl. XXII. **1.5** Egyptian Museum, Cairo, JdE 49529. Photo G. Owen. **1.9, 1.11** Photo G. Owen. **1.12** EES neg. 34/5, Royal Tomb no. 26.1; Martin, *Royal Tomb* II, Pl. 13A. **1.13** After *RT* VI, Pl. XXIX. **1.14** After *RT* II, Pls. XI, XXXVI; VI, Pl. XXX. **1.15** After *AS*, Sheet 6. **1.16** EES neg. 24/41. **2.2** After *RT* V, Pl. V. **2.3** Photo David Grandorge. **2.5** After *RT* I, Pl. XXXII. **2.6** EES neg. 21/73. **2.7** After J. D. S. Pendlebury, 'Preliminary report on excavations at Tell el-'Amarnah 1930–1.' *JEA* 17 (1931), Pls. LXXVI, LXXVII. **2.8** EES neg. 24/15. **2.9** EES. **2.10** After EES archive plan (Emery plan A). **2.11** After *RT* VI, Pl. XIV. **2.12** After TA, Pl. VIII.2, and see p. 10. The block is in the Metropolitan Museum of Art, New York, 21.9.9. **2.13** far left: EES neg. 22/77, Copenhagen, Ny Carlsberg Glyptotek ÆIN 1610. **2.15** EES neg. 24/191. **2.16** After *COA* I, Pl. XXIX. **2.23** EES. **2.24** After EES neg. 32/37. **2.25** EES. **2.27** After unpublished drawing by R. Lavers, EES. **2.30** After TA, Pl. V. **3.1** Photo David Grandorge. **3.2** After *RT* IV, Pl. XV. **3.3** After *RT* I, Pl. XXVIII. **3.4** After *RT* I, Pl. XXXIII. **3.5** EES neg 32/12. **3.6** EES neg 32/35. **3.7, 3.8** Column design by Mallinson Architects, reconstruction by Simon Bradley. **3.9, 3.10** After *RT* I, Pl. XXVII; II, Pl. XVIII. **3.12** After *COA* III, Pl. III. **3.16** Photo G. Owen. **3.19, 3.20** After EES archive material and *COA* III, 12, 188, Fig. 25; Pl. LX.5, 6, 7. **3.21** After *RT* I, Pl. XXVIII. **3.22, 3.23** Kemp, *Anatomy 1*, 284, Fig. 95. After *COA* III, 141, Pls. XXII, LXXIX, and EES archive record cards. **3.24** After EES negs 36/A 77, 78 (published in *COA* III, 141, Pl. LXXIX.7). **3.25** After EES neg. 36/A 79. **3.27** After J. D. Cooney, *Amarna Reliefs from Hermopolis in American Collections*, New York, The Brooklyn Museum 1965, 73, no. 46. Previously published with figure **3.28** in Kemp, *Anatomy 1*, 290, Fig. 96. **3.29** Egyptian Museum, Cairo JdE 29746/34176. After *RT* V, 10, Pl. XXI and collation. **3.30** After *COA* III, Pl. XIIIC. **4.1** After *COA* III, Pl. XIX. **4.2** After EES neg. 33/O 23 and *COA* III, 162, nos. 128, 129; Pl. LXXXIX. **4.3** Hieroglyphic copy after *COA* III, Pl. LXXXIII.V. **4.4** After *TA*, Pl. XLII.19; *COA* III, Pl. XIX. **4.5** See P. Payne, 'Recovering animal bone at the house of the high priest Panehsy.' *JEA* 92 (2006), 45–52, Fig. 17. **4.6** After *COA* III, Pl. XX. **4.7** EES negs 35/A 70b and c; also *COA* III Pl. XXXIX.1. **4.8** After *COA* III, Pl. XVI. **4.12** After *COA* III, Pl. XIIIB. **4.13** Based on plans by Wendy Horton. **4.14** EES neg. 36/O 37. **4.15** EES neg. 34/O 36. **4.16** After *COA* III, Pls LXX.7, LXVIII.6, LXVIII.9; *TA*, Pl. IX. **4.17** After *TA*, Pl. II. **4.18, 4.19** After *RT* VI, Pl. XXVIII. **4.20** After *RT* I, Pl. XVIII; III, Pl. XXXIII. **4.21** After *RT* III, Pls. IV, V and figures on p. 6. **4.23** EES neg. 24–25/139. **4.24** EES neg. 23/113. **4.26** EES (no neg. no.). **4.27, 4.28** 1923 drawings by F. G. Newton, EES. **4.29** After EES archive plan. **5.2** EES. **5.3** After *RT* IV, Pl. XXVI. **5.4** Helen Fenwick, with additions by Anna Stevens. **5.5** After *RT* IV, Pl. XXI. **5.8, 5.9, 5.10** After *AS*, Sheets 1, 7. **5.11, 5.12, 5.13** After *AS*, Sheets 3, 7. **5.14** After Kemp and Stevens, *Busy Lives* I, 475, Fig. 10.1. **5.15** EES. **5.16** EES. **5.17** After Kemp and Stevens, *Busy Lives* I, 509, Fig. 10.13. **5.18** EES. The lefthand sherd is in the Ashmolean Museum, Oxford (1936.644). The righthand sherd is in the Egyptian Museum, Cairo (JdE 59164). **5.19** EES. **5.21** After Kemp and Stevens, *Busy Lives* I, 177, Figure 2.44. **5.24** EES. **5.27** EES neg. 23/31; F. G. Newton, 'Excavations at El-'Amarnah, 1923–24.' *JEA* 10 (1924), 289–98, Pl. XXVI.1. **5.29** EES neg. 21/7. **5.31** Photo G. Owen. **6.1** After *COA* I, Pl. XVI. **6.2** After *COA* I, Pl. XVI. **6.3** EES neg. 22/29. *COA* I, Pl. XVII.3. **6.4** Left to right: after *RT* VI, Pl. XXVIII; *RT* IV, Pl. XXV; after *RT* VI, Pl. XXVIII; after Freed, et al., *Pharaohs*, 148, 256, Cat. 175; after *RT* VI, Pl. XXVIII. **6.5** Kemp and Stevens, *Busy Lives* I, 357, Fig. 4.16, 360; II, Chapter 1. **6.6** EES neg. 26/50. *COA* II, Pl. XVIII.2. **6.7** *COA* I, 68–69, Pl. XVIII.2. EES neg. 21/44. **6.8** After Borchardt and Ricke, *Wohnhäuser*, Taf. 21. **6.9** EES neg. 24/68. **6.10** EES neg. 23/19. **6.11** Egyptian Museum, Cairo, JdE 55520. EES negs 30/O 21a, 21b. *COA* II, 47, Pl. XLII.3. **6.12** Egyptian Museum, Cairo JdE 62780. After EES neg. 33/O 56; also *COA* III, 124, Pl. LXXVII.3. **6.13a** EES neg. 24/192. **6.13b** Glasgow. EES neg. 33/O 77. *COA* III, 125, Pl. LXXVII.2. **6.13c** British Museum, London. EES neg. 26/97. **6.13d** Egyptian Museum, Cairo JdE 53022. EES neg. 28/107. *COA* II, 22, Pl. XXXVI.3. **6.14** British Museum, London, 55147 (vessel), 55148 (tube), 55149 (strainer). EES neg. 21/523. *COA* I, 24, Fig. 5. **6.17a–e** EES neg. 22/44. *COA* I, 18, Pl. XXI.3. **6.17f** EES neg. 22/4. *COA* I, 85, Pl. XXI.4. **6.19** Photo EES neg. 36/O 17. *COA* III, 141, Pl. LXXVIII.9. **6.20** Kemp and Stevens, *Busy Lives* II, 53–57. **6.21** Photo EES neg. 36/O 48. **6.22, 6.23** Kemp and Stevens, *Busy Lives* I, 381–83. **6.24, 6.25** After *COA* II, 59–61, Pls IX, XLIII, and EES records; also Kemp, *Anatomy* 1, 245, Fig. 82. **6.26** After *AR* V, 270, Fig. 12.12. **6.27** A. J. Legge, in Kemp and Stevens, *Busy Lives* I, 447, Fig. 8.2. **6.28** EES neg. 21/37. T.E. Peet, 'Excavations at Tell el-Amarna: a preliminary report.' *JEA* 7 (1921), 169–85, Pl. XXVII.2. **6.29** Kemp and Vogelsang- Eastwood, *Textiles*, 194, Fig. 6.25; 197, Fig. 6.29. **6.30** Kemp and Vogelsang-Eastwood, *Textiles*, 166, Figs 6.1, 6.2; 236–38, Figs 6.68, 6.69, 6.70, 6.71. **6.30d** *RT* III, Pl. III. **6.31** Drawn and described by A. Boyce, in *AR* VI, 338–39, Fig. 11.1. **6.32** University of Louisiana, Forensic Anthropology and Computer Enhancement Services (FACES) Laboratory (by courtesy of Mary Manhein). **6.33** Data supplied by J. Rose and M. Zabecki. **7.1** Egyptian Museum, Cairo, JdE 65041. After *COA* III, Pl. XXXI. **7.2** After Borchardt and Ricke, *Wohnhäuser*, Hausplan 2. **7.3** After *COA* II, 64, Pl. XV. **7.4** EES neg. 30/112. After *COA* II, Pl. XXIII.3. **7.5** Object in Ägyptisches Museum und Papyrussammlung, Berlin, Inv. 21193. Drawing after R. Krauß, 'Der Bildhauer Thutmose in Amarna.' *Jahrbuch Preußischer Kulturbesitz* 20 (1983), 119–32, esp. 120, Abb. 44, 45. **7.6** Egyptian Museum, Cairo, JdE 59291. EES negs 32/O 65, 66. **7.7** EES. **7.8** Egyptian Museum, Cairo, JdE 46954. After *COA* I, 97, 104, Pl. XXVIII.1–3. **7.9** A. Boyce. See Kemp and Stevens, *Busy Lives* II, 118, Fig. 10.14. **7.10** Kemp, *JEA* 67 (1981), 15, Fig. 6. **7.11** After EES neg. 21/48, also 21/78. See also B. J. Kemp, 'Wall paintings from the Workmen's Village at el-'Amarna.' *JEA* 65 (1979), 48, Fig. 1; *COA* I, 60, 75, Pl. XVIII.3. The reconstructed Bes figures are based on T. M. Davis, et al., *The Tomb of Iouiya and Touiyou*, London, Constable 1907, Pls. XXXIII, XXXIV. **7.12** After EES negs 28/O78, 80, 81; also *COA* II, 35, Pl. XXXVIII.1–3. **7.13a** Cincinnati Art Museum, 1921.279. After EES neg. 21/521. *COA* I, 25, Pl. XII.2; also Stevens, *Religion*, 144, 228, 247. **7.13b, c, d** Cincinnati Art Museum, 1921.280–81. After EES negs 21/528, 531. *COA* I, 25, Pl. XII.4–5. **7.14** See Kemp and Stevens, *Busy Lives* II, 240–41, Pl. 17.1. **7.16** EES neg. 23/2. Stevens, *Religion*, 222, Fig. II.13.4. **7.17** Egyptian Museum, Cairo, JdE 53249. After EES negs 28/115, 117a. *COA* II, 43, Pl. XXXVII.1–4. **7.20** Photo G. Owen. **7.21** After *RT* III, Pl. I. **7.22** After *RT* III, Pl. XXII. **7.23** After *RT* II, Pl. XXIV. **7.24** After *AR* VI, 449, Fig. 15.25. **7.25** British Museum, London, 63635. After *COA* III, Pl. CIV; also 90, 92, Pl. LXXIV.9. **7.26** Contours by Helen Fenwick. **7.27** Mary Shepperson. **7.28** Photos Melinda King. **7.30** Photo G. Owen. **7.31** After Martin, *Royal Tomb* II, Pls 34, 35, room alpha, wall A. **7.32** Photo G. Owen. **8.1** Brooklyn Museum. After J. D. Cooney, *Amarna Reliefs from Hermopolis in American Collections*, New York, The Brooklyn Museum, 1965, p. 74. Previously published in Kemp, *Anatomy* 1, 298, Fig. 100. **8.2** After Izre'el, *Tablets*, Pls XXII, XL, XLIII; also Kemp, *Anatomy*, 2, 294, Fig. 106. **8.3** After *AR* V, 47, Fig. 2.17; 53, Fig. 2.23; 54, Fig. 2.24. **8.4** After *AS*, Sheets 7 and 8. **8.5** Ashmolean Museum, Oxford. EES neg. 30/O 8. *COA* II, 46, Pl. XL.2. **8.6** Egyptian Museum, Cairo JdE 66728. EES neg. 31/O 12. *COA* II, 74 **8.7** Glasgow. EES neg. 36/O 16. *COA* III, 140, Pl. LXXIX.10. **8.8** Egyptian Museum, Cairo JdE 66727. EES neg. 36/O 16. *COA* III, 31, Pl. LXXIX.10 **8.9** Egyptian Museum, Cairo JdE 64982. EES neg. 34/O 90. *COA* III, 65, Pl. LXXIII.5. **8.11** EES archive card 36/9. **8.12** Egyptian Museum, Cairo JdE 66717. Kemp and Stevens, *Busy Lives* II, 294, Fig. 19.11. **8.13** After *COA* II and A. Boyce, *AR* VI, 364, Fig. 11.10. **8.14** Kemp and Vogelsang-Eastwood, *Textiles*, 274, Fig. 8.2; 287, Fig. 8.9; 291, Fig. 8.12; 340, Fig. 9.24; 349, Fig. 9.33; 362, Fig. 9.44. **8.15** After Kemp and Vogelsang-Eastwood, *Textiles*, 279, Fig. 8.7; 290, Fig. 8.11; 301, Fig. 8.17; 304, Fig. 8.18; 356–57, Figs 9.38a and b; bone points from grid 12, Kemp and Stevens, *Busy Lives* II, 449–51. **8.16, 8.17** After *RT* III, Pls. XVII, XVIII. **8.18** Ägyptisches Museum und Papyrussammlung, Berlin, 21359. **8.19** EES. **8.20 top left**: Egyptian Museum, Cairo JdE 59287. EES neg. 32/O 34; **top right**: Egyptian Museum, Cairo JdE 59288. EES neg. 32/18; **bottom**: Egyptian Museum, Cairo JdE 59286. EES negs 32/O 73, O 74. **8.21** After *AR* I, 41, Fig. 4.1, with additional details from field records. **8.22** EES. After *AR* I, 45, Fig. 4.3.

Plates: I Egyptian Museum, Cairo, JdE 98915. **II** Ägyptisches Museum und Papyrussammlung, Berlin, 21300. **III** Egyptian Museum, Cairo, JdE

44870. **IV** Musée du Louvre, Paris, N 381. **V** Egyptian Museum, Cairo, temp. acc. no. 30/10/26/12. **IX** Photo G. Owen. **XI** Helen Fenwick. **XIII** Museum of Archaeology and Anthropology, University of Cambridge, 37.889. **XIV** F. G. Newton after *COA* I, Pls XXXVII, XXXVIII. **XV** F. G. Newton after *COA* I, Pl. XL. **XX** Line drawing after Weatherhead, *Paintings*, 92, Fig. 62; painted dado at the bottom after Weatherhead, *Paintings*, 86, Fig. 60. **XXI** Ashmolean Museum, Oxford 1893.1. **XXII** Painting by F. Weatherhead, see Weatherhead and Kemp, *Main Chapel*, Col. Pl. 3.6. **XXIII** Weatherhead and Kemp, *Main Chapel*, Col. Pl. 3.2. **XXIV** After *TA*, Pl. V, with painted dado added. **XXV, XXVI** After Kemp and Stevens, *Busy Lives* I, Col. Pl. 1. **XXVII** After *COA*, I, 18, Pl. VIII.3; *COA* I, 32, obj. 22/583, Pl. VI.4; *COA* II, 65, obj. 30/675, also 10–11, Fig. 3. **XXX** After *COA* II, 109, Pl. XXIII.4 and a watercolour copy by Hilda Pendlebury in the EES archives. **XXXI–XXXIV** EES. **XXXVI, XXXVII** Models and photos by Eastwood Cook; concept by Mallinson Architects. **XXXVIII** Model and photo by Eastwood Cook; concept by Mallinson Architects and Kate Spence. **XXXIX** See *AR* I, 28, Fig. 2.11A. **XL** See *AR* VI, 140, 144, Fig. 3.4, no. 22. **XLI** Photo G. Owen. **XLII, XLIII** Model and photo by Eastwood Cook; concept by Mallinson Architects. **XLIV** After Weatherhead and Kemp, *Main Chapel*, Col. Pl. 3.4. **XLV** British Museum, London, EA 74101. **XLVI** Musée du Louvre, Paris, E 17357. **XLVII** Egyptian Museum, Cairo. **XLVIII** British Museum, London, 55193. **XLIX** Kemp and Stevens, *Busy Lives* II, 280–83, Fig. 19.9, Pls 19.5, 19.6. **L** See Kemp and Stevens, *Busy Lives* II, 259–60, Pls 19.2, 19.3. **LI** See *AR* V, 164, Fig. 8.5. **LIII** See Kemp and Stevens, *Busy Lives* II, 365, Fig. 21.1.

Index

Arabic or roman numbers in **bold** refer to illustrations.